296.71
B47   Biale, David.
          Gershom Scholem:
       Kabbalah and counter-
       history.

296.71
B47   Biale, David.
          Gershom Scholem:
       Kabbalah and counter-
       history.

Gershom Scholem

Kabbalah and
Counter-History

Gershom Scholem

photo Aliza Auerbach

Gershom Scholem

Kabbalah and Counter-History

David Biale

HARVARD UNIVERSITY PRESS
Cambridge, Massachusetts
and London, England
1979

*For my mother Evelyn
and my father Jacob*

Printed in the United States of America

*Publication of this book has been aided by a grant
from the Andrew W. Mellon Foundation*

Library of Congress Cataloging in Publication Data

Biale, David, 1949-
  Gershom Scholem.

  Bibliography: p.
  Includes index.
  1. Scholem, Gershom Gerhard, 1897-   2. Scholars, Jewish
—Germany—Biography.   3. Scholars, Jewish—Israel—
Biography.
BM755.S295B5   296.7'1 [B]   78-23620
ISBN 0-674-36330-2

Acknowledgments

I have had the rare privilege of working with Amos Funkenstein, whose precise formulations, original suggestions, and rigorous criticisms made an incalculable contribution to this work without ever restricting my creative autonomy. I consider our relationship to have been a profound experience.

Paul Mendes-Flohr and Jacob Katz (Hebrew University, Jerusalem) both helped me with the original conceptualization of the work. Professor Katz read and criticized the manuscript. The manuscript was also read in part or in whole by Arnold Band and Hans Rogger (University of California, Los Angeles), Martin Jay and Robert Alter (University of California, Berkeley), and Leon J. Goldstein (State University of New York at Binghamton).

In the summer of 1975 while in Jerusalem, I discussed my work with Nathan Rotenstreich, R. J. Z. Werblowsky, and Werner Kraft. I owe a special debt of gratitude to Gershom Scholem, who granted me two personal interviews that summer. Upon my completion of the manuscript, Professor Scholem sent me a list of criticisms which proved very useful in making revisions. We did not always agree on matters of interpretation, but he was able to save me from a good many factual embarrassments. He was also generous enough to give me permission to publish for the first time a letter he wrote to Zalman Schocken on why he decided to study the Kabbalah.

My friends have been my best teachers and most merciless critics and editors. I thank Gabriel Motzkin, Michael Nutkiewicz, Jeremy Popkin, David Sorkin, and Noam Zion. Leon Wieseltier deserves special mention for the invaluable suggestions and criticisms he gave me during the revision of the manuscript. Our conversations have been a source of intellectual inspiration for me, and, I hope, for him as well.

I would like to thank William B. Goodman of the Harvard University Press for his many kindnesses and Dolores Kundrat and Ellen Forman for assisting with the final typing.

It is a pleasure to be able to acknowledge with gratitude the institutions which supported this project financially and made it possible for me to finish it so quickly: The Social Science Research Council, the National Foundation for Jewish Culture, and the Regents of the University of California.

Finally, Rachel Biale contributed perhaps the most to this work. She has been my intellectual partner since its inception and has read every page critically more times than she cares to remember. Together we developed the insights and organization that guided this study to completion.

D. B.

Jerusalem - Los Angeles - Berkeley - Binghamton

Contents

He regards it as his task to brush history against the grain.

—Walter Benjamin

Introduction

REFLECTIONS ON THE
SCIENCE OF JUDAISM

While still a student in Germany in 1917, Gershom Scholem, then twenty, met Gustav Steinschneider, the grandson of the great nineteenth-century Jewish bibliographer, Moritz Steinschneider. Scholem relates in a later reminiscence that he was struck by the remarkable contrast between the young Steinschneider, torn between Communism and Zionism, and his famous grandfather.[1] The elder Steinschneider, one of the pillars of the rationalist school of Jewish historiography, generally called the *Wissenschaft des Judentums,* allegedly said that Jewish scholarship had "only one task left: to give the remains of Judaism a decent burial."[2] Scholem must have considered the younger Steinschneider's oscillation between Jewish nationalism and revolutionary cosmopolitanism as both proof and refutation of his grandfather's pessimism. On the one hand, the assimilation of German Jewry had gone so far by the Weimar period that the young Steinschneider, along with most of his generation, had virtually no conception of the heritage of historical Judaism. In calling Moritz Steinschneider "the most central figure in the group of learned liquidators of Judaism,"[3] Scholem clearly lays part of the blame for this sorry state of affairs at the doorstep of the grandfather's generation. Alienated from traditional Judaism, but equally alienated from the liberal bourgeois politics and culture of the older generation, many young Jews turned to revolutionary Communism as a new source of identity. On the other hand, the very existence of a Jewish alternative to assimilation or revolution—Zionism—must have seemed to Scholem proof that Judaism remained very much alive.

Scholem's sketch of the contrast between the two generations of Steinschneiders suggests in capsule form the theme of this study: Scholem's own rejection of German-Jewish life through his radical revision of nineteenth-century German-Jewish historiography, represented here by Moritz Steinschneider. Against the predominantly

rationalist bias of the nineteenth century, he created almost single-
handedly the academic study of Jewish mysticism. The virtual
monopoly that Scholem and his disciples have achieved in interpreting Jewish mysticism itself demands a study of Scholem's work.

Scholem's remarkably lucid and accessible writings have succeeded in reaching an audience far wider than the narrow circle of
Judaica scholars. The great interest of recent years in the Kabbalah
is due almost exclusively to Scholem's growing popularity as an
historian of religion and an authoritative spokesman for Judaism.
Diverse intellectuals from the writer Jorge Luis Borges to the literary critic Harold Bloom have taken to quoting the Kabbalah as interpreted through Scholem's eyes. How has he succeeded in making
such an ostensibly alien and obscure subject so compelling and relevant to secular Jews and non-Jews alike? Since scholars and non-
scholars will be forced for many years to read the Kabbalah
through Scholem's interpretations, it is imperative to reconstruct
the assumptions and influences that lie behind his historiography.

A study of Scholem cannot be limited, however, to his activities
in the Kabbalistic archives. His revolt against the Wissenschaft des
Judentums was part of a larger revolt against German-Jewish life.
Already a radical Zionist before World War I and immigrating to
Palestine in 1923, Scholem rejected on a political and cultural level
the German-Jewish world that had produced the Wissenschaft des
Judentums. Moreover, in returning to Judaism from a secular background but without adopting orthodoxy, Scholem developed a
theological response of his own to the rational theology of the nineteenth century. Through the prism of his historiography, we can
discern Scholem's positions on the political, cultural, and theological issues that confronted his generation.

Scholem not only took up cudgels against the nineteenth-century
rationalists, but also frequently came into conflict with the dominant opinions of his own time. He developed many of his ideas in
lifelong controversy with Martin Buber, perhaps the most out-
standing Jewish thinker of the last generation of German Jewry. Although many of his initial assumptions about the irrationalist nature of Judaism were similar to Buber's, Scholem parted ways with
the great religious philosopher during World War I and charted his
own course.

√ Scholem has defined himself as a "religious anarchist."[4] Although the precise meaning of the term must emerge from the various contexts of Scholem's work, we may begin with a preliminary
definition of anarchism as a philosophy that recognizes no single
source of authority. Scholem's anarchism must be distinguished
from nihilism, which rejects all sources of authority, and from

liberal pluralism, which claims that all sources of authority are equally valid. I shall try to show that Scholem took an anarchistic position on the issues he confronted and that this position can help to organize his views into a coherent and original philosophy of Jewish history.

Behind Scholem's anarchistic thought lies a powerful and extraordinary personality. Rebellious and individualistic by nature, there is something of the "demonic" anarchist in Scholem's character. As interesting as it would be to explore in depth the man behind the historiography, this study has the more modest goal of simply trying to understand what Scholem has said and how it fits into an intellectual tradition. Where necessary, I have referred to matters of personal and intellectual biography, but only as it helps to illuminate Scholem's thought. In part, this avoidance of biography stems from a conclusion I have come to concerning Scholem's intellectual development. He arrived at certain definite positions on political, cultural, and historiographical questions at a very early age—on some issues even before the age of twenty. With a few exceptions, he did not significantly alter views throughout his career. This striking constancy of intellectual position is surely what made Scholem such a formidable figure in the eyes of his contemporaries during his youth, since he was already dead certain about many questions which they still debated. On the other hand, there is no evidence that Scholem's adherence to certain positions ever petrified into dogma. He has had the remarkable capacity to continue developing and elaborating his ideas in new and subtle ways without significantly changing their substance. His personal anarchism has perhaps prevented him from becoming stodgy or stale. Again, I have no "deep-structure" explanation for this phenomenon, nor do I attempt one in this study.

Scholem's anarchistic philosophy of Jewish history is a highly individualistic response to the crises of his time. He offers us no concrete "program," since his philosophy is the personal solution of a unique academic historian. By studying such a nonconformist figure, we do not necessarily gain direct knowledge of the general character of Scholem's generation, for he was often as much at odds with his contemporaries as with his elders. It is perhaps only today, when the programmatic philosophies of German-Jewish intellectuals have vanished in the smoke and ashes of the Nazi holocaust, that we can evaluate Scholem's lifework not only as an achievement in Jewish historiography, but also as a lasting contribution to modern Jewish thought. Although perhaps idiosyncratic, Scholem's philosophy may illuminate indirectly the political and cultural options open to the last generation of German Jews.

SCHOLEM'S "REFLECTIONS ON THE SCIENCE OF JUDAISM"

Scholem's relation to the Jewish historiographical tradition is not only central to his enterprise as an historian, but is also symptomatic of his whole intellectual makeup. Scholem acquired many of the tools of his scholarly trade by himself; an autodidact since childhood, he must be regarded as a thinker sui generis. Although he developed many of his central ideas on his own, he often did so in polemical struggle with his predecessors and contemporaries. I shall attempt to point out where I feel that Scholem has deliberately borrowed from other thinkers, but also where his ideas may be the unconscious product of an intellectual climate of opinion. No person is ever entirely aware of the ideas he has absorbed from his environment, even as he creatively appropriates and transforms them for his own purposes.

The historiographical tradition with which we most often find Scholem in conflict is the Wissenschaft des Judentums. Athough all secular study of Jewish history to the present day may be called *Wissenschaft des Judentums*, I shall use the term in a more specific sense to refer to those nineteenth-century scholars, particularly in Germany, who created modern Jewish historiography. By use of the definite article I mean to suggest that the nineteenth-century historians can be regarded as a school. In treating them as such, I am aware of the many qualifications and exceptions that might bring such a claim to grief, but I believe that Scholem himself relates to the Wissenschaft des Judentums in this way. In fact, Scholem generally refers to the nineteenth-century historiography as the *Wissenschaft vom Judentum*, indicating by this less common variant that he has in mind a school with a particular point of view rather than, generically, all of modern Jewish Studies. Since this is a book about Scholem and not modern Jewish historiography as a whole, I shall consciously adopt some of the points of view of my subject where this may serve to reconstruct his position.

Scholem's polemical relationship to the Wissenschaft des Judentums goes back to the early stages of his intellectual development. As early as 1920, as a student about to begin his work in Jewish /mysticism, Scholem planned to write an essay on "the suicide of Judaism in the so-called *Wissenschaft vom Judentum.*"[5] Postponed for a quarter of a century, the essay was written in highly passionate Hebrew in 1945 under the title "From Reflections on the Science of Judaism."[6] Subtitled "A Jubilee Lecture That Was Never Delivered,"[7] Scholem intended his remarks to reflect as much on the contribution of the Institute of Jewish Studies at the Hebrew University, which had just celebrated its twentieth anniversary, as on the Wissenschaft des Judentums itself. The question underlying his presentation was whether the new nationalist historiography had indeed corrected the errors of the nineteenth century.

Throughout the essay, Scholem adopts a highly polemical and even satirical tone toward the Wissenschaft des Judentums, which has led many to consider it his declaration of war against his predecessors. To a certain extent, the essay is now considered to have depicted the Wissenschaft des Judentums in an unfairly negative light and to have simplified an historiographical movement that contained many different tendencies.[7] Without disputing that the piece reflects Scholem's perception of the Wissenschaft des Judentums and does not even pretend to be a balanced historical account, I believe that a careful analysis of its "hidden message" reveals that his attitude toward his predecessors is much more ambiguous and positive than is generally believed. By a close examination of the essay, we will find a remarkable example of Scholem's dialectical philosophy of history at work.

Scholem believes that the Wissenschaft des Judentums failed because it was torn apart by three interrelated contradictions: objectivity versus apologetics, romanticism versus rationalism, and constructive versus destructive criticism. The nineteenth-century scholars professed the goal of historical objectivity, but because of the equally pressing political needs of emancipation, they used their historiography just as their homiletics for apologetic purposes. Apologetics demanded that Judaism be portrayed as a familiar rather than a foreign belief. Scholem refers to one particularly outrageous example of such apologetics: a sermon published by a nineteenth-century Jewish preacher entitled "Our Patriarch Jacob—the Model of a City Councilman" (*Unser Erzvater Jakob das Vorbild eines Stadtverordneten*). He comments contemptuously: "the prince of the nation in the guise of a petty bourgeois."[8] Here is a theme to which we will return: for Scholem, there is something fundamentally antithetical between true Judaism and "bourgeois culture." The overweening desire of partially acculturated Jews to enter the bourgeoisie motivated an apologetic stance that sapped Judaism of any authenticity.

Apologetics in the service of emancipation led to the second contradiction, between romanticism and rationalism. The early nineteenth century was an age of romantic nationalist historiography. But particularly in Germany, this romanticism often became antisemitic in its emphasis on a reconstituted German nation. The Jewish historians, though professing romantic ideals of using the

past to inspire pride in Jewish identity, hitched their star to enlightenment rationalism. Concerned to enter the intellectual "salon" of
nineteenth-century Europe and aware that it would only be open to
them if based on universalist, rationalist principles, the Jewish intellectuals emphasized the rationalist aspects of Judaism and scru-
pulously avoided what went on in the cellar.[9] Irrationalism or
mysticism was swept under the rug, as were the revolutionary or
apocalyptic tendencies in Jewish messianism. Social history was all
but ignored in the desire to portray Judaism as an intellectual religion. The Wissenschaft des Judentums wrote *Geistesgeschichte* in
which the *Geist* was predominantly rational.

Frequently steeped in rationalist ideas of progress, many nineteenth-century historians believed that Judaism's rational side was
reaching fulfillment in modern times. Historiography's purpose
was to contribute to this elevated goal by purging Jewish history of
all vestigial irrationalism: The Wissenschaft des Judentums wanted

> to remove the irrational stinger and banish the demonic enthusi-
> asm from Jewish history through exaggerated theologizing and
> spiritualizing. This was actually the decisive original sin. This
> terrifying giant, our history, is called to task . . . and this enor-
> mous creature, full of destructive power, made up of vitality,
> evil and perfection, must contract itself, stunt its growth and de-
> clare that it has no substance. The demonic giant is nothing but a
> simple fool who fulfills the duties of a solid citizen and every de-
> cent Jewish bourgeois could unashamedly bid him good-day in
> the streets of the city, the immaculate city of the 19th century.[10]

This passage reads almost like a Nietzschean manifesto or a statement of Bergsonian vitalism from the turn of the century. Indeed,
critics have attacked Scholem for extolling the "Dionysian" in Jewish history against the "Apollonian" spirit of the nineteenth century. We shall see that Scholem's position is considerably more
complicated than one might assume from this passage, for he uses
the word "demonic" in a much more positive sense than the English
suggests. Like Goethe's interpretation of the word *dämonisch*,[11]
Scholem conceives of demonic irrationalism as a creative force: destruction is necessary for future construction. As opposed to the
harmonious idea of progress adopted by the nineteenth-century
historians, Scholem's vision of Jewish history is a stormy dialectic
of constructive and destructive forces. We shall examine in particular Scholem's argument that the demonic Sabbatians of the seventeenth century prepared the ground for less destructive movements
in the eighteenth, such as Hasidism and Enlightenment.

By suppressing the "irrational," the representatives of the Wissenschaft des Judentums considered Judaism moribund since they ignored precisely those elements that gave it vitality. This rationalist bias led them to their undialectical view of Jewish history and precluded the possibility of future life: The Wissenschaft des Judentums "became the mouthpiece of the [Jewish] bourgeoisie for whom the slogans of destruction and construction are equally infuriating because they want to go to sleep. This sleep is known as gradual progress, preservation of the status quo through reform."[12] For Scholem, the Zionist revolutionary, the complacent reformism of bourgeois German Jewry held no promise for the future, and the fatal affection for the status quo infected the historiography of the period.

The nineteenth century's rationalism led directly, according to Scholem, to a tendency to "spiritualize" Judaism and freeze it in rigid theological dogma.[13] The sin of the Wissenschaft des Judentums was not just one-sided rationalism, but *dogmatic* rationalism. Judaism was defined by one and only one theological principle, although its formulation might vary from thinker to thinker. Scholem argues that this dogmatism reveals a fundamental misunderstanding of the history of Jewish theology. His own position does not culminate in a monolithic theology, but in an account of contradictory formulas. He maintains that Jewish theology, encompassing both rationalism and demonic irrationalism, is *anarchistic:* it yields no one authoritative formula or dogma. The very vitality of the Jewish tradition lies in this anarchism, since dogma, in Scholem's view, is by definition lifeless. Scholem engages the nineteenth century precisely on its own territory of Geistesgeschichte and radically revises its conception of the nature of the Jewish Geist.

The final contradiction in which the Wissenschaft des Judentums became entangled was between the destructive and constructive poles of the secular historical method: "The conservative and destructive tendencies in [historical] science are bound up with one another. Historical criticism as a scientific method cannot escape this essential dialectic." Historiography, like Jewish history itself, must involve a dialectic between romantic affirmation and demonic destruction. For Scholem, historical reasoning by nature is destructive, but out of the eradication of the moribund aspects of a tradition, historical criticism can "elevate the vestiges of the past to symbols of [new] life." The Wissenschaft des Judentums lost this dialectical tension, however, and because it perceived its subject as moribund, it did not use historical criticism to rescue elements of the past for building a vital future. Instead, it regarded all of the past as equally irrelevant to the present, thus laying the basis for a positivistic, antiquarian method: the burial of the historical corpse beneath mounds of indiscriminate facts. The final consequence of apologetics and dogmatic rationalism was the study of the past for its own sake, divorced from the present: a "terrifying rite of burial."[14]

Scholem does not lay the blame for the mistaken rationalist interpretation of Judaism solely on the Wissenschaft des Judentums. As the "academic mortician" of Judaism, nineteenth-century scholarship was more a symptom than a cause of the general rigor mortis of nineteenth-century Judaism. Scholem implies that historiography was necessarily doomed to failure in nineteenth-century Europe.[15] The conflict between Jewish romanticism and the desire for emancipation and assimilation was characteristic of all German Jewish life. Because the European nations were not prepared to assimilate the Jews without demanding that they alter their identity beyond recognition, Jewish historiography had no choice but apologetics. Scholem's criticism of the Wissenschaft des Judentums must be read as a Zionist critique of the possibility of a healthy Jewish life in Europe as a whole: although the Wissenschaft des Judentums started its career in the beginning of the nineteenth century with some laudable romantic goals, the social context prevented it from surviving the three contradictions mentioned above. For Scholem, the failure of Jewish historiography in the nineteenth century was only one aspect of the general crisis of Jewish bourgeois liberalism.

Scholem believes that Zionism has made possible a fundamental revision of the perspectives of Jewish historiography.[16] No longer must historiography serve as a handmaiden to political apologetics or theological dogmatism. Jewish history can be considered "from within." For Scholem, objective historiography is guaranteed by Zionism because Zionism is by definition antidogmatic: it stands above all particular interpretations of Judaism and is the one common denominator that unites all Jews. We will examine in the final chapter whether this claim of objectivity holds up in Scholem's own historiography.

Scholem notes that some of the nineteenth-century writers were close to the nationalist position he advocates. He mentions specifically Heinrich Graetz and Nachman Krochmal, but points out that they were either remarkable exceptions or ignored altogether.[17] Even Graetz and Krochmal failed to treat the Kabbalah satisfactorily from Scholem's point of view, although their "failures" would provide him with some fruitful sources. Against the theological historians of his day, Graetz proposed a definition of Judaism as the sum total of all its historical manifestations. Whereas Graetz failed to accomplish this kind of pluralistic historiography in Europe because of the hostile demands of the age, Scholem maintains that he can fulfill Graetz's program in the land of Israel. He accepts Graetz's historicist definition of the "essence" of Judaism, but rejects the possibility of realizing it without a Jewish national homeland. He implicitly claims to complete Graetz's program by giving equal weight to the irrationalist factors in Jewish history which Graetz was compelled to ignore or denigrate.

With other radical Zionists, Scholem argues that historiography, no less than any other sphere of Jewish life, needs national "normalization" in order to flourish. He explicitly rejects Chaim Nachman Bialik's belief that the Wissenschaft des Judentums could have succeeded had its language been Hebrew.[18] Language in and of itself could not effect the revolutionary change necessary for a new historiography: Zionism had to take the correct impulses in the Wissenschaft des Judentums and quite literally transplant them to the new soil of Israel.

Despite Scholem's belief in the importance of Zionism as the basis for a new historiography, he never understood national "normalization" to mean chauvinistic nationalism. As a youth in Germany during World War I, he became inalterably opposed to the degeneration of modern nationalism and developed great sympathy for political anarchism. His Zionism was always a revolt against the authoritarian and jingoistic tendencies in nationalism to which Zionism was also prey: the Jews must not be "like all the other nations."

His essay on the Wissenschaft des Judentums was directed as much against his nationalist colleagues at the Hebrew University as against the nineteenth century. If the Wissenschaft des Judentums had degenerated into pure antiquarian negation, the new nationalist historians often went to the opposite extreme: uncritical glorification. Desiring to restore pride in Jewish history, they frequently reverted to the pious affirmations of the orthodox, but in a nationalist idiom:

We came to rebel but we ended up continuing [in the same path]. . . . All these plagues have now disguised themselves in nationalism. From the frying pan into the fire: after the emptiness of assimilation comes another, that of nationalist excess. We have cultivated nationalist "sermons" and "rhetoric" (melitza) in science to take the place of religious sermons and rhetoric. In both cases, the real forces operating in our world, the genuine demonic remains outside the picture we have created.[19]

By committing an error diametrically opposite to that of the Wissenschaft des Judentums, the nationalists had fallen into the same dogmatic trap.

To borrow from Nietzsche's terminology in his *Use and Abuse of History*, Scholem renounces both "antiquarian" and "monumentalist" historiography, calling instead for a "critical" historiography which would combine romantic, nationalist ideals with critical method. The Wissenschaft des Judentums started out with such a balance, but because of the contradictions imposed on it by its historical context, its critical side went out of control and became pure negation and antiquarianism. Some of the nationalists, Scholem suggests, have gone to the other extreme of pure affirmation and have also lost the critical method.

Against both of these extremes, Scholem proposes a third course: a Zionist historiography with a critical method. If the Wissenschaft des Judentums wanted to liquidate the Jewish tradition, Scholem promises a "liquidation of the liquidation" (*hisul ha-hisul*).[20] His formulation is just close enough to Hegel's "negation of the negation" to suggest to his audience his dialectical relation to his predecessors. His is not a simple negation of the past but a dialectical appropriation of it: "We wanted to return to science with all its rigor and without compromise as we found it in the writings of Zunz and Steinschneider, but we wanted to direct it towards construction and affirmation."[21] The Wissenschaft des Judentums, although enmeshed in paralyzing contradictions, nonetheless developed the secular historical method that Scholem advocates: "[Their] program would have been appropriate had it been directed towards the building of the Jewish nation."[22]

Scholem's hidden positive relation to the Wissenschaft des Judentums emerges unexpectedly from the very language he uses ostensibly to criticize them: "The optimism famous in their opinions is a lie and a mask—there is something of the *sitra ahra*, from the other side entirely, which emerges from their actions . . . I must confess that the figures of Zunz and Steinschneider have attracted me [for a long time] . . . they are truly demonic figures."[23] By calling Zunz and Steinschneider, whom he takes as representatives of the most destructive side of the Wissenschaft des Judentums, "demonic," Scholem implies that the rationalists' negative relation to the Jewish tradition has a structural similarity to Sabbatian antinomianism. Just as the Sabbatian heresy had a constructive side, so the demonic element in the Wissenschaft des Judentums—its critical historical method—must be the key to future constructive historiography.

Scholem's exploitation of his predecessors calls for the appropriation of their critical method, but inversion of their rationalist priorities:

> Factors that have been emphasized and were considered positive from the world-view of assimilation and self-justification require fundamental new criticism in order to determine what their actual role was in the development of the nation. Factors which were denigrated will appear in a different, more positive light from this point of view . . . It is possible that what was termed degeneracy will be thought of as a revelation and light and what seemed to [the nineteenth-century historians] impotent hallucinations—will be revealed as a great living myth . . . not the washing and mummification of the dead, but the discovery of hidden life by removal of the obfuscating masks.[24]

Here in a nutshell is Scholem's whole program: Where the Wissenschaft des Judentums saw only an historical corpse, Scholem finds "hidden life." He accepts the nineteenth-century estimation that if one considers only the rational aspect of the Jewish tradition, Judaism appears dead indeed. But by also considering "degeneracy" and "impotent hallucinations" as equally legitimate within Judaism, one discovers hidden life—a "great living myth," which Scholem finds in Jewish Gnosticism and the Kabbalah.

The historian must search beneath the surface, in the "cellar" of Jewish history to find his living subject. Scholem applies this methodology to his study of the Wissenschaft des Judentums itself. He comments that "not everything takes place on the plane of the obvious. This *Wissenschaft* has a hidden history of its own."[25] The "obvious" is assimilationist negation. But this "demonic" destructive side is also a virtue since it lays the basis for critical historiography. The Wissenschaft des Judentums provides Scholem with the critical method necessary for overturning its own rationalist conclusions and discovering the "great living myth."

I shall call Scholem's historical method of unearthing the "hidden virtue" from the Wissenschaft des Judentums "counter-history." I mean by this term the belief that the true history lies in a subterranean tradition that must be brought to light, much as the apocalyptic thinker decodes an ancient prophecy or as Walter Benjamin spoke of "brushing history against the grain." Counter-history is a type of revisionist historiography, but where the revisionist proposes a new theory or finds new facts, the counter-historian transvalues old ones. He does not deny that his predecessors' interpretation of history is correct, as does the revisionist, but he rejects the *completeness* of that interpretation: he affirms the existence of a "mainstream" or "establishment" history, but believes that the vital force lies in a secret tradition.

For Scholem, the Kabbalah, a suppressed and esoteric tradition, holds the key to the continuing vitality of Judaism. Where the nineteenth century saw mysticism and myth as roadblocks to the forward progress of Jewish history, Scholem sees them as the motor forces. There is a great similarity between Scholem's views and the "counter-histories" of a number of writers at the turn of the century, particularly Martin Buber and M. Y. Berdichevsky, who were influenced strongly by Nietzsche. Counter-history became a powerful tool of protest against both the normative orthodox tradition and the rationalist Judaism of the Enlightenment. However, Scholem's counter-history is significantly different from those of the "Jewish Nietzscheans" and he developed his position partly in rejection of them. As with his relationship to the Wissenschaft des Judentums, Scholem's approach to the radical historiography of his own day represents a third course. His counter-history must be seen as a dialectical negation of both rationalist historiography and the nationalist response to it.

1.   *The Nineteenth-Century Legacy*

Scholem's relationship to the Wissenschaft des Judentums was conditioned by ambiguities in the school itself. From the outset, the nineteenth-century historians argued for a nondogmatic historiography which should have given equal weight to forces other than rationalism in Jewish history. In fact, one of the most common criticisms of the Wissenschaft des Judentums is that it was indiscriminating in its use of sources: all facts were considered equally important. But rationalist and apologetic assumptions, partly imposed by the demands of the times, worked against this program and demoted nonrational forces to a lower status in Jewish history. This tension between the promise of an all-inclusive, objective historiography and the conscious denigration of certain elements in Jewish history would prove fruitful for Scholem. He would exploit the ambiguities in the Wissenschaft des Judentums to construct his own position, which would rest on very different assumptions.

Since we are interested in the Wissenschaft des Judentums from the perspective of Scholem's historiography, we cannot examine all of the achievements of nineteenth-century scholarship. I will treat only selected examples of the relationship of the Wissenschaft des Judentums to irrationalism in Jewish history.

The term "irrationalism" will appear frequently in this work and it deserves some provisional definition, despite the danger that any definition will be incomplete and inadequate. The use of such an ambiguous term is necessary because it plays a central role in Scholem's vocabulary, and I have attempted to define it as I believe Scholem uses it. Since the late nineteenth century, irrationalism has been understood primarily as a psychological category. For Scholem, however, irrationalism is a term in the philosophy of religion. It is a mode of intuitive cognition which is based neither on observation of the phenomenal world nor on logical deductions. The religious irrationalist, or mystic, relates his experience in symbolic images rather than through logical propositions and, although the images may be drawn from the real world, the things symbolized do not correspond to observable reality. Hence, the *sefirot* images which symbolize God's emanations do not seem to describe verifiable entities in the world, but the Kabbalist nonetheless believes that they are representations of the essence of reality. Since the irrationalist does not make a logical argument, his symbols may involve logical contradictions. Scholem insists that Jewish mysticism addresses the central questions of medieval philosophy, but its paradoxical formulations, although perhaps solutions to these questions, would not be comprehensible to a philosopher. In Scholem's definition, Jewish mysticism is a self-contained tradition that developed in close proximity to Jewish philosophy, but was never merely a branch of or aberration to philosophy. The term "irrationalism" rather than, say, "nonrationalism" is more faithful to Scholem since Jewish mysticism, in his conception, is not just the negation of Jewish rationalism but forms a discrete discipline in its own right.

"Irrationalism" is not, of course, equivalent to mysticism, but with that caveat, I will take the liberty of frequently using the two terms interchangeably. Moreover, Jewish mysticism is not the equivalent of "Kabbalah" but, following convention, I will generally use Kabbalah in its broadest sense to refer to the whole phenomenon. The only exception will be in discussion of the history of Jewish mysticism, in which the term Kabbalah denotes the particular mystical movement that developed in Provence and Spain in the late twelfth or early thirteenth centuries.

DER VEREIN FÜR KULTUR UND WISSENSCHAFT DER JUDEN

The Wissenschaft des Judentums emerged in Germany in the period of romanticism. However, its deep affiliations with romantic philosophy and historiography help us very little in determining in advance its relationship to irrationalism. There were as many romanticisms as there were romantics. Certain thinkers like Hegel, who are occasionally considered romantics because of their emphasis on historical development, tried to solve the epistemological problems posed by the later Enlightenment from a rationalist viewpoint. But against this rational idealism, one finds romantics like Schelling, Hölderlin, and Baader who considered irrational myths as legitimate as the products of reason.

Historicism is generally considered the legacy of German romanticism, although, as Ernst Cassirer has shown, its seeds were already sown during the Enlightenment.[1] Under the influence of thinkers like Herder and Ranke, romantic historiography often glorified the unique spirit of each nation against the universalism of the Enlightenment. The history of each Volksgeist was equally "close to God." The development of philology as a discrete discipline contributed toward this view. In 1795, Friedrich August Wolf published his *Prolegomena to Homer*, which set out to show that Homer's writings were really composed by a number of writers. Wolf is therefore considered the founder of modern philology, although similar critical studies of the Bible had already been undertaken by Spinoza, Richard Simon, and Jean Astruc. Wolf's disciple, August Boeckh, defined the goals of the new philology in his monumental *Encyclopaedie und Methodologie der philologischen Wissenschaften*. As opposed to "history," which was understood as merely an account of political events, philology would "present in every people its entire mental development, the history of all aspects of its culture." Moreover, philology was to be free of all dogma and would use the same hermeneutical principles on any text: "If a sacred book is of human origin, it must be understood according to human rules in the usual treatment applied to books."[2]

Hence, the new historicism, with philology as its handmaiden, aspired to become an objective science (*Wissenschaft*) which would apply its tools to the whole culture of a nation. The emphasis on philology necessarily directed the focus of the new science to literature, perhaps to the detriment of nonliterary sources, but the goal of this historicism was to be all-inclusive. Since all nations were judged to have equally legitimate cultures, romantic historiography, at least in theory, was less interested in tracing universal progress than in extolling the glory of each Volksgeist.

The romantic desire to understand each Volksgeist in its unique historical context (in Ranke's famous phrase: *wie es eigentlich gewesen*) was doomed to reach a crisis in the twentieth century as philosophers of history realized that such reconstruction could never be accomplished "objectively." Moreover, the entrenched nationalism inherent in German romanticism often undermined the promise of historiography to give each Volksgeist equal treatment.

The Wissenschaft des Judentums was the stepchild of the new German historiography and was heir to all the ambiguities and tensions of its parent. In the wake of the "hep-hep" riots of 1819, a group of enlightened young Berlin Jews, deeply troubled by the setbacks to full Jewish emancipation and by the breakdown of traditional Jewish identity, met to form the Verein für Kultur und Wissenschaft der Juden.[3] This society, which has justly been considered the founding group of modern Jewish historiography, was caught between two often conflicting goals: the romantic desire to pro-

mote Jewish national identity and the rationalist need to show that
the Jews were like all other men and therefore deserved full emancipation.

The members of the Verein wanted to use history to restore Jewish pride, and they therefore frequently adopted the notion of a
unique Jewish Volksgeist that developed through history. With
other romantics, they were interested in rejuvenating the native
spirit of their nation which they thought the Enlightenment had
undermined. Eduard Gans, president of the Verein, argued that the
Enlightenment had freed the "subjective spirit" of individualism
from the fetters of religion, but that no new communal ties had
come to replace them: "The break with the intimacy of the old existence has indeed occurred, but the deeper return to this intimacy
has not taken place. The enthusiasm for religion and the strength of
old relationships has vanished, but no new enthusiasm has broken
forth, no new set of relationships has been built."[4] With the waning
of religion, the Jewish spirit had progressed to a new stage of liberation, but without some new community this liberation remained
negative. Gans and his colleagues saw the Verein as a fraternal and
intellectual solution: the historical study of Judaism would bind
them together in a new community, a new synagogue. For Gans, a
disciple of Hegel, the new ties would be founded in a synthesis between the liberated "subjective spirit" and the "objective spirit" of
historical science: "Arise you who set science (Wissenschaft), the
love of your own people and benevolence, above all else; arise, at-
tach yourselves to this noble Verein, and see the messianic age
breaking forth in the strong fraternal union of such good men."[5]
Wissenschaft was to become a messianic substitute for religion in a
secular world.

The debt which the early Wissenschaft des Judentums owed to
German historicism is perhaps most evident in the work of Leopold
Zunz (1794-1886), the member of the Verein who had the most impact on later Jewish historiography.[6] In 1818, a year before the
Verein was formed, Zunz published a programmatic essay entitled
Etwas über die rabbinische Litteratur. Zunz, who was a student of
Wolf and Boeckh, pleads for a new Jewish scholarship which would
have as its subject not just Jewish law, as it did for traditional Jewish scholars, but the whole range of Jewish literature. Moreover, he
argued forcefully for a nondogmatic historiography that would
neither impose contemporary norms on the past nor seek to make
the past "a norm for our own judgements."[7] Zunz, then, set the
stage for the new Jewish Wissenschaft, which was to be at once
philologically critical, nondogmatic and all-inclusive. Here was a

program that might well have fostered the serious study of the literature of irrationalism as a legitimate part of the totality of Jewish literature.

Immanuel Wolf, another member of the Verein, elaborated some of these ideas in 1822 in his seminal essay, "Über den Begriff einer Wissenschaft des Judentums."[8] Adumbrating a theme that would be characteristic of much of the Wissenschaft des Judentums, Wolf argued that the essence of Judaism was "the idea of the unconditioned unity in the all" (die Idee der unbedingten Einheit im All).[9] This monotheistic idea had been revealed to the Jews at the beginning of their history, but had not been fully understood then. Under Hegel's influence, Wolf argued that, as ideas develop through their historical manifestations, men acquire greater understanding of them. All intellectual and speculative movements in Jewish history contributed toward ever greater consciousness of the original monotheistic idea, and historical science must include all these movements in its inquiry.

Wolf's essay, like Zunz's, was a covert attack on rabbinic Judaism. The difference between the old rabbinic view of Judaism and that of the new Wissenschaft was that the rabbis had a one-sided, dogmatic opinion of what is properly Jewish:

> Since then, and until the present day, the rabbis confined themselves to their scholastic preoccupations. But that is the nature of scholasticism: to follow the letter of a tradition assumed to be holy and inviolable, to develop from within it every aspect of human knowledge and thus to hamper every free, individual, and living movement of the human mind and to preclude any rational and independent understanding of the infinite idea.[10]

The new historical science was objective and independent because it recognized all Jewish intellectual movements as equally legitimate. In partial anticipation of Scholem, Wolf even suggested that the true development of the "infinite idea" is reflected less in the mainstream of rabbinic literature than in the more peripheral movements such as the Essenes, the Sadducees, Hellenistic Jewish philosophy, and the Kabbalah.[11] Wolf believed that this "counterhistorical" development of the monotheistic idea culminated in the work of Baruch Spinoza.

Wolf's antidogmatic, all-inclusive notion of the Wissenschaft des Judentums might have been conducive to an unbiased evaluation of Jewish mysticism, but certain basic assumptions in the essay undermined this promise. Wolf looked for the essence of Judaism in intellectual movements: his Geistesgeschichte was the search for a rationally comprehensible idea. His model was Spinoza, who had tried to conceptualize his metaphysics with geometric logic. There could be no place for the Kabbalah's symbolic imagery in this history of the monotheistic idea.

Eduard Gans had already laid the basis for the exclusion of the Kabbalah from the "essence" of Judaism. In his third address to the Verein,[12] he argued, following Hegel, that consciousness tries to understand itself through reality. Since Gans understood consciousness as reason, he implied that whatever is not rationally comprehensible is not real. Furthermore, he defined unreal products of the imagination as historically transitory. Whatever is not real and cannot be comprehended by rational Wissenschaft need not be banned from true Judaism since it has already vanished. Therefore, as an assumed product of the imagination, the Kabbalah could appear to Wissenschaft as illusory, without any real and enduring existence in Jewish history.

The identification of rationalism with monotheism further subverted nondogmatic historiography. Although some nonconformists like Solomon Ludwig Steinheim disputed this equation,[13] the mainstream of the Wissenschaft des Judentums held that Jewish monotheism is the most rational of all religions, a *Religion der Vernunft*. They believed that the very idea of monotheism logically demands that Judaism be reduced to a single set of noncontradictory ideas: one God, one "essence" of Judaism. Any contradictory principles would undermine a strictly monotheistic view of the world, since a religion of reason governed by contradictory ideas would violate the most elementary axiom of rationalism, the law of noncontradiction. The Kabbalah's use of multiple emanations to describe God must have seemed therefore to subvert both reason and monotheism.

Why had rationalism crept in as a dogma to subvert the historicist idea of an all-inclusive historiography? The answer is that the early Wissenschaft des Judentums was not only engaged in promoting Jewish pride, but also in fighting on another front: to use historical evidence to prove that the Jews deserved complete emancipation. The Jews, they argued, were culturally prepared for emancipation since their culture was not fundamentally primitive or alien in relation to Western culture. This goal, already enunciated by Zunz as one of his reasons for writing the *Etwas über die rabbinische Litteratur*, required emphasis on those elements Jews shared with non-Jews and therefore naturally tended toward rationalism. The new German nationalist historiography, although it provided them with critical tools, could not attract these young scholars, particularly since it often excluded the Jews from its vision of a united Germany. The historiography of the early Wissenschaft des Judentums was therefore often closer to eighteenth-century rationalism than to nineteenth-century romanticism.

Torn and distorted by these contradictory forces, the early Wissenschaft des Judentums imposed rationalist principles of selectivity on its romantic goal of a history of the whole Jewish Volksgeist. The contradictions which beset the Verein für Kultur und Wissenschaft der Juden did not have only abstract consequences: when the Verein failed to fulfill its utopian communal and religious ideals, some of its members, like Gans and Heinrich Heine, escaped the tragic tensions by conversion to Christianity.[14]

The legacy of the Verein, both positive and negative, was not lost, however. In the years following its demise in the 1820s, the standard of the new historiography was carried by a whole generation of scholars. Still, the intrinsic tensions that discouraged study of Jewish irrationalism continued to plague Jewish scholarship. Zunz himself did not entirely ignore Jewish mysticism in his encyclopedic discussion of Jewish literature, but in an essay written at the same time as his *Etwas*, he bewailed the degeneration of the Kabbalah in the sixteenth century.[15] Abraham Geiger, perhaps the most prominent theoretician of German Reform Judaism as well as a great scholar, held that Jewish mysticism was a roadblock to the progressive change he saw as the essence of Jewish history.[16] Moritz Steinschneider, the great bibliographer of the Wissenschaft des Judentums, who actually discovered and described many Kabbalistic manuscripts, expressed the hope that one of his discoveries, composed by the medieval German Pietist Eleazar of Worms, might never be published.[17] Even nineteenth-century scholars such as S. D. Luzzato, who cannot be suspected of radical rationalism or assimilationism, considered the Kabbalah heresy. Similarly, the Eastern European enlightener, Judah Leib Mises, wrote that "most of the opinions of the Kabbalah resemble those of the idolators."[18]

HEINRICH GRAETZ ON THE KABBALAH

The tension between all-inclusive historicism and antipathy to Jewish irrationalism is a prominent feature of the work of perhaps the nineteenth century's greatest Jewish historian, Heinrich Graetz (1817-1891). Graetz's diatribes against the Kabbalah are notorious in Jewish historiography. But Graetz merits more extensive examination than the other scholars already mentioned because his work was informed by a Jewish nationalism not so very far from Scholem's. Indeed, in his essay on the Wissenschaft des Judentums,

Scholem mentions Graetz as one of those whose approach differed drastically from that of the mainstream.

Early in his career, Graetz set out his historicist, perhaps proto-nationalist position in a programmatic essay, "Die Konstruction der jüdischen Geschichte," in which he attacked both Reform and Orthodox thinkers of his day for trying to dogmatize Judaism by giving it a theological definition.[19] Graetz argued that each attempt to isolate an "essence" of Judaism leads only to a partial truth; although Reform and Orthodox were partially right, only a combination of their ostensibly contradictory definitions could produce a whole picture of Judaism. Graetz's goal was to realize Wolf's all-inclusive definition of Judaism. The various dogmatists had erred in trying to learn the nature of Judaism from *a priori* philosophical reflections. Graetz maintained instead that Judaism is the product of the totality of its history; only by assembling all the data of Jewish history could Judaism be defined inductively or on the basis of an *a posteriori* investigation. This historicist program was to become almost precisely Scholem's own credo a century later. Graetz solved the problem of the contradiction of definitions historically: as history developed, it produced new manifestations of the Jewish spirit. These manifestations might appear contradictory when considered ahistorically, but they could be harmonized as reflections of different stages of history.[20]

Graetz's desire to divorce history from theology suffers from internal contradictions. If each period of Jewish history manifested an autonomous principle of Judaism, what is the common denominator that ties them together? How does the principle of historical development harmonize contradictory definitions while still preserving some concept of Judaism to which a traditional Jew, like Graetz, could subscribe? In his repeated use of the metaphor comparing Judaism with a "kernel" (*Kern*) surrounded by different "shells" (*Schale*),[21] Graetz suggested that such a common denominator exists. Judaism actually retained its essential character even as it historically changed its outer form.[22]

Graetz identified this essential kernel as the "concept of an extra-mundane God" (*überweltlichen Gottesidee*).[23] This idea appeared at the beginning of Jewish history as a product of the struggle against paganism. Paganism cannot be defined only as a belief in many gods: it is the principle of immanence or the identity of God and nature. Similarly, Judaism cannot be reduced to "mere" monotheism, which is a negative principle, but is actually the principle of transcendence or the subordination of nature to an autonomous God. In all of their historical creations, the Jews have tried to realize concretely this principle of transcendence.

In his effort to avoid a dogmatic definition of Judaism, Graetz nevertheless slipped one in through the back door. As Zacharias Frankel noted in his appended criticism to Graetz's essay,[24] the reduction of monotheism to a secondary principle is either heresy or a semantic game. Since Graetz certainly did not intend heresy, we might suspect that he avoided a purely religious definition by suggesting a broader idea of Judaism which still functioned like a religious dogma. Any historical phenomenon, such as the Kabbalah, that does not satisfy the principle of transcendence must be excommunicated from Judaism.

Graetz belied his own promise of an inductive immanent historiography from the outset. Not only did he define the basic idea of Judaism in an essay at the beginning of his career, but he did so at the beginning of the essay. Graetz's dogmatic definition of Judaism was not an unfortunate result of certain unconscious biases, but a symptom of the same basic problem that plagued his Reform opponents: the need to find a principle that precedes Jewish history and directs its development.

One might even argue that the very notion of an extra-mundane God precluded an immanent historiography. A transcendent God is a force outside history which somehow plays the guiding role in historical events. A totally immanent history would unfold without outside interference. According to Graetz's definitions, immanent history would be "pagan." If Jewish history is guided from outside history, then historiography would have to take suprahistorical forces into account: historiography would no longer be an account of the immanent interplay of historical forces. Abraham Geiger's criticism of Graetz, that his history lacked an "inner driving force," was therefore correct, if for the wrong reasons:[25] Graetz's historiography was guided by an external theological principle just as his conception of Jewish history was not entirely immanent.

With many other nineteenth-century thinkers, Graetz held that the idea of a transcendent God went through a gradual and progressive process of purification throughout Jewish history. Following the Hegelian division of history into triads, which was beloved of many Jewish historians, Graetz postulated three periods of Jewish history: political (First Temple), religious (Second Temple), and reflective (Diaspora). The idea of a transcendent God attained its purest expression in the last period when it "immersed itself in the inwardness of reflection . . . Judaism became scientific scholarship (*das Judentum wird Wissenschaft*)."[26] Graetz called the last phase of his period of reflection the time of "philosophical-critical Judaism," and the dates he assigned to it (1760-1850) suggest that this latest form of Judaism was equivalent to the Wissenschaft des Judentums itself.[27] Graetz therefore believed that Jewish history was progressive and culminated with the new historical science. His belief in progress and in the superiority of rational reflection (the theme of the last period of Jewish history) make him more the child of the eighteenth-century rationalism or Hegelian idealism than of romantic historicism: although he has been compared to Ranke, he was not really an historicist for whom all ages are "equally close to God."[28] The transcendent principle of monotheism rather than the interaction of immanent forces determined the goal of history and the priorities of the historian.

The issue of transcendence versus immanence was a crucial one for the nineteenth century.[29] As much as writers like Graetz tried to secularize historical processes, they still resorted in the end to some suprahistorical force, whether Absolute Spirit or the idea of an *überweltliche Gott*. They were unable to establish history as a fully autonomous realm. We will see that Scholem would not only attempt to achieve a completely immanent historiography, but would do so by attacking the centrality of belief in a transcendent monotheistic God. He would claim that mythical ideas, often verging on pantheism or polytheism, accompanied transcendent monotheism throughout Jewish history. By throwing doubt on the centrality of a transcendent God in Jewish religion, Scholem would be able to avoid some of Graetz's problems: instead of progressing toward ever more abstract reflection on a single idea of God, Jewish history represents the continual conflict between contradictory ideas of God.

With this background in Graetz's rationalist philosophy of history, we can understand better the place he assigned mysticism in Jewish history. Mysticism was part of the period of reflection, but it was faulty reflection.[30] When Graetz labeled the Kabbalah *unjüdisch*,[31] he did not necessarily mean that it was a foreign doctrine but that it deviated from the mainstream of Jewish speculation concerning the idea of God. It was an extreme reaction to rational philosophy.

Since Graetz considered Jewish Gnosticism to be a form of philosophy and not mysticism, he dated the first Jewish mysticism to the Gaonic period (early Middle Ages).[32] Mysticism emerged as a *by-product* of the medieval philosophical defense of Judaism. The rationalist Mutazila school of Islamic philosophy prohibited attributing any human attributes to God, a position that was then adopted by Jewish rationalists. Believing that such arguments undermined the God of the Bible, defenders of Jewish orthodoxy went to the opposite extreme and composed blatantly anthropomorphistic literature, such as the *Shiur Koma* and *Alfabeta d'Rabbi Akiva*.

Thirteenth-century Kabbalah developed in a similar fashion. To nonphilosophical Jews, Maimonidean philosophy seemed to undermine traditional Jewish belief. Their defense of the tradition resulted in exaggerated and extreme irrationalism. They resorted to fantastic descriptions of the deity and abandoned all rational speculation.[33] In order to convince their coreligionists that their doctrines were authentically Jewish, the Kabbalists composed shameless forgeries in the names of the Talmudic authorities. The most famous of these late forgeries was the *Zohar*.[34]

Why did Graetz, who was so committed to the principle of historical development, consider that a late date for the *Zohar* would downgrade its importance? Graetz's main objection to the *Zohar* was that it was pseudepigraphic. We might speculate that he opposed pseudepigraphic literature because it refused to take its correct place in history. Given his firm notion of historical progress, an attempt by a recent movement to claim antiquity would be a sign of its reactionary character: Kabbalistic pseudepigraphies must have seemed to Graetz attempts to turn back the clock. Thus, where philosophy was willing to adopt new weapons to defend Judaism, mysticism rebelled against progress. Incapable of naively returning to the prephilosophic past, the Kabbalists concocted outlandish, exaggerated imitations of Talmudic legends and claimed they were authentic. To Graetz, the more "absurd" the Kabbalistic symbols, the less likely that they were authentically old. Graetz could not understand the religious motive behind pseudepigraphy and therefore considered such literature worthless. Scholem would accept much of Graetz's dating, but radically alter his evaluation of pseudepigraphy.

For Graetz, then, mysticism arose from the failure of philosophy to convert all of Jewry to its doctrines. The danger in philosophy, he implied, is that as it injects new life into Judaism by its new reflections on the Jewish *Gottesidee*, it necessarily undermines earlier conceptions of Judaism.[35] The attempt by reactionaries to turn back the clock comes in response to this perceived threat, but the mystical solutions they propose are even more dangerous. Graetz showed that each major philosophical movement in Jewish history was accompanied by a mystical reaction: the *Shiur Koma* at the time of Sa'adia Gaon, the thirteenth-century Kabbalah after Maimonides, Sabbatai Zevi together with Spinoza, and Hasidism at the same time as the Haskalah (Enlightenment). Concerning the last pair, Graetz wrote: "History in its generative power is as manifold and puzzling as Nature. It produces herbs and poisonous plants, lovely flowers and hideous parasites. Reason and unreason seemed to have entered into a covenant to shatter to atoms the gigantic structure of Talmudic Judaism."[36] At each critical juncture in Jewish history, when speculative thought was in ferment, it was accompanied by its "dark side": Jewish mysticism.

As a by-product of philosophy, Jewish mysticism could have no autonomous history of its own. Graetz pointed out some structural similarities between thirteenth-century Kabbalah and earlier motifs, but he rejected any continuous mystical tradition. Each outburst of irrationalism was unrelated to earlier or later outbursts; each must be understood solely in the context of its own time. This denial of a history of mysticism finds expression in Graetz's ironic appropriation of the Kabbalistic metaphor of the kernel and the shells. The kernel was the original idea of Judaism, and the various shells its historical manifestations. But the Kabbalah was a shell upon a shell, a parasitic accretion with no organic connection to the inner seed. Since only the kernel has a history as it produces new shells, the Kabbalah could not qualify as a legitimate focus for the historian.

The continuous battle between rational speculation and mystical exaggeration is the key to understanding Graetz's image of his own enterprise. For Graetz, the age of speculation reached its apogee with the Wissenschaft des Judentums, the philosophical-critical period. But the danger of any philosophical approach, as the history of the Kabbalah teaches, is that it can create a mystical backlash. How can the modern historian, as a representative of "philosophical speculation," avoid this calamity?

Graetz suggests an answer in his doctoral dissertation on Gnosticism and Judaism. In the foreword, he explicitly compares Gnosticism to modern pantheism, by which he almost certainly meant German idealism.[37] The Jewish Gnostics did not deny their Jewish ancestry by apostasy but tried to smuggle foreign ideas into Judaism.[38] Despite his protest that the dissertation had only academic interest, there can be no doubt that Graetz intended it as an historical allegory for the contemporary danger of Reform. The Reformers, like the Gnostics, proposed a new philosophical definition of Judaism, but if their way were followed it could produce a severe mystical reaction. The moden historian must fulfill the moderate role of Rabbi Akiva in fighting the new Gnosticism. He must seize the tools of modern historicism, as created by German idealism, and turn them to the defense of the authentic Judaism just as Akiva learned Gnosticism in order to defeat it.

Graetz's treatment of Jewish mysticism was influenced at the outset by rationalism and by his conception of his own enterprise as an
historian. The Kabbalah could serve only the negative didactic purpose of warning Jews of contemporary dangers. Historiography,
by definition, could not treat irrationalism positively lest it undermine its own essential pedagogical purpose.

KABBALISTIC SCHOLARSHIP IN THE NINETEENTH CENTURY

The overwhelmingly negative attitude of the great scholars of the
Wissenschaft des Judentums toward irrational phenomena in Jewish history reinforces the supposition that Scholem single-handedly
created the field of Kabbalistic scholarship. Without for a moment
diminishing his contribution, it is crucial to realize that Scholem
could not have accomplished what he did from scratch—he had
predecessors. Not only did they supply him with the historical and
philological methods necessary for his work, but, in many cases,
they did the initial spadework in the Kabbalistic sources themselves. Steinschneider discovered many of the Kabbalistic manuscripts in European libraries and thus prepared the bibliographical
ground for future work. Graetz himself, despite his negative attitude, demonstrates extensive knowledge and understanding of the
mystical sources. Although Scholem reserves some of his sharpest
criticism for Graetz, we shall see how great his debt is to this particular nineteenth-century precursor.

Much of the research done on Jewish mysticism in the nineteenth
century was a continuation of earlier orthodox scholarship. In the
eighteenth century, for instance, Jacob Emden undertook a comprehensive critical study of the *Zohar*, using techniques not so remote from those of modern historiography.[39] In the nineteenth century, traditional scholars such as M. H. Landauer, D. H. Joel, and
Eljakim Milzahagi continued in Emden's footsteps and Scholem has
explicitly recognized their contributions.[40]

Of particular importance in nineteenth-century Kabbalistic
scholarship is Adolf Jellinek (1820-1893), who collected and published many Kabbalistic manuscripts in his multivolume *Bet ha-
Midrash*, a work that Scholem consulted extensively in his earliest
studies. Jellinek was one of the least tendentious of the nineteenth-
century Jewish scholars of the Kabbalah. His two careful studies of
the authorship of the *Zohar* are exemplary, not least because
Graetz and later Scholem accepted their fundamental conclusions.[41]

One way in which it became possible for nineteenth-century historians, even if they were sympathetic to rationalism, to treat the
Kabbalah seriously was to consider it a branch of Jewish philoso-

phy, an assumption Scholem would have to reject. D. H. Joel, in his *Die Religionsphilosophie des Sohar und ihr Verhältnis zur allgemeinen jüdischen Theologie* (1849), tried to harmonize the *Zohar*, certainly one of the more "mythological" works of the Kabbalah, with Jewish philosophy. David Neumark, the historian of Jewish philosophy who took perhaps the most favorable view of the Kabbalah, argued in 1907 that the Kabbalah was part of the inner dialectical development of Jewish philosophy.[42] He opposed Graetz's assertion that the Kabbalah was merely an irrationalist reaction against philosophy and, as such, not a legitimate part of Judaism.

The effort to give the Kabbalah a legitimate place in Jewish history by subordinating it to the history of Jewish philosophy demonstrates the limits to which rationalist nineteenth-century scholarship was prepared to go. It is worthwhile to examine this point in greater detail by looking at one nineteenth-century philosopher of Jewish history who not only devoted much serious attention to the Kabbalah, but also must be counted as one of Scholem's most important precursors. Nachman Krochmal (1785-1840) cannot be understood in the same categories as the German Wissenschaft des Judentums. Although he was strongly influenced by the German idealism which had played such a role in the Verein, he lived his whole life in Galicia, wrote in Hebrew, and remained an orthodox Jew.[43] Krochmal was part of the dawn of the Eastern European Jewish enlightenment whose program tended to be much more nationalist than that of its German counterpart. Unlike Zunz, Steinschneider and others of the western Wissenschaft des Judentums, Krochmal did not believe that historical study was possible because Judaism was dead, although he did see the emergence of historical science as proof of "the end of days."[44]

Krochmal argued that the Jews are subject to the same laws of history as the rest of nations, but where all other nations disappear after undergoing the inevitable processes of rise, maturity, and decline, the Jews' relationship to Absolute Spirit (his idealist term for God) allows them to overcome the decline phase of each cycle of history and enter into a new cycle. In this way, Krochmal preserved the traditional concept of *nezah yisrael* (eternity of Israel) while at the same time treating the Jews as a nation within history.[45]

Krochmal's desire to harmonize an historical approach to Judaism with traditional categories came out of the influence of historicism. As opposed to the hardening attitude of orthodox rabbis in Eastern Europe, such as Moses Sofer's, Krochmal recognized that escape was no solution: only by adopting and transforming secular modes of thought could Judaism be preserved. Krochmal believed that the main challenge to Judaism in the early nineteenth century was secular historiography. In the introduction to his *Moreh Ne-vukhe ha-Zeman* (Guide to the Perplexed of the Time), he suggests that the best response to historical criticism of traditional Judaism is an historicist defense.

Each generation of Jews had possessed its own "mode of investigation" (*darke ha-limud*) by which it adopted principles of non-Jewish philosophies in order to reinterpret the original biblical revelation. Maimonides, in his own *Guide for the Perplexed*, had sought to defend Judaism against Aristotelian philosophy by enlightened use of Aristotle himself. Historicism could do the same thing for nineteenth-century Judaism by giving Jewish tradition an historical interpretation. Krochmal intended his *Guide* as a whole to be an ambitious history of Jewish thought rather than, as is commonly conceived, a purely theoretical philosophy of history.

By adopting Maimonides' title for his historicist work,[46] Krochmal was not only applying Maimonides' method to his own time, but also subtly suggesting that Maimonides' "mode of investigation" was no longer relevant. By asserting that each mode of investigation was relevant only for its own time, but not for all generations, he was following one of the cardinal principles of historicism. Yet historicism allowed him to preserve earlier modes as legitimate and, indeed, commanded that they be the prime objects of his mode of investigation: an historicist philosophy of history must consist of interpretations of past philosophies.

Since the historicism he adopted dictated that all earlier speculative movements be granted legitimacy, Krochmal necessarily started with the assumption that Jewish history is pluralistic rather than monolithic. This is one of the main principles that Scholem took from historicism. However, since Krochmal was a rationalist, he searched in the plethora of speculative movements for ideas that would correspond, no matter how inadequately, to his own. Those ideas he did not regard favorably became the cause for the ultimate degeneration of past modes of investigation. His ambiguous treatment of the Kabbalah is a case in point.

The unusually positive attitude Krochmal adopted toward the Kabbalah, already noted by a number of commentators,[47] was a consequence of this historicist philosophy. In chapter six of the *Guide*, he seems to equate the Kabbalists' "secret of the unity and the faith" (*sod ha-yihud v'ha-emunah*) with Maimonidean philosophy, Neoplatonism, and modern Idealism.[48] He refers to all of these speculative movements as "sciences of the faith" (*hokhmot ha-*

emunah), by which he means conceptual systems for converting sensual images (ziyurim) into "concepts of the understanding" (musagim sikhliyim) and, finally, into the most abstract "concepts of the reason" (musagim tvuniyim), all terms borrowed from Kant.[49] Anticipating Scholem, Krochmal also shows the striking similarities between Gnosticism, which he evidently considered another legitimate speculative philosophy, and the Kabbalah.[50] They shared such notions as the hidden God and the hypostatization of God's attributes. We shall see that Scholem elaborated these suggested similarities into a coherent theory of the Kabbalah as a persistent form of Jewish Gnosticism. Hence, the Kabbalah in Krochmal's system is one among a number of legitimate modes of investigation or "sciences of the faith."

On the other hand, Krochmal makes it clear that the Kabbalah was suited only to a certain historical period. It was a peculiar phenomenon of his third cycle of Jewish history which began after the Bar Kokhba revolt in the second century and went into decline following the death of Nachmanides (thirteenth century), coming to its nadir with the 1648 pogroms and Sabbatianism.[51] The Kabbalah precisely followed the course of this third cycle.[52] It flourished from the time of Alexandrian Jewish philosophy, reached maturity during the Gaonic period, and began to decline after the death of Nachmanides. Interestingly, Krochmal dated the "classical" Kabbalah of the thirteenth century to the phase of decline. The final denouement of the Kabbalah in the Sabbatian movement suggests other parallels between Krochmal's conclusions and Scholem's. Krochmal evidently believed that Sabbatianism was caused by a degenerated form of Gnostic Kabbalah, a conclusion that Scholem adopted without the pejorative value judgment.[53]

In Krochmal's philosophy of Jewish history, the Kabbalah degenerated into antinomian messianism because its epistemology or science of the faith was not perfect. Indeed, all sciences of the faith of earlier historical periods were in some sense defective, or else they would have survived the cycles of Jewish history. The Kabbalah, Krochmal suggests, "began with reason"[54] but degenerated into "feverish imagination" (retihat dimyonam). The mystic rejects the sensual world and relies solely on an "inner eye," which begins to conceive angels and other beings "with pure or no matter" and with which the mystic tries to unite himself. At the end, the mystic imagines that he is one with God.[55] Whereas the rationalist epistemology, which Krochmal took from Kant, also strives for abstraction from the sensual world, mystical abstraction is illusory and actually conceals mysticism's fundamental sensuality. The "inner eye" of imagination is misleading because it causes us to believe that there are such things as beings without matter. Correct epistemology does not renounce sense perceptions, but abstracts *from them.*[56] In his rejection of sense perceptions, the mystic becomes entangled in sensual representations, such as the hypostatization of God's attributes as angels. Krochmal presumably believed that the Kabbalah's vivid symbolic pictures of God's emanations were just such sensual products of the imagination. The rationalist, on the other hand, is able to rise above sensual modes of representation by rooting his conceptualizations in sense data. The Kabbalist takes the seemingly easier path of a direct flight to the divine but paradoxically remains very much grounded in sensuality; the rationalist attains greater heights by his slow and systematic ascent.

The Kabbalah may have asked the proper questions, but it arrived at an inadequate answer because its way of conceptualizing was imaginative rather than rational. The Kabbalah necessarily declined during the third cycle of Jewish history because its epistemology was inherently flawed. Nevertheless, the Kabbalah played an important preservative role in Judaism during the early part of the third cycle as a partial science of faith.

The Kabbalah's ambiguous position as a partially correct science of faith is due to the intermediate status that Krochmal assigned to imagination in his epistemology. Like Spinoza and Kant, Krochmal seems to have believed that imagination is an unclear but not entirely untrue form of reasoning. Through imagination, one might arrive at some kind of truth. Even if the Kabbalah was the product of imagination, it was still a partial manifestation of rational spirit, as was the case with the polytheistic religions.[57] Krochmal suggests a hidden comparison between the Kabbalah and the religions of the Gentile nations. He refers to the various partial spirits of the nations with the biblical attributes of God such as "splendor" (*tiferet*), "courage" (*gevurah*), "wisdom" (*hokhmah*), and "understanding" (*binah*).[58] With minor changes, his list corresponds to the names of the Kabbalistic *sefirot*. The Kabbalah was, then, a kind of compendium of all the divinities of the nations; it was on a higher level than the religions of these nations because it included all of their partial spirits—but its mode of representation was sensual.

As a confirmed historicist, Krochmal was able to treat the Kabbalah as a valuable historical source while still restricting it to an inferior level of cognition. As an intermediate type of cognition—between pure sensuality and pure abstraction—the Kabbalah occupied a "middle" stage in Jewish history, a mode of investigation relevant to the third cycle of Jewish history. Krochmal did not exclude the Kabbalah from his history of Judaism, but he subordinated its imaginative or irrational epistemology to his own idealistic rationalism. He was not able to grant irrationalism autonomous status of its own, but his historicist method, which suggested that all intellectual movements in Judaism are equally legitimate, and many of his substantive conclusions about the nature of the Kabbalah resurface in Scholem's historiography.

Krochmal is a cogent example of the fundamental tension in the Wissenschaft des Judentums between an objective method and a rationalist bias. The achievements of the nineteenth-century Jewish historiography, even in the field of the Kabbalah, were due in large measure to the "positivistic" spirit engendered by the new philology. Along with general European historiography, particularly in Germany, the Wissenschaft des Judentums believed in the importance of gathering and presenting historical "facts" in a totally objective manner. This mania for minute facts often led to indiscriminate historiography. But we have also seen how pervasive rationalism frequently undermined positivistic historiography and directed the historian toward emphasis on particular facts to the denigration of others.

Scholem would reject both positivism and rationalism. The notion of "counter-history" does not argue for an indiscriminate presentation of facts as the guarantee for historical objectivity and nondogmatism. Scholem asserts the importance of choosing certain facts over others as more "vital" and for finding that vitality in irrationalism. However, in its ideal of a nondogmatic historiography and even in some of its fundamental research in Kabbalistic sources, the Wissenschaft des Judentums prepared the ground for Scholem and indeed for all subsequent historians.

CHRISTIAN KABBALAH

The Wissenschaft des Judentums was not Scholem's only predecessor, for by the nineteenth century, Christian scholarship of the Kabbalah was sometimes already far ahead of its Jewish counterpart. It is indicative of the problematic character of the Wissenschaft des Judentums that Scholem acknowledges much more openly and positively his debt to Christian Kabbalistic scholars than to his Jewish predecessors.

Christian scholarship of the Kabbalah may have been more attractive to Scholem precisely because it was often based on counter-historical assumptions of its own, tied up with the emergence of Christian Kabbalah as a mystical movement. Christian Kabbalah considered Jewish mysticism a hidden ancient tradition, a vital movement in the heart of the petrified legalisms of rabbinic Judaism. In the late fifteenth century, Pico della Mirandola and Johannes Reuchlin discovered the Kabbalah as part of their quest for the common origin of all religions. They considered the Kabbalah an esoteric Christian movement within Judaism which predated the appearance of Christianity itself. Scholem considers Reuchlin's *De arte cabbalistica* (1517) to have originated scientific Kabbalistic research in Europe, and he has remarked facetiously that "if I believed in the transmigration of souls I could have perhaps sometimes thought that under the new conditions of research, a kind of reincarnation of Johannes Reuchlin . . . [has taken place]."[59]

Out of partly mystical motives, a number of Christian scholars in the subsequent years carried on Reuchlin's work and produced a significant body of literature on the Kabbalah which was available to Scholem when he began his own research.[60] Of particular importance was the work of Franzose Guillaume Postel (1510-1581) and Christian Knorr von Rosenroth (1636-1689). Knorr's *Kabbala Denudata* (1677-1684) contained translations of an enormous variety of Kabbalistic sources, including the relatively new Lurianic Kabbalah.

In the nineteenth century, a Christian Romantic of Franz Baader's school, Franz Joseph Molitor (1779-1860), attempted to combine Christian Kabbalah with romantic idealist philosophy and historiography. In the tradition of Christian Kabbalah, Molitor believed that the Kabbalah was an ancient secret tradition that originated with Adam. He held that it was "the true inner soul of Judaism itself, the vital principle (*lebendige Princip*) of the whole progressive development of Judaism."[61] It is not hard to imagine the impact this statement must have had on Scholem, coming as it did from someone writing at the same time as the Wissenschaft des Judentums.

Molitor divided Jewish history into three ages: masoretic, legal, and historical-mystical.[62] In the first and at least early second stages, the Jewish tradition integrated the Kabbalah with the exoteric law. When the Talmud was written down, the two began to separate, at which point Christianity emerged to renew the law from outside by appropriating and transforming the Kabbalistic tradition. Within Judaism, the codification of Jewish law in the Middle Ages by Maimonides and Karo destroyed the unity of Jewish tradition (*Verfall des Ganzen*).[63] The Kabbalah emerged as an independent, recognizable discipline in the thirteenth century precisely during the period when the law was being codified. The age of mysticism could only begin when the law "expelled" the Kabbalah, but the penalty the law paid was fossilization through loss of its inner vital force. The recovery of the Urtradition, which Molitor felt was needed to revitalize Christianity as well as Judaism, was only possible in the modern age. By infusing romantic philosophy with the fruits of historical research, Militor believed that he could transform the decayed tradition: modern historiography became the handmaiden of Christian mysticism.[64]

The counter-historical idea that the Kabbalah was the "vital" principle of Jewish as well as Christian history set Molitor apart from his Jewish contemporaries. Scholem adamantly rejected Molitor's Christological ideas, but Molitor's positive treatment of the Kabbalah clearly made a much greater impression on him than did the writings of the Wissenschaft des Judentums. As an adolescent, Scholem acquired Molitor's *Die Philosophie der Geschichte oder über die Tradition* and recommended it to his friend Walter Benjamin as the best book on the Kabbalah.[65] It is possible then that Scholem's early positive attitude toward the Kabbalah was more a result of his reading of Molitor than of any Jewish historian. For Christian romantics, particularly those fascinated by myth and mysticism, the Kabbalah did not pose the same sort of dilemmas it did for enlightened Jews.

A more positive attitude toward irrationalism within Jewish circles would have to await the revision of historiography which came in the wake of Jewish nationalism at the turn of the century. Jewish romanticism was a belated movement, coming several centuries after the period that produced Molitor's work. Scholem's own intellectual development began with the Jewish romanticism of the turn of the century, but his relationship with it was stormy and ambivalent.

Revision and Revolution

The rise of Jewish nationalism at the end of the nineteenth century brought about a revision of Jewish historiography. In his *Etwas über die rabbinische Litteratur*, Zunz had argued that modern historiography was only possible because Jewish history was over, a sentiment echoed by Steinschneider.[1] Jewish nationalism emphatically asserted that the death of Judaism was merely a nineteenth-century illusion and that resurrection was possible in the form of a national movement. This new consciousness necessarily affected the writing of Jewish history. As the belief in emancipation and acculturation eroded under the hammer blows of the new political antisemitism at the end of the century, the old rationalist assumptions of Jewish historiography lost their persuasiveness. Where universalism, rational monotheism, and emphasis on intellectual history had once governed historiography, new interpretations focused on nationalist themes, the role of irrational myth, and social movements as legitimate aspects of Jewish history.

One of the most often-quoted of the new historians was Simon Dubnow (1860-1941), who lived most of his life in Eastern Europe. Against Graetz, for whom the Jews had only had autonomy intellectually during the Diaspora, Dubnow maintained that the Jewish people were always creative socially. In the introduction to his *Weltgeschichte des jüdischen Volkes* (1925), he argued that the only objective view of Jewish history is sociological.[2] The Jewish people had never ceased to exist as a nation and had always created political communities, even in Diaspora. Dubnow's history was also a response to Zionism, since he showed the continuity of political community after the fall of the Second Commonwealth. Yet he shared with the Zionists the emphasis on the national-political character of Judaism as against the spiritual-religious definition of the Wissenschaft des Judentums.

The nationalist emphasis on social movements led to interest in possible historical models for the rejuvenation of the Jewish people. Such a model was often found in Hasidism, the pietistic social movement of the eighteenth century. A whole movement of writers, including S. A. Horodezky, M. Y. Berdichevsky, Y. L. Peretz, Yehuda Steinberg, Hillel Zeitlin, and Martin Buber, collected and rewrote Hasidic tales and composed studies of Hasidism, winning such a wide audience that the appeal of this "Neo-Hasidic" revival continues even today. Many of these writers themselves either came from Hasidic families or grew up in Hasidic environments, and when they became *Maskilim* (enlighteners), they often rejected Hasidism as a symbol of the degeneration of Judaism, thus reflecting a typical Wissenshaft des Judentums prejudice. But in their search for a national tradition, they returned to the eighteenth-century sources of Hasidism, often drastically reinterpreting the sources to suit their own more secular purposes.

Scholem started his own literary activities in the Hasidic field by translating the Hebrew manuscript of several chapters of Horodezky's *Die Religiöse Strömungen im Judentum* (1920) into German.[3] Later, following Shai Hurwitz, he became extremely disillusioned with the uncritical enthusiasm for Hasidism. We shall see that his controversy with Martin Buber over the interpretation of Hasidism actually goes back to the period shortly after World War I when he rejected the whole Neo-Hasidic revival.

The "discovery" of Hasidism was a consequence of the increasing influence of Eastern European Jewish intellectuals in Jewish historiography. The nationalist movement of the end of the century, for political and historical reasons, found most of its intellectual adherents among the Jewish intelligentsia of Eastern Europe. Frequently rebels against the traditional yeshiva world in which they were educated, but unable to enter Russian universities, they became an impatient vanguard of revolution, and many of them ultimately joined the ranks of the pioneers in Palestine. From a sociological perspective, an examination of those who revised the Wissenschaft des Judentums must focus on a circle of intellectuals far larger and more diverse than the academicians and seminarians of the nineteenth century. Journalists, essayists, writers of fiction, and poets all tried their hand at the writing of history as a way of substantiating their social and cultural programs.

The revision of the Wissenschaft des Judentums therefore owed a great deal to the Jewish intellectual revival in Eastern Europe at the end of the nineteenth century; the Eastern intellectuals made a particular impact because many of them came to Central Europe to study. Although tensions between the German Jews and the Ostjuden ran high, the encounter between Eastern European Jewish culture and its German counterpart in the years before World War I proved particularly fruitful for Jewish intellectual life. In the German universities, the young Easterners absorbed German scientific methods and applied them to the nationalistic Jewish concerns and traditional backgrounds they brought with them from Eastern Europe. The influx of Eastern European Jews of Central Europe had an important impact on Scholem because, congregating as many of them did in Berlin, they offered him a model for Jewish commitment which he could not find among German Jews.

Scholem is unquestionably the product of the romantic revision of the Wissenschaft des Judentums which took place in Central and Eastern Europe in the first decades of the twentieth century. Yet his relationship to this important intellectual movement cannot be defined precisely without examining first the varieties of revisionist historiography available to him. One cannot properly speak of *a* revision of Jewish historiography since there were as many different revisions as there were writers. It is possible to discern a number of significant trends that offered positive or negative models to Scholem. I will label these the "conservative" and the "counter-historical" revisions. The conservative historians sought to uncover phenomena that had been ignored by the nineteenth century, but they resurrected traditional values in the service of the new nationalism. The counter-historical revision was revolutionary: instead of refurbishing old values, it radically overturned tradition and found its historical models in the suppressed or heretical movements of the past.

The radical counter-historians can, in turn, be divided into two groups. The idea of a revolutionary "transvaluation of values" comes from Nietzsche, and this type of counter-history, represented for our purposes by M. Y. Berdichevsky and Martin Buber, was influenced by Nietzsche's Lebensphilosophie, which was highly popular among certain Jews studying at Central European universities at the turn of the century. These Nietzschean counter-historians particularly sought to establish myth, which both orthodox and rationalist scholars had denigrated, as the driving force of Jewish history. The second group of radicals, represented here by S. I. Hurwitz and Zalman Rubaschoff, were less wedded to Nietzschean slogans and provided Scholem with a model for a counter-history without Nietzsche.

THE CONSERVATIVE REVISION OF THE WISSENSCHAFT DES JUDENTUMS

The revision of Jewish historiography in the twentieth century owed much to Eugen Täubler (1879-1953) and his efforts to create a

nonsectarian Akademie für die Wissenschaft des Judentums.[4] Täubler recognized that most Jewish historiography had been undertaken either by self-supporting scholars or by teachers at one of the
rabbinical seminaries, such as the Liberal Hochschule in Berlin or
the Conservative seminary in Breslau. Since there were practically
no chairs of Judaic studies at any universities in Germany, Täubler
wanted to create a secular institution to train graduate students and
support research. Under the influence of Dilthey's Lebensphilosophie, he severely criticized the nineteenth-century scholars for dogmatism and positivism and sought to broaden the notion of Wissenschaft des Judentums to include disciplines previously ignored,
including the Kabbalah. Täubler's Akademie never succeeded in
training graduate students, but it did fund research fellows and
publish a *Korrespondenzblatt.* Begun in 1919, it served as an important precursor to the Hebrew University's Institute for Jewish
Studies, which opened its doors with almost identical goals only a
few years later, in 1924.

Scholem himself had only peripheral contacts with the Akademie, but a large number of his future colleagues at the Hebrew University were products of the Akademie. Two of them, Ben-Zion
Dinur (Dinaburg) and Fritz Yitzhak Baer, are the most important
for our purposes because they have been associated with a nationalist interpretation of Jewish history. It is in fact likely that Scholem
had Dinur in mind in his sharp criticism of his nationalist colleagues.

Dinur (1884-1972) substantially accepted Dubnow's critique of
the Wissenschaft des Judentums, but rejected his notion of migrat-
ing national centers in Diaspora.[5] For Dinur, there had always been
only one national center, the land of Israel. Throughout the centuries of exile, the land of Israel acted as a spiritual and physical
force in uniting the Jewish people. The messianic desire to return to
the land, regardless of its various expressions, remained the common thread in Jewish history, up to and including the Zionist
movement. Dinur's focus on political messianism was a response to
the universalized messianism of Reform Judaism.

Baer (b. 1888) similarly recognized a common nationalist thread
that linked all of Jewish history together: "A single unified period
contains the history of our nation from the first days of the first
hasidim [during the Maccabean revolt] until the period of the
spread of the modern enlightenment. Throughout this whole long
period, religious, social and historical concepts rule Israel."[6] The
religious, social, and historical concepts that united Jewish history
in this long period Baer identified as *hasidut,* or the values of social

piety. The ḥasidim rishonim during the Maccabean revolt created the pietistic social values that would sustain Judaism. Every movement in Jewish history which Baer favored expressed these values; philosophical movements endangered them.[7]

Against the philosophical prejudices of the nineteenth century, Baer emphasized social values that were at once political and religious and represented the "common people." He included mysticism in his pantheon of national movements in Jewish history, but gave it a purely pietistic and social interpretation.[8] The Kabbalah, represented by such books as the *Raya Mehemna*, voiced the social concerns of the pious artisan class in Spain. Mysticism therefore fulfilled a positive role in Jewish history for Baer, and he transformed it into a pillar of Jewish nationalism. Both Baer and Dinur treated mysticism more positively than did the Wissenschaft des Judentums, but they also subordinated it to other forces, such as messianism or social pietism. Like the rationalists, they relativized irrationalism to support their own conceptions of Jewish history: mysticism was not a movement in its own right.

We find among these examples of revisers of the Wissenschaft des Judentums an attempt to rid Jewish historiography of its rationalist bias. No longer bound by the apologetic concerns of some of the nineteenth-century historians, scholars introduced new nationalist and sociological interpretations. Although the new nationalist historiography could just as easily adopt apologetic arguments of its own to justify Jewish nationalism, its ideology was fundamentally different from that of the Wissenschaft des Judentums. However, the new historiography remained relatively conservative because the revisionists merely restated certain orthodox assumptions in new language. They gave the concept of *klal yisrael* (the community of Israel) a secular, political meaning and adopted such traditional values as social piety and messianism as the guiding principles of their historiography. In their renunciation of universalism and rationalism, they were returning to premodern concepts.

THE NIETZSCHEAN REVOLUTION

The counter-historical method that Nietzsche developed as part of his nihilistic transvaluation of values (*Umwertung alles Werten*) offered a revolutionary way of exploiting historical evidence to subvert historical conventions. Nietzsche's theory of counter-history had a significant impact on a number of Jews at the turn of the century, notably Berdichevsky and Buber. Scholem himself found Nietzsche's nihilistic philosophy abhorrent and had no further interest in Nietzsche's work after reading *Also Sprach Zarathustra*.

However, there is a certain affinity between some of Scholem's radical historical categories and Nietzsche's. Scholem's only partial rejection of Nietzsche was probably mediated through his reading of Berdichevsky, whom Scholem respected despite his nihilism. Later we shall see how Scholem, who has defined himself as a follower of Berdichevsky's moderate opponent, Ahad Ha-am, gave Ahad Haam's thought a radical interpretation based in part on Berdichevsky's philosophy of history.

In his "Use and Abuse of History," Nietzsche asserted that we need history "for life and action, not as a convenient way to avoid life and action."[9] He distinguished between three types of history: monumental, antiquarian, and critical. Monumental history wants to serve as a model for action, but it "lives by false analogy."[10] It chooses particular events from the past as models but then falsifies them to fit present conditions. As a result, "whole tracts of [the past] are forgotten and despised; they flow away like a dark unbroken river."[11] Antiquarian history is the usual answer to monumental history. Instead of glorifying certain events, it preserves all of the past indiscriminately. Antiquarian history is the particular vice of patriotic and positivistic historians: they know how to preserve but not to create. Critical history is the correct reaction to antiquarianism. It asserts that "every past is worth condemning."[12] "Life in any true sense is absolutely impossible without forgetfulness . . . the unhistorical and historical are equally necessary to the health of an individual, a community and a system of culture."[13] But along with destruction of the past, critical history suggests constructive use of history by interpreting the past mythically: "it is an attempt to gain a past a posteriori from which we might spring, as against that from which we do spring."[14] Up to this point, critical history seems no different from monumental history. The fundamental difference is that critical history is counter-history: it dialectically transforms monumental history by finding its models from the past in unconventional or heretical phenomena. Critical history shatters the sort of historical "monuments" beloved of monumental history and discovers the true models beneath the rubble.

Nietzsche's slogan of the transvaluation of all values meant that there is no such thing as value in itself, no concept of absolute "true and false" except as tools of orientation and action.[15] He attacked all dogmatic values as "standing truth on her head and denying all perspective."[16] Where dogmatism claims that there is only one truth, this "truth" is actually only one perspective among many. All philosophies that claim objective truth are mere illusions: "every philosophy also conceals a philosophy, every opinion a hideout, every word a mask."[17] When the masks are stripped off, one discovers a new perspective, contrary to the first: "The exoteric sees things from below, the esoteric looks down from above. There are heights from which even tragedy ceases to look tragic."[18]

Nietzsche defined useful history as that which is concealed beneath various dogmatic masks, such as Socratic philosophy and Christianity. Much of Nietzsche's work was devoted to exposing the true nature of these dogmatisms and discovering the Dionysian perspective suppressed by them. Nietzsche's "counter-gospel"[19] of Christianity is an excellent example of his counter-historical technique. For all his opposition to Jesus' teachings, Nietzsche asserted that the real history of Christianity is that "there has been only one Christian and he died on the cross."[20] Jesus stood outside all dogmatic religions. After his death, Christianity degenerated as it became a Church: "one constructed the church out of the antithesis of the Gospel . . . The history of Christianity is the history of progressively cruder misunderstandings of the original symbolism."[21] Historical Christianity not only suppressed all true religious impulses but even its own origins. In the end, Nietzsche concluded that original Christianity and nihilism were similar: "their purpose is set only on destruction."[22] But nihilism at least did not claim dogmatic certainty and could therefore lay the basis for a new order.

MICHA YOSEF BERDICHEVSKY (1865-1921)

In their efforts to cut all ties with traditional history, particularly of the Diaspora, the revolutionary Jewish nationalists in Eastern Europe could borrow a ready-made vocabulary from Nietzsche. Perhaps the most radical Jewish Lebensphilosophe and spokesman against the tyranny of Jewish history was Berdichevsky.[23]

Berdichevsky adopted Nietzsche's attack on the "malignant historical fever." In a seminal pasage, called "On History" (1899), Berdichevsky bemoans the enslavement of Israel to history:

A fire burnt on the eternal altar and a priest came and stuck a ritual knife into our belly. And the blood flowed and was mingled with the sacrificial fire. The worshipers fell on their faces and cried out to god . . . "save us from the cloud that rises and covers everything." And god answers: "You are my children. I have molded you in an iron kiln. You cannot die and yet your life is not life. You are a nation of history and I gave you books."[24]

In this short parable, we see Berdichevsky's typical mythopoeic style. He takes a traditional symbol, such as the cloud that pro-

tected the Jews leaving Egypt, and inverts it into a destructive
image. Priests and rabbis had emasculated Israel by turning the
vital natural religion of the people into an abstract, spiritualized
doctrine called "Judaism." The "books" represent the historical tradition. But like some kind of grotesque fossil, castrated Judaism
cannot die a merciful death; it continues to limp along in a "life that
is not life." Enslaved to its books, to its stultifying history, Israel
had lost its original vitality. Berdichevsky believed that written traditions are devoid of vitality. His counter-history began, then, with
a systematic inversion of positive traditional symbols into negative
ones, and with the suggestion that the original impulses of the nation were quite the opposite of those imposed on it by "historical
Judaism." His translation of Nietzsche's slogan "in order to build a
house, one must first destroy a house" has a particular Jewish resonance: "in order to build a temple, it is necessary first to destroy a
temple."[25] The temple of rabbinic Judaism must be razed before a
new temple can be erected.

Berdichevsky argued that Jewish history contained the sources
for a revolutionary counter-tradition: with Nietzsche, he believed
that the solution to history must come from history itself.[26] In anticipation of Scholem, he asserted that "there is not one literature of
the Hebrew, no one spirit given from one shepherd, but instead
many different literatures that were born and developed at varying
times, according to different spiritual conditions and also according
to different material boundaries."[27] Jewish history was not monolithic or dogmatic, but consisted of a variety of conflicting traditions. In one of his early essays, Berdichevsky disputed the common belief that Israel stands for ethics whereas ancient Greece
represents natural religion and physical strength.[28] All these values
could be found competing within the Jewish tradition itself. The
struggle between the sword and the book is the one constant theme
in Jewish history, for, in the words of the sages, which Berdichevsky deliberately misinterpreted for his own purposes, "the sword
and the book descended from heaven coupled together."[29]

Berdichevsky was particularly attracted to the suppressed tradition of the sword as evidence of Israel's vitalistic and naturalis-
tic impulses. In his portrayal of the Hebrews as a vital people of nature, he clearly borrowed from the Nietzschean Lebensphilosophie.
Since the traditions of the sword and of identification with nature
had been suppressed by the rabbis, Berdichevsky was forced to find
his counter-tradition among the heretics, those who "refused to
take part with us, refused to be counted with us, and, yet, how
much more are they connected with us."[30] We hear in this state-

ment an echo of Immanuel Wolf's call to find the true Judaism in movements outside rabbinical Judaism—but Berdichevsky wanted a much more radical definition of Judaism to emerge from his counter-history.

In *Sinai und Gerizim*, his last work, Berdichevsky argued that the struggle between sword and book began even before the revelation at Sinai. His goal was to show that the real religion of the Jews was a religion of nature and that Moses' antinatural Torah was a late imposition.[31] Berdichevsky claimed that evidence of this pre-Sinaitic law could be found in the series of blessings and curses mentioned in Deuteronomy 27 and 28. He believed that the curses corresponded in a rough way to the ten commandments, but were concerned with the political process of governing a nation, such as "cursed be he who removes his neighbor's landmark."[32] These blessings and curses were associated with Joshua, under whom they were uttered after the conquest of the land on Mount Gerazim and Mount Ebal. This "Torah" of Gerizim was a deliberate nationalist counterpart to Moses' "ethical" Torah. Berdichevsky elevated Joshua to the same status as Moses, as a legislator of a tradition of his own, and depicted many of the Moses stories as later imitations of the more genuine Joshua stories.

Berdichevsky took many of these theses directly from the Christian biblical criticism current in Germany at the time.[33] Although his writings on the Bible are perhaps his least known, they are his most radical, for they undermine the uniqueness of the revelation at Sinai. By basing his own myth of true Judaism on another "divine" revelation, Berdichevsky subverted the monolithic character of rabbinic Judaism at its very foundations.

Borrowing from Nietzsche's critique of ethics,[34] Berdichevsky accused the prophets of sapping Israel's vitality by substituting ethics for life. The national fiber was so weakened that Israel was ultimately exiled from its land. In this startling inversion of the rabbinic explanation of exile as a punishment for the Jews' sins, Berdichevsky agreed that the Jews were responsible for their own exile, but not because they had sinned. On the contrary, by adhering too closely to prophetic ethics, they lost the will to live.[35] Since, according to the traditional conception, Moses himself was the first prophet, all of "Judaism" from Sinai on was an unnatural perversion of national life and was to blame for the exile.

The struggle between sword and book continued in the post-biblical tradition. Berdichevsky identified it in the controversy between the schools of Shammai and Hillel and, later, during the Great Revolt against Rome, between the school of Yavneh and the nationalist Zealots.[36] Throughout the Middle Ages, the rabbinical party achieved supremacy and established its view as the sole definition of Judaism. However, many counter-traditions, including the Kabbalah, emerged to challenge the rabbis and were responsible for sustaining a spark of vitality in Judaism: "Pharisees opposed Sadducees, Karaites opposed rabbis and the Kabbalah and esoteric doctrines opposed the explicit . . . In other words, nothing genuine exists except when one extreme party does the thing completely and without tolerant compromising."[37] That none of these movements of opposition could even remotely be identified with the militaristic traditions of the sword shows the ambiguity of Berdichevsky's terms. But in stressing the common critical function served by all these traditions, he succeeded in pointing out that the rabbis had no easy monopoly.

Berdichevsky's favorite counter-movement in Jewish history was Hasidism. He argued that the Hasidism of his own day had degenerated into little more than the despised rabbinic Judaism, but its original, eighteenth-century doctrines were radically opposed to the mainstream. Berdichevsky's interpretation of Hasidism reflected his own radical critique of traditional Judaism much more than it did historical reality: his description of an antinomian Hasidism conformed more closely to Sabbatianism than to the real Hasidism.[38]

Berdichevsky was darkly pessimistic about the Judaism of his time. When emancipation was granted, the implicit prophetic and rabbinical opposition to Jewish nationalism became manifest: free to enter Western culture, enlightened Jews quickly surrendered their national identity and professed Judaism solely as a religion.[39] The prophetic tradition was therefore not just antinationalist but inherently assimilationist. Berdichevsky conceived of the age of emancipation and Enlightenment not as a break with the Middle Ages, but as their logical culmination, indeed, as the final result of the ethical Torah. He attacked the moderate cultural Zionists, such as Ahad Ha-am, for accepting the prophetic assumptions of the Enlightenment and thereby falling into the trap of the normative tradition.

Berdichevsky's solution to the seeming triumph of prophetic Judaism in the Enlightenment was the mythopoeic recreation of the suppressed counter-tradition. In both his fiction and his scholarship, he tried to evoke what he thought to have been the vital tradition of Mt. Gerizim. In stories like "Parah Adumah" (Red Heifer),[40] he portrayed the brutal, orgiastic side of Jewish society by transforming traditional symbols into myths of his counter-tradition. He devoted his scholarship to a similar goal. His implicit assumption was that the esoteric history was transmitted through legends and half-whispered myths.[41] Folklore rather than mainstream historiography was the discipline for uncovering these traditions.

Berdichevsky's revision of the Wissenschaft des Judentums was a curious mixture of critical historiography and mythopoeic Nietzschean literature. At the beginning of his career, he rejected all of Jewish history and unabashedly rewrote Jewish sources as modern myths. But in his later life he became much more of an academic, perhaps reflecting his growing belief that his counter-history actually existed in the early biblical and rabbinic sources themselves and did not have to be created. In the later collections of his early nihilistic essays, he often deleted references to Nietzsche:[42] the Nietzschean "mythmaker" who had wanted to escape the burden of history gradually himself became an historian.

Martin Buber (1878-1965)

Buber's early philosophy of history, developed before World War I, closely resembles Berdichevsky's. As Scholem has pointed out, both Buber and Berdichevsky tried to combine "revolutionary utopia [with] archaic hankering for a creative primordial time (Urzeit)."[43] The desire for a violent break with all of Jewish history mingled uneasily with the romantic urge to find a revolutionary tradition hidden in Jewish history itself. Like Berdichevsky, Buber found a model for his counter-history in Hasidism, and he may even have been influenced by Berdichevsky's Hasidic anthologies from the turn of the century. Buber's own German translations and rewritings of Hasidic tales helped to create a positive image of Hasidism among German Jews in the first decades of the century.[44]

The similarities betweeen Buber and Berdichevsky have much to do with the fact that both were influenced by Nietzsche in their youth. Although Buber later renounced Nietzscheanism, his early views on history, with which Scholem grappled during the World War I period, were shaped by his interpretation of Nietzsche. In 1895, Buber's first literary project, subsequently abandoned, was a translation of Zarathustra into Polish. Upon Nietzsche's death in 1900, he published a eulogy: "Nietzsche erected before our eyes the statue of the heroic man who creates himself. Nietzsche placed against the comfortable, painless life the life of passion and danger . . . Against the God of Genesis he brought a great adversary; the God of becoming, in whose development we may share."[45] Unlike Berdichevsky, Buber ignored Nietzsche's nihilism and atheism and, with many of his contemporaries of the Nietzschean Neue Gemeinschaft circle, gave Nietzsche a mystical interpretation.[46] Buber, who does not seem to have suffered the traumatic experience of breaking with Jewish tradition, did not feel Berdichevsky's need to annihilate the past before building a new world. His counter-history was never as destructive or as antireligious as Berdichevsky's, since he was far more interested in inward mystical experience. Buber's reinterpretation of Jewish history may have been more attractive to young German Jews than Berdichevsky's because it took this break with the past for granted. Most young German Jews at the beginning of the twentieth century, like Scholem, were already one or two generations removed from traditional Judaism.

Like Berdichevsky, Buber conceived of Jewish history as a constant struggle between opposing forces: "The history of the development of Jewish religion is really the history of the struggles between the natural structure of a mythical-monotheistic folk-religion and the intellectual structure of a rational-monotheistic rabbinic religion."[47] Buber drew the battle lines in Jewish history between folk myth and philosophical-legal institutions, a distinction Scholem adopted with his own particular modifications. Following Arthur Bonus' *Der neue Mythus*, Buber distinguished between religion and religiosity.[48] Religiosity draws its vitality out of myth, whereas religion is the lifeless institutionalization of religious feeling: "The personal, unique and inaccessible religiosity of the individual soul has its birth in myth, its death in religion."[49]

In his lecture "Myth in Judaism," Buber polemicized against those scholars who believed that myth was alien to biblical Judaism. He argued that "every living monotheism is filled with the mythical element and remains alive so long as it is filled with it."[50] Buber's definition of myth in his early work was somewhat blurred, for he seems to have considered any spontaneous form of religiosity to be mythological. He did not distinguish carefully between myth and mysticism and considered them equally legitimate. In his later writings, however, he would attack Gnostic myth in Judaism as a foreign disease and extol Hasidism for liberating mysticism from myth.[51]

Buber borrowed the notion of the necessarily lifeless character of legal institutions from Christian biblical scholarship, which argued that the original vital impulses in Judaism were destroyed when Judaism became an institutionalized religion under the priesthood. Against the Christian position, however, he attempted to legitimize Judaism as a religiosity that had never lost its vitality. Yet, because he accepted the Christian idea that institutionalized religion lacks vitality, his attempt to find myth in Judaism seems like an irrationalist form of nineteenth-century apologetics.

Buber traced the struggle between mythical religiosity and religion to the very origins of Judaism. There were basically two dominant types in Jewish history: the prophet and the priest. Moses, the archetypal prophet, was the one who "listens only to the voice, acknowledges only the deed. Aaron is the mediator, as accessible to the voices as to the voice . . . The prophet wants truth; the priest power."[52] The priests were therefore responsible for translating the living relationship with God into a body of petrified symbols, from religiosity to religion.

Those who codified the written law were the natural heirs to the priests. For Buber, both priest and scribe viewed the law as "a sum of prescriptions . . . thwarting instead of promoting living religiosity." Like Berdichevsky, he attacked all "written" law as antithetical to life: "The Bible triumphed not only over all other writings, it triumphed over life."[53] All those interested in freezing the religion in written form, whether priests or scribes, were the enemies of true Judaism. In grouping priests and scribes (or rabbis) together, Buber implied that the public rivalries between these two factions, historically known as Sadducees and Pharisees, were little more than window dressing: both groups were interested in establishing a monolithic, dogmatic religion. In this way, priestly religion became rabbinic Judaism, which Buber called "official Judaism."

Unlike Berdichevsky, Buber found his model for the minority opposition to "official Judaism" in the prophets. Buber did not emphasize the ethical message of the prophets in his early prewar writings as much as he did in his later "Hebrew humanism," but he stopped short of Berdichevsky's Nietzschean critique of Jewish ethics. Championing the prophets left Buber in a difficult position, however, for the prophets had attacked mythology. But Buber argued that the prophets had only rejected polytheistic mythology, for which they substituted their own monotheistic "myth."[54]

Buber believed that the real message of the prophets was preserved throughout Jewish history by a "subterranean" (*unterirdische*) counter-tradition sustained by the heretic and sectarian communities.[55] The Rechabites, Essenes, and early Christians were all links in this chain. Throughout the Middle Ages, the antiofficial tradition led a subterranean life, preserved by small Kabbalistic sects and only occasionally surfacing in messianic movements. Only with Hasidism did "subterranean Judaism" emerge above ground and become a genuine folk movement.[56] In his early writings, Buber regarded Hasidism as a revolt against the dogmatic rigidification of the law: "every man, by living authentically, shall himself become a Torah, a law."[57]

Buber borrowed his approach to history directly from Nietzsche.

In his essay on the translation of the Bible (1926), he outlined three
possible views of history. One might regard history as a source of
authority and derive laws from certain past events. This would be
the "monumentalist" approach of the rabbinical tradition. On the
other hand, one might see history as a "promiscuous agglomeration
of happenings," an "antiquarian" collection of random events with
no evident meaning or lesson. Buber favored a third alternative,
which he claimed was also the Bible's:

> According to the Biblical insight, historic destiny is the secret
> correlation inhering in the current moment. When we are aware
> of origin and goal, there is no meaningless drift; we are carried
> along by a meaning we could never think up for ourselves, a
> meaning we are to live—not to formulate. And that living takes
> place in the awful and splendid moment of decision.[58]

History was neither an external source of authority nor utterly devoid of meaning. By making a decision in the "current moment,"
one could recover the hidden meaning of history and thus create a
continuum of otherwise unrelated events.

Buber does not make it clear whether the historian actually re-
covers the suppressed tradition or creates it by imposing meaning
on the past. Is the historian's decision an act of free creativity, or
does the historical myth speak through him? Did Buber advocate
the writing of new myths using ancient images or the discovery and
dusting off of old ones? In the introduction to his rewritten collection of Baal Shem Tov tales, he discussed this issue but did not
really resolve it. Rather than elucidating the actual life (wirkliches
Leben) of the Hasidim, he wanted to capture the mythic essence of
Hasidism: "I have received [the Hasidic tales] and told them anew. I
have not translated them . . . I carry in me their blood and spirit."[59]
Buber wrenched the myth out of its historical context and "restored
it to its original condition."[60] He claimed poetic license to identify
the myth under layers of historical rubble, just as he found the
"mythical" message of the prophets beneath their antimythical pos-
ture. Whether the original condition of the myth corresponded to
historical reality was ultimately unimportant.[61]

Buber's notion of counter-history was a response to the perceived
failure of the Wissenschaft des Judentums. In his article on "Jüdische Wissenschaft" (1901),[62] he criticized Jewish historiography
for its philological and positivistic tendency to fragment Jewish
history into many tiny problems. The Wissenschaft des Judentums
corresponded to that type of historiography which sees the past as
a meaningless "promiscuous agglomeration of happenings." Buber

rejected this antiquarian response to the orthodox derivation of authority from the past. The nationalist reaction to orthodoxy should not be to deny any coherent pattern to history, but to construct a useful counter-history. Buber's explicit attack on the Wissenschaft des Judentums was directed more against its positivism than against its dogmatic rationalism, but his glorification of myth makes it clear how radically he rejected the rationalist interpretation.

SHAI ISH-HURWITZ (1860-1922)

The mythopoeic revision of Jewish historiography was intended to salvage something viable from Jewish history. It was a nationalist response to the perceived dogmatism of orthodox and rationalist views of Jewish history. Berdichevsky and Buber, the chief representatives of this radical position, tried to discover a hidden myth in Jewish history, but the result was often a thoroughly ahistorical poetic rewriting of history as myth. Shai Ish-Hurwitz,[63] an Eastern European contemporary of Berdichevsky's who also came to Berlin before World War I, mounted the most lucid attack on the mythopoeic writers. Hurwitz refuted the "Neo-Romantics" with a counter-history of his own. In Hurwitz we find an alternative to the Nietzscheans which still falls in the category of radicalism.

In his earliest writings, Hurwitz took a stand against traditional Judaism similar to Berdichevsky's, proclaiming in a slogan that Berdichevsky later adopted: "Israel [the nation] takes precedence over the Torah."[64] In a number of controversial articles written during the first decade of the century,[65] Hurwitz iconoclastically assaulted almost every interpretation of Judaism, whether orthodox, rationalist, or secular nationalist. Like Berdichevsky, he ridiculed Ahad Ha-am's "spiritualized nationalism" and argued that there were only two alternatives facing modern Jews: negation of the exile or assimilation.

Hurwitz conceived of his task as *avodat berurim ba-yahadut* (work of clarification in Judaism).[66] He adopted the notion of clarification from Nachman Krochmal, who had described his historical method as clarified science (*mada' mevorar*). History was to clear out the underbrush of romanticism, superstition, and pious dogmatism and reveal the true path from past to future. The job of historical study was to free the Jew from exaggerated admiration for the past and to show matters in their true light. Hurwitz argued against monolithic interpretations of Jewish history and tried to show the pluralism of Jewish belief, a theme characteristic of all counter-history. He even disputed the centrality of monotheism in Jewish history and demonstrated recurrences of non-monotheistic ideas

from the Bible onward.[67] Hurwitz thus gave a classically historicist
definition of Judaism: "I do not consider Judaism to have a metaphysical essence, possessing an abstract reality of its own standing
outside the boundaries of space and time. Rather, in all the generations and ages, [Judaism] is nothing but the sum of all the tendencies of 'the Jewish heart.' "[68]

At this point Hurwitz parted company with the Nietzscheans,
who also asserted the pluralism of Jewish history. Hurwitz violently attacked the Neo-Hasidic movement of Peretz and Berdichevsky
for trying nostalgically to reconstruct an imagined Hasidism.[69] He
was the first to name and describe this literary and historiographical movement but he did so in order to condemn it. The Neo-Hasidim, like the orthodox, had distorted the past for their own purposes: historical Hasidism did not at all conform to their mythical
picture of it.[70] Hurwitz attacked Hasidism for negating Jewish nationalism.[71] The Hasidim had turned mystically inwards and had
made their peace with exile. The Zaddik had become a "personal
Messiah" and the nationalist impulse in Jewish messianism had
been totally suppressed.[72] So Hasidism had failed to contribute
anything significant to Jewish history and had certainly never been
the force for renewal imagined by the Neo-Hasidim. In his own refutation of Neo-Hasidism Scholem adopted almost all of Hurwitz's
critique of Hasidism as a quietistic movement: for Scholem, as for
Hurwitz, the search for models of vitality in Jewish history led elsewhere.

Hurwitz was critical of the Neo-Hasidim for abandoning objective historiography and inventing a Hasidism that never existed.
His passion for historical objectivity was related to his general sympathy for rationalism and for the Jewish Enlightenment (*Haskalah*).
He argued that the Haskalah's negative relation to Jewish tradition
had a constructive impulse behind it since it demanded that the
Jews "leave exile and that they strive for a new center of life."[73] This
hidden nationalism was misdirected toward assimilation into European life, but this was not the fault of the Maskilim. In their rejection of the exile, they had dialectically prepared the ground for
Zionism.

Hurwitz attacked the Neo-Hasidim for "searching for pearls in
piles of garbage,"[74] and found solace in rationalism. In what sense,
then, was he more radical than the Wissenschaft des Judentums
save for his vehement nationalism? The difference between Hurwitz and earlier rationalists lay in his counter-history, which, although it was not based on irrationalism, was sympathetic to all
forms of heresy: "If Judaism is not to be asphyxiated by the fumes

of its own breath, it must keep an open corridor to let in a fresh breeze from outside . . . All heretics of every ilk must find a place for themselves in Judaism."[75]

Like Scholem several decades later, Hurwitz found an example of such a vital heretical movement in Sabbatianism: "Those romantic authors who want to find traces of the desire for 'revival and renewal' in mystical tendencies . . . have gone to the wrong address. Not Hasidism, but Sabbatianism is where we should search for this desire."[76] Despite its bizarre and extreme manifestations, Sabbatianism was a truly nationalist movement, dedicated to renewal of the nation. Moreover, and again in anticipation of Scholem, Hurwitz argued that Sabbatianism was the dialectical cause of all the important Jewish movements of the eighteenth century, including the Haskalah:

> In its striving for revival and renewal, in its love for beauty, aesthetics and liberation of hearts and in its desire for renewal of the Hebrew language in order to redeem the Hebrew spirit . . . [Sabbatianism] became the father of modern Hebrew literature which was no small cause of the Haskalah movement . . . On the other hand, Sabbatianism influenced greatly the rise of syncretism in Israel and prepared the ground for . . . Jacob Frank and also for Hasidism.[77]

Hurwitz also compared Sabbatai Zevi to Herzl and commented, in response to vociferous Zionist criticism, that he meant this as a compliment.[78] The modern movement of Jewish nationalism could take the great messianic movement of the seventeenth century as a glorious precursor.

Hurwitz then traced a dialectical thread from Sabbatianism through the Haskalah to Zionism. In rejecting the counter-history of the Neo-Hasidim, he adopted another, if anything, more radical one. He wanted to clear away the romantic and mystical nonsense from contemporary conceptions of Jewish history but, unlike Krochmal, who considered Sabbatianism to have been one of the mot dangerous and obscurantist movements in Jewish history, Hurwitz valued Sabbatianism as much as he did rationalist philosophy.

ZALMAN RUBASCHOFF (1889-1973)

Zalman Rubaschoff, a generation younger than Buber, Berdichevsky, and Hurwitz, adopted a position similar to Hurwitz's on Sabbatianism. The future third president of the State of Israel was

particularly important in the revision of the Wissenschaft des Judentums since, as a close friend of Scholem's in Berlin during World
War I, he had a significant impact on Scholem's approach to Jewish
history.[79]

Rubaschoff received his initial academic training before the war
at the Baron Günzburg's Academy for Jewish Studies in St. Peters-
burg, the first nonrabbinical institute of its kind.[80] He studied under
Dubnow, among others, and, as a young nationalist, contentiously
opposed the Baron's insistence that the program in Jewish history
focus solely on intellectual developments. Later, in Berlin, he published several influential articles criticizing the Wissenschaft des Judentums. He argued against Zunz's belief that the creation of university chairs in Jewish studies would lead to a revival of Judaism.
The emancipation of Jewish scholarship would not bring about
emancipation; on the contrary, only an inner Jewish national revival would produce real Jewish scholarship.[81] Scholem reproduced
this argument over a quarter of a century later in his "Reflections
on the Science of Judaism."

Rubaschoff also attacked the Wissenschaft des Judentums in an
introduction to a republication of Eduard Gans's addresses to the
Verein.[82] Pointedly entitled "Erstlinge der Entjudung" (First Fruits
of De-Judaization), Rubaschoff's essay revealed his ideological purpose in publishing the addresses: to warn young Jewish scholars
that academic assimilation was impossible. The failure of the Verein, Rubaschoff contended, was not due to the inherent impossibility of a revival of Judaism on secular grounds, as Heinrich Heine
had argued, or that the Verein members were uncreative, as Graetz
later claimed. Rather, no synthesis between Judaism and German-
ism was possible then; nor was it any more likely in the twentieth
century. Revitalized Jewish scholarship would only come as a result
of national revival.

In his own historical studies, Rubaschoff displayed conspicuous
interest in those heretical movements scorned by the Wissenschaft
des Judentums. As early as 1912 he argued that "since the idea of
redemption and [national] revival was alien to Graetz's generation,
he related to the [Sabbatian] movement in a way that he had inherited from R. Jacob Emden and which was sanctified by Moses Mendelssohn."[83] Like Hurwitz, Rubaschoff interpreted Sabbatianism as
a revolt against rabbinical authority.[84]

Rubaschoff also wrote a small study in 1920 on the eighteenth-
century Frankist movement, an extreme vestige of Sabbatianism.[85]
Although a number of much more serious studies of Frankism already existed, including one by Graetz,[86] Rubaschoff's little book

was unique for its attempt to treat the Frankists sympathetically. He felt alienated from their strange and grotesque actions, but nevertheless tried to understand them as "brothers" who "like me sat on the benches of the *ḥeder;* before the very same book we opened the depths of our souls and absorbed certain wretched and terrible impressions of life."[87] The same overwhelming desire to escape the oppressive life of traditional Judaism must have motivated these heretics as well. Rubaschoff compared Frankism unfavorably to Sabbatianism, since the latter was a messianic movement directed toward the land of Israel. But he suggested that Sabbatianism was the garden in which Frankism grew, "the same garden in which we all have roots."[88] Jewish nationalism, as well as Frankism, had its roots in the soil cultivated by Sabbatianism: as Scholem would also argue, the great messianic movement was a source for all the efforts at self-liberation that followed.

The revolutionary counter-histories of Berdichevsky, Buber, Hurwitz, and Rubaschoff, whether or not influenced by Nietzsche, constituted the radical wing of the nationalist revision of the Wissenschaft des Judentums in the early twentieth century. Scholem belongs to this radical revision, and we shall see how he borrowed from these specific writers in constructing his own interpretation of Jewish history. At the same time, his relationship to both the conservative revisionists and some of the radicals was as contentious as his relationship to the nineteenth-century historiography. His work struck out in new directions, which were frequently informed by his ambivalent feelings toward Buber, a relationship whose roots go back to Scholem's youth during World War I.

3.   *From Berlin to Jerusalem*

The intensive reading he did in Jewish history, and the influence of the writings of Martin Buber, produced Gershom Scholem's rebellion against the assimilated culture of his parents. During World War I, however, he became critical of Buber's mystical approach to both Judaism and the war. He also repeatedly attacked the German Zionist youth movement. In uncompromising opposition to both the bourgeois German-Jewish culture of his parents' generation and the "mystical" youth counter-culture, Scholem struck out on his own course, which led to emigration to Palestine in 1923. At the same time, he developed his own path in historiography: rejection of the rationalist Wissenschaft des Judentums but, equally, rejection of the mythical-mystical approach of Buber and Berdichevsky. These choices in politics and historiography were closely linked in Scholem's development. His decisions to move to Palestine and to study the Kabbalah grew out of the crucible of World War I and, although he responded to the stormy historical events in Palestine and Europe of the next half-century, he was to adhere to the basic positions he took as a youth.

Scholem has detailed his personal development in those early years, first in a number of interviews and then in two memoir accounts in German, *Walter Benjamin—Die Geschichte einer Freundschaft* and *Von Berlin nach Jerusalem*. My task here, however, is not to reconstruct Scholem's biography, but to examine the major themes in his intellectual development.

Scholem was born in Berlin in 1897. At that time, Berlin had long been the center of German-Jewish population, and Jews were active in many areas of cultural and intellectual life. Historians have frequently noted, as did Berlin Jews themselves, that there was a special Berlin-Jewish spirit, exemplified by a particularly sardonic form of humor.[1] Scholem himself still fondly uses idioms from the Berlin dialect (*berlinisch gesprochen*).[2]

The Scholem family came to Berlin in the beginning of the nineteenth century, and Scholem's grandparents were already embarked on the road to cultural assimilation. Scholem's father, a printer who earned a comfortable living at his trade, was almost completely assimilated. He worked on the Day of Atonement and observed other Jewish holidays only in a perfunctory way. Although Arthur Scholem experienced some social antisemitism, he never felt himself significantly excluded from German society. The family celebrated Christmas as a national folk holiday, complete with Christmas tree and carols played on the piano for the benefit of the Christian house-servants. Scholem relates that he ceased to participate in these family celebrations when, in 1911 after becoming a Zionist, his mother gave him a picture of Theodore Herzl as a Christmas present.[3]

Why Scholem chose to reject his parents' lifestyle and opt for a radical alternative raises issues I can touch on only superficially. It is interesting to note that three of the four Scholem sons gravitated toward relatively extreme political options. While Erich Scholem, the second oldest, followed the moderate politics of his father, the eldest son, Reinhold, joined the staunchly nationalist Deutsche Volkspartei. Werner, the third son, joined the Social Democrats and served during the Weimar Republic as a Reichstag deputy for the German Communist Party. Scholem completed the diverse picture by avowing Zionism. He notes in his autobiography that "the completely different directions which we four brothers took in these years were typical for the world of the Jewish bourgeoisie and demonstrate how little an ostensibly common environment determines the path of young people in each individual case."[4] In the relatively tolerant atmosphere just before World War I, all options seemed open to German Jews, and the Jewish world was neither politically nor culturally monolithic. Faced with a Jewish community that did not hold much appeal, and a German society still uneasy about its Jewish citizens, young Jews frequently opted for the more radical alternatives, usually socialism or Zionism, but occasionally right-wing German nationalism.

It is likely, too, that something in the Scholem family itself created an atmosphere of rebellion among the sons. Although the personalities of the other three brothers cannot be fully determined, Scholem was a veritable *enfant terrible* in his youth. By his own account he was contentious and iconoclastic. If there was any source for these rebellious personality traits, it was his father, whom he

describes as aloof and hot-tempered.[5] His relationship with Arthur
Scholem, who was rarely in the house, seems to have been marked
early on by personal tensions, which later took the form of political
arguments. He was much closer to his mother, about whom he relates a number of touching anecdotes in *Von Berlin nach Jerusalem.*[6]

Scholem expressed his revolt against his parents' bourgeois lifestyle by affirming his Jewish identity. It is not at all clear why he
chose this mode of rebellion. As he himself relates, he had little
contact with Judaism in his home, and the obligatory hour of religious studies at school left him cold. However, in the summer of
1911, his teacher, Moses Barol, who otherwise provoked only
boredom, showed the class a copy of Graetz's *Geschichte der Juden.* Scholem, already interested in history, began to read Graetz at
the Jewish community library and was inspired by the nineteenth-
century historian's implicit nationalism.[7] A year or so later he read
Buber's *Drei Reden über das Judentum* as well as his collections of
the Hasidic legends of the Baal Shem and Nachman of Bratzlav.
Buber's writings had an immediate impact.[8]

Unlike the other Jews of his generation who were also inspired by
Buber, Scholem began to study the traditional sources of which
Buber seemed a living representative. With the aid of a former reli-
gious-school teacher and later on his own, he began to learn Hebrew, and was able to master spoken Hebrew years before he emigrated to Palestine. Knowledge of the modern language, still in the
process of renewal, was extremely rare among German Jews, including such spokesmen as Buber, so that Scholem quickly became
a curiosity among his contemporaries. His command of Hebrew
would enable him to become one of the first translators into German of such modern Hebrew writers as S. Y. Agnon.

In 1913 he began to study the Talmud at one of the Berlin Jewish
communal schools in a program organized voluntarily by unpaid
teachers. He was particularly influenced by one teacher, Isaac
Bleichrode, who later came to Jerusalem.[9] In the same year, Scholem joined the Agudat Yisrael, the orthodox group founded to
oppose Zionism. Although he did not agree with the group's anti-
Zionist politics, he was attracted to it because it offered opportuni-
ties to study Jewish texts. Scholem seems to have entertained some
thoughts of becoming orthodox at this time, but the ritualistic side
of Judaism held little interest for him personally. He left the Agudat
Yisrael in 1914, although he continued to study with various orthodox teachers until his departure for Palestine in 1923.[10] Unlike Ernst
Simon, another assimilated German Jew who became a Zionist and

emigrated to Palestine, Scholem's reawakened Jewish identity did not cause him to tend toward ritual observance. On the other hand, he was not content, like many other young German Zionists, to express his identity solely through a secular political movement. Even at the age of seventeen or so, he was beginning to define his idiosyncratic relation to the Jewish tradition: not satisfied to consider himself a Jew simply because he was a Zionist, yet also not willing to embrace orthodoxy, he sought his identity in the passionate study of Jewish sources.

Scholem became a Zionist in 1911 at the age of fourteen, mainly as a result of his new interest in Judaism. Zionism was not, of course, only a movement of the young in Germany in this period. Scholem's uncle, for instance, active in the German Zionist organization and a printer by trade, published the Zionist journals *Die Welt* and *Die Jüdische Rundschau*.[11] But the Scholem family considered this lone Zionist something of a harmless eccentric, and Scholem himself, though sympathetic to his uncle's dissatisfaction with German-Jewish life, viewed much of adult Zionism as only a modified form of assimilationism. Indeed, German Zionism was often more a reaction to the social antisemitism of Wilhelmian Germany than it was a concrete political program. This "Zionism" largely fulfilled its psychological and social function once it produced Jewish fraternal and athletic organizations similar to the exclusive gentile clubs.[12]

The Zionism of the youth was a different matter, although it did not produce a large wave of immigration to Palestine until 1933. Young Jews were swept up by the "youth culture" of the period, which, in protest against industrial society and bourgeois culture, longed romantically for a new "organic" community and a return to a mythical harmonious Volk. They saw themselves as a separate class of society, one of whose main expressions was the Wandervogel youth movement. The Wandervogel, loosely organized in groups throughout Central Europe, believed that the common experience of wandering in nature would instinctively create a new community.[13]

Many German Jews joined the Wandervogel in the early years of the twentieth century.[14] Most were from assimilated backgrounds and, although their revolt was against the lifestyle of their parents, it had little to do with the question of Judaism. After about 1912, however, antisemitism in the German Wandervogel increased and many Jews felt compelled to leave.[15] Partly in response to this growing antisemitism, a group of young Jews in Berlin in 1912 formed the Blau-Weiss, a Jewish version of the Wandervogel,

which quickly spread throughout Germany and Austria and became the dominant Jewish youth movement. Although the Blau-
Weiss professed Zionism from its inception, even a cursory examination of its journal, the *Blau-Weiss Blätter*, reveals preoccupation
with idyllic descriptions of country outings and virtually no concern with Zionist ideology.[16]

Scholem never joined the Blau-Weiss, although he had connections with some of its members and later published a savage critique of it in one of its own journals. He joined the Jung-Juda, a
Zionist youth club in Berlin, and, during the war years, became its
leader, turning it into one of the most radical Zionist youth groups
in Central Europe. A number of the members of Scholem's group
later emigrated to Palestine and helped found Kibbutz Beit Zera in
the Jordan Valley.[17]

BUBER AND THE ZIONIST YOUTH MOVEMENT

The reigning spiritual leader of the German Zionist youth movement was Martin Buber, and Scholem's first knowledge of Buber
must have been through friends in his Zionist circle. By the time
Scholem became something of a follower of Buber's in the years
before the war, Buber was already in his thirties and had been a
Zionist since the turn of the century. His age and his equally prophetic and enigmatic style made him a charismatic figure. Buber
appeared as the keynote speaker at numerous student Zionist gatherings throughout Central Europe and exercised influence as far
east as Galicia.[18]

Buber's attraction lay not only in his charisma but, more important, in the mystical philosophy he used to buttress his Zionism. He
tried to show that Judaism had authentic myths of its own to serve
in this time of intense spiritual quest. Western rationality, Buber
argued, perceives the world as a multiplicity of sense perceptions,
whereas Judaism strives for unity of man with the world.[19] Despite
its bourgeois institutions, Judaism is essentially the antithesis of
Zivilization since it is a true "religiosity" (*Religiosität*) as opposed
to a sterile and ritualistic "religion." Buber turned into a virtue the
liberal antisemitic accusation that Judaism is not suited to modern
Western society: the alien "Oriental" spirit of Judaism made it a relevant belief for youth in full revolt against nineteenth-century liberalism and Western civilization.

Buber emphasized that Zionism was not so much a solution to
antisemitism as it was a vehicle for Jewish spiritual rebirth.[20] With
emancipation, the Jews had increasingly adopted Western rationalism and were losing their Oriental spirit. The long years of exile in

the West, and particularly the century following emancipation, had taken their toll. The Jewish question was therefore not one of anti-semitism, for "there is more at stake than the fate of a particular people . . . at stake are arch-human (*urmenschliche*) and universal-ly human matters."[21] Zionism meant the return of the Jews not only to their Oriental homeland but, more significantly for Buber, to their Oriental mentality. By the "unconditioned deed" of returning to Zion, the Jews could escape the atomized existence of the West, and could also pose an alternative to the West itself.

Buber's early Zionist argument was based on his *Erlebnismystik*, which, as Paul Flohr has shown,[22] was substantially different from the dialogic philosophy he espoused after World War I (although its categories prepared the way for his *I and Thou*). Buber believed that there are inner experiences (*Erlebnisse*) which are ontologically and epistemologically different from experiences through sense per-ception (*Erfahrung*). Where sense perception leads to a fragmented picture of the world, Erlebnisse are intuitive experiences of unity with the world and the highest Erlebnis is unity with the Absolute. Buber took the category of Erlebnis from Dilthey's epistemology and Simmel's sociological Lebensphilosophie.[23] The experience of unity with the Absolute was not a social category for Buber, how-ever, as it was for his teacher Simmel, but an individual, mystical one.[24] The new community (*neue Gemeinschaft*) Buber envisioned would be based on the intuitive affinity among all those individuals who partake of this Erlebnis.[25] Although those who share the ex-perience of the Absolute need not, or cannot, communicate with one another in the social realm, Erlebnis nonetheless impels them toward some new, revolutionary community. This community would be free of all externally imposed restrictions and would be motivated by the internal, intuitive understanding among its mem-bers, all fellows in the same *Erlebnismystik*.

Despite the nonsocial premises of Buber's mysticism, the young Zionists who followed him were attracted by the notion of a com-munity based on inner experience. Like Buber's, their own experi-ence of Germany was less a reaction to antisemitism than it was disillusionment with bourgeois rationalism. The universal and exis-tential interpretation Buber gave to Zionism as a new community had an immediate resonance for these assimilated young Jews. They could identify with the general youth culture and its con-cerns, claiming to follow a philosophy universalist in substance if nationalist in form. Buber's notion of a community based on shared experience corresponded closely to the Wandervogel ideal: the ro-mantic transcendence of the everyday world through the experience of nature would create the feeling of comradeship between the wanderers. Buber later abandoned Erlebnismystik in favor of a much more social doctrine of dialogue in the real world—but the Zionism he preached throughout his life was always a vehicle for some higher religious philosophy. This relativization of Zionism was particularly meaningful to young Jews who sought neither a return to orthodox Judaism nor a nationalist solution to antisemitism, but a philosophy like that of the Wandervogel. For many, however, the great Erlebnis preached by Buber came first not through Zionism but during World War I.

Historians have long noted the pervasive and liberating feeling of community experienced by the belligerent nations in the first days of the outbreak of World War I. To many of the young people who rushed off to enlist, like Rupert Brooke in England, the war brought a sense of liberation from the stifling somnolence of the prewar years. In those first months of the war, German Jews were also swept up by the waves of ecstatic patriotism. Although antisemitism did not disappear during the war, many assimilated Jews felt that they were for the first time accepted fully by German society. The war gave them a chance to prove their patriotism and was perhaps the last and most powerful argument in the long struggle for full emancipation.

German Zionists were no exception to the general war fervor. As Moses Calvary, one of the leaders of the Blau-Weiss, wrote in 1914: "And *Deutschtum?* You know that I had to struggle less for my German than for my Jewish conviction, that I really became a Zionist not out of Jewish but rather human instincts . . . A defeat of Germany would not only destroy our beloved homeland, our material possessions, our social being, but also a great part of our inner world."[26] It is particularly interesting to examine the ideological justifications the Zionists gave for these common emotions. For some Jewish nationalists, the war was an opportunity to avenge the sufferings of Russian Jews.[27] This argument was simply a Jewish version of the general fear and hatred of Russian absolutism which brought even the Social Democrats to vote for war credits in August 1914. Some Zionists argued that the war gave Jews a chance to prove their manhood, as "new Maccabees."[28] The Zionists in Central Europe had emphasized "physical culture," or what Max Nordau called "muscular Judaism," as a way of creating a new Jewish man, and the war gave the Jews an opportunity to prove themselves.

Buber's defense of the war is of special interest to us because it had such a great impact on Jewish youth. With the outbreak of hostilities, Buber mobilized his mystical philosophy for war service, writing to Hans Kohn in Prague: "Never has the concept of the *Volk* been such a reality for me as in the last weeks. A sincere and great feeling also prevails amongst the Jews."[29] At a gathering of Berlin Zionists at Hanukkah in December 1914, Buber extolled the war as a liberating experience similar to the war of the Maccabees.[30] Although Jewish troops might be fighting one another, they were nonetheless fighting for their Jewishness. The war itself was but an outer symbol for the inner mystical liberation that all Jews would experience by taking part in it. Here seemed to be the Erlebnis he had longed for, and the Jews were full participants in it. They would "deepen their experience of community (*Gemeinschafterlebnis*) and out of it build their Judaism anew."[31] Scholem was in the audience that heard Buber's remarks and he was "scandalized."[32] It is likely that this was the beginning of his critical attitude toward Buber which was to grow throughout the war.

Buber expanded on his Hanukkah address in April 1916 in the first issue of his monthly journal *Der Jude*, which became the main forum for the Jewish spiritual revival in Germany in the years immediately after the war and in which Scholem himself published some of his first articles on the Kabbalah. In the lead editorial entitled "Die Losung" ("The Watchword"), he argued that the war would destroy the illusion of an atomized society and no one, Jew or non-Jew, would want to return to his fragmented antebellum existence. The war had proven to be the greatest mystical experience of Buber's prewar philosophy: "Through the Jewish *Erlebnis* of this war, which has violently shaken the Jews and caused them to feel responsibility for the fate of their community, a new unity of Judaism has emerged."[33] The war would lead the Jews to Zionism as the new community and would teach them the mystical value of nationalism. But Buber hastened to add at the end of his article that Zionism did not propose to add one more belligerent nation to the world, but to serve as a force to bind nations together in peace. It is significant that Buber adopted roughly the same prowar argument as the anti-Zionist Hermann Cohen; although they engaged in a debate over Zionism during the war, they agreed that Jewish support for German nationalism would lead to a peaceful world.[34]

Buber's mystical Zionist defense of the war had quite an impact on the Jewish youth groups.[35] One follower of Buber, Heinrich Margulies, who was a member of the Herzlring, a Zionist group of nonprofessional employees, wrote an article in *Die Jüdische Rundschau* which prompted an angry response by Scholem.[36] Adopting

Buber's terminology, Margulies explained that those who remained
on the home front during the war feared that they would miss the
rebirth (Neugeburt) experienced by the soldiers, but the civilians
were still consecrated (weihen) by the holiness of the struggle
(Heiligkeit des Kampfes). The assimilationists had argued that the
war made Zionism superfluous since antisemitism had substantially disappeared in the first flush of national unity. But it was precisely Zionism that had prepared the Jews for war by extolling the
virtues of community, self-sacrifice, and desire for salvation of the
Volk. In short, Zionists made the best patriots. Zionism had remained isolated before the war, but with the war Zionists and German nationalists recognized each other as brothers: "In the tumult
of the crowd we sensed our melody and suddenly community (Gemeinschaft) engulfed us . . . As this experience (Erlebnis) was entrusted to us . . . so it came about that we were drawn to the war
not despite our being Jews but because we were Zionists." Here was
a faithful application of Buber's doctrine that Zionism and the war
were mystical allies.

SCHOLEM AND THE WAR

Opposition to the war in Germany in the first two years was extremely limited.[37] A small splinter group of Social Democrats, led
by Karl Liebknecht, Hugo Haase, and Rosa Luxemburg, rejected
their party's support for the Kaiser's Burgfrieden. Scholem's brother Werner, who had become a Social Democrat some two years
earlier after a short flirtation with Zionism, identified with the antiwar radicals. When Werner returned to Berlin in September 1914,
he found his younger brother equally opposed to the war, and the
two frequented the fortnightly illegal gatherings of the Social Dem-
ocratic minority in a small cafe in Neukölln.[38] Scholem was much
impressed by Liebknecht, who had originally voted for war credits
in August 1914 but reversed his position in a dramatic speech in the
Reichstag at the end of the year.[39]

Scholem's opposition to the war was not, however, prompted by
socialist arguments; his involvement with the antiwar faction was
only through his brother and, when Werner was drafted in 1915, he
stopped attending the secret socialist meetings. Although Werner's
influence may have helped him adhere to his opinions against the
tide of patriotism, he seems to have arrived at them on his own.
This tentative conclusion raises the difficult question of how Scholem, at the age of sixteen, could have opposed the war from the
outset without any external instigation, especially since the prowar
feeling in Germany was almost universal in the first months of
fighting.

If there was any one factor that caused Scholem to reject the war, it was his radical Zionism. To be sure, Zionism by itself can hardly explain his position, for, as we have seen, most of the Zionists, including the youth movements, were swept up in the war fever. However, Scholem interpreted Zionism as a call to abandon Europe and its political and cultural concerns. Many of Scholem's companions in the Jung-Juda also opposed the war, and much of Scholem's antiwar activity was centered in this group. Since it appears that he was the leader of this faction of the Jung-Juda, his friends were probably less of an influence upon him than a source of support. Lacking further evidence, one can only conclude that Scholem's radical interpretation of Zionism was probably the product of his iconoclastic and uncompromising personality: in his politics as in his historiography, he set his own course.

Scholem first expressed his antiwar position in writing in February 1915, reacting to Heinrich Margulies' article in *Die Jüdische Rundschau*. With a number of friends from the Jung-Juda, he drafted a letter to the Zionist newspaper protesting its publication of the prowar article. The students argued that Jewish national interests do not coincide with those of Germany or any of the other belligerents. The letter, which was also signed by Scholem's brother Werner, was shown to Arthur Hantke, the president of the Zionistische Vereinigung für Deutschland, who sympathized with its position but was afraid that its publication might lead to prohibition of the Zionist organization. In a meeting with Scholem and two of the other instigators, Hantke urged silence and the letter was never printed. Meanwhile, a student at Scholem's gymnasium, who caught sight of the letter when Scholem brought it in to collect signatures, denounced him to the school authorities. He was expelled from school for antiwar agitation, but soon continued his education at the University of Berlin under an arcane Prussian law designed originally to allow the younger sons of Junker noblemen to attend university for two years without highschool matriculation.[40] Although the only real impact of the suppressed antiwar letter was Scholem's expulsion from school, it is perhaps the first evidence of a split in the German-Zionist movement between those, like Margulies and Buber, who supported the war because of Zionist sentiments and the minority, like Scholem, who rejected the war on Zionist grounds.

Frustrated in their attempt to express their views in established organs, Scholem and his friends in Jung-Juda began to publish an underground paper that polemicized against the war and against the Germanophile tendencies in the Zionist youth movement. The paper came out three times, in the summer and fall of 1915 and the winter of 1916. A member of the group, Erich Brauer, who was a graphic artist, prepared the lithographic plates which were printed on the sly in Scholem's father's shop with the collusion of two of the employees. Entitled *Die Blauweisse Brille* (The Blue and White Spectacles), the name revealed the desire of the group to view events through a Zionist perspective, but it may have also hinted at its intent to expose the hypocrisy of the Blau-Weiss youth movement.[41]

Although written in an occasionally bombastic and childish style, the *Blauweisse Brille* is noteworthy evidence of the most radical tendencies in German Zionism. Toward both official Zionism and the war, the young members of Jung-Juda took an extraordinarily critical stand, which would have earned them little mercy at the hands of the authorities or support from the Jewish community had they been discovered. Scholem's first article in the inaugural issue of the paper was an attack on the Zionist youth movements, including the older leaders of the Jung-Juda. Reflecting this "generation gap" and his disagreement with the lack of Jewish content in the youth movement, Scholem concluded the article by calling the Jewish youth movments "Jewish movement without youth, Jewish youth without movement, youth movement without Judaism."

In the same issue of the *Blauweisse Brille*, Scholem published an antiwar poem, "Von der anderen Seite" (From the Other Side), more important for its political message than for its poetic style.[42]

> Out of the Infinite
> In front of you a star rises
> To the gates of the heavens
> Far beyond space and time
> You believe that it carries you
> You gave yourself to it solemnly,
> It was the war!
>
> But it did not lead
> As you believed in seeing
> Its sparks rising
> To the light of the primordial world.
> It was only a chimera
> Which passed through the world,
> It was the war!
>
> God on High laughs
> An incendiary world fire
> He throws from land to land
> Far through the night
> He gave it to us like a star
> With great force dragged us out,
> Out into the war.

> The game of the chimera flourished
> We trust in the derision of the heavens
> Even if the world
> Has already suffocated us in the flames.
> We call it necessity
> Noble, divine time
> (But) it is only war!
>
> But you stand and look
> Into the hearth of the fire
> Until the flames consume you
> The flaming lightning out of the fist of God
> Strikes you, you son of the stars:
> It destroys your vision of the world:
> Thank the war for it
> . . . If you can!

Scholem's was only a minor contribution to the corpus of antiwar poetry, but it reflects, if in a negative way, the mystical language used by Buber and his followers to justify the war. For Scholem, if the war was a divine necessity, it was only because the heavens are playing with us. Scholem thus turned Buber's solemn and sancti-monious "realization of the Absolute" through the Erlebnis of war into an ironic game of the Almighty.

In the second issue of the *Blauweisse Brille*, Scholem developed his antiwar position in an article entitled "Laienpredigt" (Lay Ser-mon). He attacked those who connected Zionism with the war:

> Does the way to Zion lie through the capitals of Europe? . . . We want to draw the line between Europe and Judah: my thought is not your thought, my way is not your way. We do not have so many people for you to throw freely into the furnace like Mo-loch. No, we need men who have the courage to think Jewish thoughts as their final thoughts, who have the courage of radi-calism in thought and deed, to be near their people in order not to be overcome by the intoxication between London and Peters-burg—men for whom the words "dogmatism" and "treason" only make them laugh.

The solution to the suffering of exile was not melancholy resigna-tion, but the "joy of youth," which could only be realized in Zion. The new world that would come out of the war would be the "Jeru-salem of joy."

The *Blauweisse Brille* contained a number of explicit barbs against Martin Buber, including a rather crude caricature and a parody of Buber's style. A copy fell into Buber's hands, and his re-sponse was to invite Scholem and Erich Brauer to come meet him.

By the time of the meeting in the middle of 1916, Buber had begun
to shift his position on the war, and the encounter was not as
stormy as it might have been. Although Scholem continued to dis-
agree with Buber on a number of fundamental issues until Buber's
death in 1965, their personal relationship was marked by mutual
respect, a quality Buber seems to have engendered by his great tolerance. Although Scholem was singularly critical and sharp-
tongued, especially in his youth, the unfailing courtesy and seriousness with which Buber treated him created a close friendship from
the start.[43]

If Scholem became friendly with Buber on a personal level during
these years, his attitude toward Buber's philosophy remained inalterably critical. Although he defended Buber's *Drei Reden über das
Judentum* in discussions with his friend Walter Benjamin, whom he
met in 1915, Benjamin's criticisms of the "Kult des Erlebnisses"
made a strong impression on him.[44] Benjamin was always much
more hostile to Buber than Scholem was, but Scholem quickly
came to see the connection between Buber's Erlebnismystik and
support for the war. After the war, he wrote a strong critique of the
Zionist youth movement in Siegfried Bernfeld's *Jerubbaal*, and although he did not mention Buber by name, the target is clear:

> because the youth cannot remain silent and cannot speak, can-
> not see and cannot act, they "experience" (*erlebt*). In these pages,
> the Torah has been turned into an *Erlebnis*. The vague mysticism
> to which Judaism is sacrificed on the altar of *Erlebnis* is the true
> crown of the youth movement . . . And they even "experienced"
> (*erlebt haben*) the war when that was still fashionable . . . How-
> ever, in truth, *Erlebnis* is nothing but a chimera, the Absolute
> turned into idle chatter (*Geschwätz*).[45]

Here it becomes clear how Scholem's opposition to the war went
hand in hand with his contempt for the vacuous neo-romanticism
of the youth movements. He also objected strenuously to Buber's
reduction of both historical Judaism and Zionism to mystical experiences.[46] Buber had preached the importance of realization (*Verwirklichung*) in his philosophy, and the discovery that he did not
intend to "realize" his own Zionism by emigrating to Palestine
came as a grave disillusionment to Scholem. Although he never directly mentioned the issue to Buber in their letters, it ran as an un-
dercurrent of tension between the two until Buber, forced almost
against his will by events in Germany, finally came to Jerusalem in
1938.[47]

Buber's Zionism seemed to Scholem bereft of any concrete program. Like most of his generation of German Zionists, Scholem was less attracted to Herzl's vision of Zionism as a solution to the political problems of the Jews than to its potential for answering cultural and spiritual needs.[48] Buber's brand of spiritual Zionism frequently filled this role for young German Zionists, but Scholem found his own model in Ahad Ha-am, the Zionist essayist from Odessa. Scholem came to believe that Ahad Ha-am's program for a cultural center in Palestine offered a much more realistic direction for Zionism than the mystical Erlebnis advocated by Buber.[49] In his later political writings in Palestine during the 1920s and 1930s, Scholem argued forcefully that the Zionist movement should adopt Ahad Ha-am's moderate cultural vision as its goal rather than the political maximalism of the Revisionists. Only after 1933 did Ahad Ha-am's belief in the possibility of rejuvenating the Diaspora without a mass emigration to Palestine seem to him shattered by the political events in Germany.

Another visionary who captured Scholem's admiration in the early years of the war was Gustav Landauer, the political anarchist who was assassinated following the abortive Bavarian socialist revolution of 1918-1919.[50] Landauer was close to Buber, but adamantly opposed Buber's position on the war. It is even possible that Landauer was instrumental in convincing Buber to abandon his political position, which may have ultimately led him also to abandon his Erlebnismystik.[51] Landauer's opposition to the war was based on strong moral and antiauthoritarian grounds, a position that appealed much more to Scholem than the Marxism of his brother Werner. Although Landauer never professed Zionism, he was close to Zionist circles, and his belief in the people as a cultural-spiritual force provided Scholem with a model for antimilitaristic nationalism. Landauer's vision of small anarchistic communes as a solution to the inhumanity of industrial capitalism made quite an impact on young Zionists and, together with Tolstoyan ideas from Russian populism, contributed to the ideological development of the kibbutz movement. Scholem heard Landauer speak in 1915 and became acquainted with him. He read Landauer's *Die Revolution* and *Aufruf zum Sozialismus* as well as other anarchist writings and considered himself an anarchist both in his opposition to the war and in his Zionism. Although he never accepted the anarchists' belief in the essential goodness of man or their vision of a new political order, his later identification of himself as a theological anarchist has its origin in his contact with anarchism during the war.[52]

SCHOLEM'S CONTROVERSY WITH THE ZIONIST YOUTH MOVEMENTS

The enthusiastic support the Zionist youth movements gave to the German war effort aroused Scholem's disgust and contributed to his general critique of their ideological bankruptcy. If these groups were truly Zionists, he argued, they would not "say Zion when [they] meant Berlin" and would not mix other political or personal professional aspirations with national goals.[53] Although Scholem would later fight against the Revisionists in Palestine, his uncompromising Zionism during World War I is strangely reminiscent of Vladimir Jabotinsky's "monism," which opposed the dilution of Zionism with any other political philosophy.

Scholem opposed the anti-ideological "activism" of the youth movements. The philosophy of "wandering" adopted by the Jewish Wandervogel stated that the experience of ecstatic fellowship would build the new community. Ideology as such was considered purely subjective and secondary to the shared experience. The Blau-Weiss made it a virtue to leave its ideology unarticulated and vague. Scholem argued that the notion of Gemeinschaft built on a common experience of wandering would never lead to emigration to Palestine and the building of a real community there. The ideal of wandering would not only fail to lead to Zion, but was actually counterproductive since it diverted youth from the development of ideology: once Gemeinschaft was realized in Germany, there would be no need for practical Zionism.[54]

For Scholem, ideology had objective value. Only a coherent, articulated ideology could convert the static youth groups into a real movement. In place of "experience" Scholem advocated education by example.[55] Scholem was particularly critical of the lack of any serious education in the youth movements. We have seen that his own path to Zionism was integrally connected with intensive study of Hebrew and classical Jewish texts. From his personal experience he believed that this sort of intense study was the proper program for the youth movement as a whole.[56]

Scholem argued that, without knowledge of Hebrew, the Zionist youth would have no real language but only "idle chatter" (Geschwätz). If they did not study Jewish sources, they would have no concept of history. As an example of their lack of historical perspective, Scholem pointed out that at the death of Hermann Cohen in 1918 the youth had no idea who Cohen was, except that he opposed Zionism: "the death of Hermann Cohen did not find them ready to mourn just as his life did not awaken their respect . . . At the grave of Hermann Cohen, Judaism mourned, but the Jewish youth movement knew only that he was an 'enemy.' "[57] It is striking that Scholem chose Cohen as a representative of Judaism, especially since he himself systematically rejected the liberal and rational brand of Judaism that Cohen stood for. Here is a meaningful hint of Scholem's own philosophy of history: his revolutionary assault on the positions of his predecessors never turned into negation. Even as he overturned their conclusions, he would always subordinate himself to the tradition of which they were a legitimate part.

Scholem's attack on the youth movements stirred a spirited controversy.[58] Hans Oppenheim criticized Scholem for carping from the outside and not understanding the real situation within the Blau-Weiss.[59] By defining radical Zionism as the goal of the movement and by advocating the immediate use of Hebrew, Scholem was posing utopian goals that could not be reached, given the degree of assimilation among Blau-Weiss members. By forcing too advanced ideals on its members, Scholem risked alienating a substantial portion of them. Oppenheim accused Scholem of elitism, a charge that has a certain validity. Few German Jews were gifted or motivated enough to undertake an intensive program of study in Jewish sources as a circuitous route to Zionism, and few would end up, as he did, a scholar in Judaica coming from a secular background. In Scholem's philosophy of Jewish history we will also see certain hints of elitism, although of a rather special sort.

Scholem's attacks on the Zionist youth movements touched certain sore spots already known to the members. In 1917 Moses Calvary gave a speech on "The Problem of Education of the Jewish Youth Wanderers" in which he admitted that "some claim that the appreciation of the German landscape is specifically German, that only the Germans can really 'wander'—there is some truth in this."[60] Oppenheim, in his reply to Scholem, also acknowledged that wandering through the German countryside threatened a new type of assimilation. Finally, Heinrich Margulies, whose article caused Scholem's first antiwar activity, turned against his mentor at a youth conference after the war. Margulies accused Buber of "spiritualizing" Zionism (*Vergeistung des Zionismus*), presumably by ignoring the need for a concrete program of emigration to Palestine.[61]

An indication of the impact of Scholem's critique of the youth movement can be found in Franz Rosenzweig's correspondence from this period (1919-1922). At least two of Rosenzweig's correspondents, Mawrik Kahn and Rudolf Hallo, were deeply shaken by Scholem's accusations and began to doubt the worth of their own Jewish activities.[62] Rosenzweig reassured Kahn that Kahn's involvement in Hasidism, even if contrived and unsuccessful, was a genu-

ine act (*Tun*), while Scholem's critique, because it was purely negative, was not. Rosenzweig argued that authentic action should not
be measured by the ecstatic feeling that accompanies it, and those
who emphasize ecstasy over action have forsaken the Jewish approach for the Christian. Rosenzweig's letter was a polemic against
Buber, as becomes clear from his satirical reference to "Rabbi Martin of Heppenheim" (Buber's home) as the only one to find value in
talking about ecstasy and Erlebnis. But in his critique of Buber's Judaism, Rosenzweig also attacked Scholem. Even if Scholem had
correctly criticized Buber for undue emphasis on Erlebnis, he himself had not engaged in any positive activity. Against Scholem's
withdrawal from involvement in the Zionist youth groups, Rosenzweig found Kahn's halting efforts to return to Judaism much more
genuine and fruitful.

It was to be expected that later, when Scholem met Rosenzweig,
who was not a Zionist, they would have a fierce argument.[63] But
despite the personal and intellectual tensions between them, Rosenzweig greatly respected Scholem's learning and, in the summer of
1923, invited him to lecture at the Frankfurt Lehrhaus.[64] Before
leaving for Palestine that autumn, Scholem taught classes at the
Lehrhaus on the Book of Daniel, the Kabbalah, and S. Y. Agnon.
Rosenzweig noted wryly in a letter to Joseph Prager that "Scholem
is here for the summer, and he is, as always, unspeakably ill-be-
haved, but likewise as always, brilliant."[65]

Scholem's polemics against the youth movements appeared
largely in the years during and just after the war. But a radical
change in the Blau-Weiss caused him to issue his most ferocious
attack in 1922.[66] For some years, the group had been developing toward commitment to emigrate to Palestine, a direction Scholem
certainly favored. In 1922, the Blau-Weiss proclaimed the necessity
of a power struggle in Palestine in order to establish a revolutionary colony of the young in opposition to bourgeois Zionism. Clearly influenced by the growing fascist tendencies in the German
youth movements, the Blau-Weiss restructured itself along military
lines and elevated its leader, Walter Moses, to a position of total
authority. Moses, who ended up running a cigarette factory in Palestine, declared in a speech to the revolutionized Blau-Weiss:

Freedom and obedience will be linked together to lead to a new
mentality. The hope for the fulfillment of life through the triumph of freedom will be achieved through the unshakeable
belief in the victory of power . . . Whoever serves [this proud or-
ganization], whether as a leader or as a soldier, is profoundly
connected with life, [but] whoever defects from it, becomes an
enemy and will perish with the bourgeois (*den Bürgern*).[67]

Scholem wrote a letter, signed by fourteen others, to *Die Jü-dische Rundschau* in strong protest against the new development in the Blau-Weiss.[68] His biting critique resonates with arguments from earlier polemics. The lack of ideology he had criticized earlier must have now seemed to him to have become mere reliance upon the leader's decrees, which, devoid of substantive content (*Inhalt*), "stands beyond good and evil, under the star of the vacuous intoxication of youth for power and leadership." Scholem labels this new ideology "unscrupulous mysticism" (*bedenklose Mystizismus*), thus suggesting that the Erlebnis mysticism he attacked in earlier articles had now culminated in authoritarianism and absolutism (*Verabsolutierung des Blau-Weiss*). Although the Blau-Weiss had proclaimed itself ready to establish a "culturally creative colony" in Palestine, it was still deeply enmeshed in the German matrix, taking its ideas from the German youth movement and its military metaphors from the World War experience to which it was still addicted. Lacking all connection to the Hebrew language and irresponsibly renouncing the received cultural heritage of the Jewish people (*den überlieferten Kulturbesitz des jüdischen Volkes*), the Blau-Weiss could make no contribution to the Jewish revival in Palestine and might even endanger it by its call to revolution against Zionist institutions. A great abyss (*Abgrund*) separated the sterile Blau-Weiss from the figure of the pioneer (*ḥaluz*) upon whom the real hopes of the Zionist movement rested.

With these harsh words, Scholem's disillusionment with the Zionist youth movement reached its culmination. However, the issues that aroused his anger were to play an important role in the development of his later thought. His rejection of the mystical approach to both Judaism and Zionism influenced his views on both Zionist politics and historiography. He would see in the militaristic messianism of the Revisionists a reincarnation of the dangerous tendencies in the Blau-Weiss: revolutionary scorn for the Jewish tradition and lack of concrete and constructive goals. In his historiography, he would depart from the mystical and mythopoeic view of Jewish history and advocate a more sober philology.

SCHOLEM AND THE CULT OF THE OSTJUDEN

Scholem's personal life during the period of these polemics was stormy and eventful. In the beginning of 1917, his brother Werner was arrested for participating in an antiwar demonstration, and Scholem's father, enraged and embarrassed at both his sons' lack of patriotism, threw Scholem out of the house and cut off financial support for about a year.[69] Scholem moved into the Pension Struck, a boardinghouse occupied primarily by Eastern European

Jews and made his living largely by translations from Hebrew and Yiddish into German. In the summer of 1917, he was called up by the army after having successfully evaded conscription for almost two years. Like Thomas Mann's outrageous hero, Felix Krull, who feigned epilepsy, Scholem contrived to dodge the German draft by pretending to be psychotic. He was kept under close psychiatric observation for some six weeks and in January 1918 was finally ruled totally unfit for military service.[70]

The time Scholem spent at the Pension Struck in Berlin proved to be singularly important in his development.[71] Here he discovered the lively intellectual world of Eastern European Jewry. Many young German Jews in search of their Jewish roots eagerly sought out Eastern European Jews as representatives of "authentic" Judaism. Scholem later called this fascination, to which he also succumbed, "the Ostjuden cult which flourished among German Zionist youth who sought thus to express their resentment of their parents' rejection of Eastern European Jewry."[72] Before the war, the Ostjuden who had fled persecution and impoverishment in Eastern Europe were coldly received by most German Jews and were regarded as uncouth and primitive. But as a result of the war, some German Jews came to view the Ostjuden much more favorably. As soldiers on the Eastern front, they saw the Jewish communities of the East first-hand and, like Franz Rosenzweig, believed they had found "living Judaism." This wartime experience in the East may have converted some assimilated Jews back to identification with Judaism.[73]

In Berlin, too, German Jews like Scholem "discovered" the Ostjuden. A group of young Jews with strong populist leanings founded a Jüdisches Volksheim which was intended as a social and educational center for the children of poor Eastern European Jews living in Berlin.[74] This attempt to "go to the people" had little success in developing contacts with the Jewish proletariat, but it did bring together German-Jewish students with Jewish intellectuals from Eastern Europe. The Volksheim sponsored cultural evenings of storytelling and poetry, and classes were given in Hebrew and Yiddish. Scholem himself attended a number of meetings at the Volksheim and was predictably scandalized by what he describes as "the atmosphere of aesthetic ecstasy."[75] He was particularly upset by the leader of the Volksheim, Siegfried Lehmann, whose lecture on "The Problem of Jewish Religious Education" struck him as a rehash of Buber's interpretation of Hasidism, which he considered "devoid of knowledge of historical Judaism." Scholem attacked Lehmann and argued that "instead of such nonsense and chatter, it is preferable to learn Hebrew and go to the sources (zu den Quellen gehen)."[76]

One Eastern European Jew active as a lecturer at the Volksheim and who lived in the same boardinghouse as Scholem was Zalman Rubaschoff. Later the third president of the State of Israel, he was working as an editor in Berlin, and he and Scholem became close friends. Scholem learned Yiddish from Rubaschoff and probably heard for the first time of Sabbatianism and Frankism, which would later become some of his most important research subjects. In later years, Scholem wrote of his friendship with Rubaschoff: "[He] seemed in my eyes like an emissary from a distant world of living Judaism who came to awaken the dry bones of German Jewry."[77]

Among the other Eastern Europeans Scholem came to know in this period was S. Y. Agnon, the great Hebrew writer who was living in Germany at the time.[78] Scholem had first heard of Agnon in 1916 through a book published by German Zionists for Jewish soldiers, which included Agnon's story "And the Crooked Shall Be Made Straight" with an introduction by Buber. Scholem later met Agnon, and they developed a close friendship that would continue in Jerusalem until Agnon's death in 1970. Since little of Agnon's work was available in German at the time, Scholem undertook to translate a number of his stories, and he was probably instrumental in bringing Agnon to the attention of German Jewry.[79]

Scholem was undoubtedly intrigued by Agnon's ambivalent relationship to Jewish tradition, which Arnold Band has characterized in the title of his book on Agnon as "nostalgia and nightmare." Agnon, whom Scholem has called the "last Hebrew classicist,"[80] had deep roots in the traditional world of Galician Jewry from which he came, but he also regarded this world with a good deal of satirical distaste. His subtle transformations of traditional Jewish motifs into demonic and surrealist stories must have seemed to Scholem to articulate his own ambivalent attraction to the demonic side of Jewish life.

Scholem also read avidly the works of M. Y. Berdichevsky. Although he only saw Berdichevsky once in a bookstore and never got to know him, he was particularly impressed by his translations of Jewish legends into German.[81] In 1919, while studying in Bern, he met S. A. Horodezky, the popularizer of Hasidism, and worked with him on translations of the latter's works from Hebrew into German. Despite this early association, Scholem later became contemptuous of Horodezky's romantic rendition of Hasidism.[82]

All of these relationships must be considered important for Scholem's intellectual development. Among the Ostjuden he found the kind of unabashed Zionism and love for Jewish tradition which he missed in German Jewry. He wrote many of his polemics against the Blau-Weiss while living in this exile community. Although he remained in Central Europe for over six years after he left his father's house, he was already psychologically removed from the assimilated bourgeois environment of his youth, vestiges of which he also found among the Zionist youth. Scholem's first experience of "Zion," as he was to find it among the predominantly Eastern European Yishuv in Palestine, already occurred in Berlin.

THE DECISION TO STUDY THE KABBALAH

Following his escape from military service in January 1918, Scholem went to Jena, where he studied at the university for six months. In May, after receiving his official medical discharge, he left Germany for Switzerland to join Walter Benjamin, who had also gone into temporary exile a short time before. For the next year and a half, Scholem lived in Bern, attending lectures at the university and spending long and intensive hours with Benjamin. In 1919, he decided to return to Germany and earn a doctoral degree. His formal university studies up to that time had focused on mathematics and philosophy, and Scholem seriously weighed the possibility of going to Göttingen to continue in mathematics.

But another option was open: to go to Munich, which had the best collection of Kabbalistic manuscripts in Germany, and write a dissertation on the Kabbalah. Scholem's interest in the Kabbalah, which had begun around 1915, had developed into a serious passion by 1919. A bibliophile like his friend Benjamin, he had acquired an enormous number of old Kabbalistic texts and, by the time he moved to Jerusalem in 1923, already had some 600 titles.[83] Within a few years he built up one of the most formidable private libraries in Jerusalem and in 1936, in a parody of the snobbish tradition of publishing catalogs of private libraries, he issued a small pamphlet entitled "A List of Books in Kabbalah and Hasidism Needed for the Book Collection of Gershom Scholem."

Scholem's path to the Kabbalah could not have been by way of any of the standard routes, whether Jewish or academic. His orthodox tutors in Bible and Talmud were unable to answer his questions about the Kabbalah, and there were no academicians in Germany at the time who had specialized knowledge of the subject. At Munich, Scholem took his degree in Semitics with the Assyriologist Fritz Hommel, but he wrote his dissertation on the *Sefer ha-Bahir* with virtually no assistance.[84]

Scholem's fateful choice of Munich over Göttingen probably grew out of intensive conversations with Benjamin and Buber. Scholem has called his friendship with Benjamin, which dated back to 1915, "the most important of my life."[85] Although Benjamin was not a Zionist and knew very little about Judaism, he was extremely sympathetic to Scholem's concerns. United in opposition to the war, they also found many areas of common interest in philosophy and metaphysics and exerted enormous influence on each other's intellectual development. Scholem's early desire to write a dissertation on the Kabbalah's philosophy of language was probably influenced by his conversations with Benjamin on this subject. He found in Benjamin's thought a philosophy with a mystical dimension which was remote from anything available at the universities he attended.[86]

Scholem also shared his decision to study the Kabbalah with Buber, who encouraged him and was probably the only person with whom Scholem conversed seriously and frequently about his studies during the Munich period.[87] Scholem's initial interest in the Kabbalah was probably inspired in part by *Drei Reden über das Judentum* in which Buber had argued, against the Wissenschaft des Judentums, that myth must be considered a legitimate part of Judaism. Scholem's rejection of "bourgeois" Judaism was consistent with the new atmosphere among young German Jews, an atmosphere Buber helped to create.[88] But as much as Scholem's fascination with irrationalism reflected his debt to Buber, his decision to study the Kabbalah as an academic project represented something new. Indeed, it has to be understood in part as a reaction against Buber's mystical approach to Jewish sources.

In Scholem's first articles on the Kabbalah, it is possible to see how his decision to take up this field was influenced by his rejection of Buber. In 1920, he wrote a long critique of Jankew Seidmann's translations of selections from the *Zohar*.[89] Scholem accused the author of rendering the language of the Kabbalah in the style of German expressionism. He attributes the blame for this to Buber's reworking of the *Tales of Rabbi Nachman*.[90] Seidmann's language was that of "the Prague Bar Kokhba . . . but was never the language of the Zohar."[91] The address of this barb was obvious: like the Blau-Weiss, the Prague Zionist circle, which included Samuel Hugo Bergmann and Robert Weltsch, was directly under Buber's spiritual influence. In this, his first article on the Kabbalah, Scholem extended his critique of the youth movements and their linguistic style to Kabbalistic scholarship: the scholars were just as infected with Buber's "expressionism" as was the Zionist Wandervogel.

A year later, Scholem published an even more extensive article on the Kabbalah in the form of a critique of Meir Wiener's *Die Lyrik der Kabbalah*.[92] Wiener distinguished between "religion" and "ritual" in passages that seem taken verbatim from Buber's *Drei Reden*. He celebrated the spontaneous "religious" act as the true *Gotterlebnis*.[93] Scholem focused acutely on Wiener's use of the Erlebnis category in treating the Kabbalah.[94] He questioned whether the distinction between "living inapplicable Erlebnis" and "cultic, practically directed ossification of dogma" was useful in understanding the Kabbalah. The Buberian distinctions led instead to a distortion of the historical essence of the Kabbalah, since they imposed anachronistic modern categories on historical materials. The tendency Wiener inherited from Buber to unite all mysticisms under a common "vulgar expressionistic theory" destroyed the historical uniqueness of each.[95] In his later critique of Buber's ahistorical interpretation of Hasidism, Scholem made explicit against Buber those arguments he had directed against Wiener in 1921.

The main problem with Wiener's book, and the whole expressionistic approach to Judaism, Scholem seems to suggest, was that Wiener's love for metaphysical ecstasy had undermined the philological and historical discipline necessary to comprehend the Kabbalah in its historical uniqueness. In a parenthetical remark, he satirizes those like Hugo Bergmann, one of Buber's closest disciples, who desire "the resurrection of metaphysics."[96] The tendency to see *any* mystical writing as poetry that could inspire a metaphysical awakening had fostered a misunderstanding of the nature of the Kabbalah. As a technical corpus of literature, the Kabbalah required not the enthusiasm of the poet or the metaphysician, but the painstaking investigation of the philologian.

Yet Scholem was by no means hostile to metaphysics. In fact, his original impetus in studying the Kabbalah must be understood as metaphysical, for he hoped to discover in those esoteric writings certain truths that had no place in rational Jewish philosophy. But he came to believe that metaphysical truths could only be discovered through the academic tools of philological and historical criticism. As he wrote in his critique of Wiener, "profound philology can have a genuine mystical function."[97] Scholem developed this startling idea in 1937 in an aphoristic letter he wrote to Zalman Schocken in honor of the latter's sixtieth birthday, entitled "A Candid Word about the True Motives of My Kabbalistic Studies." Because this manuscript, which has never been published, is crucial for understanding how Scholem came to his decision to study the Kabbalah, I translate it in full here (the original appears at the back of the book.)[98]

In no way did I become a "Kabbalist" inadvertently. I knew what I was doing—only it seems to me now that I imagined my undertaking to be much too easy. When I was about to put on the hat of the philologian and withdraw from mathematics and epistemology into a much more dubious field, I had scarcely any knowledge of my subject, but I was full of "insights."

Three years, 1916-1918, which were decisive for my entire life, lay behind me: many exciting thoughts had led me as much to the most rationalistic skepticism about my fields of study as to intuitive affirmation of mystical theses which walked the fine line between religion and nihilism.

I later [found in Kafka] the most perfect and unsurpassed expression of this fine line, an expression which, as a secular statement of the Kabbalistic world-feeling in a modern spirit, seemed to me to wrap Kafka's writings in the halo of the canonical.

At that time however, it was Molitor's curious book, *Philosophie der Geschichte oder über die Tradition*, which, falling into my hands at Poppelauer's, fascinated me greatly. As historically unfounded as it may have been, it gave an address where the secret life of Judaism, which I had pondered over in my meditations, seemed once to have dwelt.

So I arrived at the intention of writing not the history but the metaphysics of the Kabbalah. I was struck by the impoverishment of what some like to call the Philosophy of Judaism. I was particularly incensed by three authors whom I knew, Saadia [Gaon], Maimonides, and Hermann Cohen, who conceived as their main task to construct antitheses to myth and pantheism, to refute them, although they should have concerned themselves with raising them to a higher level.

Of course, it is not a great achievement to show that myth and pantheism are "false"; I considered much more important the observation, which an orthodox Jew first made to me, that there is nevertheless something of substance in them. I sensed such a higher level in the Kabbalah, regardless of how distorted it might have been in philosophical discussion. It seemed to me that here, beyond the perceptions of my generation, existed a realm of associations which had to touch our own most human experiences.

To be sure, the key to the understanding of these things seemed to have been lost, if one is to judge according to the obtuse standard of Enlightenment which Jewish scholars had to offer. And, yet, here in the first books of the Kabbalists, which I read with ardent ignorance, I found, to my surprise, a way of thinking which clearly had not yet found a home. Molitor's deep insight, regardless of how slanted may have been the perspective of Franz von Baader from which it derived, could not have been deceptive. And perhaps it wasn't so much the key that was missing, but courage: courage to venture out into an abyss, which one day could end up in us ourselves, courage also to penetrate through the symbolic plain and through the wall of history.

For the mountain, the corpus of facts, needs no key at all; only

the misty wall of history, which hangs around it, must be penetrated. To penetrate it was the task I set for myself. Will I get
stuck in the mist, will I, so to say, suffer a "professorial death"?
But the necessity of historical criticism and critical history cannot be replaced by anything else, even where it demands sacri-
fices.

Certainly, history may seem to be fundamentally an illusion,
but an illusion without which in temporal reality no insight into
the essence of things is possible. For today's man, that mystical
totality of "truth" (*des Systems*), whose existence disappears
particularly when it is projected into historical time, can only become visible in the purest way in the legitimate discipline of
commentary and in the singular mirror of philological criticism.
Today, as at the very beginning, my work lives in this paradox,
in the hope of a true communication from the mountain, of that
most invisible, smallest fluctuation of history which causes truth
to break forth from the illusions of "development."

The full meaning of this seminal and fascinating text will emerge
gradually throughout the remainder of this book. Here, in a nutshell, are the motives behind Scholem's belief in the necessity of
philological criticism as the only path to historical and metaphysical truth. From his reading of Franz Josef Molitor, whose book is
more a metaphysical than an historical study of the Kabbalah,
Scholem was inspired to see in the Kabbalah the key to the "secret
life of Judaism." He found in the mystical theses that "walked the
fine line between religion and nihilism" a possible model for his
own precarious balancing act between tradition and secularism.
Where rational Jewish philosophy, culminating in Hermann Cohen, had tried to suppress the most relevant, potentially heretical,
message of the tradition, the Kabbalah had succeeded in raising
myth and pantheism to "a higher level" and thus in rescuing something of value from them. The Kabbalah was perhaps the answer to
philosophical and metaphysical questions that philosophy had
failed to answer or deliberately avoided. Yet Scholem was not prepared to surrender himself to the mystical abyss, as had the neo-
romantics of the youth movement. The only legitimate path back
to the mystical reality of the Kabbalah lay through "the misty wall
of history," which could only be penetrated with the tools of philological criticism. Here, then, is Scholem's belief that the essence of
an historical phenomenon can never be recaptured directly, but
only through the indirect means of commentary. The historian and
not the philosopher possesses the key to metaphysical truth.

What was the "secret life of Judaism" to which Scholem felt himself attracted? He hints that it must lie in phenomena nominally considered peripheral or even heretical by the normative tradition. In a recent interview, he reconstructs the metaphysical goal that guided him in his decision to study the Kabbalah:

> I was interested in the question: does Halakhic Judaism have enough potency to survive? Is *Halakhah* really possible without a mystical foundation? Does it have enough vitality of its own to survive for two thousand years without degenerating? I appreciated *Halakhah* without identifying with its imperatives . . . This question was tied up with my dreams about the Kabbalah, through the notion that it might be the Kabbalah that explains the survival of the consolidated force of the Halakhic Judaism.[99]

Scholem's decision to study the Kabbalah was not based solely on the fact that it had been "ignored" by the nineteenth century; it might be the very key to understanding the survival of Judaism. As a nonorthodox Jew, yet deeply committed to the sources of Jewish tradition, he saw in the Kabbalah an alternative to halakhic orthodoxy, an alternative he might follow by becoming not a Kabbalist but an historian.

In 1923, Scholem emigrated to Palestine, but without the intention of continuing his work on the Kabbalah as a profession. He fully expected to earn his living as a highschool mathematics teacher. When he arrived in Palestine, the Hebrew University was still a dream and there were no avenues to an academic career. But the library of the nascent university was already in existence and by a fortunate coincidence and some financial juggling by Samuel Hugo Bergmann, the chief librarian, Scholem obtained a position as Judaica librarian.[100] After the university opened in 1925, he became lecturer and later professor of Jewish mysticism, a position he virtually created for himself as a result of this happy, if unexpected, turn of events.

Scholem's rejection of the political and cultural ambience of German Jewry in the World War I period led him simultaneously to radical Zionism and the historical study of the Kabbalah. Though these decisions were made on different planes of thought and involved different sorts of commitments and actions, they emerged together from the same matrix of events. Scholem's path from Berlin to Jerusalem, both literal and metaphorical, was a lonely one, for he had to revolt against both his parents' generation and his own. Franz Rosenzweig's characterization of Scholem in a letter to Rudolf Hallo in 1921 captures the individualistic nature of Scholem's return to Zion and to Judaism: "[Scholem] is *actually* without dogmas (*dogmenlos*). One cannot catechize him at all. I have never seen anything like it among Western Jews. He is perhaps the only one there is who has actually returned home (*Heimgekehrte*). But he has returned home alone."[101]

4. Theology, Language, and History

Scholem's rejection of Buber's mystical approach to Jewish sources came out of the political experience of the war period. However, the political and cultural dimensions of the Buber-Scholem controversy are rooted in profound philosophical and theological differences about the nature of revelation and tradition in Judaism. Although Scholem is, of course, primarily an historian and not a theologian, I believe that his rejection of Buber's metaphysics and espousal of "objective historiography" are based on significant theological assumptions of his own. Scholem's theological justification of historiography must be considered an important contribution to modern Jewish theology, especially as an attempt by an historian to wed secular historiography to a religious tradition.

Partly in response to developments in liberal Christian theology, Jewish theologians by the end of the nineteenth century were attempting to define an "essence of Judaism" (*Wesen des Judentums*).[1] This movement, perhaps represented best by Leo Baeck's book of that name, was no more than the culmination of similar efforts we have already traced in earlier Jewish historiography. Like its Christian counterpart, the "essence of Judaism" was generally defined as rational or "prophetic" ethics to demonstrate the identity between Judaism and modern culture. But also like its Christian counterpart, rational Jewish theology quickly encountered a crisis.[2] As theologians came to question modern cultural assumptions, they redefined Judaism as fundamentally *alien* to modern culture. Buber's argument that Judaism is an oriental religion was part of this general rejection of occidental culture.

The crisis of Jewish theology is most clearly illustrated in the work of Hermann Cohen (1842-1918), who articulated in his early

writings the most extreme version of rational religion. Cohen reduced religion to rational ethics and argued that God is no more
than a methodological principle. In his later writings and particularly in his posthumous *Religion der Vernunft aus den Quellen des
Judentums,* Cohen altered his position. Without abandoning his
abstract methodological God, he argued now that religion cannot
be reduced to universal ethics since religion deals with man as an
individual. Man requires something beyond ethics in order to deal
with his existential situation. Cohen's late position became the basis
for modern Jewish existentialism as developed by Franz Rosenzweig and Martin Buber, and, indeed, Buber took his I and Thou
terminology from Cohen himself.[3]

The Jewish existentialists contested the reduction of Judaism to a
principle of reason. Buber as a religious anarchist rejected the notion of an authoritative revelation and historical tradition.[4] Out of
hostility toward both orthodox halakhic Judaism and rational Jewish philosophy, Buber rejected the burden of tradition and created
his counter-history by a subjective, mythopoeic "act of decision."
Scholem also labels himself a religious anarchist, but we shall see
that he means something quite different from Buber. In fact, Scholem's theology must be considered a consistent attack on and alternative to existentialism. Like Buber, Scholem revolted against the
philosophical attempt to define an essence of Judaism and argued
that Judaism actually consists of an anarchistic plurality of sources.
However, where Buber's rejection of rationalism led him to ahistorical irrationalism, Scholem's led to historiography.

Buber and Scholem each offer answers to the crisis of rational
Jewish theology. I believe that the fundamental difference in their
responses lies in their disagreement about the ability of the historical tradition to communicate with the secular Jew. Since the possibility of communication with a religious tradition depends ultimately on one's view of the nature and efficacy of language to
transmit divine revelation, my discussion of the theological dimension of the Buber-Scholem controversy will focus to a great extent
on language. Though neither Buber nor Scholem ever engaged in
technical language philosophy, both developed views on language
which were crucial to their theologies. We shall see that Scholem's
position is particularly close to that of Walter Benjamin and may
well have been derived in part from Benjamin's early metaphysical
speculations on language.

The problem of language is particularly acute in the evaluation
of mystical experiences, since the mystic must express his experience of the infinite in finite language. Moreover, most mystics feel

an extraordinary desire to communicate their experience, even as they acknowledge the impossibility of doing so. How is the historian of religion to evaluate these linguistic expressions? There are two discernible solutions. The first is to argue that language has an inferior status to revelation and is unable to communicate more than a pale shadow of the original experience. In the face of revelation, man is quite literally dumbstruck and only later tries to translate divine silence into inadequate human speech. The essence of the mystical experience is silence; there is no relationship between it and the language used to describe it. This would be Buber's position.

The second position, which both Scholem and Benjamin adopted, argues that language itself is of divine origin and that the experience of revelation is linguistic. Since language is equivocally both divine and human, a basis exists for using language to communicate an experience of the divine. The profound implication of the language question is whether divine revelation must remain a silent, individual experience or whether it can become a public, communicable tradition, for a reliable tradition demands belief in the language in which it is conveyed.

Buber's Ahistorical Mysticism

Buber's Erlebnismystik was one of the alternatives offered to rational Jewish theology in the early twentieth century. Although his postwar dialogic doctrine of I and Thou is much better known, I shall focus on Buber's earlier thought since it had the greatest impact on Scholem.

Buber combined his metaphysical speculations with investigations in the history of religions. In the years before the war, he was interested in collecting mystical experiences of all sorts. His ecumenical anthologies of mysticism, particularly his Ekstatische Konfessionen (1909), contributed to the growing interest in irrational traditions. Like the philosopher of religion Rudolf Otto, whose classical work Das Heilige appeared in 1917, Buber wanted to establish a certain suprarational experience common to all forms of mysticism and indeed to all genuine religions.[5] We have seen that he defined this experience as Erlebnis or mystical union with the Absolute. With the later Hermann Cohen, Buber wanted to establish the irreducibility of religious experience to any other concept: the experience of the noumenal world was ontologically and epistemologically different from any other experience.

In the introduction to his Ekstatische Konfessionen, Buber develops his theory of language in the context of his general metaphysics. Following Hume, he argues that the world we perceive with our senses is no more than a fragmented bundle of perceptions: "I give the bundle a name and call it World, but the name is not that unity that is intuitively experienced (*erlebt wird*) . . . Language is perceptual knowledge (*Erkenntnis*), but the experience of ecstasis is not [this sort of] knowledge."[6] According to this view of language, which Buber seems to have taken from Fritz Mauthner,[7] language evolves out of the "naming" of perceptions. There is actually no distinction between perception and language: they are cognitively identical. Language therefore never signifies anything more than the perceptual datum with which it is connected. Whatever I call "world" refers only to my sense perceptions and does not capture the essence of the world.

According to Buber, perceptual experience (*Erfahrung*) is not the only kind of experience available to man. Intuitive-ecstatic experience (*Erlebnis*) yields not a fragmentary "picture" of the world but a lived unity. While Erfahrung can be conceptualized in words and, indeed, is essentially linguistic, Erlebnis is beyond all words and perceptions: "Unity of the I . . . now it is no longer a bundle [of perceptions]; it is a fire."[8] The true ecstatic experience, Buber argues quoting Meister Eckhardt, is silent: "The one that I mean there is wordless."[9] Because the Erlebnis is utterly silent, the mystic is also completely lonely: "He has no longer any community with him, no collectivity. Language, however, is the function of community." Without an effective language to communicate his experience, the mystic is left totally alone, although Buber postulates a theoretical community of all those who had had a genuine Erlebnis. Yet this abstract community does not require any communication between its members. It is also not clear whether the community of mystics could have any historical continuity or whether it must remain only a theoretical construct.

Despite the inherent silence of the mystical experience, the mystic is forced to articulate his experience. Buber calls this the "will to speak the unspeakable" (*Sagenwollen des Unsagbaren*).[10] The mystic tries to save something of "the timeless in time" from the memory of his experience. This memory becomes the origin of myth, which for Buber was a symbolic representation (*Sinnbild*) of the original experience. Although Buber maintains that the myth which arises out of mystical experience is more than mere psychological fantasy, he is vague about its ability to communicate the essence of the experience. Symbols, Buber suggests, might actually block Erlebnis: "Under the leadership of the priest . . . the symbol became a substitute [in Judaism] for a living communion with God."[11]

The application of these ideas to Jewish mysticism can be found in Buber's *Tales of Rabbi Nachman*, a work that served to establish the Jews' mystical "credentials." Buber claims that the Jew's orientation toward action rather than sense perception conditions him for Erlebnis. The Jewish "soul" is especially attuned to nonauditory, intuitive experience:

There is in the soul of the Jews a kernel, a certainty, a substance [which is] to be sure not sensory, objective, but rather active [and] subjective. This is pathos . . . Pathos is often enough degraded into rhetoric . . . but again and again, pathos liberates itself and becomes purer than before . . . When communicating itself, because it can do nothing else, it feels nonetheless the unreliability of all communication, the ineffability of all intuitive experience.[12]

The Jews have a healthy skepticism about language, characteristic of mystics. Buber particularly admires Rabbi Nachman's reluctance to write down his teachings. With Nachman, the Kabbalah became what it had never truly been before: an *oral* tradition that "could create its power not out of books, but out of actual life with men and in them."[13]

Following the *Formgeschichte* school of biblical criticism at the turn of the century, Buber valued oral traditions over written texts. If all communication was suspect, the written word was a particular offender. In his work on the stories of the Baal Shem Tov, the founder of Hasidism, Buber argues that the authenticity of the tales was suggested by their oral prehistory, a contention that Scholem, who was far more suspicious of oral traditions, criticized strongly.[14] Hence Buber considered Nachman's teachings particularly trustworthy because he failed to write them down.

According to Buber, Nachman had a theory of two types of speech: "He avoided the word which only gives a hasty and unreliable sense-impression (*Sinneseindruck*) . . . but the word which arises out of the foundation of the soul like an organic form, a rich and profound experience (*Erlebens*) was a great thing for him . . . The word formed late. With him the teaching is first of all an experience (*Erlebnis*) and only then becomes thought which is [the] word."[15] This somewhat mystifying passage seems to mean that most language is connected to the sensual world, although Erlebnis produces another type of language which is still considerably removed from the experience itself. This second type of "elevated" language may correspond to the mythical language alluded to in the *Ekstatische Konfessionen*.

Does this elevated speech communicate essential truth? According to Buber, Nachman believed his teachings to "have no clothes." The tales themselves became the clothes of his mystical experiences: their purpose was to awaken disciples and "plant the truths of life in [their] hearts."[16] By not writing down his teachings, and instead clothing them in oral tales, Nachman sought to lead his disciples themselves to write down the tales: "out of them and not out of the soul of the Master the word is born."[17] In other words, the mystic's own report of his experience has no relevant content of its own. His purpose is to excite an emotional response in an audience not privy to the experience itself. Writing becomes the task of the disciple and the written tale carries no essential relationship with the original experience: the disciple gets his mystical illumination secondhand. Buber saw his own task as similar to that of Nachman's disciples, although even one step farther removed from the original Erlebnis. By "retelling rather than translating" the articulated experience of the mystics, he claimed not to communicate the content of their personal encounters with the Absolute, but merely to try to strike a sympathetic chord in his reader, perhaps helping him to have his own Erlebnis. If the reader has such an experience, he can never know if it is ontologically similar to that of the original mystic, since the language in which the original experience is conveyed has only pedagogic value.

Buber's mystical skepticism about language shifted only slightly after the war with his new dialogic philosophy. In one of his essays in the 1930s on translating the Bible, he notes:

The Word of the Bible is nowhere a mere "expression" for an intellectual or spiritual concern, whether of an "ethical" or of a "religious" kind, nor for a factual content, historical or legendary, but it is a transmitted *Word*, a Word which was once spoken form . . . The coining of this Word is itself its very essence, its original nature . . . its rhythm is the necessary form in which it revealed and entrusted itself to the memory of the people.[18]

Buber's new attention to words and communication still rested on a somewhat skeptical view of language. The *word* of God has no factual content, nor does it convey any: its essence lies in its poetical rhythm and its sound patterns rather than in its communicative substance. The translation of the Bible, which Buber meant to be read aloud, was to have a lyrical impact on the listener.[19]

Buber's *I and Thou* (1923) also reveals that his later position on language had not changed markedly from his Erlebnismystik. The true dialogue of an I with a Thou is beyond language: "Only silence toward the Thou, the silence of all tongues, the taciturn waiting in the unformed, undifferentiated, prelinguistic word leaves the Thou free and stands together with it in reserve where the spirit does not manifest itself but is. All response binds the Thou into the It-world."[20] The "basic word" (*Grundwort*) spoken between "spiritual essences" (*geistigen Wesenheiten*) is the highest form of dialogue, but it takes place beyond everyday language: "We hear no Thou but feel addressed . . . with our being we speak the basic word, unable to say it with our mouths."[21] This form of communication is not human language, but occurs in some silent ethereal space: "Man receives, and what he receives is not a 'content' but a presence, a presence as strength."[22] The silent experience of the presence of the Thou seems ontologically very similar to Buber's earlier Erlebnis, although the object of the experience is no longer the Absolute by a concrete Other.

Buber's linguistic skepticism resulted in his disparaging of history and tradition. If language is incapable of communicating the essence of a revelatory experience, then how can a tradition based on revelation have any authority? Tradition is merely conventional and artificial: it is part of the linguistic realm of Erfahrung, since it cannot effectively communicate Erlebnis. Tradition might have the quality of pedagogic inspiration Buber ascribed to Rabbi Nachman's tales, but it cannot transmit divine truth. On the contrary, Buber held that tradition actually stands in the way of revelation. As he wrote to Rosenzweig in their important exchange of letters in the 1920s on revelation as a source of law: "It is only through man in his self-contradiction that revelation becomes legislation . . . I cannot admit the law transformed by man into the realm of my will if I am to hold myself ready as well for the unmediated word [of God directed to a specific] hour."[23] As we have seen, the "unmediated word of God" was, for Buber, something essentially different from ordinary language. Divine revelation has no authoritative content: it cannot create a continuing tradition. Buber's religious anarchism was a result of this bifurcation of revelation and normative tradition. Since tradition is "merely" a human creation, it has no authority over a man transfigured by the liberating experience of revelation.

Revelation for Buber was an event outside of history. He terms it a "primordial phenomenon in the present" (*gegenwärtiges Urphänomen*).[24] Revelation shatters the continuum of the everyday world of history; it has no existence outside of the "here and now" (*Jetzt und Hier*). In a passage reminiscent of Nietzsche's "eternal return of the same," Buber says of the relation of revelation to history: "Revelations . . . are, according to their nature, nothing other than the eternal, ever-present revelation, the revelation of the here and now. Never and nowhere has something happened which did not also happen in the here and now. But there is also a history; there is nevertheless a qualitative difference [between] historical moments."[25] History and time are human creations. From God's perspective, revelation is always in the here and now but, from a human perspective, it occurs in time. Buber implies that he who is truly open to revelation transcends man-made history and appropriates the divine perspective of the here and now. From his new vantagepoint, history and tradition lose their compelling force.

We have seen that Buber did not consider mystical experiences capable of generating a meaningful history of tradition. Hence his counter-history was not really a history at all, but merely a subjective reconstruction, or "retelling," of mystical experiences from the past designed to edify or inspire his readers. The "true" Judaism did not actually have a history since Buber's own theology undermined the very possibility of history. Like Graetz, Buber did not ultimately believe that Jewish mysticism had a history, but as opposed to Graetz and the rational historicists, he turned this conclusion into a virtue: lack of a history is the mark of those higher experiences that cannot be communicated.

SCHOLEM'S EARLY WRITINGS ON LANGUAGE AND THEOLOGY

In his early attack on Buber's Erlebnismystik, Scholem had sought to affirm the validity of history and tradition for the secular Jew. In order to do so, he adopted a much more positive attitude toward language as the vehicle for transmission of the tradition. Against Buber's "mysticism of silence," Scholem developed a theology in which revelation and tradition were linguistic experiences: he grounded the authenticity of tradition in the efficacy of language. Since Scholem is not a mystic, it would be a grave error to claim without careful consideration that his position resembles the one he attributes to the Kabbalah. However, from a number of articles, both early and late, we can discern that there is a remarkable similarity between his conceptions and the Kabbalah's.

Philosophy of language was one of Scholem's earliest academic interests. As a student of mathematics, he wrote a seminar paper under Bruno Bauch defending mathematical logic as a legitimate approach to language. In 1916 he read Wilhelm von Humboldt's *Sprachphilosophische Schriften* and Fritz Mauthner's *Beiträge zur einer Kritik der Sprache.*[26] After transferring his academic focus from mathematics to the Kabbalah, he initially considered writing a dissertation on the linguistic theory of the Kabbalah, a project he only completed fifty years later.[27] The evidence is compelling that Scholem's intellectual origins cannot be understood without reference to his interest in philosophy of language.

From 1917 to 1923, Scholem undertook many translations from Hebrew to German and from Yiddish to German. His interest in translation and language in general was in part a result of his fervent attachment to Hebrew, which sparked the bitter debate with the Blau-Weiss. In a letter to Scholem in 1917, upon receiving his translation of the Song of Songs into German, Benjamin wrote:

> Your love for the Hebrew language can only express itself in the German as respect before the essence of language and the word . . . In other words, your work remains apologetic because it expresses the love and honor of an object which is not in its own sphere. Now, it is not fundamentally impossible that two languages could go together in one sphere: to the contrary, this constitutes all great translation . . . However, for you, the German language will never be quite as close as the Hebrew and for that reason, you are not the "summoned" translator of the Song of Songs.[28]

This passage is an early reflection of Benjamin's theory of translation, developed later in his "The Task of the Translator," that the translator must consider all languages equally reflective of pure language. While it is possible that Benjamin's criticism of Scholem was accurate when Scholem was young, in later life Scholem came to regard German with virtually the same reverence.

Under the influence of Hölderlin's translation of Pindar,[29] Scholem developed the view, similar to Benjamin's, that translation should not make reading easier for the reader, since the great works of literature and their translations are not written "with the reader in mind."[30] In a review of three translations from Yiddish to German by Alexander Eliasberg,[31] Scholem argues that Yiddish is a difficult language to translate because its religious stratum is preserved in Hebrew. Translation of religious terms into German destroys the linguistic levels that make Yiddish a unique synthesis of a number of languages. Under the spell of the "cult of the Ostjuden," Scholem refers to Yiddish as a "warm" language (since it combines Hebrew and German) as opposed to German, which is "cold." Eliasberg responded that Scholem seemed to want not translation but transliteration of the Yiddish text into Latin characters.[32] As Ernst Simon has noted, in his own translations of mystical texts Scholem often preserves certain key terms in the original language of the text to reflect their technical meaning, although they might be equally foreign to the original.[33]

Scholem was also critical of the first samples of the Buber-Rosenzweig Bible translation, which appeared in the 1920s.[34] He set forth his critique in a number of letters to Buber starting in 1926, when Buber sent him the Genesis translation.[35] Buber himself called Scholem's comments "the most serious I have encountered, actually the only serious critique."[36] Scholem contended that Buber had adopted an elevated style (*Tonhöhe*) or, more precisely, a *niggun* (melody) for the prose passages in Genesis. Buber had imposed the flowery *Jugendstil* he still favored on texts whose original character was much more prosaic. In later years, after his position on language had changed somewhat, Buber toned down the high poetic style of the translations from the 1920s. Scholem praised the final version when it finally appeared in 1961, noting the "distinct urbanity of your new version" as against the "element of fanaticism" in the first.[37]

Buber's problem in the early translations, Scholem implied, was that he considered revelation an ecstatic experience that deserved the poetic language of "pathos." Buber believed that the inability of the mystic to convey his experience forces him to imprecise, poetic expression. Scholem first attacked this idea in 1922 in his critique of Meier Wiener's *Lyrik der Kabbala*, which was inspired by Buber's Erlebnismystik. Scholem rejected Wiener's assertion that "religion is too imprecise (*ungenau*) for [us] to grasp its whole being":

> This is actually a most successful and outstanding formulation of a groundless concept of religion which can only be established or confirmed by grasping the central fact of religion, revelation, as an amorphous, ecstatic experience (*Erlebnis*) which only (makes sense), if at all, on the plane of inwardness, while its external emanations remain entirely fuzzy. [Revelation should rather be understood] as an auditory phenomenon, which always appeared to both the philosophers of religion and theoreticians of language, as well as to the mystics [including] the Kabbalists, as exactly definable (*exakt bestimmbar*).[38]

Wiener had mistranslated mystical texts because he had assumed that mystics express their experiences in fuzzy poetic language. Mystical sources often appear unclear not because the mystic was confused but because the modern reader cannot decipher the text. For someone who does not know Latin, even Caesar's *Gallic Wars* might appear to be "mystical."[39]

In his earliest writings on religion, Scholem already began to develop a different position on the nature of mysticism and revelation. Revelation is not a silent Erlebnis, but an auditory experience that can be expressed in language.[40] Translation of Kabbalistic texts is possible because the Kabbalists themselves considered their language a precise, technical vocabulary and not arbitrary and emotive poetry. These texts are not well served by poetic translations; they cry out for scientific philology. The very self-conception of the medieval Kabbalists defines the kind of scholarship required to decipher their texts. Since the Kabbalists viewed language positively, Scholem believed with the Wissenschaft des Judentums that the philologian, whose working assumption is the continuity of a linguistic tradition, is the proper interpreter of Kabbalistic texts.

While in these early reviews (1920-1922) Scholem seems to include all religions in his argument, he is far more cautious in later formulations to refer only to Judaism and to distinguish carefully between the Kabbalah and other mystical traditions. Where Buber and other historians of religion in the early twentieth century tried to establish the common basis of all religious experience,[41] Scholem argues that, historically, each type of mysticism had its own unique tradition: "Only in our days has the belief gained ground that there is such a thing as an abstract mystical religion."[42] Without denying the similarities between mystical traditions, Scholem focuses obstinately on Jewish mysticism as a self-contained historical tradition.

THE KABBALAH'S LINGUISTIC MYSTICISM

In the introduction to Major Trends in Jewish Mysticism, in which he seeks to establish the unique characteristics of Jewish mysticism, Scholem focuses on the question of language and, in a footnote, suggests that this was his major area of disagreement with Buber:

[The mystics] continuously and bitterly complain of the utter inadequacy of words to express their true feelings, but, for all that, they glory in them; they indulge in rhetoric and never weary of trying to express the inexpressible in words. All writers on mysticism have laid stress on this point. Jewish mysticism is no exception, yet it is distinguished by two unusual characteristics, which may in some way be interrelated . . . First of all, the striking restraint observed by the Kabbalists in referring to the supreme experience; and secondly, their metaphysically positive attitude towards language as God's own instrument.[43]

The Kabbalists were less interested in describing their own experiences than in mystical commentary on earlier texts. The biographical literature, Scholem claims, is far inferior in Jewish mysticism to the theoretical. Hence, Jewish mysticism differs from many other traditions in its lack of interest in personal experience and its emphasis on a tradition of scholarly commentary. Scholem's own studies of the Kabbalah focus on "theoretical" Kabbalah and his occasional treatment of practical "experiential" Kabbalah, such as the prophetic Kabbalism of Abraham Abulafia,[44] is designed to prove the rule by reference to the exception.

Scholem believes that the defining characteristic of Jewish mysticism as commentary on a secret tradition has its origins in a unique and explicitly positive attitude toward language. Commentary is not only the proper mode of Jewish mysticism, but is actually required because of the divine origin of traditional texts. An essential connection exists between commentator and text because of the divine character of language: "Language in its purest form, that is, Hebrew . . . reflects the fundamental spiritual nature of the world . . . Speech reaches God because it comes from God . . . All that lives is an expression of God's language."[45]

In his article on "The Name of God and the Linguistic Theory of the Kabbalah,"[46] Scholem argues that linguistic mysticism developed in two stages. In the *Sefer Yitzirah*, which he dates to the second or third century, the twenty-two letters of the Hebrew alphabet and the ten cardinal numbers were the tools of creation: "the clear opinion of the author is that every created thing has a linguistic essence which consists in any conceivable combination of these fundamental letters . . . This conception of the essence of the Creation is closely linked with the linguistic conception of magic."[47] In the thirteenth century, however, linguistic magic became linguistic mysticism: the letters and numbers were not tools created by God for magical purposes, but emanations of God's own essence. God's name was conceived as equivalent to his essence and as the means by which he created the world. Creation was a linguistic process in which God's name became material.

For the thirteenth-century Kabbalists, creation and revelation were identical events: both were linguistic "autorepresentations" of God.[48] The Torah, read mystically, was nothing but a series of esoteric divine names. The hidden structure of the Torah was equivalent to the structure of the world, and the task of the Kabbalist was to decipher the common linguistic essence of creation and revelation: "The Torah, as the Kabbalists conceived it, is consequently not separate from the divine essence, not created in the strict sense of the word; rather, it is something that represents the secret life of God, which the Kabbalistic emanation theory was an attempt to describe."[49]

According to the Kabbalists, the divine language consists solely of divine names and has no grammar. Scholem notes that for the Kabbalists the essential name of God paradoxically "has no 'meaning' in the traditional understanding of the term . . . It has no concrete signification."[50] God is not meaningless, but, we might say, "meta-meaningful"; he is the source of all meaning. Words, on the other hand, do have meaning since their purpose is to communicate information. How, then, does the divine language, which has no concrete meaning, become the source of all meaning? Against Buber's "unmediated word of God," Scholem argues that the Kabbalists believed that revelation must be mediated since communication with God can only take place by indirect discourse.[51]

The dialectical translation of the divine revelation into human language is possible because of the equivocity of the divine name. The paradox of a human-divine language is inherent in the Hebrew phrase for the Tetragrammaton, *shem ha-meforash*. Scholem shows how the sixteenth-century Kabbalist Moses Cordovero offered two etymologies for this expression: it could either mean "explicit" (*l'faresh*—to make explicit) or "hidden-separate" (*l'hafrish*—to separate).[52] That the very Hebrew expression for the essential name of God contains these contradictory meanings suggests that language itself, which originates in the name of God, is equivocal. In the process of creation and revelation, God's hidden name becomes an explicit, communicable word. The divine name becomes dialectically the source of all meaning.

Scholem argues that the ability of language to be at once divine and human lies in its capacity to symbolize.[53] He argues that, for the Kabbalists, symbols are the means for describing God indirectly. Unlike allegory, the symbol is not imposed arbitrarily on a mystical event, but has the inherent power to evoke an intuitive understanding:

> If allegory can be defined as the representation of an expressible something by another expressible something, the mystical symbol is an expressible representation of something which lies beyond the sphere of expression and communication, something which comes from a sphere whose face is, as it were, turned inward and away from us . . . The symbol "signifies" nothing and communicates nothing, but makes something transparent which is beyond all expression.[54]

Symbols, like the divine name, have no concrete signification, but they become dialectically the expression of the inexpressible source of meaning.

For the Kabbalists, symbols are not arbitrary or subjective, but have an essential inner connection with what they symbolize. Symbols are therefore the residue of divine names in human language. The great faith the Kabbalists had in language was a result of their belief in symbols as the bridge between human and divine language. In the modern, technological world in which man's fantasies have been isolated to a private world of subjective symbolism, the disappearance of public symbols has become, according to Scholem, a "great crisis of language."[55] We might add that Buber's linguistic skepticism was a reflection of his own secularism since he could no longer believe in language as capable of symbolizing the ineffable.

THE KABBALAH'S PLURALISTIC CONCEPT OF TRADITION

The Kabbalistic notion of revelation, according to Scholem, is of an auditory experience in which the name of God is translated into human language and thereby becomes comprehensible. The divine name "is not a communication which provides comprehension . . . it becomes a comprehensible communication only when it is mediated."[56] Revelation is therefore a meaningless experience until it is mediated through human language, and this mediation is justified by the divine origin of the language:

> Here revelation, which has yet no specific meaning, is that in the word which gives an infinite wealth of meaning. Itself without meaning, it is the very essence of interpretability . . . We now face the problem of tradition as it presented itself to the Kabbalists. If the conception of revelation as absolute and meaning-giving but in itself meaningless is correct, then it must also be true that revelation will come to unfold its infinite meaning . . . only in its constant relationship to history, the arena in which tradition unfolds.[57]

Since there is "no immediate, undialectic application of the divine word," revelation only acquires concrete meaning in an historical tradition. Revelation is the source of all meaning and, indeed, of all life. In the words of the sixteenth-century Kabbalist Meier Ibn Gabbai, whom Scholem quotes extensively, revelation is not a one-time event, but a "fountain [which] is never interrupted . . . Were it to be interrupted, for even a moment, all creatures would sink back into their non-being."[58] Revelation is continually necessary to sustain the world, but without a tradition of commentary and interpretation to translate God's word into concrete reality, revelation would have no relation to the world and the "fountain" would cease.

How did the Kabbalists understand the interpretive tradition created by revelation? They clearly saw themselves as legitimate interpreters of revelation, even when their interpretations seemed to contradict the literal meaning of scripture. In fact, the Kabbalists justified the paradoxical character of their interpretations in theological categories. Ibn Gabbai, for instance, wrote that the "everflowing fountain" generates many "diverse ways of interpretation" but

> the differences and contradictions do not originate out of different realms but out of the one place in which no difference and no contradiction is possible. The implicit meaning of this secret is that it lets every scholar insist on his own opinion and cite proofs for it from the Torah; only in this manner . . . is the unity [of the various aspects of the stream of revelation] achieved. Therefore, it is incumbent on us to hear the different opinions.[59]

Every interpretation has divine sanction and, indeed, conflict of opinions is required to "unite the stream." Against a monolithic or dogmatic conception of Judaism, Ibn Gabbai called for an open marketplace of interpretations.

Scholem believes that the Kabbalistic doctrines of revelation and tradition are the very opposite of those of the nineteenth-century rationalists, "whose aim was an apologia based on the possible rationality of Judaism in a context which seemed to admit only unequivocal dogmatic formulations."[60] For the Kabbalists, since the source of revelation is a name unbound by any specific meaning, each word in the Torah can be interpreted *equivocally* in an infinite number of ways. The quintessence of revelation, says Scholem,

> is no longer the weight of the statements that attain communication in it, but the infinite number of interpretations to which it is open. The character of the absolute is recognizable by its infinite number of possible interpretations . . . Infinitely many lights burn in each word . . . Each word of the Torah has seventy— according to some, 600,000—faces or facets. Without giving up the fundamentalist thesis of the divine character of the scriptures, such mystical theses nevertheless achieve an astounding loosening of the concept of Revelation. Here the authority of Revelation also constitutes the basis of the freedom in its application and interpretation . . . Legitimacy was also accorded to progressive insight and speculation, which could combine a subjective element with what was objectively given . . . In principle, then, every one of the community of Israel has his own access to Revelation, which is open only to him and which he himself must discover.[61]

The right to interpret revelation in an infinite number of potentially
contradictory ways comes from revelation itself.[62] Not only was
the law revealed at Sinai, but so was the right, even obligation, to
interpret and reinterpret revelation.

Scholem argues that this potentially anarchistic theology is moderated and regulated by the concept of tradition.[63] The Kabbalists
believed that the tradition is authoritative because it is grounded in
revelation. The infinite meaning of revelation only unfolds gradually in an historical tradition, which, presumably, is open-ended
since there are an infinite number of possible interpretations. At
any given moment in history, the immediate reality of revelation
cannot be recaptured without recourse to the mediation of tradition. In other words, there is no pure experience of revelation but
only a tradition of interpretations of revelation to which one can
refer. To be sure, revelation guarantees the sanctity of any interpretation, but only to the one who submits himself to the whole
historical tradition of interpretation. Recognition of the authority
of tradition also grants the freedom to reinterpret it in new and radical ways: "That voice which calls forth incessantly from Sinai is
given its human articulation and translation in Tradition, which
passes on the inexhaustible word of Revelation at any time and
through every 'scholar' who subjects himself to its continuity."[64]

SCHOLEM'S ANARCHISTIC THEOLOGY

When Scholem speaks of "every scholar," does he also mean
himself? In the various articles referred to above on language and
theology, Scholem writes in the detached voice of an historian of
the Kabbalah, and it is often extremely difficult to discern whether
he identifies with the views of his sources. His tantalizing but reti-
cent hints that he himself might hold these positions have driven
some of his interpreters to despair.[65] Our examination of his earliest
writings suggests certain similarities between his own views on language and theology and those he later ascribed to the Kabbalah. In
addition, there exists a little-known article from 1932 where Scholem speaks in his own voice and does not conceal his theology behind the mask of the Kabbalah.

The article is a critique of Hans Joachim Schoeps's book, *Jüdischer Glaube in dieser Zeit*.[66] Schoeps, a well-known historian of
religion, is one of the more curious products of the German-Jewish
symbiosis.[67] A Prussian monarchist, he believed in the years before
the Nazis that German Jews, as opposed to the Ostjuden, could live
in harmony with a nationalistic German state. In the early 1930s he
was active politically in propagating his right-wing Völkisch ideas.

Needless to say, his political views, which were anathema to most German Jews, were enough to guarantee his theological reflections a hostile reception in the Jewish community, but he compounded his difficulties by a radical theological position permeated with Karl Barth's dialectical Protestantism.[68]

With many thoughtful Jews of his generation, Schoeps strongly criticized the liberal rationalist theology of the nineteenth century and searched for a radical religious solution to the problem of secularization. Schoeps rejected the oral law and whole Jewish legal tradition, and wanted to resurrect a biblical theology based on a doctrine of irrational revelation. Man believes in God not because revelation is in harmony with his reason, but precisely the opposite, because the content of revelation is paradoxical. Schoeps borrowed much of his existentialist terminology from Kierkegaard and Barth, but he also found a Jewish source for his ideas in the nineteenth-century iconoclastic theologian Salomon Ludwig Steinheim. In his *Offenbarung nach dem Lehrbegriff der Synagogue* (Revelation According to the Teaching of the Synagogue), Steinheim had argued that the belief in creation out of nothingness is the central dogma of Judaism and runs counter to the teachings of rational philosophy. Against the liberal rationalists of the nineteenth century, Steinheim saw Judaism as a religion of irrational revelation. Like Kierkegaard, with whom Schoeps compares him, Steinheim believed that revelation had no intelligible content and that Jewish tradition was merely conventional and artificial.[69]

Schoeps adopted Steinheim's idea of reconstructing the putative biblical faith in irrational revelation as a solution to the crisis of rational Jewish theology. Like Scholem, Buber, and others, he discovered a counter-tradition in Judaism, running from Judah Ha-Levi to Steinheim, which acclaimed the unique irrational message of Jewish revelation.[70] At the same time, he attacked the Zionists for trying to place Judaism on a secular basis. For Schoeps, Judaism was primarily a religious faith, and in studies of the historical interaction of Jews and Germans, he argued that, from a secular perspective, Jews were part of Germany.

As might be expected, Scholem violently objected to Schoeps's identification of Jewish secular fate with Germany. Although he himself had criticized the "Zionist secularization of Judaism," Scholem considered Jewish fate, both secular and religious, to be unique and distinct from Europe. He particularly criticized Schoeps's emphasis on German Jews, which he believed distorted the unique national character of Jewish history as a product of the totality of world Jewry. Schoeps's counter-history itself was a distortion since it relied on philosophical sources when it could have found a much more fruitful source in the Kabbalah. By constructing his irrationalist critique of nineteenth-century Jewish rationalism on a philosophical counter-tradition, Schoeps fell into the same trap as did the apologists: he construed a dogma of Judaism which excluded the totality of Jewish sources.

Scholem confesses his admiration for Steinheim's irrationalist nonconformism, but he rejects an irrational dogma as vehemently as he does a rational one. By attempting to return to a biblical theology of *creatio ex nihilo*, which Scholem argues is anachronistic for biblical theology in any case, Schoeps had attacked the Jewish concept of tradition. Scholem compares Schoeps's "neutralization of Jewish historical consciousness" to Karaism in the Jewish sphere and Barthian theology in the Protestant. If Schoeps wanted to overcome history with an ahistorical faith, why did he reject only the oral law? Was not biblical revelation equally absurd to a modern man concerned with "the contemporary understanding of existence" (*heutigen Daseinsverständnis*)?

Against Schoep's abrogation of tradition, Scholem suggests his own theological position in a few sentences that are formulated in terms virtually identical to those he ascribes to the Kabbalah:

> Revelation is, despite its uniqueness, still a *medium*. It is [the] absolute, meaning-bestowing, but itself meaningless that becomes explicable (*das Deutbare*) only through the continuing relation to time, to the Tradition. The word of God in its absolute symbolic fullness would be destructive if it were at the same time meaningful in an unmediated [undialectical] way. Nothing in historical time requires concretization more than the "absolute concreteness" of the word of revelation.[71]

There is no such thing as an unmediated concrete word of God. God's revelation is abstract and infinite, but because it linguistically "bestows meaning" (*Bedeutung-Gebendes*), it can be concretized by man. The interpretive tradition has its source in revelation, but it is necessary to render revelation comprehensible. Revelation and tradition are an indivisible unity. Schoeps had reduced Judaism to an ahistorical faith because he failed to understand the essential function of tradition and the impossiblity of "pure" faith. Without tradition, the "voice" (*Stimme*) of revelation necessarily loses its force:

> The voice which we perceive is the medium in which we live, and where it is not [the medium], it becomes hollow and takes

on a ghostly character in which the word of God no longer has [an] effect, but instead circumvents . . . The residue of the voice, as that which in Judaism is the tradition in its creative development, cannot be separated from it [the voice].

Against Schoeps's ahistorical, dogmatic theology of belief, Scholem calls for a return to historical consciousness. Not the suprahistorical Erlebnis of Martin Buber, but concrete historical experience (Erfahrung) must be the basis for revitalized Judaism. Scholem ends his polemic against Schoeps with a phrase from Kant: "I am not orthodox, but it is evident to me that without the restoration of such a 'fruitful *bathos* of experience' (*fruchtbaren bathos der Erfahrung*), which arises out of the reflection and transformation of human words in the medium of the divine, nothing of your project can be realized." The equivocity of divine-human language creates the historical tradition whose authority must be recognized even by Jews in a secular age.

In his reply to Scholem,[72] Schoeps argued that he and Scholem were perhaps representatives of two opposite tendencies in Jewish history, which he syncretistically labeled "critical-protestant" and "ontological-catholic." Could tradition have any meaning without belief in the immediate word of God? Scholem, although he professed belief in God, had only tradition, while he, Schoeps, sought to revitalize tradition by returning to original revelation. Schoeps wrote: "You will not find any answer here through science (*wissenschaftlich*), because to this question [the question of revitalized Judaism] only the answer through existence (*mit der Existenz*) can be convincing."[73] Schoeps thus incisively laid out the fundamental theological dispute between himself and Scholem: faith versus history.

Scholem's "Open Letter" to Schoeps must be read as an antiexistentialist manifesto and, although he specifically attacks Schoeps's dialectical theology, he must have had in mind the other "ahistorical" existential Jewish theologies of that time, notably those of Buber and Rosenzweig. Rosenzweig's view of language as he developed it in his *Star of Redemption* was actually much closer to Scholem's than to Buber's: "The manifestation (*Offenbarwerden*) that we are looking for here must be one that is essential revelation and nothing more. That is to say, however, it should be nothing else than . . . the self-negation of a purely silent essence through an audible word."[74] However, Rosenzweig considered the Jews a people outside history, whereas the essence of Scholem's position is that the Jews are subject to the laws of history.[75] Rosenzweig's opposition to the Zionist attempt to "return the Jews to history," which so enraged Scholem, must be seen as a consequence of his ahistorical view of Judaism. More important, Rosenzweig's "ahistoricity" led him to a different understanding of tradition. The revelation at Sinai, if not literally "law-giving," was at least a "command" (*Gebot*) for Rosenzweig.[76] The command of Sinai created a legal tradition that the secular Jew approaches as a given. One is free to accept of reject parts of the tradition according to one's personal progress on the "path" of the halakhah, but the nature of the tradition is both legal and fixed.[77]

Scholem's understanding of tradition is much broader than Rosenzweig's: "Tradition as a living force produces in its unfolding another problem. What had originally been believed to be consistent, unified and self-enclosed now becomes diversified, multifold and full of contradictions. It is precisely the wealth of contradictions, of differing views, which is encompassed and unqualifiedly affirmed by tradition."[78] Rosenzweig termed Scholem's position "nihilism,"[79] but I believe that he misunderstood the difference between nihilism and Scholem's religious anarchism. When Scholem calls himself a religious anarchist, he means that the historical tradition, which is the only source of knowledge we have of revelation, contains no one authoritative voice. All that can be learned from the study of history is the *struggle* for absolute values among conflicting voices of authority.[80]

Scholem is an anarchist because he believes "the binding character of the Revelation for a collective has disappeared. The word of God no longer serves as a source for the definition of possible contents of a religious tradition and thus of a possible theology."[81] Yet we have seen that he affirms belief in God as intrinsically "meaningless" but nevertheless "meaning-bestowing."[82] God stands as the unknowable origin of the tradition and as the guarantor of its legitimacy. But like Maimonides, Scholem does not believe that it is possible to make any meaningful positive statements about Him.[83] Left without direct access to revelation, he still has the literary sources of tradition about which statements can be made because their language is guaranteed by God. Scholem does not abrogate the authority of tradition, as would a secular nihilist, but asserts its pluralistic message.

Against both the Jewish existentialists and their rationalist predecessors, Scholem asserts that commentary and not theology is the correct discipline for understanding Jewish tradition:

Truth is given once and for all, and it is laid down with precision. Fundamentally, truth merely needs to be transmitted.

The originality of the exegete (*Schriftgelehrter*) has two aspects. In his spontaneity, he develops and explains that which was transmitted at Sinai, no matter whether it was always known or whether it was forgotten and had to be rediscovered. The effort of the seeker after truth consists not in having new ideas but rather in subordinating himself to the continuity of the tradition of the divine word and in laying open what he receives from it in the context of his own time. In other words: not system but commentary is the legitimate form through which truth is approached.[84]

Against the nineteenth-century search for a systematic definition of Judaism, Scholem asserts that the process of commentary is itself the vessel in which the truth of revelation is carried. The commentator is not "original" as a philosopher might be in deductively deriving a definition of Judaism from *a priori* principles. Rather, his originality consists in letting the sources speak through him; the legitimacy of his new interpretation is guaranteed by his subordination to the sources of the tradition.

The "audacious freedom of interpretation" which this theory of tradition suggests derives from Scholem's understanding of the dialectic between the written and oral law in Judaism. Interestingly enough, he quotes as his source none of the numerous Jewish analyses of this relationship, but the Christian Kabbalist, Molitor:

Every written formulation is only an abstracted general picture of a reality which totally lacks all concreteness and individual dimension of real life . . . The spoken word, as well as life and practice, must therefore be the constant companions and interpreters of the written word, which otherwise remains a dead and abstract concept in the mind . . . In modern times, where reflection threatens to swallow up all of life, where everything has been reduced to dead, abstract concepts, that old inherent reciprocal relationship between the written and spoken word, between theory and practice, has been totally displaced.[85]

Molitor suggests that the oral law reinvigorates the written by giving it a concrete interpretation: God's revelation can only become concrete through the mediation of revelation. The written word is here a metaphor for revelation, while the spoken word suggests the commentary on revelation. The tradition is only called oral metaphorically to suggest its freedom as against the ostensibly fixed and dogmatic character of the written text. Scholem recognizes that the actual notion of "writing" in Judaism, and particularly in the Kabbalah, is very different from this metaphorical usage: "For the Kabbalists, linguistic mysticism is at the same time a mysticism of writing. Every act of speaking . . . is at once an act of writing and every writing is potential speech."[86]

The notion of an oral tradition, even when actually written down, is Scholem's model for interpretive freedom. The oral tradition gains its efficacy precisely from its detached perspective on revelation: "The Torah is the medium in which knowledge is reflected; it darkens as it brings with it the essence of the tradition, radiating into the pure realm of the 'written,' that is to say, [of] unusable teaching. [The teaching] only becomes usable where it is 'oral,' in other words, where it is transmittable."[87] Because it is expressed in the language of men, the oral tradition can be transmitted, and it is usable because it can be interpreted and commented upon. But because it is already historically removed from revelation, tradition guarantees a certain freedom: it becomes the possession of men who interpret it according to their lights.

The importance Scholem attributes to historical perspective can be seen in his refusal in 1930 to translate Rosenzweig's *Stern der Erlösung* into Hebrew.[88] He found a magical, even demonic connection between the work and the spirit of the German language which made the *Stern* incomprehensible. The *Stern* would only become translatable in some future generation "that will no longer feel itself addressed in such an immediate fashion by the themes most pertinent to the present time . . . Only when the enchanting beauty of its language will have worn off . . . shall this testimony to God be able to assert itself in all its undisguised intent."[89] The language of an experience of God requires historical perspective in order to become part of a transmittable and translatable tradition.

The interpreter of tradition, living perhaps centuries after the original revelation, receives revelation through the mediation of tradition, a tradition to which he adds. Interpretation for Scholem is a creative activity that sustains the ever-growing tradition, but only the interpreter who takes upon himself the burden of tradition and does not try to leapfrog directly back to revelation is granted legitimacy.[90]

KABBALIST OR HISTORIAN?

There is a strong suggestion in the preceding argument that Scholem considers the work of the historian to be very similar to that of the Kabbalist. Both are engaged in detached commentary on a tradition. In his rejection of both the rationalist and the existentialist definitions of Judaism, does Scholem adopt the theology of the Kabbalah as a model for his own theological justification of historiography? Does he hold that the secular historian is the modern incarnation of the traditional commentator? Does historiography serve the same function as the oral tradition of the Kabbalah in reinvigorating a decaying written tradition?

The similarity between Scholem's own theological formulations and those he ascribes to the Kabbalah seems too striking to be coincidental. He clearly feels a strong affinity with his sources. The most remarkable evidence of this affinity is the first of his "Zehn Unhistorische Satze uber Kabbala" (Ten Unhistorical Aphorisms about the Kabbalah):

> The philology of a mystical discipline such as the Kabbalah has something ironic about it. It is concerned with a veil of mist (*Nebelschleier*) which, as the history of the mystical tradition, hangs around the body, the space of the matter itself. It is a mist, however, which [the tradition] generates out of itself.
>
> Does there remain for the philologian something visible of the law of the thing itself or does the essential disappear in the projection of the historical? The uncertainty in answering this question belongs to the nature of the philological enterprise itself and thus contains the expectation, from which this work lives, of something ironic which cannot be severed from it. But doesn't such an element of irony lie already even more in the subject of this Kabbalah itself and not only in its history?
>
> The Kabbalist claims that there is a tradition whose truth can be transmitted. An ironic claim since precisely that truth which is the issue here is anything but transmittable. It can be known, but not transmitted and precisely that which is transmittable in it, it no longer contains. Authentic tradition remains hidden; only the decayed (*verfallende*) tradition chances upon (*verfallt auf*) a subject and only in decay does its greatness become visible.[91]

Scholem uses explicitly Kabbalistic language in this extraordinary statement to describe his own enterprise as an historian of the Kabbalah.[92] He is concerned with an esoteric discipline that can only become the subject of historiography when it is no longer esoteric, when it has "decayed" into a public tradition. Hence the historian of the Kabbalah can never be sure if he is dealing with the thing itself or only with its historical shadow. Similarly, the Kabbalist claims to transmit the secret essence of revelation; yet the hidden character of that truth cannot be transmitted. When the Kabbalist describes the indescribable in human language, he too can never be sure of the truth of his words. This problematic relationship is reenacted in modern terms in the tension between Scholem as secular historian and his subject.

Still, the very fact of a distance between Scholem and his subject suggests that he cannot be considered a Kabbalist. The anarchistic theology that underlies his philosophy of history is not identical to the position of the Kabbalah. The Kabbalists were not full-fledged anarchists because they believed in the authority of normative Jewish law. However, the anarchism that lurked *in potentia* in their theology could become explicit in secular historiography, which is not yoked to this authority. Even if the modern historian believes that there is a God, his assumption is that the only meaningful statements he can make are about the pluralistic historical tradition. Scholem therefore sees the Kabbalists as his precursors and Kabbalistic theology as the precursor to his theological anarchism—but they are not the same. Modern historiography is a new development in the history of commentary in which the Kabbalah was an earlier stage. Unlike Buber, Scholem does not identify fully with his sources, but maintains his historical detachment, a detachment that, however, is characteristic of all commentators, secular or religious. In this way, Scholem is able to claim that secularism, as embodied in the modern historical method, is "part of the dialectic of the development *within* Judaism."[93]

Scholem's transformation of the traditional Jewish notion of commentary into historiography suggests that he views historical science, no matter how "secular" or radical, as the modern form of Judaism. In Scholem we have the fulfillment of the desire of the nineteenth-century Wissenschaft des Judentums to find a secular substitute for religion in historiography. Indeed, in his "Open Letter" to Schoeps, Scholem points out that his own position is much closer to Graetz's historicism than to twentieth-century theology. But as opposed to the Wissenschaft des Judentums, Scholem argues that an anarchistic plurality of interpretations, and not just rationalism, must characterize historical Judaism. It might well be argued that such anarchism of interpretations was already an implicit possibility in nineteenth-century historicism: witness, for instance, Nachman Krochmal's suggestively radical idea that each age has its own legitimate "mode of investigation," a phrase similar to Ranke's claim that "each age is equally close to God." If each period's way of interpreting revelation is legitimate, the historian must treat each with equal favor. Scholem may be seen as the dialectical fulfillment of the original impulse in the Wissenschaft des Judentums, since nineteenth-century Jewish historiography laid the basis for anarchistic historicism but belied its promise by generally succumbing to a rationalist, dogmatic theology. Scholem's anarchism provides Jewish historicism with a theological rationale it did not achieve in the nineteenth century.

BENJAMIN'S INFLUENCE

Scholem's position on language and theology is illuminated by the early writings of Walter Benjamin. Although it is hard to demonstrate the direction of influence in a close friendship, I believe that Benjamin developed his views on language before Scholem, who was five years his junior, and he may be considered one of Scholem's predominant sources. In November 1916, Benjamin promised to send to Scholem his essay "Über Sprache überhaupt und über die Sprache des Menschen," whose linguistic theory bears a remarkable resemblance to that which Scholem ascribes to the Kabbalah.[94] Whether or not Benjamin actually influenced Scholem on these matters, he explicated his point of view much more systematically than Scholem, and Scholem was well aware of Benjamin's formulations.[95]

Scholem regarded Benjamin as primarily a metaphysician of language engaged in "mystical linguistics."[96] He has emphasized this side of Benjamin's work against those who claim the later Benjamin as a genuine Marxist theoretician.[97] In despair over his friend's flirtation with Marxism, Scholem wrote to Benjamin in 1931: "You could be a figure of high importance in the history of critical thought, the legitimate continuer of the most fruitful and genuine traditions of Hamann and Humboldt."[98] Scholem felt that Benjamin's Marxism was only a superficial jargon which hid a much more profound religious sensibility. Like many other Germans in the 1920s, Scholem and Benjamin found certain strains in the Enlightenment and German romanticism which inspired their own thinking.[99] Scholem saw in Benjamin an intellectual heir to the philosophers of language, who, like Humboldt, had tried to discover the "inner spirit" of language common to mankind or, like Hamann, had struggled to define the mystical relationship between human and divine language.[100]

Benjamin's attitude toward language was irreconcilably opposed to Buber's; in fact, the first expression I have found of his position appeared in a letter he wrote to Buber attacking Buber's use of language.[101] Buber had invited Benjamin to contribute to his new journal, Der Jude. Like Scholem, Benjamin found repugnant the prowar tone of Der Jude, and particularly of Buber's editorial "Die Losung." In July 1916 he turned down Buber's invitation in a letter whose contents were known to Scholem.[102] Besides protesting that he had not yet developed his Jewish position sufficiently to write an article on a Jewish topic, Benjamin attacked the prowar position of *Der Jude* and particularly the connection between Buber's support for the war and his use of language. Benjamin's first statement on language was, then, a result of his opposition to the war, just as the war prompted Scholem to develop his own position against Buber.

Benjamin accused Buber of writing political propaganda; Buber had put language at the disposal of military action and language had therefore lost its independence. In war propaganda, Benjamin suggested, words have no autonomy of their own but become the obedient servants of action, the "preparation of the motives of action." Buber held that ultimate experiences are ineffable. Benjamin evidently understood Buber to be suggesting that the essence of action is also ineffable: language can, at best, prepare the motivations for action by exciting the emotions, but it has no essential relationship to action itself. Benjamin argued that, in Buber's writing, language had become "impoverished, weak acts."

Benjamin believed that language in itself is a form of powerful action: "I do not believe that the word stands somewhere farther away from the divine (*Göttlichen*) than does 'real' action." He argued against Buber that there is no sphere of experience which is ineffable: the true task of language is "the crystal-clear elimination of the unsayable (*Unsagbare*) in language. Only where this sphere of the wordless in its ineffable pure power is opened up, can the magic sparks spring between word and . . . act . . . Only the intensive directing of the words into the kernel of the innermost silence will achieve true action." Against Buber's mystical depreciation of language, Benjamin proposed a magical theory in which language itself becomes an action: to speak is to make.

Benjamin's new theory of language must also be understood as a pacifist critique of Buber's wartime Erlebnismystik. Satirically employing one of Buber's favorite mystical expressions, the "realization of the correct Absolute" (*Verwirklichung des richtigen Absoluten*), Benjamin implied that the glorification of action above words in prowar propaganda was the consequence of Erlebnismystik. For Benjamin, if language had been conceived as a form of legitimate action, it would have been turned against the war; in his Marxist period in the 1930s, he would see language as one of the only remaining weapons against fascism.

Benjamin's critique of Buber's philosophy of language was part of his general rejection of Lebensphilosophie. As Ernst Cassirer has noted, the "philosophers of life" held that life "seems to be given only in its pure immediacy . . . The original content of life cannot be apprehended in any form of representation, but only in pure intuition."[103] For Benjamin, it was precisely through language that the essence of life could be grasped. Benjamin also argued forcefully against the nominalist theory of language as "an arbitrary game." As he wrote to Hugo Hofmannsthal in a polemic against the language theory of the positivistic sciences, which could as well have been directed against Buber:

> The conviction which guides me in my literary attempts . . . [is] that each truth has its home, its ancestral palace in language, that this palace was built with the oldest *logoi* and that to a truth thus founded, the insights of the sciences will remain inferior for as long as they make do here and there in the area of language like nomads . . . in the conviction of the sign character of language which produces the irresponsible arbitrariness of their terminology.[104]

For Benjamin, language is the "essence of the world" and those who consider it an arbitrary collection of signs are "spiritually dumb."[105]

Against the sign theory of language, Benjamin developed a "Kabbalistic" conception of language as symbolic, which explains his affinity with the symbolic poets of the late nineteenth century such as Mallarmé.[106] Words have both communicative and symbolic functions. On the level of communication between people, words are impregnated with conventional meanings, but they can also symbolize an ineffable essence: "Language is in every case not only the communication of the communicable, but equally the symbol of the incommunicable."[107] Following an old distinction that he took from Goethe and that Scholem adopted, Benjamin understood symbols as the opposite of allegories.[108] Allegorization starts with a general concept and then searches for a specific but arbitrary physical representation of the general idea. The allegory therefore corresponds to the arbitrary sign of the sciences. The connection between the allegory and the concept allegorized is never immediately apparent and requires explication. Symbols, on the other hand, "establish a connection which is sensually perceived in its immediacy and requires no interpretation."[109] Since the belief in symbols had waned in the modern world, the task of philosophy, which Benjamin opposed to science, is to "re-establish the symbolic character of the word, in which the idea comes to self-understanding in its primacy."[110] Language is one of the primary cognitive tools with which man gives intelligible form to chaotic sense perceptions. Benjamin saw language as a creative instrument with which the noumenal world could be recaptured from behind the curtain of phenomenal perceptions and conventional meanings.[111]

Benjamin added a theological dimension to his idealistic philosophy of language. In his early essay, "Über Sprache überhaupt und über die Sprache des Menschens," he deals with the question of how divine language can become human. God's word is equivalent to existence, but God could not have created the world by calling it directly into existence with concrete words, since God's language, by definition, is undifferentiated and infinite. Divine language seems incommensurable with human language, and therefore an immediate linguistic relationship between God and the world, Buber's "unmediated word of God," is impossible. Creation and, in fact, all interaction between God and the world must be mediated by man. God is the "source" of language, but it is man who names objects and thereby "brings the world before God." By the process of naming, man concretizes divine language and makes it human. When man names, he repeats the primordial act of Adam and reestablishes the "magic spark" between language and objects which Benjamin referred to first in his letter to Buber. The magic spark is lost when language becomes a merely conventional instrument for human communication, but in every generation man has the capacity to recover the Edenic creativity in language.

The notion of a divine language of names which underlies conventional language is very close to the Kabbalah's theory as interpreted by Scholem of the divine name as meaningless but meaning-bestowing. For Benjamin, words are encumbered with conventional meanings, but names are "the analogue to the knowledge of the object in the object itself . . . The name is super-essential; it signifies the relation of the object to its essence."[112] Benjamin distinguished between a "pure language" consisting only of names and language burdened with conventional meanings, but he argued that no particular language can be pure since each language is bound up with its own conventions. Only the totality of all languages constitutes pure language.[113] Translation is therefore one of the best means to liberate men from the conventions of their own particular language: "The task of the translator is to release in his own language that pure language which is under the spell of another, to liberate the language imprisoned in a work in his re-creation of that work."[114]

Translation not only recaptures pure language, but also enriches the vocabulary of a particular language by drawing on the metaphors of another.[115] Like Humboldt,[116] Benjamin believed that language is not a given but an "activity" in which man is constantly creating new forms: language is always growing. Benjamin's divine *Ursprache*, or primordial pure language, could never be fully recovered since language never stands still. The mythical Adam named objects and created language *ex nihilo*, but we inherit our language from the past. As we try to recover the pure language beneath the layers of conventional accretions, we also add to the language by creating new words and reinterpreting old ones. The philosophical job of interpreting language in order to purify it is actually creative since it adds new layers to the pure language. The concept of an Ursprache was therefore only an abstract hypothesis for Benjamin since it could never be isolated without transforming it. Once man concretizes divine language, he irreversibly alters the unmediated relation between God and the world by mediating between them. Although all authentic translation and literary criticism try to recapture the magic spark between word and object which characterizes divine language, this goal remains a utopian absolute that can be approached but never reached.

For Benjamin, divine language, represented by biblical revelation,[117] was a guarantee that ordinary human language is not merely conventional and that it has its source in the noumenal world. The whole phenomenal world is like an esoteric text that demands interpretation. Our effort to understand the essence of this world is guaranteed by the hypothesis of a divine language of names which is equivalent to the "thing-in-itself." Without this theological belief in God as the source of language and in language as the mediating tool between the mind and essential reality, the work of interpretation is meaningless.

I have suggested that Benjamin saw interpretation, of which translation is a special case, as a creative process. The totality of all interpretations constitutes the ever-growing linguistic tradition. Like Scholem, Benjamin was deeply concerned with the category of tradition and with the possibility of recovering tradition in a secular world.[118] In a letter to Scholem in 1917,[119] he criticized Scholem's essay on Blau-Weiss education in which Scholem had argued for education by example. Benjamin urged him to consider tradition as the true basis for pedagogy. Teaching by example renders the student passive and makes the student dependent on the teacher. When student and teacher are both engaged in appropriation of the tradition by creative interpretation, a community of learning is created:

I am convinced that tradition is the medium in which the student is continually transformed into the teacher . . . Whoever has not learned cannot educate . . . Education (*Unterricht*) is the only point of free unification between the older with the younger generation, like waves which throw their foam into one another. Every error in education ultimately goes back to [the idea] that those who come after us are dependent upon us. They are only dependent on us insofar as they are dependent on God and on language in which we ourselves must submerge our will in some communality (*Gemeinsamkeit*) with our children.

A tradition rooted in language, which itself originates in God's language, is the common source for all generations. This tradition, like the world as a whole, does not lie beyond a passive observer to whom it is given through either education or sense perception. Rather, the tradition is appropriated by the student as he interprets it, and education consists of a community of interpreters from different generations.

In Scholem's own views on education, expressed many years later in a discussion with Israeli educators,[120] there is an echo of Benjamin's concept of an open dialogue with tradition. Education, Scholem insists, should not reflect one dogmatic viewpoint but should expose the student to the whole contradictory wealth of the tradition:

If I were called upon to teach, I would try to show that Jewish history has been a struggle over great ideas and the question is to what extent we should be influenced by the degree of success achieved in that struggle by values which were formulated and defined in the tradition . . . At the same time, I would consider with my pupils the failures in history, matters having to do with violence, cruelty and hypocrisy.

In his pedagogy, as in his historiography and theology, Scholem believes that, unless we regard the tradition as a pluralistic constellation of forces to which each generation contributes, Judaism will lose its vitality.

Benjamin and Scholem agree that the ability of language to symbolize the ineffable guarantees tradition as the medium which connects man to the divine source of creation and revelation. For both, tradition consists of creative commentary in an effort to reestablish the essential connection between man and the source of language. Their metaphysical affirmation of language and historical tradition departs radically from Buber's ahistorical mysticism and, I believe, constitutes an important response to the crisis of Jewish theology in the twentieth century.

SCHOLEM AND THE CRISIS OF JEWISH THEOLOGY

Gershon Weiler, in an article on "The Theology of Gershom Scholem,"[121] argues that Scholem does not define what he means when he says that he believes in God. In order to make meaningful statements of belief about God, Scholem should have addressed himself to the Maimonidean problem of the attributes of God, which he seemingly evades. Weiler claims that Scholem has fallen into the same logical difficulty as "the modern Protestant theologians, the existentialists and even Buber . . . They all speak as if there is some hidden [essence] which is revealed in experience alone but they continue to use the name 'God.' "[122] Weiler posits only two theological alternatives: either the logically meaningless "experiential" theology of Buber or Maimonidean rationalism.

I believe that Scholem, along with Walter Benjamin, has charted a third theological course. He does not accept Buber's conception of revelation as experience. On the other hand, although he accepts Maimonides' reluctance to assign any positive attributes to God, he is not interested in rational theology. With Benjamin, he sees God as the origin and guarantor of the process of interpretation he calls tradition. The tradition on which he, as a modern historian, comments is itself testimony to the original impetus of divine revelation; yet it does not permit any meaningful statements about revelation itself or its divine source. The only meaningful statements one can make are about the tradition, the province of the historian and commentator rather than of the theologian. Scholem's theology is therefore an antitheological argument for historiography, but historiography conceived as one more interpretive contribution to the ever-growing tradition.

Does Scholem deserve a place in the history of Jewish theology in the twentieth century? I suggested at the beginning of this chapter that the crisis of Jewish theology, embodied in the thought of Hermann Cohen, represented a watershed in theological speculations. The failure of rational theology is normally considered to have led to the existentialism of Rosenzweig and Buber. Scholem's explicit rejection of these two thinkers suggests that his own position may constitute an alternative response to the crisis of theology.

Cohen was the explicit starting point for Buber and Rosenzweig. In the last chapter we saw that the young Scholem was also well aware of Cohen and, although he criticized his contemporaries for not appreciating the Marburg philosopher, Cohen represented for him the dogmatic attempt to purge myth and pantheism from Jewish history. Scholem began his career in conscious opposition to Cohen's rationalism. But it is significant that just as Cohen's late thought pointed toward existentialism, it also hinted at the opposing direction that Scholem himself would pursue in his rejection of the existentialists: historical study of Judaism. Although it would be erroneous to claim that Scholem "borrowed" any of his ideas from Cohen, his position may be judged in retrospect as, dialectically, both a continuation and a refutation of Cohen's rational theology.

In his *Religion der Vernunft,* Cohen suggests two concepts of God. One is a personal God with whom the suffering individual can enter into dialogue, and the other is a restatement of his older concept of God as an abstract methodological principle. Although the new concept was to become a fruitful source for Buber and Rosenzweig, it is striking how closely the methodological God-concept resembles Scholem's theological position. In his chapters on "God's Uniqueness," "Creation," and "Revelation," Cohen argues that God's uniqueness is the exact opposite of the pluralistic world; yet it is not the negation of the world.[123] Instead, God is conceived as an "originative principle" (*Ursprungsprinzip*), meaning a principle that is the origin of other dialectically opposing principles.[124] Revelation is a similar process where "the eternal, which is removed from all sense experience, therefore from all historical experience, is the foundation and the warrant of the very spirit of national history."[125] God is the origin and guarantor of the permanence of the world and of the historical tradition. We immediately recognize that, despite the difference in terminology, Cohen's dialectical concept of God is very similar to Scholem's idea that God is meaningless but meaning-bestowing.

Like Scholem, Cohen considers the tradition a body of exegetical interpretations for which the model is the oral law: "The oral law is spontaneous, as the 'fruit of the lips,' whereas the written tradition is stamped on brazen tablets. [The oral law is also] not an immediately finished product, but an open one, one that always continues to be produced."[126] The tradition contains a variety of principles and interpretations, which Cohen readily admits often appear to contradict one another.[127] This notion of a pluralistic, open-ended tradition looks very much like Scholem's concept of tradition.

There is also a striking resemblance between Scholem and Cohen on the issue of the relationship of the modern interpreter to the tradition. In a rather compressed and enigmatic section of the introduction to the *Religion der Vernunft,* Cohen argues that the exegetical method of the traditional oral law is not "formal logical deduction."[128] In other words, the biblical exegete does not merely deduce his interpretation from the biblical text. Instead, he discovers his own thought in the text by a process of interaction between himself as a thinker and his source (*Quelle*):

First, thought is thought, whether it occurs in the Haggadah as a moral thought in the imaginative style of poetry, or in the Hala-

chah as a law for which, as for all other thoughts, one will subsequently find the sanction in the Bible . . . Otherwise, it would be
almost inconceivable that the memory of the talmudic scholar
could find in the great treasure of biblical words and its sentence
structure the analogy exactly appropriate to the case at hand . . .
Logic confers seriousness upon the imagination, because the
imagination is sustained and supported by the stern objectivity
of the problem.[129]

This exegetical philosophy, in which interpretive originality and
the objective message of the text are harmonized, is not only the
method of the Jewish tradition—it is Cohen's own method. He too
argues that the nature of Judaism can only be determined by a dynamic interaction between the modern philosopher and the historical sources.[130] In other words, for Cohen, the modern interpreter of
tradition operates with the same logic and principles of interpretation as can be found in the tradition itself. The philosopher of history therefore continues the work of interpretation and becomes
part of tradition. In a similar way, Scholem argues that the secular
historical method is already anticipated by the tradition itself. He
"discovers" a possible precursor of his own theology in the sources
he studies. Since his exegetical philosophy is not alien to the tradition, he, as a modern historian, continues the work of commentary.

Despite these remarkable similarities, there is a fundamental difference between Scholem and Cohen. Cohen claims that the apparent contradictions between interpretations within the tradition are
an illusion. All these interpretations are actually united by the concept of reason, and it is the task of the philosopher of Judaism to
discover this unifying reason in the sources.[131] Scholem rejects the
idea that a philosophical concept can impose unity on an intrinsically pluralistic tradition. The contradictions within the tradition
are not an illusion, but an essential consequence of the unfolding of
the infinite meanings of revelation. The only possible definition of
Judaism is the totality of the contradictory principles that make up
Jewish history. Since there is no *a priori* philosophical essence of Judaism, but only a plurality of historical sources, historiography
and not philosophy is the proper discipline for the modern Jew.
Where Cohen found his precursors in the philosophical tradition,
Scholem finds his in the pluralistic commentaries of the Kabbalah.

Although Cohen defined Judaism as solely a religion of reason,
his claim that the tradition is pluralistic prepared the ground for the
subversion of his own rationalism. By developing the notion of a

pluralistic tradition to its logical conclusion, Scholem has overturned Cohen's philosophical rationalism and addressed the crisis
of Jewish theology in an original way. Judaism can only be understood on the basis of the totality of Jewish sources, a totality that
can be grasped only by historical study of these sources themselves.
Scholem's historiography of Jewish mysticism, the core of his
oeuvre, is a contribution to just such an enterprise. It is in the history of Jewish mysticism that Scholem finds the seeds of modern
secularism and his own religious anarchism.

5.   *Mysticism*

S cholem's anarchistic theology is based on the assumption that Jewish history is pluralistic. There are several distinct traditions, often contradictory, whose very conflict is the cause of Judaism's vitality. Scholem finds one such conflicting tradition in the Kabbalah, for the Jewish mystics challenged the normative legal and philosophical interpretations of Judaism. The role Scholem believes that mysticism played in revitalizing Judaism will be the predominant subject of this chapter. We shall see how his dating and periodization assumptions form the basis for his overall view of the central position of mysticism in Jewish history.

Scholem suggests that the vital force in Jewish mysticism stemmed from its willingness to appropriate mythological symbols:

Authoritative Jewish theology, both medieval and modern in representatives like Sa'adia, Maimonides and Hermann Cohen, has taken upon itself the task of formulating an antithesis to pantheism and mythical theology, i.e. to prove them wrong. What is really required, however, is an understanding of these phenomena which yet does not lead away from monotheism; and once their significance is grasped, that elusive something in them which may be of value must be clearly defined. To have posed this problem is the historic achievement of Kabbalism.[1]

By confronting and assimilating rather than rejecting myth, mysticism was able to expand the definition of monotheism in productive directions. Scholem identifies this myth with a form of Gnosticism and sees the history of Jewish mysticism as an underground resurgence of Gnosticism in the Middle Ages. Scholem's discovery of Gnosticism, a potentially heretical dualistic myth, in the heart of Jewish monotheism suggests how broad is his definition of Judaism.

The statement quoted above also reveals something of Scholem's own program. Medieval rational theology tried as much as possible to demythologize monotheism, and the nineteenth-century theologians and historians exemplified by Hermann Cohen cast the medieval arguments in modern terms. Scholem's assertion that Judaism is not the enemy of all myth is in the Kabbalistic tradition of postulating a "monotheistic myth." He hints that, just as the Kabbalists expanded the philosophical concept of monotheism to include myth, he too would expand the nineteenth-century definition of Judaism to include irrationalism and myth.

In his effort to recover the "great living myth" in Jewish history which had been ignored or suppressed by the Wissenschaft des Judentums, Scholem seems to follow the path of counter-historical thinkers such as Buber and Berdichevsky, for whom vitality consisted in a hermetic subterranean myth. We have seen, however, that Scholem forcefully rejects their subjectivist and antihistorical approach to Jewish mysticism. He defines Jewish mysticism as a coherent tradition of commentary rather than as a series of discrete mystical experiences. The Kabbalah was a theosophical system of speculations about the nature of God and his relation to the cosmos. Since the Kabbalah was a speculative, theoretical movement, it could be subjected to the kind of philological historiography used for the history of philosophy: categories could be precisely defined and the history of the use of *termini technici* traced philologically. Scholem could treat Jewish mysticism like a philosophical system because the Gnostic myth, which he believes the Kabbalah adopted, addressed philosophical questions and used philosophical language. Jewish mysticism, he argues, was at once a philosophy employing mythical images and a myth written in philosophical language.

Scholem's idea that the Kabbalah was a synthesis of myth and philosophy closely resembles certain nineteenth-century views, some of which we have already discussed. Rationalists like Krochmal and Joel considered the Kabbalah a part of the history of Jewish philosophy, although inferior to pure rationalism. David Neumark opposed Graetz's assertion that the Kabbalah was merely an irrationalist reaction against philosophy and could not, therefore, be considered a legitimate part of authentic Judaism. Neumark attributed great antiquity to the Kabbalah and saw it as a "latent parallel" to philosophy.[2] The Kabbalah absorbed and "remythologized" the language of Jewish philosophy, and philosophy itself adopted images from mysticism.

Scholem's view combines parts of the nineteenth-century and radical twentieth-century positions. He agrees with Neumark against Graetz that the Kabbalah was not an obscurantist reaction against philosophy and that the Kabbalistic myth was impregnated with philosophical terminology.[3] On the other hand, he argues that the origins of the Kabbalah were independent of philosophy and that the Kabbalah had its own history. But he condemns the Buber-Berdichevsky claim of a subterranean self-contained tradition as "naive and incapable of withstanding historical examination."[4] Scholem does not reject the notion of an underground Judaism, for he too proposes a counter-history in which the esoteric elite of Kabbalists play a central role. But he objects to the idea that the counter-tradition has no connection with the mainstream. He claims repeatedly that Jewish mysticism was a movement at the very heart of rabbinic Judaism and not at its periphery. Mysticism was an original movement with its own unique history which nonetheless occupied a central place in rabbinic Judaism and even shared the terminology of its philosophical "enemy." Scholem therefore returns to a nineteenth-century rationalist position concerning the philosophical nature of the Kabbalah, but he transvalues it for his own purposes: although the Kabbalah resembled and borrowed from philosophy, it was a legitimate, independent discipline that proved more vital than philosophy.

For Scholem, as for many thinkers at the beginning of the twentieth century, irrational forces have a unique character that cannot be reduced to rationalism.[5] He regards unconscious or irrational forces as autonomous and perhaps even the hidden power behind man's reason: "Reason is a great instrument of destruction. For construction, something beyond it is required . . . I believe that morality as a constructive force is impossible without religion, without some power beyond pure reason."[6] Scholem believes that the constructive forces in history have their source not in reason but in irrationalism and myth. But like Freud, Scholem does not glorify irrationalism without qualification, for irrational forces also have an explosive and destructive potential. Scholem parts company with irrationalists like Nietzsche, Buber, and Berdichevsky because he fears the consequences of such forces. An anarchist, but not a nihilist, Scholem believes in the rational regulation of irrationalism, and in his historiography he strives for a rational account of the history of irrationalism. Like Shai Hurwitz, Scholem is a counter-historian who recognizes the impact of irrationalism on Jewish history, but does not necessarily identify with it.

Periodization and Dating

The central role Scholem assigns to mysticism in Jewish history can be detected in his approach to problems of periodization and dating. Since the Renaissance, the dating of the *Zohar*, the most important text of Jewish mysticism, has been a litmus test for attitudes toward the Kabbalah.[7] Hostility toward irrationalism often expressed itself in a late dating of the *Zohar*, which would undermine the book's own claim to antiquity. Yehudah Arye Mi-modena in the seventeenth century and Jacob Emden in the eighteenth both disputed the *Zohar*'s antiquity. Emden was motivated by hostility to the Sabbatians, who used Zoharic interpretations as proof for their messianic claims. Emden respected the Kabbalah, but he wanted to show that at least some portions of the *Zohar* were recent and thereby attack the Sabbatians for creating a new religion.[8]

Many of the historians of the nineteenth-century Wissenschaft des Judentums continued Emden's work, often with greater hostility toward irrationalism and with more radical conclusions. Zunz, Geiger, and Graetz all accepted a late date for the *Zohar*, regarding it as an unholy forgery. M. H. Landauer argued that it was written in the thirteenth century by the ecstatic mystic Abraham Abulafia.[9] Adolf Jellinek, who was relatively sympathetic to the Kabbalah, argued the position popularized by Graetz in less sympathetic tones, that Moses de Leon, who lived at the end of the thirteenth century, was at least one if not the only author of the *Zohar*.[10]

Orthodox defenders of the Kabbalah in the nineteenth century, such as David Luria, frequently offered an early date for the *Zohar* in order to validate the *Zohar*'s claim to have been written by Shimon bar Yohai in the second century C.E.[11] Adolf Franck, in the middle of the century, concluded that the Kabbalah as a whole originated with ancient Persian religion and that this antiquity was reflected in the *Zohar* which itself contained ancient as well as more recent strata.[12] Eljakim Mehlzahagi and Ignatz Stern at about the same time took a similar "documentary" approach, concluding that the *Zohar* was an ancient text reworked and edited in more recent times.[13] These traditionalist arguments were taken up with new vigor by some of the nationalists who revised Jewish historiography in the early twentieth century. Hillel Zeitlin (1871-1942), who had helped introduce Graetz to the Yiddish-reading public, advanced arguments against Graetz for the antiquity of the *Zohar*, thus hoping to legitimize it as a genuine part of the national literature.[14] For all these historians, whether for or against the Kabbalah, antiquity was a criterion for authenticity.

The young Scholem was initially motivated by similar concerns. In 1925 he wrote to Chaim Nachman Bialik outlining a program for the study of the Kabbalah.[15] Scholem wholeheartedly supported Bialik's idea of a new nationalist Wissenschaft. Scholem argued that insufficient attention had been paid to the internal history of

the Kabbalah, a clear reference to the tendency of Graetz and
others to deny the Kabbalah its own history. As we have already
observed, Scholem's initial motivation in studying the Kabbalah
went beyond a mere academic interest. He wrote to Bialik: "Does
the Kabbalah have value or not? It is impossible for one to escape
from or avoid this question, which is beyond mere philology. I will
admit to you without embarrassment that this philosophical interest is at my side throughout my philological and historical investigations." Scholem wanted to establish that the Kabbalah had
played a significant role in Jewish history and that therefore its
ideas had more than passing import. But if the history of the Kabbalah was truncated by the discovery that it was all the invention
of a few medieval intellectuals, its importance might diminish:
"Was the Kabbalah in fact the invention of two or three people
from Maimonides' generation or is there rather here a real 'tradition' (Kabbalah) from the days of the Gaonim and Amoraim? It is
clear that our views of the development of the religion of Israel generally after the Second Temple will be greatly influenced by these
investigations if the conclusion is positive." Although Scholem
does not explicitly say so, it appears that the philosophical value of
his philological investigations would be much enhanced if the Kabbalah were shown to be an ancient tradition.

It is likely that the concern to prove antiquity caused Scholem to
choose to edit a critical edition of the puzzling and pivotal Sefer
Bahir as the subject of his doctoral dissertation, which he completed in 1923. In his notes, and even more in later writings, he suggested that this late twelfth-century or early thirteenth-century text
was based on ancient midrashim and that it served as the link between the "ancient Kabbalah" and the Kabbalistic movement of the
thirteenth century.[16]

In his first article on the Zohar,[17] Scholem followed similar dating considerations. Entitled "Did Moses de Leon Write the Book
Zohar?" it was a cautious attack on the Graetz-Jellinek argument
that the Zohar was a forgery. Scholem concluded that Moses de
Leon made copies of the Zohar in the early 1290s, although he rejected Graetz's view that he forged the whole text for pecuniary ad-
vantage.[18] He argued further that de Leon referred to actual written
midrashim when he quoted the Zohar in works written under his
own name. If he had forged the Zohar in the 1290s, then he must
also have forged the midrashic quotations in his earlier works; this
seemed unlikely to Scholem. It was more probable that Moses de
Leon used the Zohar as a source for his own writings and that his
obscurities might be explained by the fact that he did not fully un-

derstand the ancient Zoharic passages he quoted. Although Scholem stated his arguments tentatively, it is clear that he wanted to prove that there were ancient strata in the *Zohar*.

Between 1931 and 1935 Scholem began to revise his early dating of the *Zohar*.[19] By 1938 he asserted with absolute confidence that the *Zohar* was written at the end of the thirteenth century and that Moses de Leon was the author of almost all of it.[20] In this startling reversal, which stands today despite occasional challenges,[21] Scholem substantially accepted Graetz's conclusions of a late date for the most important text of the Kabbalah.

Scholem's new position hinged on careful philological study of the *Zohar*'s language.[22] He argued that the text's corrupt and bombastic Aramaic was medieval with a strong admixture of Spanish, thus betraying its pseudepigraphical character. The uniformity of style pointed to a single author, with the exception of the *Raya Mehemna* and *Tikkune ha-Zohar* sections. Scholem also solved numerous dating problems by showing that the *Zohar* was composed in stages, starting in the late 1270s. Previous scholars had dated the strongly philosophical section, *Midrash ha-Ne'elam*, later than other sections of the text since they assumed that the more mythological passages had to be much earlier. Scholem inverted this "evolutionary rationalism," speculating that the author was initially a Maimonidean who was gradually attracted to the Kabbalah. The author had composed the *Midrash ha-Ne'elam* before he fully abandoned philosophy and then quoted from it in later additions written in the 1280s. He then wrote the other sections in the 1280s and early 1290s.

Scholem identified Moses de Leon as the author by comparing the *Zohar* with de Leon's known writings. Where previously he had held that de Leon did not understand the *Zohar* when he quoted from it, Scholem now argued that de Leon manipulated Zoharic passages with complete familiarity and that de Leon's admitted writings were deliberately intended to whet the public's appetite for the eventual publication of his masterpiece.

Having returned substantially to Graetz's position, Scholem had to deal with the old charge of forgery. It was here that he made an important contribution to the argument by reevaluating the role of pseudepigraphy as a legitimate aspect of the history of religions:

Pseudepigraphy is far removed from forgery. The mark of immorality which is inseparable from falsehood does not stain it, and for this reason it has always been admitted as a legitimate category of religious literature of the highest moral order . . . The Quest for Truth knows of adventures that are all its own and in a vast number of cases has arrayed itself in pseudepigraphic garb. The further a man progresses along his own road in this Quest for Truth, the more he might become convinced that his own road must have already been trodden by others, ages before him.[23]

The pseudepigrapher identifies himself with a former age because he believes in the eternal significance of his message. Pseudepigraphy is not forgery, but a proclamation of the continuity of a hidden tradition. The Kabbalah as a whole, even when it did not engage in pseudepigraphy, was metaphorically pseudepigraphical, Scholem intimates, because it claimed to be an ancient esoteric tradition (*Kabbalah*). The Kabbalists considered their doctrines "old as the hills" even as they generated new interpretations, because they defined their work as an interpretation of revelation that had always been in the tradition.[24] Even when the Kabbalists recognized that their sources were recent, they regarded them as revivals of a genuine hidden tradition and therefore authentically ancient. Scholem points out, for example, that the fourteenth-century Kabbalists may have doubted the *Zohar*'s claim of antiquity without for a moment rejecting its veracity.[25]

In Scholem's defense of pseudepigraphy as part of his late dating of the *Zohar*, we see how he transvalued the accepted dating assumptions in Kabbalistic scholarship. Both Graetz and Zeitlin, modern historians who arrived at opposite conclusions about the *Zohar*, assumed that antiquity was a necessary prerequisite for the value of a text. Scholem rejected this assumption. Although he often tries to place the dating of Jewish mystical texts as early as possible, his *Zohar* dating shows that he was not bound to the old assumptions. Recent texts could have as much vitality and religious authenticity as the ancient.

Scholem then accepted Graetz's accusation of pseudepigraphy, but made it a virtue, since pseudepigraphy became a means for legitimizing a creative work as part of a hidden tradition. The authority of tradition is recognized, but the freedom of literary creativity is preserved. Graetz rejected pseudepigraphy because it subverted his notion of historical progress: the Kabbalah was not a genuine product of the progressive development of Jewish consciousness, and its retreat into pseudepigraphy in the *Zohar* proved as much. In inverting this negative evaluation of pseudepigraphy, Scholem had to revise Graetz's concept of "progress" in Jewish history. The desire of the thirteenth-century Kabbalists to claim antiquity was not a sign of degeneracy, but characteristic of a certain development in the history of the Jewish religion. Scholem's rejec-

tion of the old dating assumption—antiquity equals authenticity—
required a new proposal for the periodization of Jewish history.

In the lectures on "Major Trends in Jewish Mysticism" in which
he presents his new position on the *Zohar*, Scholem suggests a new
periodization of Jewish history which would give mysticism a much
more central place than in earlier schemes. As opposed to Graetz,
he assumes that mysticism is "a definite stage in the historical development of religion and makes its appearance under certain well-
defined conditions."[26] The history of religions follows a three-stage
scheme: myth, institutionalization, and, finally, attempts to recapture the original myth. In the first stage, "the abyss between Man
and God has not become a fact of inner consciousness. That, however, is only while the childhood of mankind, its mythical epoch,
lasts." This is the period of "the immediate consciousness of the in-
terrelation and interdependence of things, their essential unity
which preceds duality . . . the truly monistic universe of man's
mythical age."[27]

The second period is the stage of "religion," which "signifies the
creation of a vast abyss, conceived as absolute, between God, the
infinite and transcendental Being, and Man, the finite creature."
This is the period when man becomes conscious of the gulf that sep-
arates him from God and when God reveals himself only in rare
theophanies. Because man no longer communicates naturally with
the gods, as he did during the mythical stage, it becomes necessary
to institutionalize revelation in order to give some continuity to the
voice of revelation. In Judaism, the second stage is represented by
the legal institutions of rabbinic Judaism. The overwhelming characteristic of the second stage is alienation from God. When man becomes conscious of the fact of alienation and of the inadequacy of
institutions to bridge the abyss between himself and God, religion
enters into a crisis.

In the third period, a time of self-reflection, religion becomes
problematic and demands an ideology which comes to the rescue of
the tradition by giving it a new interpretation.[28] The idea that the
third stage of a religion is a period of self-reflection is reminiscent of
a typical motif in the Wissenschaft des Judentums, for which self-
reflection meant philosophy. Scholem agrees that philosophy is an
"ideology of Judaism," but he argues that it failed to address the issues raised by the crisis of "classical religion." Only mysticism, as
a "romantic" attempt to recapture the unity of the original myth,
attacks head-on the alienation and dualism of the second period:
"Mysticism does not deny or overlook the abyss; on the contrary,
it begins by realizing its existence, but from there it proceeds to a
quest for the secret that will close it in, the hidden path that will

span it."[29] When the mystic attempts to restore the immediacy of
the original stage of religion, he consciously uses the old myth, re-
fracting it through the prism of the religious experience of the second stage. Mysticism is therefore the dialectical synthesis of myth
and transcendental religion: it is self-reflective myth.

Scholem takes his distinction between classical and romantic religion from Leo Baeck's famous essay "Romantische Religion."[30]
Baeck was one of the foremost Jewish polemicists against liberal
Christian theologians like Harnack, and he acclaimed Judaism as a
classical religion against the romantic "mystical-pietistic" reaction
of Christianity. Although he adopts Baeck's terms, Scholem overturns Baeck's negative view of romantic religion and thereby comes
close to accepting the Christian assumption that legal institutions
are religiously stifling, an assumption Buber shared. However, he
adamantly rejects the idea that legal institutions have no validity.
He tries to show that halakhic Judaism remained alive throughout
Jewish history, but that the cause of its vitality was the irrational
forces within it. Scholem here is perhaps closer to Molitor, who
saw the Kabbalah as the vital force within Jewish law as well as in
Christianity. It may even be that Scholem derived his three-stage
periodization from Molitor, who had developed a similar idea that
the Kabbalah represents the third period of Jewish history.[31] If we
strip away his Christological emphasis and ignore his lack of methodological historical research, we find in Molitor a remarkable
anticipation of Scholem's fundamental approach to the Kabbalah.

THE THREE STAGES OF JEWISH HISTORY

How does Scholem apply his periodization model to Jewish history? Biblical Judaism is frequently considered the monotheistic opponent of myth. Scholem does not dispute that elements in biblical
Judaism fought against myth, but he argues that Judaism never succeeded in totally purifying itself from it.[32] Biblical monotheism
oscillated between unashamed anthropomorphisms and their prophetic condemnation. The biblical text is the record of the struggle
between the mythical and transcendental stages of the Jewish religion. Since philosophical questions concerning the nature of God
did not matter to the authors of the Bible, they did not suppress or
expunge the mythic strata in their tradition.[33]

In Scholem's opinion, the rabbis in the Talmudic period were the
first to feel uncomfortable with biblical anthropomorphisms, and
they therefore treated them as mere metaphors.[34] The rabbis expressed their hostility toward myth in an antimagical theory of the
legal commandments. The Jew does not affect the cosmos when he

fulfills the law; each commandment is rather a "rite of remembrance" by which the Jew evokes the historical event that established the law: "the ritual of rabbinical Judaism makes nothing happen and *transforms* nothing. Though not devoid of feeling, remembrance lacks the passion of conjuration, and indeed, there is something strangely sober and dry about the rites of remembrance with which the Jew calls to mind his unique historical identity."[35] As representatives of the "institutional" stage of Jewish religion, the rabbis were evidently concerned to confirm the unbridgeable abyss between God and man in their legal theory: revelation could not be recreated, so performance of the commandments became a metaphysically passive act of remembrance.

Scholem intimates that the rabbis were not fully conscious of the problematic nature of a transcendent religion. Only the encounter with Greek philosophy introduced the theological issues and philosophical vocabulary which would make naive monotheism problematic and require religious ideologies to meet the new crisis of religion. The attraction of Greek philosophy lay in its monotheistic assumptions; it could provide a sophisticated vocabulary for the crystallizing sense of God's transcendence since it had already developed philosophical models of a transcendent God. The abstract God of Greek philosophy was, however, fundamentally incompatible with the personal God of the Bible, who had created the world out of his own free will in time.[36] Under the intellectual challenge of Greek monotheistic philosophies, the monotheistic religions—Judaism, Christianity, and Islam—were forced to adopt the vocabulary of their pagan opponents in order to defend their heritage. Religious thought in the Middle Ages had to try "to preserve the purity of the concept of God without loss of His living reality."[37]

In Scholem's view, medieval religious philosophy failed to achieve this synthesis. Maimonides, for instance, purged the image of God of any positive attributes in order to preserve the philosophical concept of God's unity. Philosophy similarly failed to deal adequately with the halakhah. Maimonides' historical explanation for the origin of the commandments could only erode the religious conviction that had previously motivated Jews to perform them: "To the philosopher, the halakhah either had no significance at all, or one that was calculated to diminish rather than to enhance its prestige in his eyes."[38] The philosophers reduced the rabbinical "rites of remembrance" to meaningless artifacts. For Scholem, then, philosophy set out to rid Judaism of vestigial myths and ended up losing the God of the Bible who had revealed his law at Sinai.

Given Scholem's definition of the third stage of the history of a religion as the attempt to recapture God's "living reality," philosophy could not belong to the third stage of the history of Judaism. To be sure, Jewish philosophy was a conscious "ideology of Judaism," but it could only state with clarity the fact of God's transcendence and therefore articulate the crisis of transcendence already implicit in the "classical" period. Philosophy was more the swansong of the second stage. The failure of philosophy represented the crisis of rabbinical Judaism as a whole.

Mysticism would have to be the true response to the crisis of religion: a genuine attempt to recapture God's immediacy in full awareness of his transcendence. However, we shall see that Scholem's discussion of the history of Jewish mysticism does not conform to a strictly temporal periodization. The second stage began perhaps as early as the Bible and was articulated first in the Talmudic period; it continues, as orthodox rabbinical Judaism, even today. Mysticism, which Scholem calls the great "counter-attack" against the failure of philosophical Judaism,[39] had emerged in the early Talmudic period and in fact developed within rabbinical Judaism itself. The second and third stages were chronologically equivalent. Rather than a period of law and rationalism preceding a period of irrationalism, these opposing forces were inextricably interwoven in Jewish history. For Scholem, rabbi and mystic were not always mutually exclusive categories, since some great legal authorities were also mystics:[40] Scholem's history of Jewish irrationalism is not self-contained, but is rather a history of constant interaction with normative halakhic Judaism. His periodization of Jewish history is not chronological but conceptual, and is linked to his implicit rejection of linear progress in history.

THE MYSTICAL COUNTER-ATTACK

The mystics could not simply return to the mythical stage in Judaism, since they were conscious of the transcendence of God. Mysticism had to start with the fact of a hidden God (*deus absconditus*) and harmonize him with the God of the Bible. The new mystical synthesis could not naively resurrect the anthropomorphic myths in the Bible which both rabbis and philosophers discredited as metaphors. The mystics suggested instead a symbolic reinterpretation of the biblical text: "the mythical images become mystical symbols."[41] Scholem therefore defines mysticism as the symbolic reinterpretation of myth, and follows Walter Benjamin in distinguishing between allegory and symbol. A philosophical allegory would consider an expression such as "the arm of God" a figure of speech, perhaps representing some philosophical concept. For the mystic, "the arm of God" is a symbol of a higher reality, an actual arm of God, although not in any way commensurate with a human arm. The mystic believes that there is a sphere of "divine reality" which, unexpressible in discursive terms, can be evoked symbolically. The symbolic reinterpretation of anthropomorphisms became necessary precisely because philosophy gradually emptied biblical images of any reference to the divine.[42]

The Kabbalah accomplished this reinfusion of symbols into Judaism by introducing the distinction between an exoteric and an esoteric exegesis of the Bible.[43] The new exegesis protected mysticism against the accusation of heretical innovation: the mystics claimed to revive an ancient esoteric tradition by symbolically reinterpreting the exoteric biblical text. By its conscious pretense of antiquity in exegesis, a kind of metaphorical pseudepigraphy, the Kabbalah was able to put the Jew back in touch with the wellsprings of his religion.

The Kabbalists "agreed" with the philosophers that, on an exoteric level, performance of the commandments was a rite of remembrance, a passive representation of a long-past event; but they added a new dimension to the ritual by symbolically reenacting the event in the performance of the commandment. This symbolic reenactment restored activism to Jewish law: "Those who carry out the *mitsvah* always do two things. They represent in a concrete symbol its transcendent essence, through which it is rooted in and partakes of the ineffable. But, at the same time, they transmit to this transcendent essence an influx of energy."[44] In the Kabbalah, the symbol or myth is also a mechanism by which man sustains and participates in the Divine. The Kabbalists' idea that symbols can communicate between God and man restored to the Jew the feeling of active participation in his fate and the fate of the cosmos.

Scholem believes that the Kabbalah developed in close competition with medieval Jewish philosophy. He argues that it was the thirteenth-century Kabbalah rather than legal-rabbinical Judaism which formed the main opposition to philosophy in the famous Maimonidean controversy in that century. Some of the more outspoken opponents of Maimonides, such as Abraham ben David (Rabad) and Jonah of Gerona, were among the leaders of the new Kabbalistic movement.[45] Rabad, for instance, is considered primarily a legal critic of Maimonides, but Scholem believes that his attack on Maimonides was motivated less by a desire to defend the legal tradition against philosophical subversion than by a feeling of intellectual competition: the Maimonidean controversy was between philosophers and mystics. The mystics felt that they had a genuine alternative to philosophy and, although they posed as defenders of the orthodox legal tradition, they were really defending their symbolic reinterpretation of the tradition.

An interesting case of this reinterpretation was the Kabbalistic claim that the philosophers had "spiritualized" Judaism by making it more abstract.[46] Not the mystics but the philosophers were the spiritualists. Ironically, the Kabbalists conceived their exegesis, with its corporeal descriptions of God, as more literal than the allegorical interpretations of the philosophers. They believed that their mystical exegesis revealed the true inner meaning of the Bible whereas the philosophers had escaped into irrelevant abstractions.

Scholem argues that when philosophy subjected monotheism to excessive abstraction, Judaism could not meet the psychological needs of the Jewish people. He notes that for Hermann Cohen "evil is non-existent . . . a power of evil exists only in myth."[47] Cohen's position suggested to Scholem the psychological bankruptcy of rational philosophy. Precisely because philosophy ignored the problem of evil and considered it "illusory" myth, the philosophers lost touch with "the elemental impulses operative in every human mind."[48] Because mysticism included myth, which expressed the "primitive side of life," it was able to address the concerns of the common man.

Scholem seems to agree with the Kabbalists that evil is not merely the absence of good, but exists in its own right. His attitude emerges in his letter to Hannah Arendt in which he criticizes her *Eichmann in Jerusalem*.[49] He says he is unimpressed by Arendt's thesis of the "banality of evil" and questions what had become of her earlier notion of "radical evil," developed in *The Origins of Totalitarianism*. If evil is nonexistent, it might be construed as banal, but Scholem is persuaded that evil is both radical and demonic and must therefore be addressed squarely as such.

Like medieval philosophers, mystics were "aristocrats of the mind," elitists who believed in the esoteric or "professional" character of their knowledge. But while the philosophers deliberately isolated their doctrines, the mystics believed that the masses participated in mystical acts, even if they were only comprehensible to initiates. Scholem notes the paradoxical nature of the mystic's involvement in society. The mystic, in his attempt to penetrate the innermost secrets of the cosmos, also claims to address the profound social and psychological concerns of man in society: "By the sheer paradox of his claim, the mystic has never failed to stir society to its depths . . . Who has done more to create historical movement than those who seek and proclaim the immovable?"[50]

The mystic, according to Scholem, stands at the vanguard of historical change since the presumed impact of his spiritual activity is not confined to a small sect. Hence the paradox of mysticism's historical influence is that, although an esoteric doctrine, it expresses the true psychological yearnings of the people.

Scholem tries to demonstrate this argument in his history of the Kabbalah by showing how Jewish mysticism remained an exclusive and elite discipline between the thirteenth and fifteenth centuries as it developed its "classical" doctrines. This "underground" existence was necessary, however, to prepare the ground for the emergence of the Kabbalah, reinterpreted by Isaac Luria in the sixteenth century, as the central theology of Judaism following the expulsion from Spain. The Lurianic Kabbalah became the leading cause of the Sabbatian messianic movement in the seventeenth century:

> If there was one general factor underlying the patent unity of the Sabbatian movement everywhere, then this factor was essentially religious in character and as such obeyed its own autonomous laws . . . Impinging on the social situation, the religious factor caused the various groups, the leading classes in particular, to join the messianic movement . . . [This religious factor] was none other than Lurianic Kabbalah.[51]

A small sect of intellectuals, seemingly isolated from the mainstream of Jewish life, formulated an esoteric doctrine that prepared the ground for the mass messianic movement of the seventeenth century. Religion, and specifically mysticism, rather than social or economic factors, was the main cause of Sabbatianism. The mystic, normally considered quietistic and self-absorbed, became a dynamic and revolutionary force in Jewish history.

For Scholem, Jewish mysticism offers a cogent solution to the religious and philosophical problems of a monotheistic belief plagued by a growing sense of God's transcendence. The mystics did not negate philosophy altogether, as Graetz suggested. They translated philosophy into their own system, a process that Scholem calls the "philosophization of the Kabbalah."[52] The success of the Kabbalah had much to do with its ability to appropriate philosophical concepts, transform them into mystical symbols, and then solve philosophical problems such as *creatio ex nihilo* which philosophy had failed to solve. The Kabbalists often believed that their reinterpretations rendered more clearly what the philosophers were trying to say.[53] Some Kabbalists, for instance, gave Maimonides' *Moreh Nevukhim* a mystical interpretation, and Moses de Leon himself was originally a Maimonidean who gradually moved away from philosophy into the Kabbalah. Scholem is interested in showing that the lines of demarcation between philosophy and the Kabbalah were not always clear, although the history of the Kabbalah should never be subordinated to the history of philosophy, as Neumark mistakenly thought. Scholem's philosophical treatment of Kabbalistic texts suggests his belief that the Kabbalah offered answers to philosophical problems, which should be of interest to philosophers. The philosophically informed account he has given of unsystematic and often mythological texts is powerful evidence of his attempt to make the Kabbalah intellectually respectable.

We are now in a better position to understand how Scholem fits into the debate between the Wissenschaft des Judentums and the nationalist revision over the proper focus for Jewish historiography. Historians like Graetz saw Jewish history primarily as *Geistesgeschichte;* nationalists, starting with Dubnow, turned their attention to social movements. Scholem rejects the nineteenth-century emphasis on intellectual history insofar as it focused predominantly on rationalism, since he maintains that philosophy failed to remain in touch with the heartbeat of the nation. But he does not adopt a sociological approach—even in his discussion of the Kabbalists themselves he scarcely treats their social life. Scholem's history of Jewish mysticism is itself *Geistesgeschichte*: the history of the theological doctrines and speculations of a small intelligentsia. Although a history of esoteric doctrines, it claims social relevance as an account of the true but unarticulated yearnings of the people and of the hidden cause of historical mass movements. Scholem implies that his *Geistesgeschichte* has relevance as social history precisely because it does not focus on rationalism: the Kabbalah's reinterpretation of primitive myth gave Jewish mysticism its social resonance and vitality.

The role mysticism played in rejuvenating rabbinic Judaism suggests once again Scholem's definition of the "essence" of Judaism. Opposed to the idea that Judaism is solely legal or philosophical, he demonstrates the importance of irrationalism within the tradition. A normative tradition need not be monolithic, for the essence of Judaism is a vital pluralism of law and mysticism, rational philosophy and irrational myth.

6.　　　　　*Myth*

What is the nature of the myth that regenerates Judaism from within? The new myth could not be a simple repetition of primitive mythology since, coming in the wake of legal and philosophical Judaism, it had to address abstract issues of no concern to the ancients. Mysticism, Scholem suggests, was a conscious reinterpretation of myth: myth refracted through the prism of philosophy. Scholem argues that myth and philosophy were fused by mysticism in order to save Jewish monotheism from its own internal problems.

Scholem believes that Jewish mysticism had a continuous history of its own, and he defines the philosophical myth that held it together from late antiquity to the eighteenth century as Jewish Gnosticism. Gnosticism was a religious movement of late antiquity.[1] The crisis of philosophical Hellenism in late antiquity produced a resurgence of religiosity in the Mediterranean area, and Gnosticism became one of the most important such movements in both pagan and Christian circles. The Gnostics proposed a dualistic theology in which the creator God was evil and the hidden God was good. Although the Gnostics expressed their beliefs in mythological images, they consciously addressed philosophical issues. Gnosticism therefore fits Scholem's criteria of a conscious, philosophical myth.

Scholem does not equate all of Jewish mysticism with Gnosticism, but rather sees in the Jewish appropriation of Gnosticism the most vital element in the Kabbalah. The most potentially heretical ideas constituted the creative force in Jewish mysticism from the very outset. As we shall see, Scholem contends that as late as eighteenth-century Hasidism, Gnostic elements continued to play a significant role.

Scholem's use of Gnosticism as the unifying myth of his history of Jewish mysticism raises some interesting questions. Since Gnosticism is an ambiguous and controversial concept, Scholem must confront the danger of defining the Kabbalah by a term that is itself unclear. He rarely commits himself to one definition of Gnosticism and often changes his meaning to suit different issues in the Kabbalah. Though this is by no means illegitimate, given the diverse character of Gnosticism, it raises the question as to exactly what he means. Scholem also uses the adjective "Gnostic" to refer to Jewish movements in the Middle Ages, long after the historical period of late antiquity when Gnosticism flourished as a recognizable movement. Again, this procedure may be justified, but it raises certain questions: Was there an actual historical connection between medieval Kabbalistic "Gnosticism" and the historical Gnosticism of late antiquity, or is Gnosticism a type of myth that recurs spontaneously? Is Gnosticism a "structure of thought" by which men respond to certain types of crises in religious rationalism? Finally, Scholem refers to the Jewish Gnostics as "orthodox."[2] Since Gnosticism, even in its less radical Egyptian manifestation, was a dualistic doctrine and therefore a threat to Jewish monotheism, how could it become orthodox? How might an heretical myth save monotheism?

JEWISH GNOSTICISM IN LATE ANTIQUITY

Scholem's history of the "monotheistic myth" begins in late antiquity, the period of Gnosticism itself. Nineteenth-century Jewish scholars, following Graetz, generally argued that Gnosticism was a Christian heresy against which Judaism, like orthodox Christianity, had to defend itself. Graetz interpreted certain *Merkabah* (chariot) speculations in the Talmud as allegories for Gnostic speculations that the rabbis successfully opposed. Graetz dated this heretical Jewish Gnosticism to the early second century, but he never suggested the possibility of an "orthodox" Jewish Gnosticism or of Jewish provenance for Gnostic ideas. Gnosticism was a foreign philosophy—it attempted to infiltrate Judaism but was decisively defeated.[3]

Nineteenth-century historiography generally dated the extra-Talmudic mystical literature, such as the *Hekhalot* (heavenly palace) hymns and the *Shiur Komah*, which describes God's physical anatomy in great detail, to the early Islamic period. By ascribing these highly embarrassing anthropomorphic and mystical texts to a time safely after the completion of the Talmud, they were able to portray rabbinic Judaism as pure and uncorrupted. Mysticism was a later reaction to Islamic rationalism and a sign of degeneration after the glorious age of the Talmud.

Scholem argues, against these views, that a widespread mystical movement existed at precisely the same time the rabbis were formulating the classical legal texts and that the materials previously dated to the seventh or eighth century were produced by orthodox Jews in the second or third century.[4] Moreover, he suggests that this mysticism was primarily Gnostic and that Jewish Gnosticism was a movement prior to and independent of Christian Gnosticism.

Scholem adopts Graetz's contention that the *Merkabah* legends were Gnostic, but he rejects Graetz's allegorical interpretation. These texts were literal descriptions of the soul's journey to the heavens rather than metaphors for theoretical speculations about esoteric knowledge. His definition of Gnosticism for this argument is taken from F. W. H. Anz's description of Gnosticism as the ascent of the soul from the alien earth back to its home in the fullness (*pleroma*) of God's glory.[5] The Jewish Gnostics, Scholem suggests, identified the biblical vision of God's throne with this Gnostic *pleroma*, but they translated the dualistic Gnostic terminology into biblical images that could be harmonized with monotheism.

This transformation of heretical myth into orthodox monotheism can be seen in Scholem's analysis of the *Shiur Komah*.[6] Almost everyone in the nineteenth century attributed the *Shiur Komah* to the early Islamic period, but in keeping with his belief in a second-century mystical movement, Scholem argues from a passage in Origen that it too must date from this early period. In the early third century, Origen wrote that the Jews placed restrictions on the study of certain biblical texts, including the Song of Songs. Scholem claims that all of these "forbidden" books were the subjects of esoteric exegesis and that the Song of Songs particularly was already interpreted in the second century as an allegory for God's body. The mystical interpretation of the Song of Songs must have served as the basis for texts like the *Shiur Komah*. Origen's statement would have to refer to the *Shiur Komah* or similar types of speculations, which were therefore part of the second-century mysticism.

Scholem argues that the *Shiur Komah* was actually an attempt by the mystics to "monotheize" Gnostic anthropomorphic themes.[7] The text refers to God as *yotzer bereshit* (creator of the world), which seems a clear allusion to the Gnostic dualism between a good hidden God and an evil creator God. The author defused this potential heresy by harmonizing the hidden and manifest "Gods." He distinguished between God's substance and appearance: the hidden divinity (God's essential substance) cannot be described, but the corporeal "glory" of God can. The *Shiur Komah* therefore described God's manifest characteristics without impinging on his hidden essence. This theme was to play an important role in the Kabbalah of the twelfth and thirteenth centuries. The orthodox reinterpretation of Gnostic dualism ensured God's unity and ineffability while at the same time employing anthropomorphic images. The Gnostic challenge was met by transforming myth into monotheism and monotheism into myth.

In his discussion of the *Shiur Komah*, Scholem shows that a Jewish Gnosticism existed before the Christian Gnosticism that emerged in the late second and third centuries. He overturns the usual assumption that the Jews borrowed Gnosticism from Christian heretics. On the contrary, the Jews provided the Christians with material for Gnosticism. In this radical thesis, Scholem partially resurrects the theory of Moritz Friedländer, A. Büchler, and others concerning a pre-Christian Gnosticism.[8] In his *Der vorchristliche jüdische Gnostizismus* (1898), Friedländer argued that Jewish Gnosticism already existed in the first century in Alexandria and that by the second century the term for heretic (*min*) meant Gnostic. Scholem accepts the hypothesized existence of an heretical Jewish Gnosticism that adopted hermetic traditions from the Greeks in Egypt, although he gives no proof of his own for this assertion. The crux of his argument is that some members of this heretical school must have combined forces with the *Merkabah* mystics to form the Gnostic groups who wrote the *Shiur Komah*.[9] These new groups remained orthodox, however, since their mysticism was within the limits of Jewish law and they wanted to preserve monotheism even as they boldly employed mythical imagery. According to Scholem, then, the early history of Jewish Gnosticism, as indeed the history of the Kabbalah as a whole, was part of the internal dialectic of Jewish history rather than a response to Christian or pagan Gnosticism.

Scholem's early dating of the Gnostic texts suggests that a mystical movement of major proportions existed precisely during the years when the Palestinian rabbis were enjoying their greatest power. The fact that the *Merkabah* legends were included in the Talmud and were attributed to well-known legal authorities suggests that, even if these figures were not themselves mystics, mysticism had a legitimate place as an esoteric discipline in intellectual Jewish circles and was a respected activity among legal scholars. The third mystical period of the Jewish religion began at the time the second, "classical," period reached its climax. In fact, the two periods cannot be chronologically separated since the rabbinical world tolerated both mysticism and legalism.

Scholem's thesis of an early Jewish mysticism that may have actually influenced Christian Gnosticism has been repeated with new emphasis by Erwin Goodenough in his monumental *Jewish Symbols in the Greco-Roman Period*. Although Goodenough was not the only one to suggest the possibility of a Jewish source for early Christian mysticism, his reliance on Scholem is illuminating.[10] Goodenough argues that the notion of a normative legal Judaism in late antiquity is a distortion perpetrated by medieval rabbis and modern scholars: Judaism in the Greco-Roman period was actually much more pluralistic. His studies of Philo and Jewish art in the period suggest to him a Jewish mysticism nourished by Hellenistic sources that existed quite apart from rabbinic Judaism and was only suppressed after a long struggle. Goodenough explicitly quotes Scholem's work as evidence for his own supposition that Judaism has always consisted of "the tension between the two types of religious experience everywhere, the religion of the vertical path by which man climbs to God . . . as over against the legal religion where man walks a horizontal path through this world."[11] Although Scholem does not go to Philo for his evidence of early Jewish mysticism, the thrust of his argument seems basically similar to Goodenough's. However, where Goodenough sees mystical Judaism as a separate current in Jewish history, Scholem is careful to point out that mysticism flourished in the very heart of legal rabbinic Judaism. Goodenough, whose knowledge of the rabbinic sources was derivative, strayed into a modified Christian argument against the vitality of legal Judaism. Although Scholem sees mysticism as a vital force in Jewish history, he does not negate the vitality of the law, since "normative" Judaism consisted of both Halakhah and Kabbalah.

After the Talmudic period, rabbinic mysticism underwent a decline in originality. The magical elements present in much of the *Merkabah* literature disappeared, and "this point is really the end of the movement as a living force; from then on it degenerates into mere literature."[12] The next major stage in Scholem's history of Jewish mysticism did not begin until the late twelfth century and then not in the Orient but in Germany, Southern France, and Spain. The renaissance of mysticism at this time developed in a movement that acquired the name "Kabbalah" (tradition). Today we use the term to apply to the whole history of Jewish mysticism but, technically and historically, it really only signifies Jewish mysticism starting from the late twelfth and early thirteenth centuries.

The sudden emergence of a prolific movement of mysticism at roughly the same time in a number of communities in Europe had already puzzled nineteenth-century historians like Graetz. We have seen that Graetz attempted to explain the new Kabbalah as an obscurantist defense of tradition against philosophy, whereas David Neumark suggested that it was a product of the internal dialectical development of Jewish philosophy. Neither was willing to grant the Kabbalah its own unique history and internal etiology. Scholem suggests just such a solution: the thirteenth-century Kabbalah was the product of an underground tradition of Jewish Gnosticism which started in late antiquity.

This belief goes back to the very beginning of Scholem's career. With the exception of his reversal on the dating of the *Zohar*, he took a radical position in his earliest writings, which he expressed in his letter to Bialik, and held to it throughout his life. His intellectual career may be seen as a steady attempt to substantiate certain extraordinary intuitions he had as a student.

Scholem's choice of dissertation topic, the *Sefer ha-Bahir*, indicated the direction his interpretation was to take. Against Adolf Jellinek, who had argued that the *Bahir* was written by Isaac the Blind at the beginning of the thirteenth century, Scholem suggested that the *Bahir*'s sources were much earlier Midrashic texts.[13] Although Scholem did not explicitly argue in his critical edition of the *Bahir* that these sources were Gnostic, by 1928 he had made the Gnostic character of the book central to his thesis.[14] The *Bahir*'s term *mal'ē*, for instance, was the Hebrew equivalent of the Gnostic *pleroma*. The cosmic tree, representing the lower seven sefirot, was also a Gnostic metaphor. Most important, the sefirot imagery, transformed from mere numerals in the ancient *Sefer Yitzirah* into hypostatizations of God's attributes, was identical to the Gnostic concept of the aeons of the hidden God. The Gnostic reinterpretation of the sefirot as attributes of God distinguished the medieval Kabbalah from all earlier Jewish mysticism and became the hallmark of all future Kabbalistic theosophy. Because the *Bahir* was the first work to introduce this notion to the Provence mystics, it was the seminal work of the new Kabbalah and the most important bridge between the old and the new mysticism.

By arguing against a late date for the *Bahir*, Scholem sought to establish the enigmatic text as the connecting link between ancient Jewish Gnosticism and medieval Kabbalah. A Kabbalistic tradition in the mid-thirteenth century itself suggested that the *Bahir* was transported from the Orient via the Hasidim of the Rhineland to Provence.[15] Scholem believes that one Aaron of Baghdad was responsible for bringing a number of Gnostic and *Merkabah* texts, perhaps including elements of the *Bahir*, from the East to Italy dur-

ing the Gaonic period whence the Kalonymide family took them to
Germany in the ninth century. In Germany, these old manuscripts
formed the basis for the Gnostic elements in Ashkenazic Hasidism.[16] From Germany, the texts were carried to Provence where
some of them were redacted as the *Sefer ha-Bahir*. It is not without
interest that this theory is close to Krochmal's description of how
the sefirot theosophy was first developed by Kabbalists in Baby-
lonia and was carried westward via Italy to Spain in various
"scrolls and small pamphlets" (*megilot v'kuntresim ketanim*).[17]

Scholem's intriguing theory was incomplete without some evidence of these underground texts. He discovered this missing link in
a thirteenth-century German commentary on the *Shiur Komah*
which quoted a work named *Sod ha-Gadol* (Great Mystery), passages of which correspond to the *Bahir*. Scholem identified this unknown work with a mystery-magical text named *Raza Rabba* (Aramaic for "great mystery") mentioned by the ninth-century Karaite
Al Kunisi.[18] The *Raza Rabba* must accordingly have been the
source for the *Bahir*, and its ninth-century terminus proves the antiquity of the *Bahir*'s traditions.

The new Kabbalah was therefore neither a result of economic-
social causes nor a reaction against philosophy, but rather an independent religious movement catalyzed in part by the impact of
the Gnostic ideas collected in the *Sefer ha-Bahir*. Scholem's emphasis on the enormous influence of written texts for the formation
of religious movements recalls his theoretical disagreement with
Buber about whether the most reliable sources for Hasidism are its
written or oral traditions.

THE KABBALAH AND PHILOSOPHICAL ISSUES

I suggested in Chapter One that nineteenth-century scholars,
notably Neander and Krochmal, saw the parallels between Kabbalah and Gnosticism and even believed that the Kabbalah may have
served as the basis for Gnosticism. Krochmal pointed out the striking similarities between the two movements in their doctrines of a
hidden God and the hypostatization of God's attributes. Krochmal
maintained that the Gnostic element continued to exert an influence
throughout the history of the Kabbalah and ultimately exploded
into heresy in the form of seventeenth-century Sabbatianism. He
also considered both Kabbalah and Gnosticism to have been forms
of philosophy permeated with myth. All of these arguments laid
the groundwork for Scholem's description of Jewish mysticism as a
synthesis of Gnosticism and philosophy, although he never explicitly mentions the resemblance of Krochmal's views to his own.

Scholem believes that the most productive interaction between the thirteenth-century Gnostic Kabbalah and medieval Jewish philosophy resulted from the exposure to Neoplatonism.[19] The Gnostic Kabbalah, represented by the *Bahir*, was a rather motley collection of symbolic images, potent in their evocative impact but limited in conceptual sophistication. The Kabbalah emerged from its Gnostic "underground" and became a coherent religious movement precisely when it began to appropriate medieval philosophy and to systematize its symbolic imagery.[20] From Jewish Neoplatonists such as Abraham bar Hiyya, Abraham ibn Ezra, and, less directly, Solomon ibn Gabirol, the Kabbalists could borrow Neoplatonic terminology.[21] Although Scholem discerns two tendencies in medieval Kabbalah, the "Gnostic" represented by the *Zohar* and the "philosophical" represented by Azriel of Gerona, the differences between them had more to do with style than with basic issues. The one relied more on mythic symbols, while the other engaged primarily in discursive speculations, but they both struggled with similar conceptual issues, principally involving the problem of creation of the world.

For the Neoplatonists, who emphasized the absolute abstractness of the One, the world is emanated unceasingly through a series of secondary emanations or middle levels.[22] The thirteenth-century mystics were particularly attracted to this doctrine because it could be "Kabbalized" by reinterpreting the emanations as sefirot. Scholem shows that this reinterpretation was actually a misinterpretation because the sefirot in the *Zohar*, for instance, were hypostatizations of God's attributes and therefore represented a movement within God himself rather than outside of him, as was the case with the Neoplatonic middle levels. Some rationalist scholars such as D. H. Joel interpreted the sefirot as external to God, thus solving the problem of his unity, since if the sefirot were actually part of God he would be fragmented into a number of parts.[23] Scholem refutes this nineteenth-century attempt to harmonize the Kabbalah with Neoplatonic philosophy by arguing that the Kabbalists were not afraid to confront certain philosophical problems and to answer them with potentially heretical paradoxes. The problem with emanationist philosophy is its inability to explain why the undifferentiated One should will itself to differentiate and thereby create the diversified world. The Kabbalah's misunderstanding of Neoplatonism was productive because it allowed for the possibility of differentiation within the divine itself, pointing toward a potential solution to a philosophical problem. By playing with heretical formulations, the Kabbalah negated philosophy, but also solved philosophical problems.

The Kabbalah attempted to solve the problem of creation by a "productive misunderstanding" of the traditional rabbinic and philosophical doctrine of *creatio ex nihilo*.[24] Scholem believes that philosophy had reached a dead end with Maimonides in trying to deduce this dogma from logical principles; it only succeeded in undermining the creator God of the Bible. The Kabbalists saved *creatio ex nihilo* and God's free will in creating the world by a Gnostic reinterpretation of the concept of nothingness. Nothingness, which was endowed with ontological reality, was not the same as non-Being. While seeming to adopt philosophical language, the Kabbalists interpreted *creatio ex nihilo* to mean that God himself is the source of nothingness: *creatio ex nihilo* paradoxically means creation out of God himself. This doctrine was a synthesis of the traditional concept of *creatio ex nihilo* and the Neoplatonic notion of emanation of the world out of the essence of God, but it was based on a mythical-Gnostic view of creation of the world out of the divine abyss.

The Kabbalists of the early thirteenth century referred to the hidden God of the Neoplatonists and Gnostics as *ayin* (nothing). They therefore solved the problem of *creatio ex nihilo* by simply equating God with nothingness. Scholem points out, however, that this solution leads to pantheism since, as in Neoplatonism, there would be no difference between God and his creation.[25] To avoid this heresy, such Kabbalists as Azriel of Gerona and Joseph Gikatila introduced a dialectical moment into their speculations: nothingness is not identical with God, but is rather the name of his first emanation or *sefirah* called *keter* (crown). Azriel identified this "nothingness" with the first Neoplatonic emanation, representing God's will. Since the first sefirah is itself the attribute of God's will, one cannot speak of God's emanating the first sefirah by an act of free will. Only the second sefirah can be said to be "created" by God's free will. Since the Bible attributes free will to God as creator, it must be referring to the first sefirah and not to the hidden *ain sof*. In other words, the Bible never mentions the *deus absconditus* because it is only concerned with God's free actions. The Kabbalists were thus able to avoid the potential dualism of Gnostic theology by postulating a dialectical development within God himself which they appropriated from Neoplatonic emanationism. At the same time, the notion that the process of creation must pass through a moment of absolute negation decisively separated God from his creation and thus avoided the problem of pantheism.

This dialectical logic reached its culmination in the Lurianic Kabbalah of the sixteenth century. In the thirteenth century, Azriel had mentioned that the hidden God is indifferent to his emanations and therefore the emanation of the first sefirah could not be properly called an act of creation. But Luria pushed the creative act back into the hidden God himself. God creates nothingness out of himself by contracting himself (*zimzum*). Every act of creation requires a space devoid of God which can only be created by God's self-negation. Despite hints of radical determinism in parts of the Lurianic Kabbalah, Luria managed to restore God's voluntarism without abrogating the philosophical requirement for his hiddenness and ineffability.[26] Scholem argues that the Lurianic Kabbalah was perhaps the most Gnostic and mythological Kabbalistic theory, for despite its geometrical terminology, it essentially wrote a biography of the innermost workings of the divine.[27]

By the infusion of myth into Judaism, the Kabbalah succeeded in preserving monotheism without sacrificing the creator God of the Bible. For the philosophers, God is a static "unmoved mover." The Kabbalah gave this philosophical concept life by infusing it with dialectical dynamism: "[God is conceived as he who is] absolutely living and whose hidden life is considered as a movement of the Endless out of itself and into itself."[28] Scholem's repeated use of the word "dialectical" and the philosophical account he gives to the Kabbalah suggest his explicit assumption of affinities between the Kabbalah and dialectical philosophies such as Hegel's and Schelling's. Through the prism of Hegel's *Logik*, he attempts to give a coherent description of what would appear otherwise a logically paradoxical and confused theosophy. Scholem's implied comparison between the Kabbalah and Hegelian philosophy is reminiscent of Krochmal's attempt to consider the Kabbalah as one of the precursors of the modern idealism, and Scholem acknowledges that Krochmal was the only nineteenth-century Jewish thinker to recognize these parallels.[29]

Scholem's relationship with philosophy is therefore ambivalent. On the one hand, he condemns both medieval and modern rationalist philosophy for evading the fundamental issues of man's psychic existence and for failing to preserve the "reality of the living God." He extols mysticism for succeeding where philosophy failed. But, on the other hand, his treatment of the Kabbalah suggests that Jewish mysticism can best be understood in the context of philosophical issues: although it had its own history apart from philosophy, the Kabbalah addressed philosophical questions and presented cogent solutions.

THE GNOSTIC KABBALAH AND JEWISH ANTINOMIANISM

Scholem's description of the Kabbalistic synthesis of myth and philosophy is no easy compromise. On the contrary, he argues that the Kabbalah was on the brink of heresy since it borrowed its myth from dualistic Gnosticism. Gnosticism frequently rejected all law as originating with the despised creator God; antinomianism became a nihilistic gesture of rebellion against his tyranny.[30] Like Krochmal, Scholem maintains that the antinomian theology of the Sabbatian movement was permeated with Gnostic elements inherited from the Kabbalah. In Sabbatianism, the history of the Gnostic myth in the Kabbalah reached its culmination, and the anarchistic potential in Kabbalistic theology became actual.

In his influential essay "Redemption Through Sin" (1937),[31] Scholem argues that the Sabbatian "mystery of the Godhead" was "nothing less than the totally unexpected revival of the religious beliefs of the ancient Gnostics, albeit in a transvalued form."[32] His analysis focuses on the thought of Abraham Cardozo, who was one of the leading ideologues of the heretical messianic movement. He points out that Cardozo inverted the usual Gnostic theme of a hidden good God.[33] For Cardozo, the hidden God, or "First Cause," did not need to reveal himself. To call him "hidden" actually confuses the issue since he could be known to reason. There was also no particular religious value in knowing him since his laws were the laws of nature. It is the creator God who revealed himself at Sinai and whom Cardozo considered the "good" God. Because of the evils of philosophy, Jews had begun to worship the *deus absconditus* instead of the creator God, but in the messianic days, which Cardozo believed had commenced with Sabbatai Zevi, the good God of Israel would again reveal himself through his Messiah. Although this conception of God was indeed dualistic, it transformed the evil creator God of the Gnostics into the God of Israel.

Perhaps more obviously reminiscent of Gnosticism was the nihilistic theology of Jacob Frank, one of the most radical of the eighteenth-century successors to Sabbatai Zevi.[34] Frank justified his antinomian behavior by a theory of a good God who was not responsible for the creation of the world or the giving of the law. He called on the worshippers of the good God to break the evil law of this world.

According to Scholem, the heretical explosion of Gnostic symbols in Sabbatianism was inherent in Kabbalistic symbolism from the outset.[35] In order to preserve a transcendent God and avoid pantheism, the Kabbalah resorted to ever more dialectical constructions, increasing the contradictions within God himself. These contradictions were resolved beyond human comprehension in the Infinite, a point on which the Kabbalah seems to have differed from medieval philosophy. But from a human perspective, the dialectical paradoxes could easily degenerate into an heretical ideology. The

Sabbatians, Scholem believes, interpreted the spiritual mysteries "materialistically";[36] they understood the symbols of God's self-contraction not as a metaphor but as an actual process within God. They interpreted the radical distinction between a hidden and a revealed God as real, thus justifying the Sabbatian Gnostic heresy. Scholem suggests that this may not have been a total misinterpretation of Kabbalistic symbolism. A symbol for the Kabbalists was an image of a real process, which is itself beyond articulation; it is not merely a human metaphor "imposed" (*übertragen*) on God. If the contradictions within God are only paradoxical from our perspective, then from God's perspective they describe material reality: God actually operates according to a dialectical logic which seems incomprehensible or paradoxical to us. In other words, the "materialistic" interpretation of Kabbalistic symbolism was justified because the symbols were meant from the outset to reflect a higher reality. The Sabbatian heresy was a logical if extreme result of the process of materialistic symbolization in the Kabbalah. The role of mythical symbols within Judaism was ambiguous because the symbols were both constructive and destructive: they were the source for the fruitful mystical reinterpretation of monotheism, but also for its heretical rejection.

The reappearance of heretical Gnosticism in late medieval Judaism returns us to one of our original questions: Was there something like an underground history of Jewish Gnosticism after late antiquity, or rather a series of unconnected recurrences of Gnostic "structures of thought"? Scholem believes in the transmission of actual Eastern Gnostic texts from hand to hand until they surfaced in transmuted form in Europe close to a millenium after their original formulation. His treatment of the origins of Sabbatianism reflects a similar opinion. As we shall see, he believes that the whole history of the Kabbalah prepared the ground for the Sabbatian Gnostic heresy. On the other hand, his justification of pseudepigraphy in his dating of the *Zohar* is a powerful argument for the spontaneous recurrence of Gnostic motifs in a thirteenth-century text. Which, then, is more representative of Scholem's interpretation of the history of Gnosticism in the Kabbalah, his analysis of the *Bahir* or of the *Zohar*?

For Scholem, the two possibilities—an actual literary history of Gnosticism versus a history of its spontaneous recurrence—are not mutually exclusive. In allowing for both possibilities, he suggests that intellectual history can never be a straightforward account of overt influences, especially if the historian tries to relate two movements separated by many centuries. The library of a medieval

Kabbalist might be limited to certain standard mystical works, but they had indirectly absorbed a long and rich intellectual tradition, including many ideas seemingly unrelated to Jewish mysticism itself. Intellectual traditions, Scholem suggests, are often hidden and reach back to remote origins. Hence it is possible that Gnostic texts, translated and transmuted, had an indirect influence on Sabbatian theology through many centuries of literary filters. At the same time, the medieval mystics undertook an intellectual project similar to that of the Gnostics: they consciously rejected philosophy by transforming it into a philosophical myth. Since religious myth, according to Scholem, tries to confront elemental and eternal human fears, it is no surprise that mythic structures of thought should recur in different generations.

Scholem interprets Jewish mysticism as the fruitful encounter between a changing tradition and the creative human mind. Traditional symbols were transformed and reinterpreted to suit the requirements of new historical periods, while the creative process itself was enriched by the incorporation of old motifs. Thirteenth-century Kabbalists absorbed not only rabbinic and philosophical materials, but also the efforts of earlier mystics to understand their own personal experience in terms of the orthodox tradition.

Kabbalah (tradition) meant the belief in mysticism as the true interpretation of Judaism and also the belief in the existence of an esoteric tradition of mystical texts. At times, this tradition actually existed, as the case of the *Bahir*, and at times it was established by pseudepigraphy, as with the *Zohar*. If the dominant trend in the mystical esoteric tradition was Gnostic, this was so because Gnosticism suited the intellectual needs of the mystics. Both the real history of Jewish Gnosticism and the original creation of "Gnostic" texts in the Middle Ages were part of the same process: the mystical reinterpretation of rabbinical and philosophical Judaism as the true "original" interpretation. There was no contradiction between antiquity and originality for the Kabbalists, since the notion of an esoteric tradition guaranteed both.

To summarize Scholem's relation to the nineteenth-century interpretation of the Kabbalah: The Kabbalah must be understood as a genuine religious movement with its own inner history. It was not a series of unconnected reactions against rationalist Jewish philosophy, as Graetz thought, or a product of the inner dialectics of Jewish philosophy, as Neumark believed. Because neither Graetz nor Neumark was prepared to admit the existence of an underground tradition of myth within Jewish mysticism, they missed the fact that the Kabbalah has its own unique history.

Scholem does not, however, accept Berdichevsky's and Buber's assertion of an entirely separate subterranean history of myth in Judaism. The recurring outbreaks of myth can be found in the very heart of rabbinic Judaism, not on its periphery. In some cases the mystics were themselves legal authorities. Although the Kabbalah has its own history, its development was intertwined with rabbinic and philosophical Judaism. By reinterpreting myth and philosophy for its own purposes, the Kabbalah created a paradoxical hybrid: "Orthodox Gnosticism." The very ability of the Kabbalah to revitalize Judaism by a mystical reinterpretation of mythical symbols relied on its proximity to the normative tradition.

Scholem therefore accepts Krochmal's description of the Kabbalah as Gnostic, but with no negative value judgment. Krochmal saw Jewish history as a progressive history of consciousness in which the Kabbalah occupied an intermediate stage. The early Kabbalah, which resembled philosophy, degenerated in the late Middle Ages into an ultimately heretical myth. For Scholem, the recurrence of myth throughout Jewish history is a positive sign of vitality. His history of the Kabbalah implicitly overturns Krochmal's belief in philosophical progress, which was characteristic of the nineteenth century in general. Even the most abstract forms of monotheism require the infusion of potentially heretical myth to preserve their psychological and spiritual relevance. On the other hand, the continual recurrence of myth in a monotheistic religion does not necessarily suggest a Nietzschean cyclical theory of history. Scholem's three-stage scheme for religious development points out the difference between the mythological period and the later conscious myth of the mystics. Religious consciousness has its own history in which man's use of myth develops and changes, but his need for myth never disappears.

SCHOLEM AND MODERN APPROACHES TO MYTH

Scholem's evaluation of myth as the driving, vital force in Jewish mysticism is related to certain attempts in German intellectual life in the early twentieth century to give greater legitimacy to the scientific study of myth. Religion, philosophy, and psychology all contributed to a new estimation of the continuing influence of "primitive" modes of thought.

Scholem's treatment of myth in Jewish mysticism shares with the counter-histories of Buber and Berdichevsky the emphasis on irrationalism as the dynamic force in history. However, his historiography must be distinguished from their attempt to create myths in order to transcend normative history. As an historian rather than a writer of myth, Scholem is a child of the *Religionswissenschaft-schule* of the late nineteenth and early twentieth centuries. Although his academic training was in mathematics and philosophy, he obtained his doctorate in Semitic philology from Munich where he came in contact with the particular methodology of the German scholars of ancient Near Eastern religions.[37]

In his famous and controversial lectures, *Babel und Bibel* (1902),[38] Friedrich Delitzsch summarized the position of the Religionswissenschaftschule, arguing that the whole Near East shared a common religious heritage consisting of a body of related myths. Delitzsch was partially motivated by academic antisemitism as he attacked the unique revelatory character of Israelite religion, but he also elucidated the basis for a comparative approach to ancient religion. He showed how the discoveries of Assyriology had shed considerable light on the Bible's true literary origins, which were not a divine revelation but part and parcel of a Near Eastern tradition predating the Israelites.

In order to show the interdependence of ancient religions, the historians of religion typically traced the transfer of certain mythological topoi from one particular religious tradition to another.[39] The main instrument for this kind of historiography became philology, which called for the precise identification of the origin and history of a particular word or motif. When Scholem calls himself a "philologian," he has in mind the philological method of tracing the history of the recurrence of Gnostic topoi throughout the history of the Kabbalah.

The Religionswissenschaftschule was itself particularly interested in Gnosticism as a religious myth that had developed throughout the Mediterranean world of late antiquity. Here was a system of thought which might prove the universality of the ancient religious mind. In the nineteenth century, scholars such as Adolf von Harnack considered Gnosticism "the acute hellenization of Christianity," meaning that it was primarily a philosophical reaction against Christianity. But Orientalists of the Religionswissenschaftschule at the beginning of the twentieth century, such as Wilhelm Bousset in his *Hauptprobleme der Gnosis* (1907), suggested that Gnosticism consisted of a variety of mythological motifs derived from many separate Oriental traditions. The new interpretation emphasized Gnosticism's mythological character as opposed to the earlier desire to consider it a type of perverse philosophy and also asserted Gnosticism's original independence from Christianity.

The problem with interpretations like Bousset's was that it became increasingly difficult to see a unified phenomenon called

"Gnosticism" underlying the welter of different mythological traditions. Was there an essential definition of Gnosticism? In 1934 Hans Jonas tried to answer this question in his *Gnosis und spätantiker Geist*. Departing from the usual philosophy versus myth argument, Jonas tried to define an essential spirit of Gnosticism, "to understand the spirit speaking through these voices and in its light to restore an intelligible unity to the baffling multiplicity of its expressions."[40] Influenced strongly by phenomenology, Jonas tried to intuit an essence of Gnosticism as a discrete religious movement that drew its vocabulary from the philosophical and mythological traditions of late antiquity. Hence Jonas defined Gnosticism as at once a philosophical myth and a mythic philosophy under the rubric of a Gnostic *religion*. The essence of this religion was the theme of alienation from the cosmos. Jonas suggested the conceptual connection between Gnosticism and modern existentialism based on this notion of alienation, which entered Western culture in late antiquity and never left it; existentialism was only its latest incarnation. A follower of Heidegger, Jonas therefore implicitly defined himself as a modern-day Gnostic.[41]

There are many similarities between Jonas and Scholem as heirs to and dissenters from the Religionswissenschaftschule. Scholem, who knew Jonas in the 1930s, also approaches the Kabbalah as a legitimate religious expression with its own unique history. Although Scholem does not limit his definition of Gnosticism to one "essence," he still relies frequently on Jonas's concept of cosmic alienation, and even quotes extensively from Jonas in his discussion of the Frankists as Gnostic heretics.[42] In the final analysis, the problem of the Kabbalah strongly resembles the problem of Gnosticism since both are characterized by a "baffling" multiplicity of expressions. Where the nineteenth-century historians saw only a chaotic jumble of incoherent texts, Scholem imposes a rational order upon his material by organizing it with the term "Gnosticism."

Jonas's comparison with modern existentialism suggests the possibility that Gnosticism as a concept might not be limited to one historical period. Scholem's "discovery" of Gnosticism in the Middle Ages, as late as Sabbatianism and even Hasidism, is a bold extension of this suggestion, although he arrived at his initial conclusions in 1928 before meeting Jonas. The Religionswissenschaftschule as a whole encouraged the tracing of Gnostic motifs beyond the world of late antiquity. These historians believed that the religious ideas developed in late antiquity would play a continuing role in the Middle Ages, often in underground heretical movements. One example of this methodology is Hans Liebeschütz's *Das alle-*

gorische Weltbild der Heiligen Hildegard von Bingen (1930). Liebeschütz, who also wrote extensively on modern German-Jewish
thought, attempted to demonstrate the reappearance of certain
Gnostic motifs in that twelfth-century Christian mystic.[43] Just as
Liebeschütz traced these themes from late antiquity to medieval
Christian mysticism, so Scholem does for the history of Jewish
mysticism. The world of late antiquity produced certain fruitful
ideas that influenced all subsequent religious thought. Proof of the
continuity of these traditions is evidence of the unextinguishable
relevance of certain powerful myths.

From a broader perspective, Scholem as an historian of religion
fits into modern attempts to give scientific explanations for the continuing role of myth in human consciousness. German romantic
philosophers such as Schelling and Baader rediscovered myth and
gave it philosophical legitimacy. The young Schelling called for a
union of the "monotheism of reason" and the "polytheism of the
imagination."[44] In his later *Philosophie der Mythologie*, Schelling
wrote about the ostensible contradiction between rational philosophy and myth: "But in this very opposition lies a challenge and a
specific task, to discover reason in this seeming unreason, meaning
in this apparent meaninglessness . . . Our intention must . . . be to
make the form itself appear necessary, hence rational."[45] Myth was
not foreign to the task of philosophy since it could be studied, like
art or literature, as a legitimate artifact of consciousness. Myth was
no more an "invention" of the mind than language. Although neither had any "objective" existence, as parts of consciousness they
both deserved philosophical investigation. Idealism made it possible to consider myth a legitimate part of the innate structure of
the mind. Scholem acknowledges his debt to Schelling's legitimization and philosophical treatment of myth in the beginning of his essay on "Kabbalah and Myth."[46]

In the twentieth century, Ernst Cassirer rediscovered Schelling's
philosophy of mythology.[47] Cassirer argued that myths are not allegories but symbols, an argument identical to Scholem's. Symbols
were central to Cassirer's philosophy as modes by which consciousness appropriates the world. All descriptions of reality, whether
myth or science, use symbols to order data. The difference between myth and science is not that the first has a distorted picture
of reality while the other sees things "as they are," but that science
is aware of its use of hypotheses (the scientific form of symbols).[48]
Still, because they are commensurable, science can be used to understand myth.

Scholem heard Cassirer lecture in Berlin in 1916-17 and, although he says he was not impressed,[49] his views on myth resemble Cassirer's. Through Walter Benjamin, Scholem came into touch with the Neo-Kantian philosophical appropriation of myth.[50] From his discussions with Benjamin about myth, as well as from his hostile reading of Hermann Cohen, Scholem in 1918 began to develop his own ideas about the Jewish struggle against mythology, and came to the conclusion that myth was never defeated by monotheism.[51]

Scholem is also intellectually close to the Jungian psychological interest in myth, although he never adopts the theory of archetypes. Jung argued against Freud that dreams should not be interpreted as fixed signs but as elastic mythological symbols. He understood symbols as "expressions of a content not yet consciously recognized or conceptually formulated."[52] Jung was able to create, at least in his own mind, a less dogmatic system than Freud's. Scholem's own description of Kabbalistic symbols has the same antidogmatic motivation: the Kabbalistic symbols are expressions of the inexpressible, evocative "names for the nameless."

Jung transposed individual dream symbolism into collective myth in his theory of archetypes.[53] A precise correspondence exists between the psychic history of an individual and the lexicon of the collective psyche. The study of myth is therefore the social dimension of individual psychology.[54] Jung theorized that dreams serve as forms of compensation for individual problems in the conscious psyche; on a collective level, myth compensates for conscious rationalism. To the extent that rationalism and materialism had increased in modern consciousness, mythical compensation had also increased in the collective unconscious.[55]

Jung's dialectic between the conscious and unconscious, repeated on the social level as myth, resembles Scholem's dialectic between rationalism and irrationalism in Jewish history. Scholem believes that myth compensates for the excessive efforts of rationalism to preserve monotheism. Jung was attacked for favoring irrationalism; so, too, Scholem has been attacked for glorifying nihilistic forces in Jewish history. But Jung pointed out that an excess of one leads to exaggerated compensation by the other. Scholem also conceives of a healthy balance between the contradictory forces in history, and does not glorify the powers of destruction. Myth is necessary, but also dangerous.

Scholem's personal connection to the Jungians came through Erich Neumann, who died in 1960 in Tel Aviv.[56] Neumann applied Jung's psychological categories to an intensive investigation of myth, notably the *Magna Mater* symbolism.[57] The similarity be-

tween Neumann's and Scholem's reevaluation of myth can be seen
in a striking passage in Neumann's *Origin and History of Consciousness*. In a discussion of sexual symbolism in creation myths,
Neumann objects to those who call these images obscene:

> the sexual symbolism that appears in primitive cult and ritual
> has a sacral and transpersonal import, as everywhere in mythol-
> ogy. It symbolizes the creative element, not personal genitality
> . . . Judaism and Christianity between them—and this includes
> Freud—have had a heavy and disastrous hand in this [personal-
> istic] misunderstanding. The desecration of pagan values in the
> struggle for monotheism and for a conscious ethic was neces-
> sary, and historically an advance, but it resulted in a complete
> distortion of the primordial world of those times.[58]

In Neumann's attack on Freud, there is a structural correspondence
to Scholem's critique of both rabbinical Judaism and the Wissenschaft des Judentums. The suppression of myth has historical justification in Judaism, but myth is fundamental to religious life. The
Kabbalah corrects the imbalance in the collective Jewish psyche.
Moreover, just as Jungians claim to have corrected the imbalance
of "repressive" Freudian psychoanalysis, so Scholem proposes his
historiography as the necessary corrective to the Wissenschaft des
Judentums.

Scholem developed many of his more general reflections on the
Kabbalah at the Jungian Eranos Conferences in Switzerland, where
Neumann was one of the guiding lights.[59] Despite his personal and
intellectual proximity to the Jungians, however, Scholem cannot be
considered a Jungian historian. As he himself says:

> In treating the history and world of the Kabbalah, using the con-
> ceptual terminology of psychoanalysis—either the Freudian or
> the Jungian version—did not seem fruitful to me. Even though I
> should have had a strong affinity to Jung's concepts, which were
> close to religious concepts, I refrained from using them . . . I par-
> ticularly avoided using the theory of archetypes.[60]

I believe that Scholem avoids Jungian terminology because of his
hesitation to reduce religious symbolism to psychology. He feels
that the limitation of symbolism to the private world of the individual creates a spiritual vacuum. There is, however, a mysterious
dimension to the world that has its source outside the psyche.[61]
Where psychologists reduce symbols and myths to products of the

mind, Scholem, with the Kabbalists, seems to believe that they have an ontological status of their own corresponding to some spiritual reality. Scholem's philosophical and philological examination of myth as a potent force in Jewish history leaves the door open for a form of genuine spirituality in a secular world.

7.   *Messianism*

Scholem's philosophy of Jewish history becomes evident from his underground history of orthodox Gnosticism. Monotheism was revitalized by the infusion of irrational myth, reinterpreted by the mystics. Rationalism and irrationalism, monotheism and myth, are dialectically interrelated. Judaism is the history of the struggle between contradictory forces, and it is that internal dialectic, rather than the infiltration of foreign ideas, which gives Jewish history its dynamism.

We have seen that the Gnostic myth Scholem finds throughout the history of Jewish mysticism barely concealed a deeply heretical impulse. Gnosticism in late antiquity was prone to antinomianism and nihilism because it believed that all law originated with the evil creator God. Jewish mysticism transformed Gnosticism into an orthodox myth, but the threat of its lapsing into heretical antinomianism never disappeared: in appropriating Gnosticism, the mystics played with heretical fire. In the Sabbatian messianic movement of the seventeenth century, the Gnostic myth finally realized its heretical potential: Scholem suggests that the extreme Gnosticism present in Sabbatian theology was but the logical culmination of the whole history of Jewish mysticism.

The congruence of heresy and messianism was, according to Scholem, no coincidence. During the Middle Ages, Jews with heretical impulses could find an outlet in conversion to Christianity or Islam: as a minority community, they were less likely to develop internal heretical sects since dissatisfaction could be relieved by leaving the community altogether. Within the Jewish world, however, "there was only one power that could bring about such an outbreak [of heresy]: that is messianism. It is the great catalyst in Judaism."[1] For Scholem, messianism served the same function as myth in ventilating the stuffy and cloistered Jewish world with an "anarchic breeze." It could do so because it was frequently the product of myth. When the potent forces of Gnostic mysticism were liberated from meditative speculation and directed toward messianic action, they produced the greatest internal upheaval of the Jewish Middle Ages, Sabbatianism. Scholem argues, moreover, that this mass messianic movement, generated by a development within Jewish mysticism, decisively undermined the traditional medieval world and inaugurated the modern period of Jewish history.

Scholem defines two types of messianism: restorative and utopian-catastrophic.[2] Restorative messianism strove for the return of the Jews to political sovereignty, particularly as it was thought to have existed under the kingdom of David. Although this type of messianism certainly preached a radical change in the Jews' exilic existence, it did so strictly in the framework of tradition: messianic times would close the circle of history by restoring the Jews to their original state, thus making possible the fulfillment of all the commandments. The utopian-catastrophic view, which Scholem frequently calls apocalypticism, envisioned instead an entirely new world, unlike anything experienced previously, except perhaps in a mythical Eden. According to the apocalyptic theory of history, the new aeon would be preceded by a sudden rupture in historical continuity, and might be characterized by a radically new law; apocalyptic messianism was therefore prone to heretical antinomianism.

For Scholem, the history of Jewish messianism must be understood as a dialectic between the traditionalist and apocalyptic poles.[3] These two contradictory yet complementary tendencies gave messianism its revolutionary dynamism and at the same time held it within certain bounds. The messianic desire for full redemption of all the Jewish people never disappeared from Jewish history, although Scholem speaks of its occasional "neutralization." With most Jewish nationalist historians, Scholem believes that messianism is one of the central themes of Jewish history, although we shall see that he defines it more radically. He castigates the nineteenth-century Jewish thinkers for distorting and suppressing what he considers the authentic forces of Jewish messianism.

THE WISSENSCHAFT DES JUDENTUMS AND MESSIANISM

Jewish thought in the nineteenth century typically renounced both the restorative and utopian poles of Jewish messianism. It is well known that Jews felt compelled by the terms of emancipation to replace their belief in a Messiah who would restore them to their ancestral homeland with an acceptance of the European nations as their only real home. The price of emancipation, exacted perhaps most brutally by Napoleon in his questions to the Assembly of Jewish Notables and the Sanhedrin,[4] was renunciation of the nationalist side of Jewish messianism.

The Jewish response to this demand was frequently not to abandon messianism altogether, but to displace its target from the land of Israel to Europe. When Joseph II of Austria promulgated his relatively enlightened *privilegium* of 1780, certain *Maskilim* (Jewish enlighteners) hailed him as the Messiah.[5] In 1822 the venerable Maskil, Lazarus Ben David, disputed the claim that belief in a Jewish Messiah is central to the Jewish tradition, arguing that "no man can reproach the Jew when he finds his Messiah in the good princes who make him equal to all other citizens and give him the hope of achieving complete fulfillment of all civic rights and responsibilities."[6] Later in the century, the Russian-Jewish poet Y. L. Gordon compared Alexander II, who had eased some of the restrictions imposed on the Jews by his predecessors, to Cyrus the Great of Persia, whom the author of Deutero-Isaiah had called the "anointed" (*mashiah*) of God.[7] All of these characterizations of benevolent non-Jewish rulers as the Messiah were part of a long tradition, but the eighteenth- and nineteenth-century appropriation of the tradition concealed a radical innovation: the Maskilim used a traditional form of praise for a congenial gentile ruler to broadcast their loyalty to the modern state. Secularized messianism had become a tool of assimilation and apologetics.

Another common Jewish reaction to the demands of emancipation was to transform messianism into universalism. Perhaps uncomfortable in transferring messianic ideals directly from the Jewish nation to a non-Jewish nation, Enlighteners like Abraham Geiger claimed that the true message of messianism all along had not been nationalism but universalism. Geiger asserted that Christianity is false universalism because it never passed through a national stage of development; but Judaism, because it did outgrow nationalism, is the true teacher of universalist messianism.[8]

If religious and political apologists purged messianism of its restorative-national aspect, nineteenth-century thinkers also actively suppressed its apocalyptic side. I have shown earlier how Nachman Krochmal and Heinrich Graetz considered Sabbatianism the ultimate perversion of Judaism. Believing in the continued, uninterrupted progress of consciousness, they denied the existence of apocalyptic breaks in the historical continuum. They considered the modern age the culmination of Jewish history, not a radical departure from it. Whereas the nineteenth-century believers in progress shared with apocalyptic messianism the belief in a new age, better than any that had preceded it, they abandoned the theory of a catastrophic break in history.

The nineteenth-century transformation of Jewish messianism found its clearest and most radical expression in Hermann Cohen, as Scholem himself suggests: "Hermann Cohen, surely as distinguished a representative of the liberal and rationalistic reinterpretation of the Messianic idea in Judaism as one could find, was driven by his religion of reason into becoming a genuine and unhampered utopian who would have liked to liquidate the restorative factor entirely."[9] In Cohen's utopian universalism, we find equally the suppression of the restorative and apocalyptic aspects of messianism. Cohen's utopianism was based on his distinction between mythology and monotheism. Mythology has no real concept of historical progress and instead harks back to an idyllic Golden Age (*das goldene Zeitalter*).[10] Monotheism, on the other hand, does not seek to return to the happiness of the Golden Age, but instead to increase knowledge of the true God. Since the process of acquiring knowledge is infinite, monotheism is necessarily oriented toward the future in which knowledge will increase. Unlike mythology, which is romantic and reactionary, monotheism is the aspiration for infinite time.[11] The messianic age will truly be an "age of culture" since it will be the age of complete knowledge. It will be a utopia in the precise sense that it does not exist now in any place but instead remains an ideal in the process of eventual realization.

Cohen defined messianism as universalism and, in his brief history of the messianic idea,[12] placed its origin in the idea of monotheism. Messianism derives from monotheism since the idea of a unique God requires a unified mankind.[13] This universalist idea was already implicit in prophetic monotheism, but it was not completely actualized in biblical times since it was expressed in Jewish nationalism. The destruction of the Jewish state was a positive event because it allowed Israel to bring its universalist message to fruition. Cohen, along with a general nineteenth-century current, therefore inverted the idea that the exile was a punishment for Israel's sins and found in it a great opportunity for the development of messianism. In his famous polemics against Zionism, Cohen argued that the Jews, as the international leaven of messianism, had superseded the need for a nation-state.[14]

As a universal religion—the "divine dew among the nations"—Judaism had come closest to realization of the messianic idea implicit in its original monotheism. Cohen saw an ultimate identity of purpose between German nationalism and Jewish messianism. The

German national spirit was "the spirit of classical humanism and true universalism,"[15] while the Jews, no longer a nation limited by place, were the international religious emissaries of the same values. In his highly patriotic series of articles "Deutschtum und Judentum," written during World War I, Cohen defended Germany as the true harbinger of the coming messianic order. Since Germany was the nation representing the Jewish religious spirit, Jews around the world owed Germany "a debt of filial piety" for fighting "the just war [in] preparation for perpetual peace."[16]

SCHOLEM'S RESTORATION OF APOCALYPTICISM TO MESSIANISM

Jewish nationalist historiography at the beginning of the twentieth century quite naturally attacked the tendency of the Wissenschaft des Judentums to liquidate the restorative aspect of messianism. Ben Zion Dinur made messianism, which he defined as the desire to return to the land of Israel, the central theme of Jewish history. Joseph Klausner also wrote extensively on the historical heritage of Jewish messianism in support of his own militant nationalism.[17]

The new historiography did not emphasize as strongly the catastrophic-apocalyptic side of messianism. The nationalists frequently wanted to prove that Zionism was the culmination and fulfillment of Jewish history rather than its abrogation. To be sure, writers like Berdichevsky, who called for a radical break with normative, exilic Jewish history, may be considered apocalyptic, but with the exception perhaps of Shai Hurwitz they rarely studied Jewish apocalyptic movements of the past in support of their own position. Even so radical a writer as Martin Buber deliberately defined Jewish messianism as prophetic and antiapocalyptic. In his essay "Prophetie und Apokalyptik,"[18] Buber argued that apocalyptic motifs entered Judaism from Iranian sources and were therefore alien to the Jewish prophetic spirit. Buber understood the true messianism not as an end of history, but as the sanctification of the world in history. In place of an "end of days," Buber substituted the possibility of redeemed moments throughout history, the "All-Day of Redemption."[19]

Scholem's great contribution to this movement of revision was his almost single-handed rehabilitation and legitimization of apocalypticism as a continuing motif in Jewish messianism. He translated into Jewish scholarship an important trend already developed in the historiography of Christianity. Liberal Christian scholars, epitomized by Harnack, had considered the historical Jesus an ethical preacher and discounted any apocalyptic interpretation of early

Christianity. Franz Overbeck, Johannes Weiss, and Albert Schweitzer overturned this interpretation of Christianity and replaced it
with the view that the original Christianity was a Jewish apocalyptic sect that revolted against the world and did not transmit an ethical message.[20]

At about the same time, other scholars of Christianity began to
discover the radical apocalyptic movements in later Christian history which had been suppressed or forgotten by nineteenth-century
rationalism. K. Holl and Ernst Bloch drew attention to Thomas
Münzer and the Anabaptists, while Albrecht Ritschl and Erich Seeberg examined the roots of radical Pietism.[21] Karl Mannheim, in his
Ideologie und Utopie (1929), analyzed the ideological functions of
different types of utopianism and gave a particularly acute account
of the character and historical role of chiliastic utopianism.[22]

Scholem must be seen as part of this rediscovery of the historical
role of apocalypticism.[23] Like his colleagues in Christian historiography, he finds vitality in Jewish apocalyptic movements which
others had dismissed as degenerate: "It has been one of the strang-
est errors of the modern Wissenschaft des Judentums to deny the
continuity of Jewish apocalypticism. The endeavors of leading
scholars to dissociate apocalyptic from rabbinic Judaism and to as-
sociate it exclusively with Christianity have contributed so much to
the modern falsification of Jewish history and the concealment of
some of its most dynamic forces, both constructive and destructive."[24] As with his investigations of the role of myth in Jewish
thought, Scholem argues that ostensibly heretical ideas actually
played a legitimate role within Jewish history and were not insidi-
ously infiltrated from the outside. Apocalypticism was not a
Christian or Iranian idea, but had its roots in the indigenous soil of
Judaism itself. In the persistent dialectic between restorative and
apocalyptic messianism in Jewish history, apocalypticism always
appeared as the vital force in messianic movements.[25] Although the
apocalyptic motif was partially suppressed in the Middle Ages by
rationalists like Maimonides, it never disappeared. Like mysticism,
it was not entirely alien to the great legal authorities:

For a number of [the great men of *Halakhah*], apocalypticism is
not a foreign element and is not felt to be in contradiction to the
realm of *Halakhah*. From the point of view of the *Halakhah* . . .
Judaism appears as a well-ordered house and it is a profound
truth that a well-ordered house is a dangerous thing. Something
of messianic apocalypticism penetrates into this house: perhaps I
can best describe it as a kind of anarchic breeze.[26]

Scholem's interpretation of Judaism therefore emphasizes the heretical and revolutionary impulses in messianism as the true driving forces in Jewish history. For Scholem, historical change, which is necessary if a tradition is to remain alive, comes through the revolutionary struggle of contradictory principles. History does not consist of eternal gradual progress, as the nineteenth century believed, but of apocalyptic ruptures. The central role that apocalyptic messianism plays in Scholem's historiography is surely a consequence of this radical view of historical change.

Scholem's attack on the nineteenth-century censorship of apocalypticism must be understood in the general context of his hostility to the attempt to impose a dogmatic definition on Judaism. By arbitrarily restricting Judaism to only certain historical phenomena, the nineteenth-century scholars had ignored the most vital forces in Jewish history. The relegation of apocalypticism to Christianity was a case in point. In his analysis of the Sabbatian theology of Nathan of Gaza, perhaps the most important Sabbatian propagandist, Scholem writes that Nathan's doctrine of

faith as independent of, and indeed outweighing, all outward religious acts and symbols is distinctly Christian in character . . . But however this may be . . . this proclamation did not provoke the reaction one would have expected if some of today's clichés regarding the 'essence' of Judaism and of Christianity were correct . . . There is no way of telling a priori what beliefs are possible or impossible within the framework of Judaism . . . The 'Jewishness' in the religiosity of any particular period is not measured by dogmatic criteria that are unrelated to actual historical circumstances, but solely by what sincere Jews do, in fact, believe, or—at least—consider to be legitimate possibilities.[27]

It is interesting that, in his refutation of nineteenth-century dogmatism, Scholem formulates his view of Jewish history in terms rather similar to Hermann Cohen's utopianism. Cohen had criticized purely restorative messianism for seeing history as a closed circle, whereas he defined utopianism as directed toward an open and unknown future. As a Zionist, Scholem is of course much more sympathetic to the restorative strains in messianism, but he too adopts a utopian approach to history. Yet he gives an antidogmatic twist quite different from Cohen's: "The phenomenon called Judaism does not end on a particular date and I do not think it is likely to end so long as a living Judaism exists. But there is something living that is beyond dogmatic definition . . . Judaism includes *uto-*

pian aspects that have not yet been discovered."[28] Like Cohen,
Scholem sees Jewish history as open-ended, but he concludes that
Judaism cannot therefore be dogmatically defined.

The study of Jewish apocalypticism and Sabbatianism in particular became a powerful weapon for Scholem in shattering dogmatic
definitions of Judaism by showing how censored "heresies" in Jewish history were just as legitimate as the normative tradition. The
argument that the Sabbatian messianic heretics were part of Jewish
history became the cornerstone of his counter-history. As a result,
his *Sabbatai Ṣevi* attracted strong criticism by several Israeli scholars, notably Baruch Kurzweil and R. J. Zvi Werblowsky, who saw
in it the extreme expression of Scholem's use of historiography to
destroy traditional concepts of Judaism.[29] These critics argued that,
by claiming that Sabbatianism was a central episode in Jewish history and that the Sabbatian theology was as important as normative rabbinical thought, Scholem had subverted any coherent
definition of Judaism. We shall return repeatedly to the substance
of these accusations, particularly those of Kurzweil, in the remaining chapters of this book.

As his student Isaiah Tishby has pointed out,[30] Scholem's effort
to legitimize the Sabbatians in Jewish history was not based solely
on the claim that a large number of Jews believed in Sabbatai Zevi.
The Sabbatian theologians must be considered legitimate Jewish
thinkers because they developed their radical theology in the vocabulary of traditional Jewish symbols. Where earlier historians
had considered the Sabbatians demented rebels devoid of theological originality, Scholem not only demonstrates the sophistication
and originality of Sabbatian theology, but also argues that its roots
were firmly implanted in the history of the Kabbalah. Sabbatianism was not an aberration of Jewish history or a wild departure
from traditional Judaism as the result of non-Jewish influences, but
a movement whose origins lay in the heart of the legitimate tradition and whose heretical theology developed as a plausible offshoot
of accepted concepts.

THE DIALECTICAL PREPARATION OF SABBATIANISM

Although Scholem had learned of Sabbatianism from Zalman
Rubaschoff in his student days, he does not seem to have con-
sidered it the focus of his Kabbalistic research until 1927, when he
discovered a manuscript in Oxford by the Marrano Sabbatian,
Abraham Miguel Cardozo.[31] His 1928 article on "Die Theologie des
Sabbatianismus im Lichte Abraham Cardosos" and his "Miẓvah ha-
Ba'ah B'avera" (Redemption Through Sin) in 1936 showed that he

viewed the apocalyptic and heretical theology of Sabbatianism as the culmination of the history of the Kabbalah.[32] By reconstructing Scholem's history of the Kabbalah as preparation for the Sabbatian outburst, we can see his dialectical philosophy of history at work. From an inward, spiritualized messianic doctrine, the Kabbalah developed into the driving force behind the mass messianic movement of the seventeenth century. Apocalyptic messianism, which never vanished from the Jewish consciousness, was cultivated and nourished until it burst onto the stage of history as Sabbatianism. In Sabbatianism, moreover, the apocalyptic elements in messianism joined forces with the underground tradition of Gnosticism in the Kabbalah to make an explosive mixture that would demolish the traditional Jewish world.

With the exception of the thirteenth-century *Sefer ha-Temunah*, which propounded a theory of historical cycles, each represented by different and contradictory Torahs,[33] the early medieval Kabbalah was not especially interested in eschatology. It focused instead on issues of theosophy and cosmogony: the beginning rather than the end of history. The ecstatic and contemplative absorption in esoteric matters of creation guaranteed "a type of individual non-messianic redemption . . . One should not see [the early Kabbalists] as followers of a movement to alter radically the style and pace of Jewish life."[34] There is a seeming contradiction between this formulation and the criteria Scholem sets up for defining Jewish messianism. He claims that Jewish messianism is characterized by its social and historical dimension, while Christianity emphasizes inner, spiritual redemption.[35] The early Kabbalah, however, which Scholem describes as a belief in "non-messianic redemption," seems to have deemphasized the traditional Jewish concern for national redemption. We have here another example of Scholem's desire to legitimize messianic expressions that would normally be excluded from Judaism, even by his own criteria.

The phrase "non-messianic redemption" suggests that mystical contemplation rather than historical activity brings liberation. Scholem is careful to indicate that he does not consider the early Kabbalah to have negated messianism but rather to have "neutralized" it. The term "neutralization," which Scholem used for the first time in 1934 in an essay on the Kabbalah after the Spanish expulsion,[36] means the suppression of the restorative and apocalyptic elements in messianism, but not their complete liquidation. By focusing on the primordial harmony of God and the cosmos, the early Kabbalah prepared the ground for a radical shift of emphasis to social redemption. This shift resulted from the trauma of the expulsion from Spain in 1492.

The desire for redemption became acute as a result of the expulsion and attendant persecutions. The Kabbalists responded to the historical crisis by transposing it to a cosmic framework: the desire for historical redemption was reinterpreted as a symbol of the mystical desire to return the cosmos to its original harmony.[37] The metahistorical concerns of the early Kabbalists prepared the way for the entrance of the Kabbalah into the realm of history: "Everything internal became external: the penetration of the Kabbalist into the profundities of creation was overturned entirely at the time of the great emotional revolution and became religious activity in the community."[38] Scholem argues that the Kabbalah moved to fill a spiritual vacuum following the expulsion from Spain: traditional Jewish theology was unable to account for the historical crisis and to offer solace, but the Kabbalah, having prepared itself in the "underground," emerged as the authoritative theology of a Judaism in crisis.

It was through the Lurianic Kabbalah, developed in Safed in the middle of the sixteenth century, that Jewish mysticism became a public, widely accepted theology.[39] The Lurianic Kabbalah proposed a cosmic myth of exile and redemption which mirrored the actual historical experience of the Jews. Luria described the exile and redemption of the Jews as a symbol for a movement within God himself: God had created the world in order to rid himself of the seeds of evil. In this catharsis (*zimzum* and *shevirat ha-kelim*), part of God went into exile from himself. The process of redemption, which actually began at the moment of catharsis, consists in restoring the scattered, exiled sparks of divinity to their primordial harmony. The process of creation thus became synonymous with cosmic exile, and redemption with the restoration (*tikkun*) of cosmic order.

The person of the Messiah was of little importance to Luria since redemption does not come "suddenly, like a thief in the night," but is a long, gradual process extending back to creation. Luria gave man an active role in the restoration of the divine sparks: each generation must fulfill its quota of "restorations." Against the belief of some secularists that Jewish messianism was always passive in the Middle Ages, Scholem's repeated emphasis on Luria's importance reveals the profoundly activist potentiality in mysticism. If the early Kabbalah was quietistic, it ultimately developed into a mystical doctrine teaching man's active role in the cosmos.

The possibility of messianic activism inherent in the Lurianic Kabbalah became explicit in Sabbatianism. The relationship between the Lurianic Kabbalah and Sabbatianism forms the cornerstone of Scholem's theory of how the Kabbalah broke out of its

cloister and became the motivating force for one of the greatest
mass movements of the Jewish Middle Ages. In the 1920s, even before his first study of Sabbatianism, he suspected the possible influence of the "apocalyptic atmosphere in Safed" in the sixteenth century on the messianic movement of the seventeenth.[40]

With the declaration of Sabbatai Zevi as Messiah by Nathan of
Gaza in 1665, Kabbalistic messianism became a social movement.
The presumed completion of the mystical restoration of divine
sparks made it possible for the new messianic age to manifest itself,
as it were, in the person of Sabbatai Zevi. The process of transformation of Kabbalistic messianism from a personal, internal concern in the early Kabbalah to a historical myth reached completion
in Sabbatian theology. The mystical "non-messianic redemption"
was transmuted into restorative messianism, but with an apocalyp-
tic-cosmic dimension. Hence the dialectic between utopian and
restorative messianism found its most potent expression not in Maimonides' rationalist political messianism, but in antinomian apocalypticism.

As if to symbolize the end of the internal mystical stage of messianism and the beginning of its external historical completion,
Nathan of Gaza banned the use of the Lurianic *kavvanot*, which
were the meditations used in prayer to hasten the restoration of divine sparks.[41] Because he believed that an entirely new aeon of history had begun, Nathan considered the Lurianic Kabbalah to be
obsolete, just as, later, radical Sabbatian theology would consider
the whole body of Jewish law obsolete: in Sabbatianism, the antinomian and revolutionary potentialities in apocalyptic messianism
became frighteningly actual.

The Lurianic Kabbalah therefore prepared the soil for Sabbatianism, only to be negated. The relationship between the two serves a
number of important functions in Scholem's work. He wants to
show that the history of the Kabbalah was the major source of
Sabbatianism and that therefore the Kabbalah had widespread historical impact despite its esoteric character. As I have already mentioned, Scholem judges Sabbatianism to have been primarily a
religious movement and therefore caused by a development in religious consciousness. This role, he argues, could only have been
played by the Lurianic Kabbalah, which provided the Sabbatians
with their messianic vocabulary even as they radicalized its meaning. By portraying Sabbatianism as part of the Jewish religious tradition and not a desperate reaction to suffering, Scholem claims to
give it authenticity and legitimacy. Finally, Scholem's extensive
treatment of Sabbatianism is based on the assumption that Sabbat-

ianism was a mass movement, encompassing all geographical areas and social groups of the Jewish world. The world-wide character of Sabbatianism is explained by the fact that its main source, the Lurianic Kabbalah, became the universal theology of Judaism in the century before the messianic outbreak.[42]

One may be permitted to wonder whether Scholem has confused the historical cause of Sabbatianism with its ideological and theological justification. The fact that the Sabbatians adopted the messianic imagery of the Lurianic Kabbalah may tell us how they conceived of themselves and their mission, but not necessarily the underlying reasons why they acted as they did. This issue points again to a fundamental characteristic of Scholem's philosophy of history: his emphasis on intellectual and especially esoteric movements as motivating forces in history.

There is also an immanent problem in Scholem's characterization of Sabbatianism as an apocalyptic movement instigated by the Lurianic Kabbalah. Scholem himself notes that Lurianic messianism was actually closer to the notion of gradual progress than to apocalypticism.[43] Luria's point of catastrophe occurred at the beginning of history rather than at the end. Moreover, apocalypticism typically teaches man's passivity in the face of the coming catastrophe; Luria emphasized man's active role. To be sure, the idea of a cosmic myth encompassing historical events is typically apocalyptic, but the crucial element of a rupture in history is missing. It would seem from Scholem's own description of the Lurianic Kabbalah that the apocalyptic element in Sabbatianism was not inherited from the Kabbalah, which had actually become antiapocalyptic, but from the atmosphere of catastrophe in the centuries following the Spanish expulsion. In other words, it is hard to understand from Scholem's presentation how the Lurianic notion of progress became Sabbatian apocalypticism except by negation, and this negation was perhaps prompted more by causes external to the Kabbalah than by the Kabbalah itself.

SABBATIANISM AND ENLIGHTENMENT

Scholem's contention of a mass outburst of apocalyptic messianism and heretical antinomianism on the threshold of the modern period implicitly challenges the rationalist belief in the progression of Jewish history from darkness to enlightenment. If Sabbatianism were only a peripheral movement, it could be dismissed as irrelevant to the mainstream of Jewish history. Nineteenth-century historiography had maintained that the modern period was inaugurated by the external influences of the new Christian tolerance and

Enlightenment in the eighteenth century. Scholem claims that the modern period was produced by a dialectic within Jewish history: Sabbatianism shook the foundations of traditional Judaism from within.[44] Religious Judaism, since it produced the Kabbalah, which in turn produced Sabbatianism, sowed the seeds of its own destruction.

Consistent with his belief in the power of ideas, Scholem focuses his account of the hidden influence of Sabbatianism on the dialectical development of Sabbatian theology. His first study of Sabbatianism, on Abraham Cardozo's heretical theology, shows how this Marrano Kabbalist turned the Lurianic Kabbalah into moral anarchism.[45] According to Luria's doctrine of the transmigration of souls, actions are neither moral nor immoral in themselves but are to be judged relative to a soul's assigned task of restoring its quota of divine sparks. Failure to fulfill one's quota meant returning in another life to do so. The question already implicit in the Lurianic theory was whether one's evil actions required punishment once one had fulfilled the assigned restoration. In other words, man was perhaps no longer responsible for evil actions in an earlier incarnation, thus annulling any moral calculus. Moreover, man's ignorance of his previous lives implied lack of knowledge of just what his assigned quota was and where he had failed. In Cardozo's thought, man's actions became a "game" (*Spiel*) or "theology of chance" (*Theologie des Hasards*) which undermined the moral certainties of traditional Judaism: "Thus it was that before the powers of world history uprooted Judaism in the nineteenth century, its reality was threatened from within. Already at that time [the time of Sabbatianism] the 'reality of the Hebrews,' the sphere of Judaism, threatened to become an illusion."[46] Once again we observe a striking example of how Scholem, in 1928, had already arrived at one of his most cherished hypotheses, which he was to develop throughout his career: Sabbatianism destroyed Judaism from within nearly a century before the Enlightenment.

In his "Redemption Through Sin" in 1936, Scholem explored in greater detail the Sabbatian doctrine of the "holiness of sin"—which was developed first to explain Sabbatai Zevi's strange antinomian actions and later became the central ideology of the movement following his apostasy. For those who remained in the movement as believers after Sabbatai Zevi "took the fez," two options were possible: to regard Sabbatai Zevi's heretical actions as unique and continue to live an outwardly orthodox life while retaining inner belief in a new messianic reality, or to emulate his apostasy. Scholem calls the first option "moderate Sabbatianism" and the second "radical."

For the moderates, the distinction between outward and inward life became acute. We have already observed Scholem's theory of the development of Kabbalistic messianism from a purely inward doctrine to an historical myth in the Lurianic Kabbalah and finally to the extreme outward apocalyptic messianism of Sabbatianism. But with the failure of the movement to achieve political-historical success, the messianic belief was again sundered: the believer now lived in the inner faith that everything in the world had mystically changed with the appearance of the Messiah, but his apostasy had held the external evidence of this change in abeyance. This "mystical schizophrenia" produced a state of mind similar to that of the Marranos and explains why some Marrano Kabbalists such as Cardozo were attracted to Sabbatianism.[47] According to Scholem, the new inner-outer dichotomy led to the splitting of identity into the private and public compartments characteristic of modern Judaism. It would seem, however, that the development of the Sabbatian mentality into the Jewish Enlightenment required at least one more inversion, which I do not find in Scholem's account: where the moderate Sabbatians remained traditional Jews outwardly and were only eschatologically "free" inwardly, the slogan of the Enlightenment was "a Jew at home and a man in the street."

The radical Sabbatians, on the other hand, solved the problem of bifurcation either by open conversion to Islam or Christianity or by violation of Jewish law in secret. The Dönmeh sect in Turkey and the Frankists in Eastern Europe prefigured the more assimilationist tendencies in modern Judaism because they chose apostasy.[48] In the case of Jacob Frank and his followers, apostasy did not mean sincere acceptance of the new religion, but a dialectical nihilism expressed through the mask of Christianity. With Frank, the doctrine of the holiness of sin reached its most demonic expression. Frankist nihilism ultimately turned outward to a desire for political liberation, and certain Frankist tracts suggested the connection between the heretical mystical doctrines and the political ideals of the Enlightenment.[49]

On a theoretical level, then, Sabbatianism prepared the ground for modern secularism and the Enlightenment. The doctrine of the holiness of sin became secular indifference to all traditional Jewish law. In an important aphorism, Scholem suggests that Reform Judaism, which has substantially banished the Halakhah from its own practice of Judaism, is a product not only of Sabbatianism but actually of the early Kabbalah:

Just as nature, seen Kabbalistically, is nothing but a shadow of the divine name, so one can also speak of a shadow of the law,

which is cast ever longer around the life of the Jews. But in the
Kabbalah, the stony wall of the law becomes gradually transparent . . . This alchemy of the law, its transmutation into transpar-
ency, is one of the most profound paradoxes of the Kabbalah . . .
[The] logical end of this process must be the rise of Jewish Reform: the shadowless, pure abstract humanity of the law, devoid
of all background but also no longer irrational. Reform is thus a
remnant of the mystical dissolution of the law.[50]

This enigmatic passage requires some explication. According to
the Kabbalists, nature is like a shadow concealing the spiritual, divine essence of the world; the law is similarly only a symbolic fab-
ric for a deeper reality. Scholem transforms this Kabbalistic motif
into something different: the law hides the true essence of the life of
the Jewish people. This passage should be read as an implicit critique of Jewish law.

Scholem then mixes his metaphors by calling the law a "stony
wall" (steinerne Mauer), which is a negative rendering of the rabbinic description of the oral law as a "fence around the Torah"
(siyag la-torah). The Kabbalah broke down this wall, presumably
by its pluralistic theory of exegesis. Apocalyptic Sabbatianism,
which Scholem does not mention explicitly in the aphorism,
formed the last stage in this alchemy of the law before the law lost
its capacity to throw a shadow around Judaism. With Reform Judaism, the dialectical interplay between the constraint of the law and
the liberating force of mysticism disappeared as law became purely
rational and abstractly universal. The secularization of the law,
Scholem implies, sealed the doom of Jewish mysticism, because
mysticism required a normative Judaism as a foil for its mystical
reinterpretation. The very rise of Reform, whose rationalism opposed equally halakhah and Kabbalah, was, however, the consequence of internal development within mysticism. Nineteenth-century rationalism and secularism were certainly a revolution in
Jewish history, but it was a revolution dialectically prepared by the
religious tradition.

Along with his theoretical studies of Sabbatianism and its hidden
intellectual connections to secular Judaism and the Enlightenment,
Scholem has tried to prove his bold claims by showing the biographical links between eighteenth-century Sabbatians and Jewish
Enlighteners. He argues particularly that among the Jewish bourgeoisie of Bohemia and Moravia, families with Sabbatian or Frankist traditions often became leaders in the new Haskalah: "Even
while still 'believers'—in fact, precisely because they were 'believers'—they had been drawing closer to the spirit of the Haskalah all

along, so that when the flame of their faith finally flickered out, they soon reappeared as leaders of Reform Judaism, secular intellectuals or simply indifferent skeptics."[51] The twentieth-century historian of atheism, Fritz Mauthner, appropriately enough, was one such descendant of a Sabbatian family, while Aharon Horin, a pioneer of Reform Judaism in Hungary, was a Sabbatian in his youth.[52] Scholem has also unearthed some extraordinary evidence of how a number of Sabbatians from Bohemia and Moravia, notably E. J. Hirschfeld and Moses Dobruschka, entered Masonic lodges at the end of the eighteenth century and introduced some radical Kabbalistic doctrines into Masonic ritual.[53] Dobruschka, perhaps the most fascinating of the whole cast of characters who followed this underground path from heretical mysticism to secular enlightenment, was guillotined during the French Revolution with Danton under the alias of Junius Frey.

In order to establish the pervasive influence of Sabbatianism on the Jewish Enlightenment, Scholem argued that a widespread movement persisted as late as a century after Sabbatai Zevi's apostasy. Even in the eighteenth century, Jacob Emden made this accusation and instituted a veritable witch-hunt for secret Sabbatians. Emden accused Jonathan Eibeschütz, one of the greatest legal authorities of the age, of Sabbatian sympathies, sparking a controversy that split the rabbinical world in Central and Eastern Europe. By the twentieth century, most of the orthodox community came to reject Emden's contentions in order to squelch the possibility that Sabbatianism was more than a passing phenomenon and to save the reputations of a number of venerable orthodox rabbis. In reviving Emden's suspicions that Sabbatianism was a major force as late as the eighteenth century,[54] Scholem incurred the wrath of the orthodox world. A concerted attack by orthodox scholars forced him for the only time in his career to answer one of his accusers in an orthodox journal.[55] He later published a special pamphlet systematically refuting his opponents.[56] The controversy is evidence that Sabbatianism remains a potentially dangerous embarrassment to modern orthodoxy, for, if Scholem's claims are correct, they show that religious Judaism in the eighteenth century was far more heterogeneous than it conceives of itself today.

The connections Scholem has drawn between Sabbatianism and Enlightenment resemble what other scholars had already demonstrated about the relationship between Christianity and the origins of the European Enlightenment. Since Max Weber, scholars have tried to portray the dialectical development of the Christian sectarian movements spawned by the Reformation into the Enlighten-

ment. Max Weber's study of the influence of Calvinism on the
"spirit of capitalism" was followed by studies of more radical heretical groups, such as the Socinians and the Anabaptists.[57] Special
attention has also been paid to the connections between mystical
Pietism and Enlightenment.[58]

Scholem sees his own work in this historiographical tradition. To
be sure, his argument of the hidden connection between Sabbatianism and Enlightenment is not entirely new, for even in the eighteenth century, Gottfried Selig and Jacob Emden suggested the
link.[59] In the twentieth century, Shai Hurwitz preceded Scholem in
describing Sabbatianism as a trailblazer of the Enlightenment.[60]
Scholem's contribution lies in systematizing and supporting these
earlier suggestions with exhaustive research as well as connecting
them with a coherent, radical philosophy of Jewish history.

This latest chapter of Scholem's work, perhaps the boldest and
most original, is also the most subject to doubt. As Jacob Katz has
pointed out,[61] Scholem's thesis is weak in terms of both intellectual
and biographical links. Despite similar attitudes toward the "yoke
of the commandments," Enlighteners need not have taken their
ideas from the Sabbatians. Scholem's examples of Sabbatians who
became Enlighteners or Reformers, as provocative as they are, constitute only a minuscule fraction of the Jews who abandoned orthodoxy for new forms of Judaism. Katz shows that even some of
Scholem's prime examples, such as Aharon Horin, may never have
been Sabbatians or, like E. J. Hirschfeld, may have discovered Sabbatianism after they had already come to Enlightenment.

Sabbatians were certainly more susceptible to assimilation because they were already outcasts from orthodox Jewish society, but
this is a sociological argument, which, although he would not reject
it, is far from Scholem's main thesis. Scholem is undoubtedly right
that Sabbatianism helped to undermine the traditional rabbinical
world much more than has been assumed, but his claim of an inherent connection between Sabbatianism and Enlightenment is probably unprovable.

Scholem's theory of how mystical heresy ushered in the modern
period of secularism and rationalism is the culmination of his attempt to show the hidden influence of mysticism on Jewish history.
His account of the development of Kabbalistic messianism into
apocalyptic heresy and finally secular enlightenment rests on his
theory of the productive conjunction of opposites: myth and
monotheism, mysticism and rationalism, apocalyptic messianism
and secularism. This theory derives from his understanding of the
role of demonic forces in history: "The desire for total liberation

which played so tragic a role in the development of Sabbatian nihilism was by no means a purely self-destructive force; on the contrary, beneath the surface of lawlessness, antinomianism and catastrophic negation, powerful constructive impulses were at work."[62] As opposed to a theory of gradual progress, history proceeds by violent ruptures. Yet these discontinuities do not mean that one historical period has no influence on the nature of its successor. The constructive potentiality of the demonic suggests that radical change and continuity are not mutually exclusive. As radically different as the Enlightenment may seem in contrast to the mystical messianism of Sabbatianism, there is a hidden connection between them since Sabbatianism unwittingly prepared the ground for secular rationalism. Where previous historians saw only unresolvable contradictions and negations, Scholem argues that continuities can be established between seeming opposites. This was the goal that Hermann Cohen had set for the philosopher of Judaism confronted by contradictions between the historical sources. But where Cohen imposed harmony by the concept of reason, Scholem demonstrates hidden connections between irrationalism and rationalism, and his evidence for these connections is historical sources.

HASIDISM AND MESSIANISM

Many Jewish nationalist writers were attracted to study Hasidism as a vital popular movement from the past. Because Jewish nationalism had to confront the question of messianism, the various interpretations of Hasidism often focused on the messianic character of the movement. Ben Zion Dinur and Scholem's own student Isaiah Tishby argued that traditional restorative messianism played a crucial role in Hasidism.[63] Dinur saw in Hasidism a forerunner of political Zionism. Tishby showed that Hasidic messianism arose with no special connection to the waning of Sabbatianism in Poland. Hasidism utilized traditional messianic formulas and was not a product, either positive or negative, of Sabbatianism. Tishby's argument was directed against Scholem's contention that Hasidism emerged as a response to the failure of Sabbatianism.

Against the messianic interpretation of Hasidism, Simon Dubnow and Martin Buber argued that Hasidism was antimessianic in a traditional sense.[64] Buber rejected apocalypticism as a legitimate aspect of Jewish messianism. He associated apocalypticism with Gnosticism, which he also considered alien to Judaism.[65] Buber's discussion of the history of the Kabbalah shows some similarities to Scholem's, but he sometimes seems closer to the nineteenth century. Buber believed that, by the time of Sabbatianism, the

Kabbalah had degenerated into Gnosticism so that its apocalyptic character was fundamentally anti-Jewish. For Buber, apocalyptic Gnosticism was an escape from the everyday world, which is the world man should try to sanctify.[66]

Hasidism, according to Buber, was a movement to return Judaism to its concern for the everyday world. Against the Gnostic tendency in the Kabbalah, Hasidism sought to "deschematicize the mystery" (Entschematisierung des Mysteriums).[67] Hasidism's contribution did not lie in a theoretical innovation in Kabbalah, but, on the contrary, in escape from the dangers of degeneration. Hasidism decisively liquidated the disastrous messianism in the Sabbatian movement by investing everyday action with divinity.

Buber's interpretation of Hasidism coincided with his general philosophy. Although in his initial writings on Hasidism during the period of his Erlebnismystik he emphasized the ecstatic quality of Hasidic mysticism, after the war he became concerned with the concrete "here and now" and saw in Hasidism the sanctification of the concrete, everyday world. Redemption, Buber now believed, could come for each individual at any moment in time. So he found in Hasidism a model for his individualistic reinterpretation of traditional messianism. Although he did not deny the national dimension of messianism, Buber believed that it would be the end result of the many concrete acts of sanctification of the "here and now."[68]

Like Hermann Cohen, Buber defined his messianism as utopian and antiapocalyptic.[69] He saw Zionism as just such a utopian attempt to sanctify the concrete world. Zionism might therefore take Hasidism as a model for its own spiritual direction:

> Hasidism is a great revelation . . . in which the nation appears to be connected by an inner tie with the world . . . Only through such a contact will it be possible to guard Zionism against following the way of nationalism of our age, which, by demolishing the bridges which connect it with the world, is destroying its own value and right to exist.[70]

Buber's emphasis on redemption in the "here and now" seems surprisingly apocalyptic. As Karl Mannheim wrote, "the only true . . . identifying characteristic of chiliastic experience is absolute presentness."[71] Even though he urged a return to the plane of historical action, the category of history served for Buber more as a metaphor for the existential present than for an historical continuum.

Scholem's own position on Hasidism is iconoclastic. Against

both the messianic and antimessianic interpretations of Hasidism he argues a third position, that Hasidism neutralized traditional messianism:

> Hasidism represents an attempt to preserve those elements of Kabbalism which were capable of evoking a popular response but stripped of their messianic flavor to which they owed their chief success during the preceding period . . . Perhaps one should rather speak of a 'neutralization' of the messianic element . . . I am [however] far from suggesting that the messianic hope and the belief in redemption disappeared from the hearts of the Hasidim.[72]

This significant statement stakes out his alternative to the prevailing interpretations. Against Dinur and, later, Tishby,[73] Scholem asserts that Hasidism was "quietistic": it avoided action to bring the Messiah and deferred messianic times to the distant future. Quoting Hillel Zeitlin, Scholem claims that in Hasidism "every individual is the redeemer, the Messiah of his own little world."[74] He tries to demonstrate that Hasidism emerged out of the vestiges of Sabbatianism in Eastern Europe as a deliberate attempt to subdue inherent apocalyptic dangers.[75]

These arguments are almost identical to Buber's and, indeed, Scholem's position appears to be much closer to Buber's than he may be willing to admit. Scholem and Buber also shared a similar political position on the relation of Zionism to messianism. Nonetheless, Scholem's notion of the neutralization of messianism was directed as much against Buber as against Dinur and Tishby. In his article in *Commentary* in 1961, Scholem accused Buber of historical falsification of Hasidism. Where Buber had tried to find his own religious existentialism in Hasidism, Scholem argued that in reality Hasidism did not sanctify the concrete "here and now": "For it is not the concrete reality of things that appears as the ideal result of the mystic's action, but something of the *Messianic* reality in which all things have been restored to their proper place in the scheme of creation and thereby deeply transformed and transfigured."[76] Scholem holds that the personal redemption of divine sparks was not an existentialist glorification of the concrete world as Buber saw it, but a Gnostic attempt to annihilate it. The messianic element that Hasidism retained, albeit divested of its national dimension, was Gnostic and apocalyptic. An historical understanding of Hasidism reveals that it is actually much more alien than Buber had thought; instead of becoming a model for modern man, it emerges as a prod-

uct of Kabbalistic messianism with the most radical elements neutralized. Buber had misinterpreted Hasidism because he started
with a definition of messianism remote from the true character of
the messianic idea in Judaism, particularly as it developed in the
Kabbalah.[77]

The famous controversy over Hasidism of the 1960s goes back to
as early as 1921 when Scholem read the manuscript of *Der Grosse
Maggid* where Buber first expressed his views on the opposition of
Hasidism and Gnosticism. He wrote to Buber arguing that Hasidism must not be understood as a rejection of Kabbalistic Gnosticism, but as a dialectical development within it.[78] Buber's attempt
to study Hasidism as a phenomenon independent of the Kabbalah,
and perhaps even opposed to it, could not gain credence unless
rooted in the history of the Kabbalah itself. Scholem was prepared
to agree that the Hasidim did not innovate in the field of theoretical
Kabbalah, but this was not because they rejected the Kabbalistic
tradition.

The argument over Hasidism is therefore an interesting example
of the difference between Buber and Scholem on the study of history. For Buber, an historical movement can be understood by
finding in it points of identification with one's own life experience.
The historical phenomenon consequently loses its historical context
and background. For Scholem, no historical movement exists in a
vacuum. Its connection to its intellectual predecessors determines
its character, and the only way a past and alien tradition can be understood is not by wrenching it out of history but, on the contrary,
by locating it precisely in its original historical reality.

By calling Hasidism a neutralization of messianism, Scholem
suggests how it fits into the history of Kabbalistic messianism. We
recall that he characterized the thirteenth-century Kabbalah in virtually identical terms. The Lurianic Kabbalah "de-neutralized"
messianism and thereby caused the apocalyptic explosion of Sabbatianism in the next century. Following Sabbatianism, the messianic impulse was once again neutralized. Scholem's terminology
leads to the conclusion that Hasidism used the language of the Lurianic Kabbalah to return Kabbalistic messianism to its original, pre-
Lurianic state. Messianism was not banished but defused.

Unlike many of his contemporaries on both sides of the Hasidism
controversy, Scholem is not overly sympathetic to Hasidism. Since
he contends that apocalyptic messianism was like an "anarchic
breeze" in the well-ordered house of halakhic Judaism, he seems to
believe that the neutralization of these forces would hinder revolutionary historical change. Like Shai Hurwitz, he finds Sabbatian-

ism much more dynamic and historically significant than Hasidism, which he characterizes as "quietistic." On the other hand, Scholem's appreciation of the historical role of apocalyptic forces does not necessarily mean identification with them. He recognizes the nihilistic potentiality in messianism which became actual in Sabbatianism. At the beginning of *Sabbatai Ṣevi* he notes: "Jewish historiography has generally chosen to ignore the fact that the Jewish people have paid a very high price for the messianic idea."[79] He conceives of his own historiography as a warning of the price that this idea may exact from the Jewish people. Scholem's personal position on messianism is necessarily complex, since he believes that the vital forces for change in Jewish history are potentially demonic and destructive; yet they may produce unexpected positive consequences. On the other hand, the realization of messianism would mean the end of the historical tradition, of the struggle between contradictory interpretations of revelation. Committed to the pluralistic flux of tradition, Scholem would have to be ambivalent at best about the messianic end of history, for the Messiah as the final authority is the ultimate representative of the monolithic interpretation of Judaism.

At the conclusion of his essay on "The Messianic Idea in Judaism," Scholem explains why messianism is inherently problematic:

In Judaism, the messianic idea has compelled a life lived in deferment, in which nothing can be done definitively . . . Precisely understood, there is nothing concrete which can be accomplished by the unredeemed . . . Jewish so-called *Existenz* possesses a tension that never finds true release; it never burns itself out. And when in our history it does discharge, then it is foolishly decried as pseudo-messianism.[80]

Against Buber, Scholem understands messianism as "the real anti-existentialist idea." The paradox of messianism is that it requires the realization of metahistorical longings in the concrete realm of history, but, as in Sabbatianism, the infusion of a cosmic doctrine into the concrete world may lead to nihilism since the real world can never fully reflect mystical reality. In order to maintain the critical dialectic of Jewish history, messianism could neither be realized nor totally suppressed: the tension of a life lived in deferment both preserved the Jewish tradition and gave it dynamism.

For Scholem, the failure of a messianic movement is not "the big lie . . . of the great actor and imposter," as the opponents of Sabbatai Zevi charged. It is rather, he writes quoting a legend of the believers, a "victory of the hostile powers rather than the collapse of a vain thing."[81] For Scholem, the hostile powers are not so much supernatural as inherent in the paradox of messianism. There is no such thing as pseudo-messianism, for just as apocalyptic messianism inevitably tries to discharge itself in the concrete world, so it is inevitably doomed to failure. Yet the forces of messianism, even when neutralized, have never disappeared from Jewish history.

8. *The Politics of Historiography*

Scholem considers Sabbatianism to have been the great watershed in Jewish history between the medieval and modern periods: all subsequent movements such as the Haskalah and Hasidism had some hidden or overt connection to it, even if they "neutralized" it. Apocalyptic messianism shook the Jewish world at its foundations, but the dialectic of rebellion and continuity, revolution and conservatism, gave Jewish history its ongoing vitality.

Given the centrality of Sabbatianism in his conception of Jewish history, Scholem would have to relate Zionism to the great messianic movement of the seventeenth century. Indeed, Zionism necessarily conjured up the question of Jewish messianism since it proposed to accomplish at least part of the messianic promise: the restoration of Jewish political sovereignty in the land of Israel. Some writers, like Dinur, saw Zionism as the explicit fulfillment of the messianic dream, while others, like Buber, were very reluctant to use traditional messianic imagery in their Zionist thought without radically reinterpreting it.

We have seen that Scholem adopted Shai Hurwitz's evaluation of Sabbatianism as the central liberating event in modern Jewish history. Hurwitz regarded Sabbatianism as a model for Zionism and Sabbatai Zevi as a seventeenth-century Herzl. Does Scholem similarly consider Zionism as latter-day Sabbatianism? We shall see in this chapter that Scholem rejects the identification of Zionism with apocalyptic messianism and defines Zionism as what I shall call "neutralized messianism." If the message of apocalyptic messianism is the obliteration of historical tradition, Scholem sees Zionism conversely as the "utopian retreat back *into* Jewish history." If Zionism is not a movement of the "end of days," what is its relationship to Jewish history as a whole? Since Scholem developed his

initial interest in the historiography of Jewish mysticism in close
proximity to his Jewish nationalism, his position on Zionism can
serve as a valuable litmus test for his historiosophical assumptions.
By examining his Zionist ideology, we will begin to solve the problem that has continually plagued his critics: What is Scholem's own
position on the historical phenomena he has described?

As we saw in the last chapter, following the publication of the
Hebrew edition of *Sabbatai Ṣevi*, a number of Israeli critics claimed
to have found a positive connection between Scholem's historical
studies and his position on Zionism. Baruch Kurzweil and R. J. Z.
Werblowsky each took Scholem to task on similar grounds of glorifying Sabbatianism as an example of the true Judaism and as a forerunner of Zionism. They both interpreted Scholem's historiography as a nihilistic, antitraditionalist force structurally similar to
Sabbatianism.

Kurzweil's argument, by far the more vituperative, provoked an
angry response from some of Scholem's colleagues, although Scholem himself did not enter the fray.[1] Despite Kurzweil's frequently
hyperbolic style, there is much in his argument that deserves serious attention. Kurzweil accused Scholem of hiding his anarchistic
theology behind the guise of an objective historian. He argued that
Scholem is far from objective toward Sabbatianism since he treats
the Sabbatians with exaggerated sympathy while lambasting their
orthodox opponents as narrow-minded fanatics. Scholem, he asserted, had succumbed to a belief in "demonic irrationalism."[2] His
view of Judaism, which Kurzweil considered roughly identical to
that of Nathan of Gaza, led directly to the secular relativization of
Judaism: "[Scholem's research on Sabbatianism] is a grandiose and
dangerous attempt to bestow on the secular interpretation of Judaism—and especially as it has been revealed since the rise of secular
Zionism—the force of continuity which is immanent to religious
Judaism itself."[3]

Kurzweil's vigorous accusations against Scholem reflected his
own general attitude toward secular Zionism. In literary essays
ranging from the Hebrew writers of the turn of the century to the
"Canaanite" movement of the 1940s and 1950s, Kurzweil castigated
secular Zionism as a disastrous and sterile departure from Jewish
tradition.[4] In his essays on Scholem, he argued that Scholem had
legitimized a dangerous precedent for "nihilism" in Jewish history.
Why, Kurzweil asked, should such messianic nihilism not reemerge
in the Zionist movement? Scholem's historiography was particularly dangerous because he had cloaked his revolutionary break
with Jewish tradition in a reinterpretation of the tradition itself as

revolutionary. Kurzweil's disagreement with Scholem was, more-over, fundamentally pedagogical: he accused Scholem of educating a whole generation of Israelis to believe that Sabbatianism was the real Judaism and that the normative legal tradition was only marginally significant.

Kurzweil acknowledged, however, that Scholem had referred in his book to "the high price which the Jewish people have paid for the messianic idea" and that this represented a more cautious attitude toward messianism. He suggested that Scholem's views must have undergone a substantial revision from his alleged sympathy for antinomianism in the 1936 "Redemption Through Sin" article to a more ambiguous position in *Sabbatai Ṣevi*:

> Scholem has come to understand that the anti-rabbinic, anti-Talmudic revolt did not solve anything. Auschwitz on the one hand and the State of Israel as its antithesis . . . contradicted his earlier conception . . . Today Scholem is far from his innocent and enthusiastic rebelliousness. It seems to me that he also became disillusioned a while ago with Judaism and the realization of Zionism and so has barricaded himself in an ivory tower of "pure science."[5]

Despite Scholem's increased moderation, Kurzweil insisted that his views still had a profound, if now unintended, antinomian effect. Scholem himself might have realized the high price of messianism, but by arguing that the Sabbatian heresy was legitimately Jewish, he had led Israeli youth into misunderstanding the essence of Judaism.

In the next chapter, I shall devote attention to Kurzweil's attack on Scholem's objectivity as an historian. I do not believe that Scholem has ever considered his historiography independent of his Zionism or that he has ever retreated into an ivory tower. My fundamental contention is that on the question of messianism, as on so many of the other basic issues he confronted, Scholem made his decisions very early and stuck to them with little substantive change. Kurzweil was wrong about a shift in Scholem's position following the Holocaust and the creation of the Jewish state, for a careful examination of Scholem's first essay on Sabbatianism in 1928 reveals that he was already aware of the dangers of extreme messianism for Zionism. He wrote at that time:

> The messianic phraseology of Zionism, especially in its decisive moments, is not the least of those Sabbatian temptations which could bring to disaster the renewal of Judaism . . . As transient in

time as all the theological constructions, including those of Cardozo and Jacob Frank, may be, the deepest and most destructive
impulse of Sabbatianism, the hubris of the Jews, remains.[6]

Despite Scholem's unequivocal denial of a positive connection
between Sabbatianism and Zionism, we must concede to Kurzweil
that statements such as these seem to contradict many of Scholem's
other assertions about the positive hidden consequences of apocalyptic messianism. Moreover, it is hard to avoid the impression
that Scholem has tried to find a precursor to his own anarchistic
theology in Sabbatian antinomianism. Are we dealing here with a
contradiction in Scholem's thought? Is he able to reconcile his attraction to the destructive, demonic elements in apocalyptic messianism with his recognition of their political hazards? Or does his
moderate Zionist position contradict his historiography, where he
is far more willing to allow free rein to heresy and destruction? I
shall try to answer these questions by turning to Scholem's personal
political development in the 1920s and 1930s. Just as the crucible of
World War I forged his decision to leave Germany for Palestine
and to undertake scholarly study of the Kabbalah, so the tumultu-
ous political events in the first decade of his life in Palestine shaped
his interpretation of Zionism in Jewish history. I believe that it is
possible to find a precise parallel between the statement in the 1928
Cardozo article and Scholem's political position in the same period.

SCHOLEM AND THE BRIT SHALOM

In order to understand Scholem's political activities in Palestine
in the 1920s and 1930s, it is important to depict briefly the general
political context of that time.[7] The political culture of Palestine in
the 1920s left little room for the liberal politics characteristic of the
Jewish professional and academic classes in Central and Western
Europe. Among the Jewish population in Palestine, the artisans and
workers tended to support the various socialist labor parties, while
the small propertied class and petty merchants who arrived from
Poland in the mid-twenties supported either the General Zionists or
the nationalistic Revisionist Party of Jabotinsky. The kind of liberal
politics espoused by most Jews in the Weimar Republic was notably
absent from the political landscape, in part because German Jews
did not come to Palestine in force until after 1933. The more radical
choices prevalent in Eastern European Jewish political life tended to
dominate the scene. Even after 1933, German Jews exercised relatively little political influence, although they were a substantial
portion of the population.

Although Scholem and his colleagues in Jerusalem often had distinct sympathies for the socialist labor movement, they were still politically isolated. Their Zionism was more the result of a cultural and moral revolt against bourgeois German culture than a nationalist reaction to political antisemitism or a desire to establish a socialist utopia. When the liberal intelligentsia, many of whom were from Central Europe, did try to enter the political arena, their motivation was more often moral than pragmatically political or fanatically ideological.

Insofar as the liberal intelligentsia crystallized into a political force, it did so largely because of the creation of institutions independent of the official Zionist agencies. Foremost among these institutions was the Hebrew University, which was established in 1925 and whose initial staff was composed of both Eastern European and German scholars. Its first chancellor, the American Jewish leader Judah L. Magnes, conceived of the university along American lines as an institution serving all the Jewish people without affiliation to any political party.[8] This nonpartisan autonomy, rare in the Palestine of those days when virtually everything was controlled by a political party, created something of a liberal enclave in Jerusalem. Following the mass immigration of German Jews to Palestine in the 1930s, the group of liberal academics in Jerusalem was strengthened as the university absorbed many refugees into its faculties. Many of these new refugees had great difficulty in assimilating the Hebrew culture they found in Palestine, and they retained the political and cultural manners they brought with them from Germany. Because they created a "little Berlin" in Jerusalem and the other towns where they settled, many German-Jewish immigrants remained politically isolated. Having come to Palestine in 1923 with a firm knowledge of Hebrew, Scholem did not have these problems of assimilation, but his social environment remained the peculiarly inbred intellectual community in Jerusalem which S. Y. Agnon has portrayed with a loving but satirical pen in many of his stories.[9]

Another influence in the milieu of the liberal intelligentsia was the activities of the German-Jewish merchant and publisher, Zalman Schocken.[10] Schocken had made a fortune in Germany in department stores but, motivated by intense Jewish concerns, had opened a publishing house in Berlin at the beginning of the 1930s. After the Nazis came to power, Schocken, an ardent Zionist, began to transfer some of his operations to Palestine and he purchased the daily newspaper Ha-Aretz, which he turned into a forum for the liberal intellectuals. He established a publishing house in Tel Aviv corresponding to his German operation, which the Nazis had shut down just before World War II. Through his publishing enterprises and his independent liberal newspaper, Schocken played an important role in creating a small liberal "counter-culture" in Palestine in the 1930s, alongside the dominant socialist labor culture. Like many other intellectuals, such as Agnon and Buber, Scholem developed close ties to Schocken who, from the mid-thirties, published many of his works in German, Hebrew, and, later, English. Scholem also began to write in *Ha-Aretz*, often reporting in detail on his Kabbalistic research for the edification of the general public.

The first political organization of the nascent academic intelligentsia was the *Brit Shalom* (Peace Alliance), formed in 1925.[11] Originally intended as a discussion forum on Arab-Jewish problems, the Brit Shalom became something of a political gadfly by proposing that the Zionist movement renounce its aspirations for majority status. The Brit Shalom based its political assumptions on Churchill's 1922 White Paper, which advocated a binational polity under the British Mandate. To its enemies, the Brit Shalom seemed to call for the Zionist movement to abandon the cardinal principles of free immigration and political sovereignty and instead seek the "levantization" of the Jewish community in Palestine. Although never able to attract popular support beyond the liberal intellectuals connected with the university, the Brit Shalom drew disproportionate attention because of the intellectual weight of some of its members. Scholem himself took an active role in the Brit Shalom from its inception until it ceased to function in 1933. He wrote a series of editorial articles in its journal, *She'ifoteinu* (Our Aspirations), as well as in the daily press.[12]

The conciliatory position of the Brit Shalom became an issue of public debate in the wake of the violent Arab riots of August 1929. The outbreak of Arab hostility provoked bitter arguments in the Hebrew press about the character and goals of Zionism, and Scholem became involved in a most revealing exchange over the relationship of Zionism to messianism in the pages of the trade-union journal *Davar* in November-December 1929.[13] The Hebrew novelist Yehudah Burla had attacked the Brit Shalom for trying to sever the national ties between the Palestinian Jewish community and the world-wide Diaspora by calling for a limit to immigration and the forging of a common identity with the Arabs. Burla's charge that the Brit Shalom sought a specifically Israeli identity as opposed to a Jewish identity for the Jews in Palestine is ironic, as well as mistaken, for in the 1940s and 1950s it was to become the slogan of the "Canaanite" (or Young Hebrew) movement whose political origins were precisely the opposite of the liberal Brit Shalom and whom Scholem vigorously denounced in later years. The ultimate consequence of the Brit Shalom's program, Burla suggested, was to "profane the nation's holy of holies—its hope for complete redemption. Our historical messianic hope exists even today in the heart of the new Israeli man in the form of political Zionism in a much more complete way than the messianic idea existed in the past in the heart of the religious Jew."

Scholem replied to Burla by rejecting the identification of messianism with Zionist politics:

> I absolutely deny that Zionism is a messianic movement and that it has the right to employ religious terminology for political goals. The redemption of the Jewish people, which as a Zionist I desire, is in no way identical with the religious redemption I hope for in the future . . . The Zionist ideal is one thing and the messianic ideal another, and the two do not meet except in the pompous phraseology of mass rallies which often infuse our youth with a spirit of new Sabbatianism which must inevitably fail. The Zionist movement has nothing in common with Sabbatianism.[14]

Here we see a political statement that corresponds to Scholem's conclusion in his first article on Sabbatianism about the dangers of messianism. The studies of Sabbatianism he had just undertaken some two years before the political controversies of 1929 provided him with an historical model of what Zionism must at all costs avoid.

The clear target of Scholem's reference to "the pompous phraseology of mass rallies" was Revisionism. The Revisionist Party was established in 1925 by Vladimir Jabotinsky, who had resigned from the Zionist Executive in 1923.[15] Jabotinsky made the goal of a Jewish majority on both banks of the Jordan River the central plank of his nationalist party. He also prophesied a coming apocalyptic catastrophe for European Jewry and called for their immediate mass immigration to Palestine. The Revisionists received much of their support from Eastern European middle-class Zionists, who could not countenance the socialist ideology of the labor parties but were more militant than Weizmann's General Zionists. Jabotinsky fostered a youth movement called *Betar*, which adopted military dress and organization. Following the riots of 1929, the Revisionists gained considerable support in Palestine as many Jews, drawing opposite conclusions to those of the Brit Shalom, saw majority status and militant tactics as the only hope for avoiding future mas-

sacres. Elements of the Palestinian Betar, under the ideologue Abba
Ahimeir, formed the first units of the militant underground which
ultimately evolved into the later terrorist Irgun and Stern groups.[16]

Revisionism, particularly in its Palestinian branch, was motivated by an acute form of secularized messianism. Perhaps the
most explicitly apocalyptic of the groups to come out of Revisionism was the Freedom Fighters of Israel (Lehi), which, under the leadership of the poet Abraham Stern, split off from the Irgun in 1940.[17]
In one poem, Stern described himself as a soldier of the King Messiah from the generation that would "force the end," the traditional
expression the rabbis used since the Talmud to condemn apocalyptic messianists.[18] Stern inverted the pejorative dictum into a battle
cry. His followers conceived of the final battle with the British as an
apocalyptic catharsis out of which they could expect only death.
The departure of the British and the establishment of a Jewish state
under the socialists in 1948 seemed to them depressingly prosaic, a
victory without revolution.[19]

The roots of this secular apocalypticism can be traced back at
least to the 1920s in the emerging ideology of Palestinian Revisionism. The poet Uri Zvi Greenberg, who, after a brief flirtation with
socialism, became one of the leading Revisionist ideologues in the
late 1920s, filled his epic poetry with apocalyptic images and in his
Rehovot ha-Nahar even adopted the literary form of the Apoca-
lypse.[20] Another of the early ideologists of Palestinian Revisionism
inspired by Jewish messianism was the literary historian Joseph
Klausner. In 1902, Klausner had written his doctoral dissertation in
Heidelberg on "The Messianic Ideas of the Jewish People in the Period of the Tannaim," which he published in an enlarged Hebrew
translation in Palestine in the 1920s. In the preface to the second
Hebrew edition (1927), Klausner revealed the political philosophy
behind his historical study:

> It is not the Hebraic, the prophetic, the Messianic-Israelite social
> conception which has become a basis for bringing about redemp-
> tion in the land of vision and promise, but a foreign social con-
> ception linked up with economic and historical materialism, to
> which the prophetic idealism is a mockery . . . Zionist social pol-
> icy cannot be based on an authoritarian materialism . . . it must
> be prophetic, saturated with the Jewish Messianic idea.[21]

The rise of Revisionism in Palestine had much to do with the desire
of the Jewish middle class to find a political ideology with which to
counter the Marxism of the labor movement. Klausner provided a
nationalistic messianism to buttress the Revisionist capitalist ethos.

Although his messianism included a universalist dimension, he considered prophetic messianism equivalent to Jewish nationalism, which was to serve as an example to all other nationalisms.[22]

Klausner's Revisionist messianism has particular relevance for our discussion because Klausner was probably the one prominent Revisionist with whom Scholem had significant personal encounters. Klausner was one of the most important professors at the new Hebrew University, and he led the nationalist opposition among students and faculty to the liberal Brit Shalom. Although the university was firmly in the hands of the liberals, Klausner could muster sufficient student activism to create disturbances. In 1927, Scholem wrote to Chancellor Magnes to complain that plans to establish a chair of Yiddish philology were threatened by "terrible chauvinistic" agitation.[23] The nationalists regarded the study of Yiddish at the Hebrew University as nothing less than the betrayal of the ideals of national renewal of the Hebrew language. According to Scholem, Klausner had personally threatened to lead students into the lecture hall the first day of classes to disrupt the lecturer, should he be appointed. Klausner's agitation had its desired effect and the chair was not established. But the threat to turn the university into a political battleground was by no means idle, for several years later right-wing students succeeded in disrupting a lecture by Norman Bentwich, who had been Attorney-General for the British Mandate and was sympathetic to the Brit Shalom.[24]

Following the 1929 Wailing Wall riots, Scholem himself was involved personally in one incident that illuminates the hysterical atmosphere of the time. Following the riots, the Va'ad Leumi established a committee under David Yellin to present evidence to the British commission investigating the incident. The committee asked Scholem, as the university expert on Kabbalah, for Kabbalistic works concerning the Wall, presumably to strengthen the Jews' historical and religious claims. Scholem refused to make books from his private library available to the committee. In a letter to *Doar ha-Yom*,[25] A. Babakov attacked Scholem bitterly for his refusal to cooperate, portraying him as a rabid anti-Zionist. In his response,[26] Scholem argued that he did not believe the question of the Wall should be decided by a judicial body, but should be a matter for political negotiation. Behind Scholem's refusal to lend his expert authority to the Jewish defense of Wailing Wall rights was his belief that the political disputes with the Arabs should be resolved on the plane of politics, irrespective of religious considerations. Here, as in his attack on Isaac Breuer's "politics of mysticism" around the same time, Scholem opposed the prostitution of mysticism and religion in general in the political arena.[27]

The events following the riots of 1929, notably the increasing strength of the militant nationalists and the polemics against the Brit Shalom, provoked something of a crisis in Scholem's thinking. Although already a rebel against "official" Zionism in Germany, he now found himself substantially isolated from the general political trends in Palestine. On 22 May 1930 he wrote to Martin Buber, who was sympathetic to the Brit Shalom and later led its successor, the Ichud, that "it would be useless to deny that the countenance of the Zionist affair has darkened for us [for the Brit Shalom] in a catastrophic way."[28] The question was not only the political controversy with the Arabs but, more important, the internal character of Zionism. The Revisionists and their messianic pretensions constituted the greatest threat to the Zionist enterprise. As he wrote in 1934, Zionism "will not find its salvation, its *tikkun*, in the wild apocalypticism of the Revisionists."[29]

In the wake of the Zionist Congress in 1931, Scholem wrote a long letter to Walter Benjamin which betrays similar despair and anguish about the future of Zionism.[30] During the Congress, the Revisionists had demanded that the Zionist organization explicitly define its end goal as majority status in all of Palestine. Although the Revisionist program was not adopted, the moderate leader Chaim Weizmann was forced to resign in a vote widely, if wrongly, interpreted as a victory for the Revisionists.[31] Scholem understood that the Revisionist resolution was principally aimed against the Brit Shalom, and in the letter to Benjamin he decried the attempt to ostracize the Brit Shalom from Zionism. He insisted that the Zionist organization had no right to define who was and who was not a Zionist. In politics, as in historiography, Scholem had no sympathy for dogmatism.

The issue that concerned Scholem the most in his letter to Benjamin, as well as in several articles he wrote at about the same time in the Brit Shalom journal, was the inability of Zionism to solve the "Jewish question." All the loud talk of mass immigration and majority status seemed to him in 1931 no better than a pipe dream. Zionism had failed precisely because it had succeeded: "It has anticipated its victory spiritually and with it lost the power to achieve it materially. It has, to be sure, fulfilled a function and indeed under enormous difficulty, which it had in no way intended. We have won too early . . . When Zionism was victorious in Berlin . . . it could no longer [succeed] in Jerusalem."[32] The dialectic of success was such that, once Zionism created a feeling of Jewish pride in European Jews, it made them feel more comfortable in Europe and thus unwittingly hindered the mass immigration it sought. In this interesting analysis, we can hear the echo of Scholem's earlier criticism of the German Zionist youth movement for not placing emigration to Palestine at the head of its agenda. But while during World War I he believed that a change in ideology could encourage immigration, by 1931 he had become much more pessimistic and felt that Zionism's Pyrrhic victory was historically inevitable. Needless to say, Scholem could not have anticipated the flight of German Jews to Palestine after 1933; he may have regarded Jabotinsky's warnings of catastrophe as just another indication of the apocalypticism inherent in Revisionism. However, in retrospect after the Holocaust, Scholem's prediction that the mass of European Jews would not come to Palestine seems all too prescient.

Scholem's despair over the possibility of mass immigration and immediate solution to the Jewish question led him to reject the messianic promises of some of his Zionist contemporaries. Messianic expectations were unrealistic since Palestine could not solve the problem of all the Jews. But "complete redemption through Zionism" was also a "falsification" of Zionist goals.[33] The Revisionist emphasis on complete redemption led to "imperialism": "The Zionist movement still has not freed itself from the reactionary and imperialistic image that not only the Revisionists have given it but also all those who refuse to take into account the reality of our movement in the awakening East."[34] Scholem believed that this political-messianic Zionism was fatally flawed: "if the dream of Zionism is numbers and borders and if we can't exist without them, then Zionism will fail, or, more precisely, has already failed."[35]

Despite the revolutionary, anti-imperialist rhetoric of these attacks on Revisionism, Scholem equally rejected the socialist Zionist desire to "normalize" the Jewish people. The goal of Zionism should not be to turn the Jews into a "nation like all the nations." The slogan of normalization seemed to him a form of assimilation and a denial of the uniqueness of Jewish history.[36]

These polemics against normalization and a political solution to the Jewish question reflect Scholem's own personal motivation in becoming a Zionist. We have seen that his own path to Zion was not a result of antisemitic experiences in the Berlin of his youth. Although political antisemitism had existed in Germany since the 1880s, and some Central European Jews such as Herzl and Nordau had been converted to Jewish nationalism by the rise of antisemitism in the West, the experience of most Central European Jews was not of virulent antisemitism. For Scholem, as for many Jewish young people, Zionism was not so much a political and economic solution to the Jewish question as a cultural revolt against their parents and a quest for new values. Scholem's definition of Zionism in an article in the 1960s still reflects his own youthful experience: "[Zionism was] a movement of youth in which strong romantic motives necessarily played a role; it was a movement of social protest whose inspiration arose as much out of the ancient but still vital call of the prophets of Israel as out of the solutions of European socialism."[37] Although Scholem was obviously aware of the pressing political and economic need of European Jews for a national state, his personal relation to Zionism was more romantic than political.

SCHOLEM'S INTERPRETATION OF AHAD HA-AM

Preoccupied more with the cultural problem of Judaism than with the political Jewish question, Scholem rejected the respective solutions of the Revisionists and socialist Zionists, advocating instead Ahad Ha-am's "cultural Zionism." As early as World War I, he had found in Ahad Ha-am the most relevant spiritual guide, and he agreed with the Russian-Jewish publicist that Zionism's main goal should be to build a cultural and national center in Palestine in order to rejuvenate Judaism throughout the world. Although bitingly scornful of his contemporaries who failed to emigrate to Palestine when he did, Scholem understood that the Diaspora was not about to disappear and that Zionism must play the central role of ensuring its spiritual vitality.[38] This philosophy was an important motif in the Brit Shalom's position on the role of Zionism, even though its opponents accused it of wanting to sever the Palestinian Jewish community from the Diaspora. In the Brit Shalom journal, Scholem strongly attacked those who wanted to "excommunicate" Ahad Ha-am from Zionism.[39]

There is, however, something problematic in Scholem's attachment to Ahad Ha-am. Ahad Ha-am's philosophy of history was close to the nineteenth-century liberal idea of uniform, gradual progress: Zionism could reinvigorate the Diaspora if it did not propose a radical break with Jewish tradition.[40] It was against this conservative notion of Zionism and Jewish history that Berdichevsky directed his Nietzschean polemics, arguing that history proceeds by a dialectic of destruction and construction.[41] Because Scholem seems to maintain a similar theory of historical change in his studies of myth and messianism, it would not seem that he could agree with Ahad Ha-am about the relation of Zionism to Jewish history. The question returns us to the original issue posed by Kurzweil: Doesn't Scholem's revolutionary philosophy of history apply equally to his position on Zionism?

Scholem himself is aware of the problematic nature of his relationship to Ahad Ha-am. He defines himself as "a radical follower of Ahad Ha-am's thought."[42] Between those who see Zionism as a continuation and fulfillment of Jewish history and those who see it as a radical break, Scholem searches for a third path. Like Ahad Ha-am, he sees Zionism as essentially secular and yet part of the Jewish tradition.[43] As long as the radical and "heretical" forces in Jewish history had contributed to the continuity of the tradition, they could be considered legitimately Jewish. Once they denied any tie with tradition and degenerated into apostasy, as was the case with Christianity and radical Sabbatianism, they broke the historical continuum. In the final analysis, Scholem's ambivalence toward Sabbatianism and his critique of both the German Zionist youth movements and the Revisionists rest on their attempts to obliterate the historical tradition.

Evidence for this can be found in Scholem's political statements after the establishment of the State of Israel in which he has attacked the Canaanite movement. The Canaanites wanted to liquidate all of Jewish history and resurrect a mythical biblical-Canaanite people in the land of Israel.[44] Scholem witheringly castigates the Canaanites for "educational murder," by which he means their attempt to sever themselves from the historical tradition.[45] Like Hans Joachim Schoeps, they are in error for trying to return to a pure biblical religion or culture without taking into account the whole historical tradition after the Bible.[46] Such a leap over history is impossible.

Scholem sees the profound inner connection between Berdichevsky's radical interpretation of Jewish history at the beginning of the century and the Canaanite revolt against history in the 1940s and 1950s.[47] The Canaanite movement, a radical offshoot of Palestinian Revisionism,[48] can be taken as an extreme symbol for all those apocalyptic movements in Zionism which Scholem rejects for trying to cut the knot with tradition.

On the other hand, Scholem considers the revolutionary character of Zionism to be its driving force. Here his view is much closer to Berdichevsky's than to Ahad Ha-am's. The socialist pioneers (halutzim) were a revolutionary vanguard driven by the desire to eradicate the exile, and Zionism owes much of its success to them.[49] Scholem sees the conservative and revolutionary forces in Zionism as dialectically interrelated: continuity and radical change are part of the same continuum. He asks: "Could there not exist between the conservative, restorative and revolutionary, Utopian-directed tendencies [in Zionism] an understanding or at least something binding, in which they could meet without annulling and negating each other?"[50]

We note in this question that Scholem uses precisely the same terms he applies to the history of Jewish messianism: messianism is a fruitful dialectic between restorative and utopian-apocalyptic forces. Messianism demands realization in the concrete world, but any attempt at such actualization is doomed to failure and to condemnation as "false messianism." Zionism necessarily conjures up such messianic pretensions but also utilizes the energies inherent in them: the socialist pioneers were motivated by unconscious messianism and an apocalyptic desire for liquidation of the old aeon of exile and suffering. In its effort to enter into the concrete realm, Zionism edges up to the messianic abyss and calls upon the messianic energies of the people. Should it give itself up entirely to apocalyptic messianism and sever the tie with Jewish history, it will fail as Sabbatianism did. But should it dissociate itself entirely from the messianic tradition, it will lose its vital dynamic. The revolutionary moment in messianism is both necessary and mortally dangerous.

For Scholem, excesses of either messianism or antimessianism are equally threatening to the continuity and development of Jewish tradition. Is there a radical interpretation of Ahad Ha-am's thought that preserves "limited" Zionism without losing messianic energies? I believe that Scholem suggests such a solution in his concept of the neutralization of messianism which we encountered in the discussion of Hasidism. There we saw Scholem's interpretation that Hasidism did not liquidate messianism but neutralized it by redirecting its energies toward the personal rather than the national realm. Hasidism quietistically deferred national redemption to the distant future. Scholem's treatment of Hasidism betrays a certain contempt for this passive neutralization of messianism; he is far more drawn to Sabbatian dynamism. He obviously conceives of the Zionist movement as more revolutionary than Hasidism because it preaches Jewish activism and does not make its peace with exile.

In his reply to Burla, however, Scholem states that the messianic redemption he longs for is not identical with Zionism, and he defers it to the distant future. Like Hasidism, Zionism should direct messianic energies to the concrete world, although Hasidism wrongly did this by annihilating reality. Scholem opposes the use of messianic images in Zionism: the language of Zionist ideology must be purely political and never religious. In this sense, his Zionism is quite different from Hasidism or, for that matter, the Haskalah, which transferred messianic imagery to European rulers. But what all three movements share, in Scholem's conception, is the utilization of messianic energies for purposes other than the immediate national redemption of Israel. If it is fair to adopt and broaden Scholem's term "neutralization of messianism," which he only applies in a specific sense to Hasidism and the early Kabbalah, we can argue that Zionism, like Hasidism and the Haskalah, is also a response to Sabbatianism. As a movement of neutralized messianism, Zionism is but one more attempt to harness the messianic energies released at the dawn of the modern age and redirect them toward constructive purposes.

These post-Sabbatian movements, despite their significant differences, were all neutralizations of messianism because they had a similar relation to Jewish history. They stretched the historical tradition, but as long as they did not end in apostasy they did not break with it entirely. Zionism utilized the messianic energies of the pioneering vanguard, but this vanguard was always conscious of its responsibilities toward the people and the tradition as a whole: it was a vanguard that was always looking back over its shoulder.[51] This characterization is reminiscent of Scholem's view of the Kabbalistic elite in earlier periods: although ostensibly isolated from the people as a whole, the Kabbalists had a strong sense of the psychological resonance of their esoteric doctrines. Unlike the philosophers who deliberately cut themselves off from the uneducated masses, the Kabbalists, in Scholem's reconstruction, always had their fingers on the emotional pulse of the nation. They were a vanguard conscious of their followers, even if the followers were not aware of following. The socialist pioneers were similarly conscious of their connection to the people. Although they might have claimed ideologically to want to do away with the religious definition of Judaism, they did not want to break with the Jewish people. Scholem defines Zionism as the undertaking of "*responsibility* for our life as a community on all planes, whether it be [our] secular, sacred or religious nature as Jews, and as nothing other than as Jews."[52] In this passage, written in 1967, we can discern an echo from one of Scholem's early polemics against the youth movements where he also defined Zionism as the taking of responsibility (*Verantwortung*).[53]

The essence of this responsibility lies in the relation of the Zionist elite to Jewish history. As Scholem argued against George Steiner, the literary critic who has affirmed the creative social role of the cosmopolitan Jewish intellectual: "[Steiner] is trying to live outside of history, while we in Israel are living responsibly, inside of history."[54] Living responsibly means to live within an historical tradition and to act in history. It is not entirely clear why Scholem assumes that action within history is only possible in a Jewish national polity, when Jews manifestly act "historically," and as Jews, even in the Diaspora. However, he regards the Zionists as those who shoulder the burden of history: "The building of the land of the Bible and the foundation of the State of Israel represent, if you will allow me to use a daring formulation, a utopian retreat of the Jews into their own history."[55] The notion of a retreat into history reminds us immediately of Scholem's own path to Zionism during and after World War I when he retreated, as it were, from Europe to Palestine and, quite literally, into the study of history as a possible source of Jewish identity.

The retreat into history is utopian for Scholem because it taps the messianic promise of the centuries. It is not apocalyptic, however, because it puts the final redemption in the future. Because the Zionists direct their efforts toward the concrete tasks of building the nation, their revolutionary drive is transmuted into a realistic fulfillment of history and not into its apocalyptic abrogation: "the difference between Zionism and Messianism resides in the fact that Zionism is acting within history, while Messianism remained on a Utopian plane."[56]

We note again how similar Scholem's understanding of messianism is to Hermann Cohen's in its deferral of messianic times to the future. Both are "utopians" in their belief that the history of Judaism is open-ended; Scholem regards Zionism as but one more stage in the tradition. The radical difference between them lies in the target of utopianism, for Cohen directed it toward abstract universalism, while Scholem sees it as a retreat from universalism to Jewish national concerns. Cohen and Scholem also part ways on the evaluation of apocalypticism. Both renounce apocalyptic messianism, but Scholem's understanding of the dialectic of Jewish history causes him to believe that apocalypticism is not overcome by a straightforward negation, but only by the dialectical neutralization of its destructive capacities.

Connection with history is the constraint that prevents Zionism from sliding into the messianic abyss. As Scholem concluded in his critique of Schoeps: "The connection of the historical with an eternal present can only be realized, it seems to me, in two ways, which are not mutually exclusive: in the medium of the apocalyptic or tradition."[57] Scholem chooses a synthesis: apocalyptic energies moderated by tradition, a solution that parallels his theological anarchism in which tradition regulates the freedom of interpretation.

Submission to tradition is, of course, a dangerous business, since it can stifle growth. Scholem believes that the nineteenth-century antiquarian interpretation of Judaism as well as religious orthodoxy sapped the vitality of living Judaism. These interpretations undermined Judaism by imposing a dogmatic definition on what Scholem considers an anarchistic plurality of beliefs. Zionism is a revolution against both orthodoxy and the nineteenth century's diluted form of Judaism. It draws its vitality as well as its stability from Jewish history precisely because it is a return to the *totality* of Jewish history: "[Zionism] was ready to identify itself with the fate of the Jews in all, I say all, its aspects—the religious and secular equally."[58] Only Zionism is by definition antidogmatic because it stands above all particular interpretations of Judaism and is the one common denominator that unites all Jews, that accepts all definitions—religious and secular—of "who is a Jew."[59]

Kurzweil was indeed correct that Scholem's Zionism cannot be separated from his historiography, for Scholem tries to integrate Zionism into Jewish history by showing that it is a product of the Jewish tradition even as it revolts against parts of it. However, Scholem's Zionism is in no sense a modern version of Sabbatianism. His adamant denunciations of those in Zionism from Revisionists to Canaanites who wanted to escape the responsibilities of the historical tradition suggest that his political position was never as "nihilistic" or "apocalyptic" as Kurzweil thought. Scholem's interpretation of Jewish history and of Zionism's position in that history is as much an objection to radical secularists as to the dogmatic orthodox. Zionism must neutralize secular nihilism on the one hand and religious dogmatism on the other, but it must do so without destroying either.

Since his intense political involvement in the late 1920s and early 1930s, Scholem has been generally silent on the pressing political questions confronting Zionism and the State of Israel. However, the debates over Zionism and messianism from that period are not merely of antiquarian interest, for they still rage today on the Israeli political stage. Those who see Zionism as a messianic movement have, if anything, grown even more powerful in recent years. Whether the demonic forces in Zionism, to use Scholem's language, will have a positive or a destructive effect on the course of Jewish history can only be determined in historical perspective, as Scholem has shown in his studies of Sabbatianism. It is therefore understandable and perhaps inevitable that Scholem as an historian has not applied the same evaluation to modern political phenomena as he has to historical events. His historiography cannot be construed as a political program but, at best, as a warning. Well attuned to both the danger and the promise of messianism, he writes:

> Little wonder that overtones of messianism have accompanied the modern Jewish readiness for irrevocable action in the concrete realm, when it set out on the utopian return to Zion . . . Whether or not Jewish history will be able to endure this entry into the concrete realm without perishing in the crisis of the messianic claim that has virtually been conjured up—that is the question which . . . the Jew of this age poses to his present and to his future.[60]

9.   *Counter-History*

The place Scholem assigns to Zionism in Jewish history can also give us some clues about the role of the Zionist historian in Jewish historiography. As we saw in the analysis of Scholem's essay on the Wissenschaft des Judentums, historiography, like every element in Jewish life, needs national normalization in order to flourish. The Wissenschaft des Judentums failed to include the irrational and apocalyptic elements of Jewish history in its definition of Judaism because its social context forced it into apologetics, dogmatic rationalism, and antiquarianism. With the loss of these vital forces, nineteenth-century Judaism became an empty shell and nineteenth-century historiography an impotent "rite of burial." Whether excessively biased toward rationalism or utterly indiscriminate in its antiquarianism, the Wissenschaft des Judentums failed to fulfill its initial promise. Still it was the first to develop a critical historical method. This valuable tool was wasted.

The rationalist historiography of the nineteenth century broke down in the beginning of the twentieth. The new nationalist historians attacked their predecessors for an apologetic and distorted view of Judaism and emphasized social and irrational factors previously ignored or despised. Scholem accepts most of the nationalist critique, but he rejects some of the nationalists for excesses in the opposite direction: they ignore the dialectic of demonic destruction and creativity which he finds in Gnostic myth and Sabbatian antinomianism. Their uncritical glorification of Jewish history is a result of an uncritical historical method.

Since Scholem rejects the Zionist slogan of "normalization" of the Jewish people, his desire to normalize historiography does not mean the absolute negation of previous historiography. The correct reaction to the Wissenschaft des Judentums is not absolute negation, but neutralization. Just as Zionism neutralized the nihilistic moment in apocalyptic messianism by redirecting its energies toward concrete tasks, so Scholem appears to argue for an historiography that will neutralize the demonic in the Wissenschaft des Judentums by translating its method into a critical, but constructive, program.

Scholem's use of the term "demonic" to describe some of the representatives of the Wissenschaft des Judentums suggests that he considers the nineteenth-century historiography structurally similar to Sabbatianism. Both sought to bring an end to Jewish history, the one by apocalyptic messianism and the other by historiographical obituary. However, if we take Scholem's argument to its implied conclusion, the relationship between Sabbatianism and the Wissenschaft des Judentums is not only structural and theoretical, but also historical. As the origin of Jewish secularism, Sabbatianism would have to be held ultimately responsible for the secular method of the nineteenth-century historians. Although Scholem never makes this argument explicitly, it is consistent with his view of the continuity of hidden Sabbatian influence.

Scholem sees a resemblance between Sabbatianism and the "demonic" method of the Wissenschaft des Judentums and he prescribes historiographical neutralization. But he also considers the nineteenth-century historians to have been representatives of the opposite tendency, toward rationalism and dogmatism. If the ultimate consequence of the Wissenschaft des Judentums was nihilistic, its proclaimed public position was more a modern incarnation of the conservative rabbinic tradition. In other words, the nineteenth-century school was paradoxically at once too radical and too conservative. Just as Jewish life as a whole in the nineteenth century stood in need of reinvigoration by the Zionist movement, so the conservative tendencies in Jewish historiography require a vitalizing revision. Historiography must do its part in the Zionist movement of Jewish revival.

The function that the new historiography, and Zionism in general, serves in Jewish history is structurally akin to the role of messianism and myth in rejuvenating the conservative tendencies in the halakhah. We recall that Scholem calls apocalyptic messianism the "anarchistic breeze" which airs out the "well-ordered house" of the halakhah. Using almost exactly the same terms, he argues that "the new evaluations and emphases which Zionism has established have brought a fresh breeze (*frischen Wind*) in a house which had seemingly been all too well-ordered (*allzu wohl geordnet war*) by the nineteenth century."[1] Scholem's anarchistic approach to Judaism may therefore be intended to play the same role in the history of historiography as messianism played in the history of the halakhah. His Zionist historiography walks the fine line between succumbing to the destructive tendencies of the Wissenschaft des Judentums and ignoring the constructive potential in its demonic method.

I have suggested labeling Scholem's neutralization of the Wissenschaft des Judentums "counter-history" since it calls for the completion of the nineteenth-century program under reordered priorities. His history of the Kabbalah stands much closer to the Geistesgeschichte of the Wissenschaft des Judentums than to the social histories or mythmaking of some of the nationalist historians. But his intellectual history of Judaism is transposed into a different key: where the nineteenth century focused on the history of Jewish rationalism, Scholem finds vitality precisely in those irrational and even heretical forces that had previously been depreciated.

In the light of the structural similarities between the role of this historiography and Jewish mysticism in Jewish history, it also becomes evident why Scholem can use the Kabbalah as an historical model for his counter-history. The Kabbalah itself was an underground movement for revival in Jewish history; yet it accomplished its work by appropriating the normative tradition and transforming it. Because it represented "freedom under authority," the Kabbalah proposed bold and far-reaching new interpretations of the tradition without destroying the tradition altogether. So, too, Scholem's historiography suggests an audacious expansion of the idea of Judaism without negating the value and legitimacy of the normative tradition. The Kabbalah, as a counter-historical interpretation of normative Judaism, becomes a suggestive model for the modern historian seeking to rejuvenate Jewish historiography in a secular age.

The Problem of Objectivity

Scholem holds that Zionism has returned the Jews to responsibility for the totality of their history. In the light of this claim, it becomes clear why the Zionist historian can be objective, since only he theoretically lives in an atmosphere that accepts all of Jewish history as equally legitimate. Scholem argues that the self-proclaimed objectivity of the Wissenschaft des Judentums "never existed and could not exist" because of the hostile political demands of the age: apologetics could use only part of Jewish history and had to suppress what was embarrassing in the struggle for emancipation. Implicit in Scholem's conception of Zionism is that objective historiography will only be possible when the Jewish people are no longer subject to the political and cultural distortions of an anomalous life in exile:

[In the wake of Zionism] the Jewish people can try to solve its problems without any squinting to the left or right; it can pose the question of confrontation of Jews and non-Jews; it can approach the clarification of the historical and spiritual issues pending between Jews and Gentiles. Such problems can now be taken up and discussed, independent of what anyone else may have to say on the subject and without regard for external considerations . . . Great perspectives have been laid open as a result of this . . . utopian retreat of the Jewish people to its own existence and the decision to engage this existence to the fullest extent—perspectives that obviously influence research.[2]

Especially in his later writings,[3] Scholem does not deny that history written in the Diaspora can be creative and objective, but he clearly feels that the success of Zionism has made this possible. Scholem does admit that nationalist historians have been just as susceptible to tendentiousness and dogmatism as historians writing in the Diaspora. The promise that Zionism will lead to objective historiography is therefore more of an ideal than an inevitable and immediate consequence of Jewish nationalism.

We have seen that Scholem's claim of historical objectivity became one of the main targets of Baruch Kurzweil's voluminous critique. Although Kurzweil's criticisms have already proven to be frequently far off the mark, they can serve as a useful foil for examining some of the key issues in Scholem's work. Kurzweil argued that Scholem's unquestionable fascination with the more esoteric episodes in Jewish history is evidence of his subjective bias. He maintained that Scholem had only substituted one bias for another: antibourgeois irrationalism for bourgeois rationalism.[4] Scholem, says Kurzweil, identifies his own anarchism with certain irrationalist trends in Jewish history while claiming to speak objectively for all of Judaism. Where Buber's anarchism was perhaps justifiable because he never claimed to be faithful to his historical sources, Scholem's is not because he assumes the pretense of objectivity.[5]

Kurzweil advanced the common observation that there is no such thing as historical objectivity since all interpretations are equally subjective.[6] Following the critique of historicism of the early twentieth century, he argued that since all historical research is "impressed with the stamp of subjective historicism," it can never understand the essence of Judaism, which Kurzweil, under the influence of Franz Rosenzweig's existentialism, believed was ahistorical.[7] Scholem's attempt to treat Judaism as a subject of history could never yield more than a subjective interpretation since historiography, as a secular undertaking, could never grasp the essential nature of an ahistorical religious faith.

Kurzweil thought that with Scholem's anarchistic Zionist historiography, the attempt of historians to understand Judaism had come to a self-destructive end. Scholem had, indeed, completed the work of the Verein für Kultur und Wissenschaft der Juden, which Kurzweil considered to be "similar to [that] of the later Sabbatians and Frankists."[8] Scholem's anarchism only made explicit the antinomianism implicit in the historical enterprise from the outset: "Soon enough, the anarchistic restlessness will turn either explicitly or implicitly against the attempt to find satisfaction in nationalist Zionism as a substitute for Judaism . . . This is the dialectic of Scholem's philosophy of history: it is the pinnacle of the Zionist conception and the beginning of its liquidation."[9] Since anarchism by definition refuses to accept any movement in history as ultimately authoritative, it must eventually turn against Zionism itself. Since secular Zionism, in Kurzweil's mind, had utterly cut its bonds to Jewish tradition, it had laid a mortal trap for itself.

Much of Kurzweil's critique does not stand up under scrutiny. Scholem's anarchism is not synonymous with Sabbatian nihilism. As an anarchistic philosopher of Jewish history, Scholem may well have fulfilled the program of the Wissenschaft des Judentums, but he did so by neutralizing its "antinomian" consequences. Scholem does not propose his historiography as a program for Zionism, for he clearly rejects the idea that two historical periods are the same and that the revolt of the Sabbatians can or should be imitated by the Zionists. Moreover, we have already examined in detail Scholem's theological refutation of the existentialist claim, adopted by Kurzweil, that Judaism can only be understood by an act of faith rather than through historical research. Scholem does not accept the idea of an "essence" of Judaism, whether deduced philosophically or intuited existentially.

Yet Kurzweil's critique, intemperate and exaggerated as it may have been, does raise certain issues we cannot avoid. On the one hand, Scholem claims that historical objectivity is possible in the wake of Zionism, and he evidently believes that the nineteenth-century promise of an all-inclusive historiography will only be fulfilled under the new conditions of the twentieth. The desire for an historicist definition of Judaism will only be possible when historians recognize that Judaism consists of many contradictory phenomena. On the other hand, Scholem's own historical work has been devoted to one aspect of the Jewish sources, the irrational. I have tried to show throughout this book that Scholem has undertaken his project not only in order to fill in the incomplete picture left by his predecessors, but because he believes that the subject of his investigations holds the key to the survival of Judaism. Scholem's as-

sumptions about the source of vitality in Jewish history are not
merely the product of long years of research but, as we have seen,
were already central to his thinking when he chose his subject in his
youth. Since Scholem has selected one aspect of Jewish history for
investigation and has claimed that it is the source of vitality, in
what sense can his work be considered any more "objective" than
that of his predecessors? Doesn't Scholem's insistence on the importance of irrationalism subvert the notion of an all-inclusive historiography and thereby become only the mirror image of the dogmatic rationalism of the nineteenth century?

We have also seen that Scholem establishes a close affinity between his secular historical method and the exegetical philosophy
of the Kabbalah. Since he is not a Kabbalist, he by no means identifies himself with the Kabbalah, but a related problem remains:
Has Scholem perhaps imposed modern concerns and categories
upon the historical sources he studies? In the early twentieth century, philosophers such as Dilthey realized that reconstruction of
the alien past was only possible if some sort of empathy could be
established between the historian and his subject. Dilthey suggested
that out of the historian's own "lived experience" (Erlebnis), a kind
of understanding (Verstehen) of the past became possible. However, this Lebensphilosophie, which claimed to solve the "crisis of
historicism," actually only translated the crisis into new terms: if
past historical contexts were really different from today's (and Dilthey believed they were), then the only type of Verstehen possible
would distort history by imposing a modern experience on an alien
one.[10]

In Jewish historiography, a similar situation arose, although out
of different concerns. The antiquarian detachment of the Wissenschaft des Judentums made Jewish history seem utterly alien to
nineteenth-century Jews. Buber's subjectivist approach to history,
influenced in large measure by Dilthey,[11] claimed to put the Jew
back in touch with his history by rewriting historical sources on the
basis of contemporary experience. Does Scholem's attempt to replace antiquarianism with a new historiography avoid Buber's
identification of present experience with historical sources, or does
he too impose modern categories on the alien world of the Kabbalah and thereby distort its historical reality?

Finally, does an anarchistic philosophy of history raise the spec-
ter of total relativism, or what Ernst Troeltsch called an "anarchy
of values"?[12] If the pluralistic sources of Judaism contradict one
another, does the effort to define Judaism solely on the basis of its
historical sources end up exploding the possibility of defining Juda-

ism at all? Such an historiography may be termed inductive, for it seeks to avoid imposition of an *a priori* principle on the sources and its goal is to let the sources speak for themselves. Does an inductive historiography based on contradictory sources lead inevitably to relativism?

These then are the three interrelated questions we must address: objectivity versus subjectivity; detachment from the historical sources versus imposition of contemporary experience on them; and dogmatism versus relativism, or *a priori* versus inductive historiography. In the rest of this chapter, I propose to outline Scholem's response to these issues, in part by reference to parallel theories that may have influenced him or with which he may have found sympathetic affinities. Scholem's philosophy of counter-history, which he shares with a number of other German Jews of his generation, suggests implicit answers to these questions, answers that attempt to avoid the rigid antinomies in which the questions have been formulated. Whether or not the theory of counter-history is philosophically satisfying matters less to us here than its role in the history of Jewish thought.

I have defined counter-history as the theory that there is a continuing dialectic between an exoteric and a subterranean tradition. The true history lies beneath the surface and often contradicts the assumptions of the normative tradition. How does such a theory answer the problems of historicism? Since Scholem has not articulated systematically his philosophy of history, we must turn to a number of theoreticians whose ideas are demonstrably similar to Scholem's and with whose work he was familiar, even if we cannot establish a precise pattern of influence.

We have seen the similarities between Scholem's counter-history and the Nietzschean counter-histories of M. Y. Berdichevsky and Martin Buber. Scholem's is an expression of a similar revolt against the traditional way of looking at the Jewish past and an attempt to recover something valuable from a frequently oppressive and alien tradition. Yet Scholem has attacked the Nietzschean approach vehemently and labeled it "naive" because its proponents hold that the history of Jewish myth is independent of official Judaism. He proposes a much more subtle theory in which the mainstream and underground traditions are connected. More important, Scholem objects to the antihistorical mythopoeic approach of the Nietzscheans and their rejection of the actual historical tradition. Against the subjective fabrication of historical myths, Scholem attempts to restore legitimacy to tradition by exhaustive immersion in the historical sources.

We must therefore look elsewhere for parallels to Scholem's theory of counter-history. Scholem's own generation of German Jews produced a good many thinkers who found paths back to religious traditions by means of counter-history.[13] Two who will be particularly helpful for our examination of Scholem are Walter Benjamin and Ernst Bloch, both highly idiosyncratic, even "heretical" Marxists who searched for possible syntheses of dialectical materialism with theology.

BENJAMIN AND BLOCH

In 1940, at the end of his life, Benjamin formulated a series of "Theses on the Philosophy of History."[14] The "Theses" are a polemic against historicism, which he says, quoting Ranke, tried to recognize the past "the way it really was." Benjamin argues that this is a misleading and hypocritical claim, since the historicist typically writes the history of the victors and therefore fails to understand that the great "cultural treasures" (Kulturgüter) of history were produced by the exploitation of the working masses: "They owe their existence not only to the efforts of the great minds and talents who have created them, but also to the anonymous toil of their contemporaries. There is no document of civilization which is not at the same time a document of barbarism."[15] Since the "anonymous" oppressed classes cannot write, they produce no sources. By allowing the sources to dictate what he writes, as if he could ignore everything he knows about history subsequent to the period he is studying, the historicist necessarily surrenders to the class bias of his sources.

For Benjamin, historiography does not consist in a false "faithfulness to the sources." The historian must continually be on his guard not to become "a tool of the ruling class" by submitting uncritically to his sources. The historicist may "recite events without distinguishing between major and minor ones," but the historical materialist approaches history out of his own contemporary concerns. By a "tiger leap into the past," the historian "blasts [an event] out of the continuum of history" and rescues its true, hidden meaning. He recognizes that "the struggling, oppressed class is itself the depository of historical knowledge."[16]

Benjamin described the process by which the historian saves the message of the oppressed class from anonymity in his phrase "to brush history against the grain" (Geschichte gegen den Strich zu bürsten).[17] The historian must read the sources against their class intent. The recovery of this secret history requires fastening on the seemingly insignificant and trivial details in the sources.[18] When the historian comes across details that immediately connect with his own experience, the tyranny of the monolithic history of the victors is shattered.

Benjamin found in Marx the key to a new concept of historical objectivity. The visible world is a myth since our perception of it is a result of "false consciousness" imposed by class bias. Historiography must demythologize the past by exposing the visible world for the illusion it is. If reality is a myth, the esoteric tradition becomes the true reality. Counter-history is not merely a revision of bourgeois historiography, the substitution of one bias for another, but an inversion of all conventions that are shown up as the opposite of their illusory appearances.

Scholem, to be sure, never had any sympathy for either Marxist language or a materialist analysis. His history of Sabbatianism pointedly argues for the importance of religious over socioeconomic factors. He was highly critical of Benjamin for distorting the true metaphysical nature of his thought by cloaking it in materialist terms. Scholem's insistence that the "true" Benjamin was a metaphysician and not a Marxist has provoked an enormous argument by recent Marxists, who find an attractive model in Benjamin.[19] But whether or not it is correct, Scholem's reading of Benjamin is strong evidence of his own antipathy toward Marxism and his belief in metaphysics as the basis for historical thought.

Hannah Arendt has noted the deep affinity between Benjamin's and Scholem's methods. Benjamin's study of the Baroque, undertaken before he became a Marxist, already reflected his desire to brush history against the grain, for he, like Scholem, took a subject that had been ignored or even considered illegitimate: "It was an implicit admission that the past spoke directly only through things that had not been handed down, whose seeming closeness to the present was thus due precisely to their exotic character, which ruled out all claims to a binding authority."[20] Scholem's remarkable ability to make the Kabbalah accessible and relevant has much to do with the affinity he has suggested between the Kabbalah's incipient anarchism and modern secularism, but this surprising affinity becomes persuasive precisely because the Kabbalah seems at first so alien.

Perhaps the most striking resemblance between Benjamin's and Scholem's theories of counter-history is in the notion that truth lies in hidden details. Scholem's work gains its brilliance not only from the lucid generalizations he has been able to apply to the Kabbalah, but also from his extraordinary attention to detail. In his disciplined hands, the fascination with seemingly insignificant facts, which for Benjamin remained largely unsystematic and eclectic, becomes a powerful historical and philological tool. The Wissenschaft des Judentums also emphasized the almost indiscriminate collection of facts. But Scholem, as against his predecessors, tries to seize upon those hidden details possessing the sparks of vitality and restore them to their proper place. As he concludes his essay on the "Science of Judaism—Then and Now":

> By genuine scholarly immersion into facts and circumstances we may be able to reorganize and reconstruct the whole from its smallest parts. Such an immersion must not shrink from the insight expressed in the magnificent saying ascribed to Aby Warburg: *Der liebe Gott lebt im Detail* [it is in minutiae that the beloved God can be found].[21]

Benjamin's concept of brushing history against the grain as a means of overturning the oppressive judgments of past historiography can serve as a useful device for understanding Scholem's relation to his own historiographical predecessors. His restoration of irrational motifs to a central place in Jewish history is frequently inspired by the ambiguities of some of the rationalist historians. Writers such as Krochmal and Graetz did not so much ignore irrationalism as deny it authenticity in Jewish history. Because these historians often investigated irrational phenomena intensively as foils for what they believed to be the true Judaism, they did much of the spadework for Scholem. By reading them against their intent, by inverting their value judgments, Scholem is often able to turn their conclusions to his own benefit, such as Krochmal's description of the Gnostic character of the Kabbalah or Graetz's dating of the *Zohar*. To be sure, these conclusions emerged first and foremost out of his own exhaustive research, but they must be situated in the historiographical tradition in which they stand. Scholem's counter-history consists of not only the transformation of the nineteenth century's critical historical method, but on occasion even the appropriation of many of its substantive conclusions, inverted by new and more positive evaluations. The recovery of the suppressed vital tradition of the Kabbalah required reading the Wissenschaft des Judentums against the grain: where the nineteenth century saw only "degeneracy and impotent hallucinations," Scholem finds the "great living myth."

Scholem's close friendship with Benjamin suggests the plausibility of considering their philosophies of history together. Another "heretical Marxist" whom Scholem knew, but with whom he was never so close, is Ernst Bloch.[22] Although Scholem condemns

Bloch's writings as "expressionistic," there are certain resemblances worth noting, particularly because they will lead us unexpectedly to another possible source for Scholem's counter-history. Bloch believes that religious heretics are the most genuine religious figures. In his recent *Atheism in Christianity*, he gives the Bible a counter-historical "class" interpretation to show that the religion of the common people was profoundly atheistic. Borrowing idiosyncratically from biblical criticism, he argues:

> It is clear that there is such an underground Bible . . . So the banner should cry not "Demythologize!"—but "Detheocratize!" Only that can do justice to the Bible's still saveable text. The Bible only has a future inasmuch as it can, with this future, transcend without transcendence . . . [There] are in fact two Scriptures: a Scripture for the people and a Scripture against the people.[23]

Although Bloch claims to be a Marxist atheist, his identification with God-fearing "atheists" throughout history exposes him for the religious thinker he is. In his *Atheism in Christianity*, he subtly transvalues atheism into a religious force.

GOTTFRIED ARNOLD

Scholem has compared Bloch to the eighteenth-century Pietist historian Gottfried Arnold, and in this I believe there lies a fruitful parallel to Scholem's own work.[24] Arnold's massive *Unparteiische Kirchen und Ketzerhistorie* (1699-1700), which has stood in Scholem's library since 1926, is an extraordinary attempt to show that the true history of Christianity is the history of the persecuted, the martyrs and the heretics: "Where suffering is, there are the pious."[25] By definition, for Arnold, Christianity is an inward religion opposed to worldly institutions. Whereas true Christianity, which is voluntary, does not coerce outward expressions of belief, secular institutions are primarily concerned with controlling man's external actions. Therefore, when the Church imposed dogma upon the *ecclesia primitiva*, it became a secular institution and forfeited its legitimacy.[26] Since persecution is one of the signs (*Kennzeichen*) of truth, it does not matter whether the persecutor is a secular institution or the Church itself: martyr and heretic are equally true Christians.

True Christianity has no external history, since its essence is the recurring inward struggle of the soul and not the fate of worldly institutions. The history of the external world is a "history of decay" (*Verfallsgeschichte*), while the true, hidden history is an ac-

count of how martyrs and heretics maintain the purity of their faith
against the coercion of the world. The apocalyptic idea that true
Christianity is a revolt against worldly history is an old one in the
Christian tradition, extending back to Joachim of Fiore and even
earlier to Augustine, and it would find a modern echo in the twentieth-century "theology of crisis."[27] Arnold's special contribution
lay in transforming this old mystical motif into the centerpiece of
his exhaustive history of the Church; his work represents a transi-
tion between theology and modern historiography.

The tension in Arnold's history came from his antihistorical theology, for the true subjects of history, he believed, are those who
negated history. Because he attempted to write a history of "antihistorical" figures, Arnold was curiously able to conceive of his
task in terms similar to objective historiography.[28] He entitled his
work *unparteiische*, by which he meant that he belonged to no dogmatic party. By definition, dogma arises out of the subsuming of
inner religious experience into worldly institutions: dogma is the
consequence of worldly history. The orthodox were the real heretics because they suppressed the freedom necessary for true religion.[29] An *unparteiische* history rises above dogmatic history and
returns Christianity to its original nonworldly impulses. Only the
persecuted have no biases, because they believe in the truth of their
inner experience and do not enforce a dogmatic belief on others.
Arnold believed that by writing a history which transcended all
"historical" parties, he could discover the true Christianity. His
counter-history was antidogmatic, but it had a definite point of
view. "Objectivity," if conceived as *unparteiische*, does not mean
disinterestedness.

Scholem's attention to the heretics and outcasts of Jewish history
is similar to Arnold's. They share the belief that an attack on dogmatism is a precondition for objective historiography. Scholem opposes the philosophers for attempting to define a dogmatic essence
of Judaism; therefore, a history of Jewish philosophy alone, although it might be faithful to its sources, would be a distortion of
Judaism. Because the Kabbalah adhered to a pluralistic theory of
tradition, which Scholem takes to be genuinely Jewish, it is the key
to a true understanding of Judaism. Hence, focusing on the Kabbalah is *unparteiische* because the Kabbalists were the antithesis of
dogma. The Kabbalah must be the source of vitality in Judaism precisely *because* it was ridiculed and suppressed by those trying to
impose a single definition.

Despite the illuminating similarities between Scholem and Arnold, there are equally illuminating differences. Arnold was himself

a Christian sectarian and therefore identified fully with his sources, whereas Scholem sees in the Kabbalah the prefiguration of secularism but does not equate them. Scholem's counter-history does not pit the inner forces of light against the outer "secular" forces of darkness. The heresy that interests him deviates not in the direction of pure inwardness but, instead, toward worldly secularism: Sabbatianism led to Enlightenment. He repeatedly insists that the category of individual inwardness is foreign to Judaism and that Jewish history unfolds in a public, communal tradition, even when its foremost representatives seem to congregate in esoteric sects. But if the age-old distinctions between Judaism and Christianity divide Scholem from Arnold, he shares with the eighteenth-century Pietist the belief that only counter-history can shatter establishment dogmas and uncover the objective truth beneath them.

SCHOLEM'S COUNTER-HISTORY

With the help of these other theories of counter-history, we can attempt to answer the three questions raised earlier. The Wissenschaft des Judentums had posed as objective by offering a positivistic and antiquarian treatment of the past, but Scholem argues that this claim was specious because the nineteenth-century historians participated in the censorship of the tradition. They confused antiquarianism with objectivity and ended up in dogmatism. Against the misleading claim of objectivity in the Wissenschaft des Judentums, Scholem elevates historical selectivity to the highest principle. Objectivity does not consist of a detached and ecumenical presentation of all the facts of Jewish history, but in the proper evaluation of those forces that lent the tradition its vitality. Scholem does not deny the validity of a history of Jewish philosophy or law, but he believes that the vitality of Jewish history can only be understood fully as a result of the impact of irrationalism. Philosophy and law could not have survived without the contribution of the demonic. Scholem's hunt for this vital element leads him to rummage about in the "dustbins of history": "Half-articulated mutterings about mystical secrets, symbols and images, all rooted in the world of esoterica and in the abstruse speculations of the Kabbalists, became transformed, in my eyes, into invaluable keys to an understanding of important historical processes."[30]

I have called Scholem's counter-history an account of the productive conjunction of opposites: myth and rationalism, restorative and apocalyptic messianism. The Jewish tradition is governed by the constant dynamic conflict between these opposing forces. A static picture cannot be objective because it only reflects the con-

stellation of forces at a particular moment, obscuring the hidden
level on which future developments are being prepared. Historiography must uncover these vital forces at work, and its portrait cannot ignore the contradictions between them. Only by taking sides
as to which forces are truly vital can the correct picture emerge.

Counter-history is history written by the *engagé*. Does it therefore succumb to the imposition of the historian's own experience on
the past? I have tried to suggest that Scholem sees a structural similarity between the historian and the Kabbalist, but not an equiva-
lence. The affinity makes the Kabbalah strikingly modern and relevant, but it does not collapse into Buber's unhistorical rendering of
historical movements. Scholem is able to strike a delicate balance
between detachment and involvement, and therein lies his difference from the Wissenschaft des Judentums on the one side and Buber on the other. His subject, the Kabbalah, becomes accessible
because it prefigures modern ideas, but because it is not identical
with them it retains its own historical meaning.

Nowhere does this issue come into sharper focus than in Scholem's "Unhistorische Sätze über Kabbala." Since these aphorisms
are "unhistorical," Scholem allows himself much greater freedom in
speculating about the metaphysical message of the Kabbalah, but
the ideas he develops also permeate his own historiography. In one
of the "Sätze," he analyzes the materialistic language of the Lurianic Kabbalah and concludes: "The conception of the Kabbalists as
mystical materialists with dialectical tendencies would indeed be
utterly unhistorical, but anything but meaningless."[31] Scholem uses
this Marxist language tongue-in-cheek, for he obviously avoids a
materialist analysis of the Kabbalah; his history focuses on an intellectual elite rather than the "masses." However, the aphorism hints
at a fundamental issue: though the Kabbalists would not recognize
themselves as mystical materialists, it may be that a modern understanding of them is facilitated by deliberately applying such anachronistic categories. The problems the Kabbalists addressed are
eternal problems, and their solutions have resonance in modern
thought. At the same time, the Kabbalah cannot be considered a
modern intellectual movement, for that would distort its historical
reality: this is the reason Scholem labels his metaphysical reflections *unhistorische*. The historian must strike a balance between
applying categories from his own experience to his historical material and letting the sources speak for themselves. When Scholem, in
his discussion of the Lurianic Kabbalah, uses categories from Hegelian logic to describe the paradox of *zimzum*, he succeeds in
doing so without rewriting the Lurianic Kabbalah *as* Hegelian

philosophy. His persistent application of philosophical categories to the Kabbalah must be judged as just such a balancing effort between contemporary relevance and historical distance.

The final issue I raised concerns the tension between dogmatism and relativism, which might also be conceived as the tension between *a priori* and inductive historiography. Scholem claims that the Jewish tradition consists of a plurality of ideas and that this conclusion is the only one to be drawn from a nondogmatic consideration of all of Jewish history. Has he relativized Judaism to the point where it is impossible to make any meaningful statements about its nature?

We can gain insight into the nature of this problem by returning to Hermann Cohen's philosophy of history in his *Religion der Vernunft*. Cohen suggested the idea of a pluralistic tradition consisting of potentially contradictory sources. But he argued that the effort to define Judaism inductively, by drawing conclusions solely from the sum total of the sources, must come to grief: "The manifold appearances of alleged religion in the variety of its contradictory forms would render it impossible to find a common concept of religion, rather than secure for induction the prospect of a general concept of religion as the final goal of inductive sampling."[32] The fundamental problem with induction, Cohen suggests, is that it cannot define a subject that is still developing: "history by itself does not determine anything about the essence and peculiarity of the concept, which, in the course of history up to now, may not yet have developed to its final realization."[33] Cohen proposes a different method for overcoming the problem of the plurality of sources: "It is impossible to develop a unifying concept of Judaism out of the literary sources unless the concept of Judaism itself is anticipated as an equal project."[34]

What this seminal passage means is that the student of Judaism must first approach the sources with a hypothesis about what the essence of Judaism must be. As a result of the interaction of the hypothesis with the sources, a more precise hypothesis will emerge, which, after a long process of this sort, will ultimately result in a definition of Judaism. The final goal is to find a hypothesis that is not contradicted by any of the sources.[35] Cohen believed that such a project is possible because the essence of Judaism is reason, and the hypotheses used to organize and examine the sources are themselves generated by reason. Hence it should be possible to formulate a hypothesis confirmed by all the sources of Judaism. He held that his own definition of monotheism as a rational idea was just such a hypothesis and that with it he was able to demonstrate the underlying unity of the literary sources of Judaism. Cohen avoided the problem of induction and relativism by proposing an idealist philosophy of history in which an *a priori* concept of Judaism is used to direct investigation of the sources. Reason could construct continuities between the ostensibly conflicting sources because the essence of the sources themselves was also reason.

How does Cohen, whom Scholem rejected so vehemently, help us in evaluating Scholem? We have already seen that Scholem's theology resembles Cohen's in certain fundamental respects, but it parts company with Cohen on the nature of the tradition. Where Cohen wanted a unified concept of Judaism, Scholem rejects the prejudice for unity at the outset; Judaism is, by nature, made up of contradictory principles. If the historian attempts to impose one unified "essence" of Judaism on his sources, he will destroy the vital struggle between opposing forces. Yet Scholem does not fall into the trap of a purely relativistic and inductive historiography. He operates with a very clear *a priori* principle of vitality, even as he attempts to define Judaism according to all its historical sources. As he writes in the introduction to *Sabbatai Ṣevi:* "I have written this book on the basis of a particular dialectical view of Jewish history and the forces acting within it. But from the start, more than just this view has been at work guiding my presentation—the view itself is the outcome of a constantly renewed immersion in the sources themselves."[36] Like Cohen, he portrays his work as a dynamic interaction between the historian's hypothesis and the message of his sources. Under the impact of the sources, the historian may be forced to modify his hypothesis, but there is no such thing as the sources producing, inductively, their own conclusions. The sources can only "speak for themselves" through the mediation of the historian's organizing hypothesis, even as that hypothesis undergoes continual change and refinement.

The organizing hypothesis Scholem uses in his study of Jewish history is that irrationalism constitutes a vital force in the unfolding of the tradition. But, as opposed to Cohen's use of the concept of rational monotheism to impose unity on the sources, Scholem suggests that irrationalism is the foundation of a pluralistic tradition. Instead of leading to a definition of the essence of Judaism, it is the principle that *denies* the search for an essence.

To be sure, such a position is fraught with difficulties, since any principle used in organizing the investigation of historical sources would seem to define the essence of those sources, even if the principle rejects the possibility of an essence. Although Scholem may be susceptible to such criticism on a philosophical level, he is saved precisely because he does not attempt to transform his anarchistic position into a philosophical system. Irrationalism is a dynamic force rather than a static and eternal essence. Since history is open-ended, irrationalism may no longer serve its vital function in Judaism in the future. Yet Scholem makes no predictions because he is an historian and not a philosopher. As an historian, he works with a circumscribed number of sources. Theoretically, of course, all things are possible within Judaism. But history did develop in a certain way and it has produced a finite number of sources which, even if they contradict one another, can still yield definite conclusions. Scholem's achievement lies in arguing that there is no essence of Judaism while simultaneously daring to identify the element in history that gave Judaism its vitality. Like Cohen's, his method is not purely inductive, for he starts with certain assumptions. But by adopting an antidogmatic organizing principle, he can still claim to be letting the sources speak for themselves without distortion. His anarchism is a third alternative to relativistic pluralism and dogmatism.

Although Cohen was not an historian of the Wissenschaft des Judentums, his rationalism represents, in a general way, the stand of nineteenth-century Judaism. Scholem's relationship to Cohen may be seen as a precise philosophical model for his relationship to his predecessors in historiography. His counter-history is not a simple rejection of the Wissenschaft des Judentums, for he borrows from his predecessors even as he transforms them. So, too, we have seen than in philosophy of history as in theology, Scholem has dialectically transformed Cohen's arguments. Like Cohen, he approaches his sources with a concept with which he claims to identify the vital elements in history. But his concept is the very opposite of Cohen's rationalism, and he rejects the philosophical quest for a unified system. Both Scholem and Cohen believe in a tradition consisting of interpretations of literary sources which may conflict. Scholem has perhaps taken Cohen's suggestion of a pluralistic tradition to its logical conclusion without succumbing to Cohen's own dogmatism, on the one hand, or relativism on the other. In historical perspective, Scholem's anarchistic philosophy of history as the counter pole to Cohen's rationalism is itself proof that the pluralistic tradition of contradictory interpretations continues and did not come to an end with Cohen. And, in the same light, Scholem's counter-history demonstrates that the search for an understanding of the Jewish tradition has not reached its final conclusion.

Epilogue

BETWEEN MYSTICISM
AND MODERNITY

Martin Buber once remarked that "all of us have students, some of us have even created schools, but only Gershom Scholem has created a whole academic discipline." Scholem's investigations of Jewish mysticism have indeed forced a major revision of Jewish historiography in the twentieth century and, more broadly, of the way Jews conceive of their history and their religion. Scholem's position in the history of Jewish historiography, and particularly his relationship to the Wissenschaft des Judentums, exemplify his relationship to the various political, cultural, and religious options open to modern Jews. I have characterized Scholem's revision of Jewish historiography as a dialectical neutralization rather than an outright negation of his predecessors. This relationship to the nineteenth-century historians, marked by both continuity and rebellion, may be taken as symptomatic of his general response to the European Jewish world from which he and they originated.

In his youth Scholem uncompromisingly rejected the possibility of Jewish life in the Diaspora but, at the same time, advocated a return to the sources produced in large measure by Diaspora Judaism. His position must be understood in the context of one of the central debates in the Zionist movement since the 1890s: How should Zionism relate to the Diaspora? The most extreme position, represented by intellectuals from Berdichevsky to the Canaanites, called for the complete "negation of the exile" (shlilat ha-galut) and of the Jewish tradition interwoven with it. Despite his own adamant attack on Jewish life in Germany, Scholem never joined the camp advocating negation of the exile. As a cultural Zionist inspired by Ahad Ha-am, he saw Zionism as primarily a revolutionary solution to the cultural and spiritual problem of Judaism in a secular world. The renewal of the Jewish community in the land of

Israel must be accompanied by a revival of Judaism, which in turn might make its impact felt on the diluted Jewish culture of the Diaspora. To be sure, without the actual building of a physical community in Israel, no revival would be possible, but the settlement itself was only a means to the larger end. As an educator and scholar, Scholem has conceived of his own work as a contribution toward this ideal of cultural renewal.

Scholem has never negated the exile because his rebellion against Diaspora Jewish life was accompanied by a return to historical Jewish sources. Diaspora culture, which for many Zionists evoked only feelings of embarrassment, was for him part of the rich tapestry of Jewish tradition. We have seen that Scholem relentlessly opposed those in the Zionist movement, like the Blau-Weiss, who built their ideology without knowledge of the historical tradition, or those, like the Revisionists, whom he perceived as apocalyptic secularists intent on cutting all ties with Jewish history. He argues that the legitimate and necessary desire to revolutionize Jewish existence cannot be based on the destruction of the tradition. Emigration to Palestine, he insisted in his youth, must be accompanied by return to the sources of tradition.

For Scholem, this return to tradition did not mean adoption of orthodoxy. Zionism represented a revolution precisely because it called for a return to Judaism on a new basis. Scholem's Zionism and his decision as an historian to study Jewish sources, each intimately bound up with the other, are part of his personal solution to the problem of Judaism in a secular age, a solution nourished by his profound desire for both rebellion and continuity.

Scholem maintains that if Israel is to preserve the vital tie with tradition even as it revolutionizes it, it cannot afford to turn its back on the Diaspora, which represents the source of much of that tradition. Since Zionism must "take responsibility" for the totality of Jewish life, it must also take responsibility for the Diaspora:

The return to Zion—which is not identical with dissolving into the Levant—will have incalculable consequences for the formation of our future if it does not try to avoid the fruitful tension between the forces that find expression in that return by coming to a one-sided and all-too-easy decision in favor of one of these forces. That is true of an orientation directed to an untransformed preservation of tradition as it is of one seeking to cut us off from the roots of that tradition . . . Without the impulses coming from the new life in Israel, the Judaism of the Diaspora will fall into decay. But Israel, too, is in need of the conscious connection and relation to the whole, the service and transformation of which, in the final analysis, constitutes the justification of its existence.[1]

In these lines, written in 1969, Scholem acknowledges that the Diaspora will continue to play a significant role in Jewish life, a position he might not have been so willing to take in his youth. But it is a position ultimately consistent with his experience in Palestine of the 1920s and 1930s and with the conclusions of his studies of mysticism and messianism. Since Zionism does not represent the end of Jewish history, but yet another stage in its continual development, the pluralistic struggle of the tradition must persist: the legitimate differences between Israel and the Diaspora can be turned into a fruitful interaction that will give Judaism new vitality. Scholem's position suggests that, in the dialogue between Israel and the Diaspora, neither side should claim a monopoly. In contemporary affairs, as in history, pluralism is the key to the survival of Judaism.

The dialectical relationship between continuity and rebellion was perhaps more possible for a German Jew in the early part of the twentieth century than for the many young Jews from Eastern Europe who also turned toward Zionism during the same period. The rebellion of Eastern European Jews necessarily had to be total, for, growing up in an orthodox environment, they adopted Zionism equally as a rejection of Diaspora existence and of the orthodox way of life of their parents. Although Scholem was profoundly influenced by his contact with Eastern Jews, his own rebellion had a different origin and followed a different course. Coming from an assimilated background, his rebellion also meant return. In Scholem's career, as individual as it is, we can observe the creative interplay and tension between Eastern and Western European Jewry, a relationship that also played a significant role in the evolution of the Zionist movement.

As a German Jew, Scholem retained many more of his ties to his motherland than did his contemporaries from Eastern Europe. While they found few redeeming virtues in Eastern European culture, he never severed himself from German culture, even as he rejected Germany. Although Scholem has written in Hebrew since the 1920s, he has not given up his mother tongue. Many of his most important reflections on the nature of the Kabbalah were first delivered as lectures in German and published in that language. His recent autobiography, *Von Berlin nach Jerusalem*, is replete with idioms in the Berlin dialect, thus bearing witness to his continuing attachment to the German language of his youth. But this attachment is not mere nostalgia for times past. If the Buber-Rosenzweig translation of the Bible into German was "the tombstone of a relationship which was extinguished in unspeakable horror,"[2] his own writing is aimed at showing the German-reading public a Judaism that is still very much alive. Since Scholem is evidently persuaded that the history of the Jewish community in Germany has come to an end, he may well believe that only now can Germans begin to understand the true nature of Judaism. In a peculiar way, Scholem and many of the other German Jews who emigrated see themselves as the embodiment of what Germany might have been; only on foreign soil could true German culture flourish and, then, in the hands of those Germany most rejected.

If Scholem's Zionism represents a third course between orthodoxy and total negation of the Diaspora, it also points to a new direction in the relationship of Jews to non-Jews. In the wake of the Holocaust, Jews have felt the unavoidable need to reevaluate this historical relationship. The answers that have been proposed to this dilemma cover the whole spectrum of opinion. On the one extreme, there are those, exemplified by the nationalistic wing of the Zionist movement, who reject any dialogue with the non-Jewish world, avowing that Israel is eternally fated to be "a nation which dwells alone." On the other hand, there are those who, acting almost as if the destruction of European Jewry was a tangential incident, still seek full Jewish assimilation on nineteenth-century terms.

Since 1922, when he denounced the "fascist tendencies" in the Blau-Weiss, and the late 1920s when he attacked the "chauvinism" of the Revisionists, Scholem has opposed the extreme nationalism to which Zionism has always been susceptible. He holds no brief for those who would cut Israel's ties to the western world, just as he rejects those who would cut the tie to Jewish tradition. On the other hand, he has written bitterly against the proponents of an easy reconciliation with the non-Jewish world, symbolized at its extreme by Germany: "I deny that there has ever been a . . . German-Jewish dialogue in any genuine sense as an historical phenomenon. To a dialogue belong two who listen to each other, who are ready to perceive who the other is and represents and [to] respond to him."[3] The very terms of emancipation precluded genuine dialogue, since the price pre-Nazi Germany exacted from the Jews for admission to its society was abandonment of their identity. To attempt after the Holocaust to "renew" a dialogue that had never existed is impossible, Scholem argues, and to create a new dialogue would be an extraordinarily difficult and delicate task in which both sides would have to overcome old stereotypes without betraying the burden of history.

Against the two extremes of national isolation and facile dialogue, Scholem suggests, echoing Max Brod, a "distant love." While the modern love of the Jews for Germany—and for Europe in general—had always gone unrequited when the Jews still lived in Diaspora, perhaps a new relationship could be established in the wake of Zionism, which had achieved the geographical separation of Jews and Europeans. Just as the new self-confidence that Zionism had bequeathed to the Jews might make possible an unapologetic historiography, so might the Jewish revival in Israel lay the basis for a genuine relationship between the Jews and the nations of the world. In no sense, however, does Scholem see this new relationship resulting from the "normalization" of the Jewish people, for that would be nothing more than a nationalist incarnation of the old sin of assimilation. The Jewish people must address the non-Jewish world with confidence in their own identity and tradition, but without cutting themselves off from the non-Jewish cultures in which they had lived for so many generations. Scholem's success in becoming a major spokesman for Judaism in the twentieth century may have much to do with the fact that he has not deliberately searched for a non-Jewish audience. Instead of attempting to create a direct dialogue with the western world, he has expressed his distant love indirectly, by writing without compromise or apologetics about Jewish history in all its obscure and esoteric facets.

It is perhaps surprising, even paradoxical, that an historian dealing with the most arcane of subjects—mysticism—should have become one of the universally recognized representatives of modern Judaism. Yet, in an age radically alienated from religious traditions, the quest for spirituality finds unexpected spokesmen. The method of counter-history, which asserts that vital religious forces never disappear, may be the only way to build bridges to an alien past. It is perhaps no coincidence that many of Scholem's contemporaries, such as Martin Buber and Walter Benjamin, constructed counter-histories in their search for a path back to tradition. In these attempts there is the same mixture of traditional sources and modern concepts. Caught between a modern culture they rejected, even as they expressed their rejection in its language, and a utopian alternative—whether Zionism or Marxism—they all groped for a viable synthesis between religion and secularism.

Scholem's counter-history is based on a new understanding of tradition, quite different from the normal secular definition according to which conservatism is the sole hallmark of tradition. Scholem argues instead:

there is also a life of tradition that does not merely consist of conservative preservation, the constant continuation of the spir-

itual and cultural possessions of a community . . . There are do-
mains of [tradition] that are hidden under the debris of centuries
and lie there waiting to be discovered and turned to good use . . .
There is such a thing as a treasure hunt within tradition, which
creates a living relationship to tradition and to which much of
what is best in current Jewish consciousness is indebted, even
where it was—and is—expressed outside the framework of orthodoxy.[4]

Through his studies of Jewish mysticism, Scholem believes he has
created a place for tradition—newly conceived—in a secular world.
In an essay on Franz Rosenzweig, Scholem noted:

The God who has been banished from man by psychology and
from the world by sociology, no longer desired to sit in the heavens and he therefore gave up the seat of the quality of justice to
dialectical materialism and the seat of the quality of mercy to
psychoanalysis. He contracted himself until nothing of him remained revealed . . . But perhaps his last contraction is really
revelation? Perhaps the disappearance of God into a point of
nothingness has a higher purpose and only in a world which has
been totally emptied of him will be where his kingdom is revealed?[5]

The failure of the secular sciences of Marxism and psychoanalysis
may itself be a sign of the hidden dialectic of the divine. Only now,
in full awareness of the crisis of secularism, can the creative potential in tradition be unearthed from under the debris of centuries.
The study of esoteric Jewish mysticism is perhaps the best preparation for the contemporary search for the religious spark that is now
so well hidden. By presenting Jewish mysticism in a modern and
accessible idiom while preserving the archaic and foreign intona-
tion of its voice, Scholem has put us in touch with forces at once
alien and yet paradoxically familiar.

A Birthday Letter
Selected Bibliography
Notes
Index

A Birthday Letter from Gershom Scholem to Zalman Schocken

Ein offenes Wort über die wahren Absichten meines Kabbalastudiums

Für Sie, lieber Herr Schocken, in Erinnerung an manche Stunden freundschaftlicher Mitteilung und unverschleierten Gedankenaustauschs, zu Ihrem 60. Gesburtstag. 29 Oktober 1937.

Ich bin keineswegs aus Versehen "Kabbalist" geworden. Ich wusste, was ich tat—nur habe ich mir meine Unternehmung offenbar viel zu leicht vorgestellt. Als ich mich daran machte den Shafpelz des Philologen anzuziehen und mich aus Mathematik und Erkenntnistheorie auf eine so viel zweideutigere Position zurückzuziehen, hatte ich zwar keinerlei Kenntnisse über meinen Gegenstand, aber ich stak voller "Einsichten".

Drei Jahre, die für mein ganzes Leben bestimmend geworden sind, 1916-1918, lagen hinter mir: sehr erregtes Denken hatte mich ebensosehr zur rationalsten Skepsis meinen Studiengegenständen gegenüber wie zur intuitiven Bejahung mysticher Thesen geführt, die haarscharf auf der Grenze zwischen Religion und Nihilismus lagen.

War es doch der vollkommene und unübertroffene Ausdruck dieser Grenze, der als die säkularisierte Darstellung kabbalistichen Weltgefühls in einem heutigen Gemüt mir später Kafkas Schriften fast mit dem Glanze des Kanonischen umkleidet hat.

Damals aber war Moliters seltsames Buch "Philosophie der Geschichte oder über die Tradition," das mir bei Poppelauer in die Hand gefallen war, von faszinierender Wirkung auf mich. So unfundiert es in Historischen auch sein mochte es gab eine Adresse an wo das geheime Leben des Judentums, dem ich in meinen Meditationen nachhing, einmal gewohnt zu haben schien.

So kam ich mir der Absicht, nicht die Historie, sondern die Metaphysik der Kabbala zu schreiben. Ich stand unter dem Eindruck der Armseligkeit dessen, was man gern Philosophie des Judentums nennt. An den drei einzigen Autoren, die ich kannte, an Saadja, Maimonides und Hermann Cohen empörte mich, wie sie ihre Hauptaufgabe darin fanden, Antithesen gegen den Mythos und den Pantheismus aufzustellen, sie zu "widerlegen", während es sich doch hätte darum handeln müssen, sie zu einer höheren Ordnung aufzuheben.

Es gehörte ja nichts dazu zu zeigen, dass Mythos und Pantheismus
"falsch" sind—viel wichtiger schien mir die Bemerkung, die mir zuerst ein
frommer Jude machte, dass dennoch etwas dran ist. Solch höhere Ordnung, wie entstellt immer zur Sprache gebracht, ahnte ich in der Kabbala.
Es schien mir, dass hier, jenseits der Einsicht meiner Generation, ein Reich
von Zusammenhängen existierte, die auch unsere menschlichsten Erfahrungen betreffen müssten.

Freilich, der Schlüssel zu dessen Verständnis schien verloren zu sein,
nach dem tristen Niveau der Aufklärung zu schliessen, die jüdische Ge-
lehrte darüber anzubieten hatten. Und doch, zu erstaunlich blitzte hier, in
den ersten Büchern der Kabbalisten, die ich mit glühendem Unverständnis
las, ein Denken auf, das offenbar—berlinisch gesprochen—noch nicht nach
Hause gefunden hatte.

Molitors Tiefblick, so schief auch die Perspektive Franz v. Baaders war,
aus der er kam, konnte nicht getrogen haben. Und vielleicht fehlte gar
nichte so sehr der Schlüssel als vielmehr nur eines: Mut. Mut, in einen Abgrund zu steigen, der eines Tages bei uns selber enden könnte. Mut auch,
durch die symbölische Fläche, die Wand der Historie hindurchzusetzen.

Denn der Berg, das Korpus der Dinge, bedarf gar keines Schlüssels; nur
die Nebelwand der Historie, die um ihn hängt, muss durchschritten
werden. Sie zu durchschreiten—daran habe ich mich gemacht. Ob ich im
Nebel stecken bleibe, sozusagen, den "Tod in der Professur" erleiden
werde? Aber die Notwendigkeit der historischen Kritik und kritischen Historie kann, auch wo sie Opfer verlangt, durch nichts anderes abgegolten
werden.

Gewiss, Geschichte mag im Grunde ein Schein sein, aber ein Schein,
ohne den in der Zeit keine Einsicht in das Wesen möglich ist. Im wunder-
lichen Hohlspiegel der philologischen Kritik kann für heutige Menschen
zuerst und auf die reinlichste Weise, in den legitimen Ordnungen des Kom-
mentars, jene mystische Totalität des Systems gesichtet werden, dessen
Existenz doch grade in der Projektion auf die historische Zeit verschwin-
det.

In diesem Paradox, aus solcher Hoffnung auf das richtige Angesprochen-
werden aus dem Berge, auf jene unscheinbarste, kleinste Verschiebung der
Historie, die aus dem Schein der "Entwicklung" Wahrheit hervorbrechen
lässt, lebt meine Arbeit, heute wie am ersten Tag.

                                                        Gershom Scholem

English translation, pages 74-76.

Selected Bibliography

WORKS BY GERSHOM SCHOLEM

Note: A complete bibliography of Scholem's work from 1915 to 1978 has been published by the Magnes Press of the Hebrew University, Jerusalem (1978). The following is a partial list of the books and articles used most frequently in this study.

"Abschied—Offener Brief an Herrn Dr. Siegfried Bernfeld und gegen die Leser dieser Zeitschrift." *Jerubbaal* 1 (1918-19), 125-130.

Die Blauweisse Brille. Nos. 1-3 (1915-16).

Das Buch Bahir. Leipzig, 1923.

Devarim be-Go—Pirke Morashah u-Teḥia. 2 vols., 2nd ed., Tel Aviv, 1976.

"Did Moses de Leon Write the Book Zohar?" (Hebrew). *Mada'ai ha-Ya-hadut* 1 (1926), 16-29.

"Education for Judaism." *Dispersion and Unity* 12 (1971), 205-214.

"Erklärung." *Die Jüdische Rundschau* 97 (8 December 1922), 638.

Die Geheimnisse der Schöpfung. Ein Kapitel aus dem Sohar. Berlin, 1935.

Jewish Gnosticism, Merkabah Mysticism and Talmudic Tradition. 2nd ed., New York, 1965.

Judaica. 3 vols., Frankfurt, 1968-1973.

"Jüdische Jugendbewegung." *Der Jude* 1 (1916), 822-825.

"Jugendbewegung, Jugendarbeit und Blau-Weiss." *Blau-Weiss Blätter (Führerzeitung)* 1 (1917), 26-30.

Leket Margaliot. Tel Aviv, 1941.

"Lyrik der Kabbala?" *Der Jude* 6 (1921-1922), 55-69.

Major Trends in Jewish Mysticism. 3rd ed., New York, 1961.

Meḥkarim u-Mekorot le-Toldot ha-Shabta'ut ve-Gilguleha. Jerusalem, 1974.

The Messianic Idea in Judaism and Other Essays on Jewish Spirituality. New York, 1971.

"The Name of God and the Linguistic Theory of the Kabbala." *Diogenes* 79 (1972), 59-80, and 80 (1972), 164-194.

"Offener Brief an den Verfasser der Schrift 'Jüdischer Glaube in dieser Zeit.' " *Bayerische Israelitische Gemeindezeitung,* 15 August 1932, 241-244.

On Jews and Judaism in Crisis, ed. Werner J. Dannhauser. New York, 1976.

On the Kabbala and Its Symbolism, trans. R. Mannheim. New York, 1969.

Pirke Yisod be-Havanat ha-Kabbala u-Semaleha. Jerusalem, 1976.

Sabbatai Ṣevi. The Mystical Messiah, 1626-1676. Revised English edition, trans. R. J. Z. Werblowsky. Princeton, 1973.

"Three Sins of Brit Shalom" (Hebrew). *Davar,* 24 November 1929, 2.

Über einige Grundbegriffe des Judentums. Frankfurt, 1970.

Über die jüngste Sohar-Anthologie." *Der Jude* 5 (1920-1921), 363-369.

Ursprung und Anfänge der Kabbala. Berlin, 1962.

Von Berlin nach Jerusalem. Frankfurt, 1977.

Von der mystischen Gestalt der Gottheit. Frankfurt, 1973.

Walter Benjamin—Die Geschichte einer Freundschaft. Frankfurt, 1975.

"Wohnt Gott im Herzen eines Atheisten?" *Der Spiegel,* 7 July 1975, 110-115.

"Zur Frage der Entstehung der Kabbala." *Korrespondenzblatt* 9 (1928), 4-26.

GENERAL WORKS

Note: For a complete bibliography of works on the Kabbalah to 1927, see Scholem's *Bibliographia Kabbalistica. Die jüdische Mystik (Gnosis, Kabbala, Sabbatianismus, Frankismus, Chassidismus) behandelnde Bücher und Aufsätze von Reuchlin bis zur Gegenwart* (Berlin, 1933).

Ahad Ha-am, *Selected Essays of Ahad Ha-am,* trans. Leon Simon. New York, 1962.

Ahimeier, Abba, *Brit ha-Biryonim.* Tel Aviv, 1972.

Alter, Robert, "The Achievement of Gershom Scholem." *Commentary* 55 (April 1973), 69-73.

———— *After the Tradition.* New York, 1971.

Altmann, Alexander. "Leo Baeck and the Jewish Mystical Tradition." *Leo Baeck Memorial Lecture* 17. London, 1973.

———— *Studies in Religious Philosophy and Mysticism.* London, 1969.

———— "Theology in Twentieth Century German Jewry." *LBIY* 1 (1956), 193-217.

———— "Zur Auseinandersetzung mit der dialektischen Theologie." *MGWJ* 79, n.s. 43 (1935), 345-361.

Anz, Wilhelm, *Zur Frage nach dem Ursprung des Gnostizismus.* Leipzig, 1897.

Baeck, Leo, *Aus Drei Jahrtausenden.* Tübingen, 1958.

Baer, F. Y., "Clarification of the Situation of Our Historical Studies" (Hebrew). *Sefer Magnes.* Jerusalem, 1938.

———— "The Function of Mysticism in Jewish History" (Hebrew). *Zion* 7 (1942), 55-64.

———— "The Historical Background of the Raya Mehemna" (Hebrew). *Zion* 5 (1939), 1-44.

———— "Religious and Social Tendencies in the Sefer Hasidim" (Hebrew). *Zion* 1 (1935), 1-50.

———— *Yisrael ba-Amim.* Jerusalem, 1955.

Baron, Salo, *History and Jewish Historians,* Philadelphia, 1964.

Ben David, Lazarus, "Uber den Glauben der Juden an einen Künftigen Messias." *Zeitschrift für die Wissenschaft des Judentums* 2 (1822), 200-225.

Ben Ezer, Ehud, ed., *Unease in Zion.* New York, 1974.

Benjamin, Walter, *Briefe,* ed. T. W. Adorno and G. Scholem. 2 vols., Frankfurt, 1966.

———— *Gesammelte Schriften,* ed. R. Tiedemann and H. Schweppenhäuser. 3 vols., Frankfurt, 1972-1974.

———— *Illuminations,* trans. Harry Zohn, ed. Hannah Arendt. New York, 1969.

———— *Schriften,* ed. T. W. and G. Adorno. 2 vols. Frankfurt, 1955.

———— *Ursprung des deutschen Trauerspiels.* Frankfurt, 1972.

Bergmann, S. H., *Hogai ha-Dor.* Jerusalem, 1935.

———— "The Principle of Beginning in the Philosophy of Hermann Cohen" (Hebrew). *Keneset* 8 (1944), 143-153.

———— *Toldot ha-Filosofia ha-Hadasha.* Jerusalem, 1970.

Bin Gorion (Berdichevsky), Micha Yosef, *Kol Kitve Bin Gorion.* 2 vols., Tel Aviv, 1965.

———— *Me-Ozar ha-Aggada.* Berlin, 1914.

———— *Sinai v'Gerizim.* Hebrew trans. Tel Aviv, 1962.

Bloch, Ernst, *Atheism in Christianity,* trans. J. T. Swann. New York, 1972.

Boeckh, August, *On Interpretation and Criticism,* trans. J. P. Pritchard. Norman, Oklahoma, 1968.

Buber, Martin, *Briefwechsel aus sieben Jahrzehnten,* ed. G. Schaeder. 3 vols., Heidelberg, 1972-1975.

———— *Ekstatische Konfessionen.* Jena, 1909.

———— *Die Geschichte des Rabbi Nachman.* Frankfurt, 1906.

———— *Der Grosse Maggid und seine Nachfolge.* Frankfurt, 1922.

———— *Hasidism and Modern Man,* trans. M. Friedman. New York, 1958.

———— *I and Thou,* trans. W. Kaufmann. New York, 1970.

———— *Die Jüdische Bewegung.* 2 vols., Berlin, 1916-1920.

———— *Die Legende des Baal Schem.* Frankfurt, 1908.

———— *On the Bible,* trans. Olga Marx. New York, 1968.

———— *On Judaism,* trans. Eva Jospe. New York, 1967.

———— *The Origin and Meaning of Hasidism,* trans. M. Friedman. New York, 1960.

———— *Paths in Utopia,* trans. R. F. C. Hull. New York, 1958.

———— *Die Schrift und ihre Verdeutschung.* Berlin, 1936.

———— "Theory of Hasidism" (Hebrew). *Amot* 2 (1963-64).

———— *Werke.* 3 vols., Munich, 1962.

Bulthaup, Peter, ed., *Materialien zu Benjamins Thesen "Über den Begriff der Geschichte."* Frankfurt, 1975.

Cain, S., "Gershom Scholem on Jewish Mysticism." *Midstream* 17 (December 1970), 35-51.

Calvary, Moses, "Feldbriefe." *Die Jüdische Rundschau,* 26 November 1914, 7.

Cassirer, Ernst, *The Philosophy of Symbolic Forms.* 3 vols., New Haven, 1955.

Chomsky, Noam, *Current Issues in Linguistic Theory.* The Hague, 1964.

Cohen, Arthur A., *The Natural and the Supernatural Jew.* New York, 1964.

Cohen, Gerson D., "German Jewry as Mirror of Modernity." *LBIY* 20 (1975), ix-xxxi.

Cohen, Geula, *Woman of Violence,* trans. Hillel Halkin. New York, 1966.

Cohen, Hermann, *Ethik des reinen Willens.* 2nd ed., Berlin, 1907.

—— *Jüdische Schriften,* ed. Bruno Strauss. 3 vols., Berlin, 1924.

—— *Logik der reinen Erkenntnis.* Berlin, 1902.

—— *Reason and Hope,* trans. and ed. Eva Jospe. New York, 1971.

—— *Die Religion der Vernunft aus den Quellen des Judentums.* Frankfurt, 1919. English trans. by Simon Kaplan, New York, 1972.

Collingwood, R. G., *The Idea of History.* New York, 1956.

Danto, Arthur, *Analytical Philosophy of History.* London, 1965.

—— *Nietzsche as Philosopher.* New York, 1965.

Davies, W. D., "From Schweitzer to Scholem—Reflections on Sabbatai Sevi." *Journal of Biblical Literature* 95 (1976), 529-558.

Delitzsch, Friedrich, *Babel and Bible,* trans C. Johns. New York-London, 1903.

Dinur, Ben-Zion, *Be-Mifne ha-Dorot.* Jerusalem, 1974.

—— *Israel and the Diaspora.* Philadelphia, 1969.

Dubnow, Simon, *Nationalism and History,* ed. K. Pinson. Philadelphia, 1958.

Emden, Jacob, *Holi Ketem.* Altona, 1775.

—— *Mitpaḥat Sefarim.* Lvov, 1870; Jerusalem, 1970.

—— *Sefer Shimush.* Amsterdam, 1762.

Fishman, Samuel. "Aspects of Berdichevsky's Historiography." Diss., University of California, Los Angeles, 1968.

—— "Berdichevsky on the Meaning of History." *Judaism* 21 (1972), 104-109.

Flohr, Paul, "From Kulturmystik to Dialogue—The Formation of Martin Buber's Philosophy of I and Thou." Diss., Brandeis University, 1973.

Freud, Sigmund, *Character and Culture,* ed. P. Rieff. New York, 1963.

Freund, Else, *Die Existenzphilosophie Franz Rosenzweigs.* Hamburg, 1959.

Geiger, Abraham, *Nachgelassene Schriften,* ed. L. Geiger. 2 vols., Breslau, 1875-1878.

Glatzer, Nahum, "The Beginnings of Modern Jewish Studies." In *Studies in Jewish Intellectual History,* 27-45, ed. A. Altmann. Cambridge, 1964.

—— *Franz Rosenzweig.* New York, 1961.

Graetz, Heinrich, *Frank und die Frankisten.* Breslau, 1868.

—— *Geschichte der Juden.* 11 vols. 2nd ed., Leipzig, 1866.

—— *Gnosticismus und Judentum.* Krotoschin, 1846.

—— *The History of the Jews,* trans. Bella Lowy. 5 vols. London, 1904.

—— "Die Konstruktion der jüdischen Geschichte." *Zeitschrift für die religiosen Interessen des Judentums* 3 (1846), 81-97, 121-132, 361-368.

—— "Die mystische Literatur in der gäonischen Epoche." *MGWJ* 8 (1859), 67-78, 103-118, 140-153.

—— *The Structure of Jewish History,* trans. I Schorsch. New York, 1975.

Gombrich, E. H., *Aby Warburg—An Intellectual Biography.* London, 1970.

Gross, Walter, "Zionist Students' Movement." *LBIY* 4 (1959), 143-165.

Guttmann, Julius, *Philosophies of Judaism.* New York, 1973.

—— "Rabbi Nachman Krochmal" (Hebrew). *Keneset* 6 (1941), 259-287.

Habermas, Jürgen, "Die verkleidete Tora. Rede zum 80. Geburtstag von Gershom Scholem." *Merkur,* January 1978, 96-104.

Halkin, Simon, *Modern Hebrew Literature.* New York, 1950.

Hattis, Susan Lee, *The Bi-national Idea in Palestine During Mandatory Times.* Haifa, 1970.

Herlitz, Georg, "Three Jewish Historians—Jost, Graetz and Täubler." *LBIY* 9 (1964), 69-90.

Hodges, H. A., *The Philosophy of Wilhelm Dilthey.* London, 1952.

Hoffer, Willie, "Siegfried Bernfeld and Jerubbaal." *LBIY* 10 (1965), 150-167.

Holz, Hans Heinz, "Philosophie als Interpretation." *Alternative* 56/57 (1967).

Horodezky, S. A., *Ḥasidut ve-ha-Ḥasidim.* Berlin, 1922.

Hughes, H. Stuart, *Consciousness and Society.* New York, 1958.

Hurwicz, E., "Shai Ish-Hurwitz and the Berlin He-Atid." *LBIY* 12 (1967), 85-102.

Hurwitz, Shai, ed. *He-Atid,* I-VI (1908-1924).

—— *Me-Ayin u-Le'ayin?* Berlin, 1914.

Jay, Martin, *The Dialectical Imagination.* Boston, 1973.

—— "Politics of Translation—Siegfried Kracauer and Walter Benjamin on the Buber-Rosenzweig Bible." *LBIY* 21 (1976), 3-24.

Jellinek, Adolf, *Auswahl kabbalistischer Mystik.* Leipzig, 1853.

Joel, D. H., *Die Religionsphilosophie des Sohar.* Leipzig, 1849.

Jonas, Hans, *Gnosis und spätantiker Geist.* Göttingen, 1934.

—— *The Gnostic Religion.* Boston, 1963.

Jones, Rufus, *Studies in Mystical Religion.* London, 1909.

Jung, C. G., *Dreams,* trans. R. F. C. Hull. Princeton, 1974.

Kaufmann, W., *Gola ve-Nekhar.* 2 vols., Tel Aviv, 1961.

Katz, Jacob, "On the Question of the Connection Between Sabbatianism, Enlightenment, and Reform" (Hebrew). *Studies in Honor of Alexander Altmann.* Forthcoming.

Keshet, Yeshurun, *M. Y. Berdichevsky.* Jerusalem, 1958.

Ketavim—Lohamei Herut Yisrael. 2 vols., Tel Aviv, 1959.

Klausner, Joseph, *The Messianic Idea in Israel,* trans. W. Stinespring. New York, 1955.

Klausner-Eshkol, A. *Hashpa'at Nietzsche ve-Schopenhauer al M. Y. Bin Gorion.* Tel Aviv, 1954.

Kochan, Lionel, *The Jew and His History.* New York, 1977.

Krochmal, Nachman, *Kitve Rabbi Nachman Krochmal,* ed. S. Rawidowicz. Berlin, 1924; Waltham, 1960.

Kurzweil, Baruch, *Ba-Ma'avak al Arkhai ha-Yahadut.* Tel Aviv, 1969.

——— *Sifrutenu ha-Hadasha—Hemshekh O Mahapekhah?* Jerusalem, 1971.

Kutschera, F. V., *Sprachphilosophie.* Munich, 1971.

Lachover, F., "Revealed and Hidden in the Doctrines of Nachman Krochmal" (Hebrew). *Keneset* 6 (1941), 296-332.

Laqueur, Walter, "The German Youth Movement and the Jewish Question." *LBIY* 6 (1961), 193-206.

——— *A History of Zionism.* New York, 1972.

——— *Young Germany.* New York, 1962.

Lew, Marcel, "Hebräische Sprache und Hebräische Literatur." *Die Jüdische Studenten* 19 (1921-1922), 221-225.

Liebeschütz, Hans, *Das allegorische Weltbild der Heiligen Hildegard von Bingen.* Leipzig, 1930.

——— "Judaism and History of Religion in Leo Baeck's Work." *LBIY* 2 (1957), 8-21.

——— *Von Simmel zu Rosenzweig.* Tübingen, 1970.

——— "Wissenschaft des Judentums und Historismus bei Abraham Geiger." In *Essays Presented to Leo Baeck,* 75-94. London, 1954.

Link-Salinger, Ruth, *Gustav Landauer—Philosopher of Utopia.* Indianapolis, 1977.

Löwith, Karl, *From Hegel to Nietzsche,* trans. D. Green. New York, 1967.

——— *Meaning in History.* Chicago, 1949.

Lucas, Noah, *The Modern History of Israel.* New York, 1975.

Lunn, Eugene, *Prophet of Community—The Romantic Socialism of Gustav Landauer.* Berkeley-Los Angeles, 1973.

Mannheim, Karl, *Ideology and Utopia,* trans. L. Wirth and E. Shills. New York, 1936.

Marcus, Ahron, *Hartmanns inductive Philosophie im Chassidismus.* Vienna, 1888.

Margalit, Elkanah, *Hashomer ha-Tzair.* Tel Aviv, 1971.

Margulies, Heinrich, "Der Krieg der Zurückbleibenden." *Die Jüdische Rundschau,* 5 February 1915, 46-47.

Mauthner, Fritz, *Beiträge zur Kritik der Sprache.* 3 vols., Leipzig, 1923.

——— *Wörterbuch der Philosophie.* 3 vols. 2nd ed., Leipzig, 1923-1924.

Meyer, Michael, "Abraham Geiger's Historical Judaism." In *New Perspectives on Abraham Geiger,* 3-17. Cincinnati, 1975.

——— *Ideas of Jewish History.* New York, 1974.

—— *Origins of the Modern Jew*. Detroit, 1967.

Misch, Georg, *Lebensphilosophie und Phänomenologie*. 2nd ed., Leipzig and Berlin, 1931.

Molitor, Franz Josef, *Die Philosophie der Geschichte oder über die Tradition*. 2 vols., Münster, 1834-1857.

Moses, Siegfried, "Salman Schocken—His Economic and Zionist Activities." *LBIY* 5 (1960), 73-104.

Mosse, George, *The Crisis of German Ideology*. New York, 1964.

—— *Germans and Jews*. New York, 1970.

Nash, Stanley, "Shay Hurwitz—A Pioneering Polemicist for Truth." *Judaism* 22 (1973), 322-327.

Neander, August, *Genetische Entwicklung der vornehmsten gnostischen Systeme*. Berlin, 1818.

Neumann, Erich, *The Origins and History of Consciousness*, trans. R. F. C. Hull. Princeton, 1954.

Neumark, David, *Geschichte der jüdischen Philosophie des Mittelalters*. 2 vols., Berlin, 1907.

Nietzsche, Friedrich, *Anti-Christ*, trans. R. J. Hollingdale. Baltimore, 1968.

—— *Beyond Good and Evil*, trans. W. Kaufmann. New York, 1966.

—— *The Use and Abuse of History*, trans. Adrian Collins. Indianapolis, 1967.

Oppenheimer, Franz, "Alte und Neue Makkabäer." *Jüdische Rundschau*, 28 August 1914.

Otto, Rudolf, *The Holy. An Inquiry into the Non-rational Factor in the Idea of the Divine and Its Relation to the Rational*, trans. J. W. Harvey. 2nd ed., London, 1952.

Overbeck, Franz, *Christentum und Kultur*. Basel, 1919.

Perlmutter, Moses, *Yonathan Eybeschutz ve-Yaḥso el ha-Shabta'ut*. Tel Aviv, 1947.

Poppell, Steven, "Salman Schocken and the Schocken Verlag." *LBIY* 17 (1972), 93-117.

—— *Zionism in Germany*. Philadelphia, 1977.

Rawidowicz, Simon, *Studies in Jewish Thought*. Philadelphia, 1974.

Reinharz, Jehuda, *Fatherland or Promised Land*. Ann Arbor, 1975.

Reissner, Hanns, "Der Berliner Wissenschaftzirkel." *Leo Baeck Institut Bulletin* 6 (1963), 101-112.

Rosenzweig, Franz, *Briefe*, ed. Edith Rosenzweig. Berlin, 1935.

—— *On Jewish Learning*, trans. N. Glatzer. New York, 1965.

—— *Der Stern der Erlösung*. Frankfurt, 1921.

Rosmarin, T. W., *Religion of Reason: Hermann Cohen's System of Religious Philosophy*. New York, 1936.

Rotenstreich, Nathan, "Absolute and Change in the Thought of Krochmal" (Hebrew). *Keneset* 6 (1941), 333-345.

—— "Graetz and the Philosophy of History" (Hebrew). *Zion* 8 (1942), 51-59.

———— *Ha-Maḥshava ha-Yehudit ba-Et ha-Ḥadasha.* Tel Aviv, 1966.
———— "Krochmal's Concept of History" (Hebrew). *Zion* 7 (1942), 29-47.
Sasportas, Jacob, *Ẓiẓat Novel Ẓvi,* ed. I. Tishby. Jerusalem, 1954.
Schelling, F., *Einleitung in die Philosophie der Mythologie.* In *Sämtliche Werke,* pt. 22, vol. II. Stuttgart and Augsburg, 1856.
Schoeps, Hans Joachim, *Bereit für Deutschland.* Berlin, 1970.
———— *Ja-Nein-und Trotzdem.* Mainz, 1974.
———— *Jüdischer Glaube in dieser Zeit.* Berlin, 1934.
———— ed., *Steinheim zum Gedenken.* Leiden, 1966.
Schorsch, Ismar, "From Wolfenbüttel to Wissenschaft: The Divergent Paths of Isaak Markus Jost and Leopold Zunz." *LBIY* 22 (1977), 109-128.
———— "The Philosophy of History of Nachman Krochmal." *Judaism* 10 (1961), 237-245.
Schweid, Eliezer, "Nachman Krochmal's Philosophy and Its Relationship to the Philosophy of Maimonides, the Kabbalah, and Modern Philosophy" (Hebrew). *Iyyun* 20 (1969), 29-59.
Schweitzer, Albert, *The Quest for the Historical Jesus.* New York, 1968.
Seeberg, Erich, *Gottfried Arnold.* Meerane in Sachsen, 1923. Republished Darmstadt, 1964.
Seils, Martin, *Wirklichkeit und Wort bei J. G. Hamann.* Stuttgart, 1961.
Shand, James, "Doves among the Eagles—German Pacifists and Their Government during World War I." *Journal of Contemporary History* 10 (1975), 95-108.
Shatz, Rivka, *Ha-Ḥasidut ki-Mistika.* Tel Aviv, 1968.
Shatzker, Haim, "The Jewish-German Attitude of German-Jewish Youth at the Time of the First World War" (Hebrew). In *Meḥkarim B'Toldot Am Yisrael ve-Eretz Yisrael,* II, 187-215. Tel Aviv, 1972.
———— "Tenuat ha-Noar ha-Yehudit." Diss., Hebrew University, Jerusalem, 1970.
Shavit, Ya'akov, "The Ideology of Israeli Anti-Semitism" (Hebrew). M.A. thesis, Tel Aviv University, 1972.
———— "The Relation between Idea and Poetics in the Poetry of Yonatan Ratosh" (Hebrew). *Ha-Sifrut* 17 (Fall 1974), 66-91.
Shazar (Rubaschoff), Zalman, *Al Tilei Bet Frank.* Berlin, 1922-23.
———— *Ore Dorot.* Jerusalem, 1971.
Shochat, Azriel, *Im Ḥilufei ha-Tekufot.* Jerusalem, 1960.
Simon, Ernst, "Das dunkle Licht, Gershom Scholems *Judaica III.*" *Mitteilungsblatt des Irgun Olej Merkaz Europa,* 5 April 1974, 5-6.
———— "Über einige theologische Sätze von Gershom Scholem." *Mitteilungsblatt des Irgun Olej Merkaz Europa,* 8 December 1972, 3ff, and 15 December 1970, 4ff.
Steiner, George, *After Babel.* New York, 1975.
———— "Inner Lights." *The New Yorker,* 22 October 1973, 152-174.
Steinheim, Solomon Ludwig, *Die Glaubenslehre der Synagogue.* Leipzig, 1856.
———— *Die Offenbarung nach der Lehre der Synagogue.* Frankfurt, 1835.

Stern, Selma, "Eugen Täubler and the Wissenschaft des Judentums." *LBIY* 3 (1958), 40-59.

Strauss, Leo, *Persecution and the Art of Writing*. Glencoe, Ill., 1952.

Tal, Uriel, "Theologische Debatte um das 'Wesen' des Judentums." In *Juden im wilhelminischen Deutschland 1890-1914*, 599-633, ed. Werner Mosse. Tübingen, 1976.

Taubes, Jacob, "Krochmal and Modern Historicism." *Judaism* 12 (1963), 150-165.

Tiedemann, Rudolf, *Studien zur Philosophie Walter Benjamins*. Frankfurt, 1973.

Tishby, Isaiah, "The Messianic Idea in the Rise of Hasidism" (Hebrew). *Zion* 32 (1967), 1-45.

―――― *Mishnat ha-Zohar*. Jerusalem, 1971.

―――― *Netive Emunah u-Minut*. Ramat Gan, 1964.

Tramer, Hans, "Gershom Scholem zum 75. Geburtstag." *Mitteilungsblatt des Irgun Olej Merkaz Europa*, 8 December 1972, 3.

Troeltsch, Ernst, "Die Krise des Historismus." *Neue Rundschau* 33 (1922), 572-590.

Ucko, Sinai, "Geistesgeschichtliche Grundlagen der Wissenschaft des Judentums." In *Wissenschaft des Judentums im deutschen Sprachbereich*, I, 315-353. Tübingen, 1967.

Underhill, Evelyn, *Mysticism. A Study in the Nature and Development of Man's Spiritual Consciousness*. London, 1926.

Urbach, E. E., "Traditions Concerning Mystical Doctrines in the Period of the Tannaim" (Hebrew). In *Sefer Ha-Yovel Li-Khvod Gershom Scholem*, 1-29. Jerusalem, 1968.

Weiler, Gershon, *Mauthner's Critique of Language*. Cambridge, 1970.

―――― "On the Theology of Gershom Scholem" (Hebrew). *Keshet* 71 (1976), 121-128.

Weiss, J. G., "Via Passiva in Early Hasidism." *Journal of Jewish Studies* 11 (1969), 137-157.

Werblowsky, R. J. Z., *Joseph Karo, Lawyer and Mystic*. London, 1962.

―――― "Philo and the Zohar." *Journal of Jewish Studies* 10 (1959), 25-45, 113-137.

―――― "Reflections on Gershom Scholem's Sabbatai Zevi" (Hebrew). *Molad* 15 (November 1957), 539-547.

Wiener, Max, ed., *Abraham Geiger and Liberal Judaism*. Philadelphia, 1962.

―――― "The Ideology of the Founders of Jewish Scientific Research." *YIVO Annual of Social Science* 5 (1950), 184-196.

―――― *Die jüdische Religion im Zeitalter der Emanzipation*. Hebrew trans. Y. Amir. Jerusalem, 1974.

Wieseltier, Leon, "Etwas über die jüdische Historik: Leopold Zunz and the Inception of Modern Jewish Historiography." *Sciences philologiques et traditions culturelles nationales aux XIXe siècle*, ed. H. Wissman. Paris, 1978.

―――― "The Revolt of Gershom Scholem" and "Gershom Scholem and the

Fate of the Jews." *New York Review of Books,* 31 March 1977, 23-26,
    and 14 April 1977, 27-30.
Wolf, Immanuel, "Über den Begriff einer Wissenschaft des Judentums."
    Zeitschrift für die Wissenschaft des Judentums 1 (1822), 1-24.
Yerushalmi, Y. H., *From Spanish Court to Italian Ghetto—Isaac Cardoso.*
    New York, 1971.
Zeitlin, Hillel, *Be-Fardes ha-Hasidut ve-ha-Kabbala.* Tel Aviv, 1965.
Zunz, Leopold, *Gesammelte Schriften.* 3 vols., Berlin, 1875.
Zweig, Stefan, *The World of Yesterday.* Edinburgh, 1943.

ABBREVIATIONS

Works by Scholem:

Grundbegriffe	*Über einige Grundbegriffe des Judentums.* Frankfurt, 1970.
Jewish Gnosticism.	*Jewish Gnosticism, Merkabah Mysticism and Talmudic Tradition.* 2nd ed. New York, 1965.
JJC	*On Jews and Judaism in Crisis,* ed. Werner J. Dannhauser. New York, 1976.
KS	*On the Kabbala and Its Symbolism.* New York, 1969.
MI	*The Messianic Idea in Judaism and Other Essays in Jewish Spirituality.* New York, 1971.
MT	*Major Trends in Jewish Mysticism.* 3rd ed., New York, 1961.
SS	*Sabbatai Sevi. The Mystical Messiah, 1626-1676,* rev. Eng. ed. trans. R. J. Z. Werblowsky. Princeton, 1973.
Von Berlin	*Von Berlin nach Jerusalem.* Frankfurt, 1977.
Walter Benjamin	*Walter Benjamin—Die Geschichte einer Freundschaft.* Frankfurt, 1975.

Journals:

Korrespondenzblatt	*Korrespondenzblatt des Vereines zur Grundung und Erhaltung einer Akademie für die Wissenschaft des Judentums.*
LBIY	*Leo Baeck Institute Year Book.*
MGWJ	*Monatsschrift für Geschichte und Wissenschaft des Judentums.*

Notes

INTRODUCTION

1. *Walter Benjamin*, 116-117, and *Von Berlin*, 157-158.

2. Reported by Gotthold Weil in the *Jüdische Rundschau* in 1907 after Steinschneider's death. Scholem was responsible for making Steinschneider's remark well known. See "Reflections on the Science of Judaism" (Hebrew), *Luah Ha-Aretz* (1944-45), 102, reprinted in *Devarim be-Go*, 2nd ed. (Tel Aviv, 1976) 393.

3. *Walter Benjamin*, 117.

4. See, for example, "Reflections on the Possibility of Jewish Mysticism in Our Time," (Hebrew), *Amot* 2 (1964), 11-19; "With Gershom Scholem," *JJC*, 32-33; "Zionism—Dialectic of Continuity and Rebellion," in *Unease in Zion*, ed. Ehud Ben Ezer (New York, 1974), 279ff; and "Education for Judaism," *Dispersion and Unity* 12 (1971), 209.

5. *Walter Benjamin*, 117.

6. *Devarim be-Go*, 385-403.

7. The attempt to revise Scholem has been proposed, significantly, by two historians from the Jewish Theological Seminary, Gerson Cohen and Ismar Schorsch. The essence of these arguments is that there was a conservative Wissenschaft des Judentums which actually sought to preserve living Judaism. See Cohen, "German Jewry as Mirror of Modernity" *LBIY* 20 (1975), ix-xxxi, esp. xxv, and Schorsch, "From Wolfenbüttel to Wissenschaft—The Divergent Paths of Isaak Markus Jost and Leopold Zunz," *LBIY* 22 (1977), 109-128, esp. 114, for his attack on Scholem.

8. Ibid., 398.

9. "Science of Judaism," *MI*, 309. Many of the ideas Scholem developed in the Hebrew article in 1945 reappear in new formulations in this essay, originally delivered as an address in London in 1960. Scholem's tone is more restrained in the later essay, particularly in regard to his colleagues at the Hebrew University, but there is no evidence that his views substantially changed.

10. *Devarim be-Go*, 396.

11. See Jacob and Wilhelm Grimm, *Deutsches Wörterbuch* (Leipzig, 1860), II, 715.

12. *Devarim be-Go*, 394.

13. "Science of Judaism," *MI*, 305. See also Scholem's attack on modern Jewish theology in "Franz Rosenzweig and His Book 'The Star of Redemption' " (Hebrew), *Devarim be-Go*, 413ff.

14. Ibid., 386-391.

15. Ibid., 393-394.

16. Ibid., 398; *MI*, 31-312.

17. Ibid: for Graetz, 397, for Krochmal, 390.

18. See Bialik's "Open Letter" to the editors of *Devir* 1 (1923). For Scholem's rejection of Bialik, see *Devarim be-Go*, 395. Scholem's general response to Bialik's call for a rejuvenated Wissenschaft was very positive. See his letter to Bialik, republished in *Devarim be-Go*, and the discussion of Scholem's letter, Chapter Five.

19. Ibid., 402.

20. Ibid., 399.

21. Ibid., 400-401.

22. Ibid., 388.

23. Ibid., 391.

24. Ibid., 399.

25. Ibid., 393.

1. THE NINETEENTH-CENTURY LEGACY

1. *The Philosophy of the Enlightenment* (Boston, 1951), 197-233.

2. August Boeckh, *On Interpretation and Criticism*, trans. J. P. Pritchard (Norman, Oklahoma, 1968), 48.

3. On the Verein and the early Wissenschaft des Judentums, see Michael Meyer, *Origins of the Modern Jew* (Detroit, 1967), 144-183; Max Wiener, *Die jüdische Religion im Zeitalter der Emanzipation* (Hebrew trans., Jerusalem, 1974), 204-284; Max Wiener, "The Ideology of the Founders of Jewish Scientific Research," *YIVO Annual of Social Science* 5 (1950), 184-196; Hanns Reissner, "Der Berliner Wissenschaftzirkel," *Leo Baeck Institut Bulletin* 6 (1963), 101-112; Zalman Rubaschoff (Shazar), "Erstlinge der Entjudung: Drei Reden von Eduard Gans im Kulturverein," *Der jüdische Wille* 1 (1918), 30-42 (Hebrew trans. in Zalman Shazar, *Ore Dorot*, Jerusalem, 1971, 351-385); Sinai Ucko, "Geistesgeschichtliche Grundlagen der Wissenschaft des Judentums," *Wissenschaft des Judentums im deutschen Sprachbereich* (Tübingen, 1967), I, 315-353; Nahum Glatzer, "The Beginnings of Modern Jewish Studies," in *Studies in Jewish Intellectual History*, ed. A. Altmann (Cambridge, 1964), 27-45.

4. *Jüdische Wille*, 198 (English trans. in Meyer, *Origins of the Modern Jew*, 167).

5. Ibid., 42 (Meyer, 166).

6. Zunz's most important historical essays have been collected in his *Gesammelte Schriften*, 3 vols. (Berlin, 1875). On Zunz, see L. Wallach, *Liberty and Letters: The Thoughts of Leopold Zunz* (London, 1959), and Leon Wieseltier, "Etwas über die jüdische Historik: Leopold Zunz and the Inception of Modern Jewish Historiography," to be published in *Sciences Philo-*

logiques et Traditions Culturelles Nationales aux XIXe Siècle, ed. H. Wissman (Paris).

7. Gesammelte Schriften 1, 5n1.

8. Zeitschrift für die Wissenschaft des Judentums (ZWJ) 1 (1822), 1-24. Wolf expressed a hope quite similar to Eduard Gans's: "und soll je ein Band das ganze Menschengeschlecht umschlingen, so es das Band der Wissenschaft, das Band der reinen Vernunftigkeit, das Band der Wahrheit" (24).

9. ZWJ, 3.

10. ZWJ, 12 (rev. trans. from Michael Meyer, Ideas of Jewish History, New York, 1974, p. 149).

11. ZWJ, 11, 14.

12. Jüdische Wille, 196 (Shazar, Ore Dorot, 377-378).

13. Steinheim believed that philosophical rationalism and mysticism (by which he was thinking primarily of Neoplatonism) both claimed that the world emanates necessarily from God. Judaism, on the other hand, teaches that God created the world out of nothingness by an act of free will. Since revealed monotheism contradicts the logical tenets of rational philosophy, Steinheim understood it as irrational. See his Die Glaubenslehre der Synagogue (Leipzig, 1856), 166, 209.

14. See Hanns Reissner, "Rebellious Dilemma: The Case Histories of Eduard Gans and Some of His Partisans," LBIY 2 (1957), 179-193, and Eduard Gans (Tübingen, 1965).

15. Gesammelte Schriften 3, 81: "Und gerade wie sie (die Kabbala) mit Bibel und Masora umsprang, wütheten ihre barbarischen Jünger des 16. Jahrhunderts mit ihr selber, versinkend in den finstersten Aberglauben."

16. Geiger believed that mysticism could serve an invigorating function in the history of religion, but Jewish mysticism only played this role in Protestantism after the Reformation. In the Jewish sphere itself, mysticism was sterile. See Max Wiener, ed., Abraham Geiger and Liberal Judaism (Philadelphia, 1962), 207, 209. On Geiger, see further Hans Liebeschütz, "Wissenschaft des Judentums und Historismus bei Abraham Geiger," Essays Presented to Leo Baeck (London, 1954), 75-94, and Michael Meyer, "Abraham Geiger's Historical Judaism," New Perspectives on Abraham Geiger (Cincinnati, 1975), 3-17.

17. Quoted by Scholem in Judaica III, 260.

18. For a discussion of Haskalah attacks on the Kabbalah, see Fischel Lachover, "Revealed and Hidden in the Doctrines of Nachman Krochmal" (Hebrew), Keneset 6 (1941), 298-299. See also Scholem, "Die Erforschüng der Kabbala von Reuchlin bis zur Gegenwart," Judaica, III, 259-260.

19. Zeitschrift für die religiosen Interessen des Judentums (ZRIJ) 3 (1846), 81-97, 121-132, 361-368, 413-421; see 82-83. The essay was republished by Schocken (Berlin, 1936). English trans., Ismar Schorsch, Structure of Jewish History (New York, 1975).

20. ZRIJ, 82-83. The first to point out the precise function of history for Graetz was Nathan Rotenstreich, "Graetz and the Philosophy of History" (Hebrew), Zion 8 (1942), 51-59.

21. *Gnosticismus und Judenthum* (Krotschin, 1846), v. Also "Einleitung," *Geschichte der Juden*, 2nd ed. (Leipzig, 1866), IV, 4: "[Die jüdische Literatur] bildet den Kern der jüdischen Geschichte den die Leidensgeschichte mit einer bitteren Schale umgeben hat." Graetz seems to have borrowed his imagery from the Kabbalah.

22. *ZRIJ*, 91: "Das Judentum weiβ sich in diesen beiden Zeitraumen als eins und dasselbe, es trägt in sich dieses Selbstbewuβtsein, das bei aller Verschiedenheit ausserer Erfahrungen und innerer Metamorphosen es für sich eine untheilbare Einheit bildet."

23. Ibid., 87.

24. Ibid., 89-90n1.

25. *Jüdische Zeitschrift für Wissenschaft und Leben* 4 (1866), 146. Geiger argued that Graetz's history was not really history, but a series of stories (*Geschichten*) strung together. It was certainly correct to criticize Graetz for his tendency to render historical events into personality conflicts and amusing biographical sketches, but it should not be mistaken for lack of theological principle standing behind his conception of Jewish history. The stylistic peculiarities of the Geschichte are not a true indication that Graetz did not believe in historical development.

26. Ibid., 362-3 (trans. Schorsch, 95).

27. This periodization appeared in the *Geschichte* (vol. IV), intro. in 1st ed. (1853; see trans. in Meyer, *Ideas of Jewish History*, 233). In the second edition (1866), Graetz altered the periodization so that the third period ended with Mendelssohn and not with his own Geschichte. This emendation in the latter edition is not clear, but it may have been due to Graetz's growing pessimism about the value of his own time. In the "Konstruktion" essay, written in the 1840s, however, he put great confidence in the value of history to complete the work of philosophy. See *ZRIJ*, 420: "Findet man jetzt die ewigen Wahrheiten nicht bloβ in den Gedanken des Geists, sondern in den Thaten des Geistes . . . und ganz besonders in den Evolutionen der Geschichte: so hat das Judenthum nur diesen Standpunkt einzunehmen, und seine philosophische Rechtfertigung muβ ihm leicht werden."

28. See Salo Baron, *History and Jewish Historians* (Philadelphia, 1964), 269-276, also Rotenstreich, *Zion*, 56, for a critique of Baron's comparison of Graetz and Ranke.

29. Hermann Cohen's theology was the most thoroughgoing attempt to establish the absolute transcendence of the Jewish God. To this end he argued that Jewish monotheism is not simply the belief in God's unity but, more precisely, in God's uniqueness (*Einzigkeit*). See especially his "Einheit oder Einzigkeit Gottes," *Jüdische Schriften*, ed. Bruno Strauβ (Berlin, 1924), I, 87-100, and *Die Religion der Vernunft aus den Quellen des Judentums* (Frankfurt, 1919), chap. 1, "Die Einzigkeit Gottes." Cohen argues that pantheism affirms a principle of unity which it applies to God and the world. If the principle of unity is applied only to God, then the world is negated. Only a notion of *uniqueness* can preserve a transcendent God and affirm the world as *correlating* with God (*Religion der Vernunft*, 100ff.). Mysticism is a doctrine of God's *immanence* similar to pantheism. In his

early writings, Cohen considered himself a Spinozist and asserted that the
Kabbalah was a Jewish precursor to Spinoza's pantheism ("Heine und das
Judentum," *Jüdische Schriften*, III, 9ff). In his later writings, Cohen re-
nounced Spinoza and attacked mysticism for positing a false identity between God and the world, thus subverting God's transcendent uniqueness
(*Religion der Vernunft*, 125-127). Mysticism is predicated on an aesthetic
rather than an ethical consciousness and is therefore fundamentally alien to
reason which is the essence of ethics (*Ethik des reinen Willens*, 2nd ed.,
Berlin, 1907, 221, 306). For Cohen's analysis of Graetz on these issues see
"Grätzens Philosophie der jüdischen Geschichte," *Jüdische Schriften*, III,
203-213.

30. *ZRIJ*, 372.

31. *Geschichte*, VII, 65.

32. "Die Mystische Literatur in der gaonischen Epoche," *MGWJ* 8
(1859), 67-78, 103-118, 140-153. Graetz distinguished sharply between
thirteenth-century Kabbalah and Gaonic mysticism, which knew nothing
of the four worlds of the later Kabbalah and wrote in Hebrew rather than
in pseudo-Aramaic. By attributing "Kabbalistic" doctrines only to the thirteenth century, he tried to refute David Luria's dating of these concepts to
the Gaonic period. See also *Geschichte* (2nd ed.), VIIn3 and 421ff.

33. *Geschichte*, VII, 64-77: "Die Kabbala is ein Zerrbild, welches die
jüdischen und die philosophischen Ideen in gleicher Weise verunstaltet."

34. Graetz, *History of the Jews*, trans. Bella Lowy (London, 1904), IV,
12: "His genuine writings however were not sufficiently noticed and had
brought him in little fame and money. Moses de Leon then hit upon a much
more effective means for opening hearts and purses wider. He commenced
the composition of books under feigned but honored names."

35. Graetz treated Maimonides, Spinoza, and Mendelssohn as both re-
juvenators and underminers of traditional Judaism. On Maimonides, for
instance, see *History*, III, 501: "And since in the end thinkers will always
remain the guides and leaders of men . . . it can be said with justice that Judaism is indebted to Maimuni for its rejuvenescence." But, on the other
hand, see ibid., 484: "Maimuni's theory, consistently followed out, is calculated to undermine Talmudical Judaism."

36. Ibid., V, 397.

37. Graetz took this idea from G. B. Jaesche, *Der Pantheismus* (1826-
1832), and Ferdinand Christian Baur, *Die christliche Gnosis* (1835). I thank
Professor Scholem for these references.

38. *Gnosticismus*, 35.

39. For Emden's dating of the *Zohar*, see *Mitpaḥat Sefarim* (Lvov,
1870; Jerusalem, 1970).

40. *Judaica* III, 260-261.

41. *Moses de Leon und sein Verhältnis zum Sohar* (Leipzig, 1851), and
Beiträge zur Geschichte der Kabbala (Leipzig, 1852). See also *Bet ha-Mid-
rash*, 3rd ed., 2 vols. (Jerusalem, 1967).

42. *Die Geschichte der jüdischen Philosophie des Mittelalters* (Berlin,
1907), I, 46-48, 63-95.

43. For Krochmal's biography, see Simon Rawidowicz's introduction to *Kitve Nachman Krochmal* (Berlin, 1924; 2nd ed., Waltham, 1960), 17-98. On the question of the influence of German idealism on Krochmal there is an extensive literature. The main issue is that of Hegel's influence. Zunz, who was the first to publish Krochmal's *Guide* in 1851, claimed that Krochmal discovered Hegel late in his life and was profoundly influenced by him. See Zunz, *Gesammelte Schriften*, II, 155-156. The most extensive attempt to prove Krochmal's association with Hegelianism was by J. L. Landau, *Nachman Krochmal, ein Hegelianer* (Berlin, 1904). Landau was subjected to a devastating attack by Simon Rawidowicz in "War Nachman Krochmal Hegelianer?" *Hebrew Union College Annual* 5 (1928), 435-582 (English trans. in Rawidowicz, *Studies in Jewish Thought*, Philadelphia, 1974, 350-387), and in *Kitve Nachman Krochmal*, 160-201. Rawidowicz noted the influence of other idealists, such as Fichte and Herder, and of Vico. More recently, Jacob Taubes attempts to revive the Hegelian argument by claiming that "what Hegel did to Christianity [in historicizing it], Krochmal did to Judaism." See "Krochmal and Modern Historicism," *Judaism* 12 (2) (1963), 150-165. I am in agreement with Rawidowicz that Hegel was not the main idealist influence on Krochmal, but also with Taubes that the structure of Krochmal's historicist arguments was so similar to Hegel's that one may speak of Krochmal's interpretation of the history of Spirit quite apart from the question of actual influence.

44. *Moreh Nevukhe ha-Zeman* (Guide) in Rawidowicz, ed., *Kitve Nachman Krochmal*, 249. Krochmal claimed that the rabbis in the Talmudic period already used a "modern" form of historical interpretation, which they had to suppress since it was ahead of its time. However, at the "end of days" (*be-aharit ha-yamim ha-rabbim*) these ideas could be revealed, suggesting that Krochmal's philosophy of history, since it makes explicit the esoteric rabbinic historicism, is itself a sign of eschatological times. Taubes was the first to point out Krochmal's connection of historicism with eschatology. He takes his evidence from a passage similar to the one quoted above from the *Guide*, 255 (see Taubes, 160).

45. *Guide*, chap. 8. On the problematics of Krochmal's philosophy of history, see Nathan Rotenstreich, "Krochmal's Concept of History" (Hebrew), *Zion* 7 (1942), 29-47, and his "Absolute and Change in the Thought of Krochmal" (Hebrew), *Keneset* 6 (1941), 333-345.

46. Krochmal died before the *Guide* could be published. In 1851, Leopold Zunz published it under the present title, which he claimed, on the basis of a number of letters Krochmal had written, to have been the title Krochmal himself picked. See Zunz's introduction to *Moreh Nevukhe ha-Zeman* (Lemberg, 1863), 6.

47. Lachover, *Keneset*, 300ff; Eliezer Schweid, "Nachman Krochmal's Philosophy and Its Relationship to the Philosophy of Maimonides, the Kabbala and Modern Philosophy" (Hebrew), *Iyyun* 20 (1) (1969), 29-59.

48. *Moreh Nevukhe ha-Zeman*, 30. Krochmal took his arguments on the connections between Kabbalah, Gnosticism, and Neoplatonism from August Neander, *Genetische Entwicklung der vornehmsten gnostischen Systeme* (Berlin, 1818), esp. 1-22: "Einleitung: Elemente der Gnosis im

Philo." Neander's study may have also been Hegel's source when the latter wrote "Die Kabbalistische Philosophie, gnostische Theologie beschäftigen sich alle mit diesen Vorstellungen, die auch Philo hatte," *Werke* (Glückner ed.), XIX, 26. On Krochmal's metaphysics, see Julius Guttmann, "Rabbi Nachman Krochmal" (Hebrew), *Keneset* 6 (1941), 259-287, and his *Philosophies of Judaism* (New York, 1973), 365-391.

49. In his Hebrew-German lexicon of Krochmal's philosophical vocabulary (*Kitve Nachman Krochmal*, 211-218), Rawidowicz uses Kantian terms: *ziyur* is *Vorstellung*, *musagim sikhliyim* are *Verstandesbegriffe*, and *musagim tvuniyim* (or *musage binah*) are *Vernunftsbegriffe*.

50. *Guide*, chap. 15.

51. Ibid., 112.

52. Ibid., chap. 15, esp. 258.

53. Ibid., 271.

54. Ibid., 271: "pathu be-sekhel."

55. Ibid., chap. 1.

56. Ibid., 12.

57. Krochmal believed that every religion, no matter how primitive, possessed some form of spirit. Even idolatry is not mere fetishism. See *Guide*, 29, where Krochmal derives this idea from a peculiar interpretation of the Talmud's dictum that worshiping the "spirit of the mountain" (*gada de-har*) constitutes a more serious form of idolatry than worship of the mountain itself. Krochmal argues that this actually proves that even idolators worship a "spirit," thus making idolatry much more positive than the rabbis intended.

58. Ibid., 35.

59. *Judaica* III, 237. See also Scholem's "Zur Geschichte der Anfänge der christliche Kabbala," *Essays Presented to Leo Baeck*, 158-193, and F. Secret, *Les Kabbalistes chrétiens de la Renaissance* (Paris, 1964).

60. In *Von Berlin*, 181-182, Scholem relates how he acquired Knorr von Rosenroth's *Kabbala Denudata* in 1922. On Christian Kabbalistic scholarship, see *Judaica* II, 247-258.

61. *Die Philosophie der Geschichte oder über die Tradition* (Münster, 1834-1857), I, 10.

62. Ibid., II, 8.

63. Ibid., I, 35-36.

64. Ibid., I, 17: "Unserer Zeit scheint es vorbehalten zu sein, allmälig wieder zu einigen, was in fruhëren Jahrhunderten gewaltsam auseinadergerissen worden und so das alte Leben in neuer Gestalt wieder hervorzurufen." See also II, 4, where he discusses the role of "unsere neuere Philosophie" (idealism).

65. *Walter Benjamin*, 53, and Benjamin's letter to Scholem of June 1917, *Briefe* (Frankfurt, 1966), I, 136-139.

2. Revision and Revolution

1. Zunz, *Gesammelte Schriften*, I, 4: "Aber gerade weil wir zu unserer Zeit die Juden . . . vielleicht oft ohne es zu wollen oder zu ahnen die neuhebräische Literatur zu Grabe tragen sehen, tritt die Wissenschaft auf und

verlangt Rechenschaft von der geschlossenen."

2. Dubnow, *Nationalism and History*, ed. K. Pinson (Philadelphia, 1958).

3. Letter from Scholem of 31 March 1978.

4. See Selma Stern, "Eugen Täubler and the *Wissenschaft des Judentums*," *LBIY* 3 (1958), 40-59, esp. quote on 49. Täubler's ideas can be found in his introductory address to the Akademie in *Korrespondenzblatt* 1 (1919), 10-19. See also *Mitteilungen des Gesamtarchivs der deutschen Juden*, I (1908) and III (1912), and in the thirty-first report of the *Lehranstalt für die Wissenschaft des Judentums* (1913). On Taubler, see B. Z. Dinur, *Israel and the Diaspora* (Philadelphia, 1969), 44-47, and Georg Herlitz, "Three Jewish Historians: Jost-Graetz-Taubler," *LBIY* 9 (1964), 69-90. On the Akademie, see Hermann Cohen, "Zur Begrundung einer Akademie für die Wissenschaft des Judentums," *Jüdische Schriften*, II, 210-218.

5. Dinur, *Israel and the Diaspora*, 33-44.

6. *Yisrael Ba'amim* (Jerusalem, 1955), 12.

7. For Baer's views on the *hasidim rishonim*, see ibid. For later periods, see "Religious-Social Tendencies in the Sefer Hasidim" (Hebrew), *Zion* 1 (1935), 1-50, and "The Historical Background of the Raya Mehemna" (Hebrew), *Zion* 5 (1939), 1-44. Baer's main scholarly work was on the Jews of Christian Spain. See his dissertation, *Studien zur Geschichte der Juden im Königreich Aragonien wärhend des 13. und 14. Jahrhunderts* (Berlin, 1913), and *Toldot ha-Yehudim be-Sefarad ha-Nozrit* (Tel Aviv, 1944-45), trans. as *History of the Jews in Christian Spain* (Philadelphia, 1961). A particularly clear example of Baer's pietistic nationalism and glorification of the common people can be found in the latter work: "As is to be expected, most of the apostates [during the period before the expulsion of 1492] whose names we know came from the wealthy and cultured classes. Jewish religious zealots rightly sought the cause of apostasy in the philosophical views of the converts and contrasted these people with the humble men and women whose simple faith withstood the test" (*Jews in Christian Spain*, II, 130).

8. See Baer's review of Scholem's *Major Trends*, "The Function of Mysticism in Jewish History" (Hebrew), *Zion* 7 (1942), 64.

9. *Use and Abuse of History*, trans. Adrian Collins (Indianapolis, 1957), 3.

10. Ibid., 16.

11. Ibid., 15.

12. Ibid., 21.

13. Ibid., 7-8.

14. Ibid., 21.

15. *Beyond Good and Evil*, trans. Walter Kaufmann (New York, 1966), sec. 108: "There are no moral phenomena, only a moral interpretation of phenomena."

16. Ibid., preface. Arthur Danto calls Nietzsche's position "perspectivism" in *Nietzsche as Philosopher* (New York, 1965), 68-100.

17. *Beyond Good and Evil*, sec. 289.

18. Ibid., sec. 30.

19. Karl Löwith so characterizes Nietzsche's *Zarathustra* in *Meaning in History* (Chicago, 1949), 211.

20. *Anti-Christ*, sec. 39.

21. *Anti-Christ*, trans. R. J. Hollingdale (Baltimore, 1968), sec. 36, 37.

22. Ibid., sec. 58.

23. On Nietzsche's influence on Berdichevsky, see Aliza Klausner-Eshkol, *Hashpa'at Nietzsche v'Schopenhauer al M. Y. Bin Gorion* (Tel Aviv, 1954). During Berdichevsky's lifetime and immediately after, there was a controversy about whether he was in fact a Nietzschean. Ahad Ha-am, Joseph Klausner, Y. L. Brenner, Chaim Tchernowitz, Yaakov Rabinowitz, and F. Lachover contended that he was not. Klausner-Eshkol has persuasively shown Berdichevsky's reliance on Nietzsche and his transformation of Nietzsche's concepts into his own system. See also Baruch Kurzweil, "The Influence of Lebensphilosophie on Hebrew Literature at the Beginning of the 20th Century" (Hebrew), in his *Sifruteinu ha-Hadash-Hemshekh O Mahapekhah?* (Jerusalem, 1971), 225-270. On Berdichevsky's philosophy of history, see Samuel Fishman, *Aspects of Berdichevsky's Historiography* (diss., University of California, Los Angeles, 1968). On Berdichevsky as mythmaker, see David Jacobson's forthcoming article, "The Recovery of Myth: M. Y. Berdichevsky and Hasidism," *Hebrew Annual Review* 2 (1978).

24. *Kol Kitve Bin Gorion* (*KKBG*; Tel Aviv, 1965), II, 19. Klausner-Eshkol has shown how Berdichevsky borrowed Nietzsche's terms in this parable (37-38).

25. *KKBG*, 34, in "Old Age and Youth" (Hebrew), written in 1898. Berdichevsky exploited the equivocal meaning of "house" (*bayit*) in Hebrew which could refer either to an actual house or to the Temple.

26. *Use and Abuse of History*, 50: "For the origin of historical culture and of its absolutely radical antagonism to the spirit of a new time and a modern consciousness must itself be known by a historical process. History must solve the problem of history."

27. *Me-Ozar ha-Aggada* (Berlin, 1914), 12.

28. "Note 8" (Hebrew), *KKBG*, II, 52-53. Berdichevsky criticizes Zev Yavitz who revived Krochmal's idea that each nation has certain characteristics which make it transient, while only Israel's national traits guarantee it eternal life. Berdichevsky seems to suggest against Krochmal's Jewish nationalism that because all nations—including Israel—are a mixture of traits, all are equally subject to the laws of history.

29. "Two Faces" (Hebrew), *KKBG*, II, 45. In the Talmudic source (BT *Shabbat* 119b), the sword represents the external threat to the Jews if they do not obey the book. Berdichevsky typically misinterprets the passage to indicate that the sword represents one aspect of Israel's own personality.

30. *Me-Ozar ha-Aggada*, 16.

31. *Sinai und Gerizim*, Hebrew trans. (Tel Aviv, 1962), 7: "the revelation on Gerizim and Ebal, which is generally thought to be the final seal on the various revelations of law in the Hexateuch (starting with Sinai), was

actually the *first;* the covenant of Gerizim was the most ancient and its value for the religion of Israel was and is greater than the value of all the other covenants, despite the fact that it was suppressed." For a similar view of Sinai as a priestly imposition on a natural religion, see David Frishman, *Ba-Midbar* (Berlin, 1923). Frishman, who was also influenced by Nietzsche, depicted the history of the masses at the time of Sinai and glorified revolts against the normative tradition. As a "history" of the *erev rav* (masses) rather than of the leadership of Israel, Frishman's stories were a conscious counter-historical revision of the Bible.

32. Ibid., 132ff.

33. See the review of *Sinai und Gerizim* in *MGWJ* 71 (1927), 141-144. The reviewer notes that Berdichevsky used contemporary scholarship in an erratic and incomplete fashion. He points out the similarity to Sellin's work on Moses which argued that Moses was deposed in the desert and that Joshua played a much more important role than the Bible attributes to him. See Ernst Sellin, *Mose und seine Bedeutung für die israelitisch-jüdische Religionsgeschichte* (1922). Freud later used Sellin for his own iconoclastic *Moses and Monotheism* (New York, 1939). Berdichevsky also claimed that Samaritan traditions supported his contentions of a special revelation at Gerizim, but scholarly studies of the Samaritans have shown their belief in Moses and the Sinaitic revelation.

34. "We and They" (Hebrew), *KKBG,* II, 47-48. Berdichevsky quotes extensively from Nietzsche's history of the degeneration of Israel from a natural religion to a religion forged by priests. See *Anti-Christ,* sec. 24-26, and *Beyond Good and Evil,* sec. 195, where Nietzsche blames the prophets for the "inversion of values . . . which marks the beginning of the slave revolt in morals."

35. "Destruction and Construction" (Hebrew), *KKBG,* II, 29-30, and "Culture and Ethics," 37-38.

36. For Berdichevsky's counter-history of the Great Revolt, see "Old Pages" (Hebrew), *KKBG,* II, 44-45.

37. "Zionism and Patience" (Hebrew), *KKBG,* II, 86-89.

38. In 1911, Berdichevsky renounced Hasidism: "We believed that we could find [in Hasidism] complete freedom of religion . . . but we found a faith confined within the boundaries of a race, and with disappointment, we had to put away the *Shivhei ha-Besht.*" "On Expansion and Contraction" (Hebrew), *He-Atid* 5 (1913), 151-172.

39. For two views of Berdichevsky's relation to the Haskalah and his place in the Hebrew revival, see Simon Halkin, *Modern Hebrew Literature* (New York, 1950), 93, and Yehezkel Kaufmann, *Gola ve-Nekhar* (Tel Aviv, 1961), 386-404.

40. *KKBG,* I, 181-184.

41. Berdichevsky's various collections of folktales began to appear in the first decade of the century, which was when Jewish folklore became a discipline. The two most important other contributions in this field were Bialik and Ravnitsky's *Sefer ha-Aggadah* (Berlin, 1908-1911), and Louis Ginzburg's *Legends of the Jews* (Philadelphia, 1909).

42. Klausner-Eshkol, 30.

43. "Bubers Aufassung des Judentums," *Judaica*, II, 144.

44. See particularly his *Die Geschichte des Rabbi Nachman* (Frankfurt, 1906), *Die Legende des Baal Schem* (Frankfurt, 1908), and *Der Grosse Maggid und seine Nachfolge* (Frankfurt, 1922).

45. "Ein Wort über Nietzsche und die Lebenswerte," *Die Kunst im Leben* 1 (2) (1900), 13, quoted and translated in Paul Flohr, "From Kultur Mystik to Dialogue: The Formation of Martin Buber's Philosophy of I and Thou" (diss., Brandeis University, 1973), 78; also 278n160, and 4. See also Grete Schaeder, *The Hebrew Humanism of Martin Buber*, trans. Noah Jacobs (Detroit, 1973), 31-37.

46. Flohr, chap. 3.

47. "Myth in Judaism," in *On Judaism*, trans. Eva Jospe (New York, 1967), 99. *On Judaism* is an English translation of Buber's *Drei Reden über Judentum* (Frankfurt, 1911), and *Vom Geist des Judentums* (Leipzig, 1916).

48. *Baal Schem*, ix. See also "Jewish Religiosity," in *On Judaism*, 80ff.

49. *Baal Schem*, ix. The contrast between myth and religion corresponds to Buber's notion of formlessness and form. In any creative process, formlessness breaks into the formed and gives it life; formlessness, like myth, is the principle of creation. See "Das Gestaltende," *Jüdische Bewegung* (Berlin, 1916), I, 204-216.

50. *On Judaism*, 99.

51. See Chapter Seven.

52. *On Judaism*, 88.

53. Ibid., 90.

54. *Baal Schem*, ix.

55. *On Judaism*, 90-92.

56. *Baal Schem*, x: "Im Chassidismus siegt für eine Weile das unterirdische Judentum über das offizielle."

57. *On Judaism*, 92.

58. From a lecture delivered in 1926, published in *Die Schrift und ihre Verdeutschung* (Berlin, 1936), 13-91; passage translated in Buber, *On the Bible*, trans. Olga Marx (New York, 1968), 7.

59. *Baal Schem*, viii.

60. *Hasidism and Modern Man*, trans. Maurice Friedman (New York, 1958), 41.

61. Buber, "Theory of Hasidism" (Hebrew), *Amot* 2 (7) (1963-64), 43.

62. *Die Welt*, 11 and 25 October 1901, and in *Jüdische Bewegung*, I, 45-58.

63. On Hurwitz, see Stanley Nash, "Shay Hurwitz: A Pioneering Polemicist for Truth," *Judaism* 22 (Summer 1973), 322-327, and E. Hurwicz, "Shai Ish Hurwitz and the Berlin he-Atid," *LBIY* 12 (1967), 85-102.

64. *Ha-Meliz* 9(6) (1883), quoted in Nash, 325.

65. Hurwitz, "On the Question of the Survival of Judaism" (Hebrew), *Ha-Shiloah* 13 (1904), 287-307, and "Two Paths" (Hebrew), *Ha-Shiloah* 16 (1907). The bibliographical journal *Ein Ha-Qoreh* 1 (1923), 98-104, lists over twenty responses to Hurwitz's first essay.

66. "On the Expansion of the Boundaries" (Hebrew), *He-Atid* 3 (1911), 130.

67. *Me-Ayin u-Le'ayin?* (Berlin, 1914), 20-22.

68. "Hasidism and Haskalah" (Hebrew), *He-Atid* 2 (1909), 69.

69. Ibid., 29ff.

70. On *Shivhei ha-Besht*, ibid., 36ff. Berdichevsky's renunciation of Hasidism appeared in Hurwitz's journal and was based substantially on Hurwitz's analysis.

71. Ibid., 76-78.

72. "More on the History of Shabbatai Zevi" (Hebrew), *He-Atid* 6 (1924), 122.

73. "Hasidism and Haskalah," 81.

74. The phrase is Nash's, based on Hurwitz in "Hasidism and Haskalah."

75. *Me-ayin u-Le'ayin?* 84.

76. "Hasidism and Haskalah," 60.

77. "More on the History of Shabbatai Zevi," 128-129.

78. "Hasidism and Haskalah," 96, and *Me-ayin u-Le'ayin?* 259ff.

79. See Chapter Three.

80. See Rubaschoff's (Zalman Shazar) memoir, *Morning Stars,* trans. S. Nordi (Philadelphia, 1967), 171-193.

81. "Der Lehrstuhl," *Der Jude* 2 (1917) (*Ore Dorot,* 385-389).

82. *Jüdische Wille* 1 (1918-19) (*Ore Dorot,* 351-385).

83. "The History of Sabbatianism in the Ukraine" (Russian), *Jewrejskaja Starina* 5 (1912), 218-221 (*Ore Dorot,* 117-121). See also "The History of Sabbatianism in Hungary" (Russian), ibid. 7 (1914), 120-123 (*Ore Dorot,* 113-117), and "Messiah's Secretary" (Hebrew), *Ha-Shiloah* 21 (1912), 36-47.

84. *Ore Dorot,* 61.

85. First published in *Ba-Adama* 6 (1920), then as *Al Tilei Bet Frank* (Berlin, 1922-23).

86. Graetz, *Frank und die Frankisten* (Breslau, 1868); A. Kraushar, *Frank i Frankiscy Polscy* (Cracow, 1895); and Meier Balaban, "On the History of the Frankist Movement" (Hebrew), *He-Atid* 5 (1913), 132-151 (later expanded into his *Le-Toldot ha-Tenuah ha-Frankit* (Tel Aviv, 1934-35) in two volumes.)

87. *Al Tilei Bet Frank,* 4.

88. Ibid., 23.

3. From Berlin To Jerusalem

1. For a critical discussion of the "Berlin-Jewish spirit" and bibliography, see Peter Gay, *Freud, Jews and Other Germans* (New York, 1978), 169-188.

2. For Scholem's childhood memories of Berlin, see *Von Berlin,* 23-24.

3. Ibid., 20-22, 41-42, "With Gershom Scholem," *JJC,* 4-7.

4. *Von Berlin,* 58. See also *JJC,* 3.

5. *Von Berlin,* 14-15.

6. Ibid., 28-32.

7. Ibid., 51-52; *JJC*, 5, 17.

8. *Von Berlin*, 60; *Walter Benjamin*, 14, 22.

9. *Von Berlin*, 63-64; *JJC*, 9; and "Greetings to a Teacher: To Abraham Isaac Bleichrode at Eighty" (Hebrew), *Ha-Aretz*, 8 October 1947, 2.

10. *Von Berlin*, 75-78; *JJC*, 9-10.

11. *Von Berlin*, 33ff.

12. On this period of German Zionism, see Jehuda Reinharz, *Fatherland or Promised Land* (Ann Arbor, 1975).

13. See Walter Laqueur, *Young Germany* (New York, 1962), and George Mosse, *The Crisis of German Ideology* (New York, 1964).

14. See especially George Mosse, "The Influence of the Volkish Idea on German Jewry," in *Germans and Jews* (New York, 1970), 77-116. On the Eastern European Jewish youth movement, see Elkanah Margalit, *Hashomer ha-Tzair* (Tel Aviv, 1971), esp. 17-55, for general background. For Germany and Austria, see Haim Shatzker, *Tenuat ha-Noar ha-Yehudit* (diss., Hebrew University), and Walter Gross, "Zionist Students' Movement," *LBIY* 4 (1959), 143-165.

15. Laqueur, *Young Germany*, 74-87, and his article, "The German Youth Movement and the Jewish Question," *LBIY* 6 (1961), 193-206.

16. See Shatzker, *Tenuat ha-Noar*. For details of formation of the Blau-Weiss, see *Blau-Weiss Blätter* 1.1 (May 1913), particularly Erich Barin, "Gleitwort." On early ideology, see *Blau-Weiss Blätter*, first several numbers. But cf. Hans Tramer, "Blau-Weiss-Wegbereiter für Zion," *Die Jugendbewegung* (Cologne, 1963).

17. *Von Berlin*, 59ff., 93; *JJC*, 8.

18. Margalit, *Hashomer ha-Tzair*, 23.

19. "The Spirit of the Orient and Judaism," address delivered in 1912, trans. in *On Judaism*, 57-78.

20. "Was ist zu tun?" *Jüdische Bewegung*, I (Berlin, 1920), 123ff. Buber's Zionism was fundamentally unpolitical and spiritual. In "Die Tempelweihe," ibid., 229-242, an address delivered on Hanukkah, 1914, Buber notes that national liberation through war was only the external manifestation of the Maccabean achievements: "Das Wesentliche ist ihm nicht der Sieg der judaischen über die syrischen Waffen, sondern die Reinigung des geschändeten Heiligtums, die durch den Sieg ermöglicht war" (p. 232). Also, in reply to Hermann Cohen, *Jüdische Bewegung*, II, 64.

21. *On Judaism*, 23.

22. Flohr, "From Kulturmystik to Dialogue," 49-107.

23. Ibid., 7, 14. See also Otto Bollnow, *Die Lebensphilosophie* (Berlin, 1958), and Rudolph Weingartner, *Experience and Culture: The Philosophy of Georg Simmel* (Wesleyan, 1960).

24. Buber's concept of *Zwischenmenschliche*, later so important in his dialogic philosophy, first appeared in his introduction ("Geleitwort sur Sammlung") to the forty-volume series *Die Gesellschaft* which he edited (Frankfurt, 1906-1912). But the ontological foundation of *das Zwischenmenschliche* was in the private mystical Erlebnis and was therefore trans-

muted into an asocial category. See Buber's remarks in a debate with Ernst Troeltsch in 1910, published in *Schriften der deutschen Gesellschaft für Soziologie* (Tübingen, 1911), and discussed and quoted in Flohr, 103-104. For Flohr's illuminating discussion of Buber's transformation of Simmel's sociological categories into "a term of ontological ethics," see 46ff.

25. Buber took the concept of a *neue Gemeinschaft* from the Nietzschean circle led around the turn of the century by the brothers Hardt. See Flohr, 58-72.

26. "Feldbriefe," *Jüdische Rundschau*, 26 November 1914, 4.

27. See editorial, "Feinde ringsum," *Jüdische Rundschau*, 7 August 1914.

28. Franz Oppenheimer, "Alte und Neue Makkabäer," *Jüdische Rundschau*, 28 August 1914, and the banner headlines in the 8 August 1914 issue: "Wir trauen, dass unsere Jugend, durch die Pflege jüdischen Bewusstseins und körperliche Ausbildung in idealer Gesinnung und Mannesmut erstarkt, sich in allen kriegerischen Tagen auszeichnen wird."

29. Buber Archive 376/I, quoted and translated in Flohr, 136.

30. "Die Templeweihe," *Jüdische Bewegung*, I, 229-242.

31. Ibid., 241.

32. Letter from Scholem, 31 March 1978.

33. *Jüdische Bewegung*, II, 11.

34. For the polemic, see Buber's "Open Letter" to Cohen in *Der Jude* 1 (August 1916), "Begriffe und Wirklichkeit," 283-289; Cohen's reply, published in his *Jüdische Schriften*, 328-340; and Buber's response to Cohen, "Zion, der Staat und die Menschheit," *Der Jude* 1 (August 1916), 425-433.

35. On the Zionist youth movements and the war, see Haim Shatzker, "The Jewish-German Attitude of German Jewish Youth at the Time of the First World War and the Effect of the War on this Attitude" (Hebrew), in *Mehkarim be-Toldot Am Yisrael ve-Eretz Yisrael* (Tel Aviv, 1972), II, 187-215.

36. "Der Krieg der Zurückbleibenden," *Jüdische Rundschau*, 5 February 1915, 46-47. See also Reinhold Lewin, "Der Krieg als jüdisches Erlebnis," *MGWJ* 63 (1919), 1-14.

37. On German pacifism during the war, see James Shand, "Doves Among the Eagles: German Pacifists and Their Government during World War I," *Journal of Contemporary History* 10.1 (January 1975), 95-108. Stefan Zweig describes the extraordinary difficulty of finding pacifists in the first days of the war and the irresistibility of the surge of patriotism, which even he admits to feeling. See his *World of Yesterday* (English trans., Edinburgh, 1943), 196ff.

38. *Von Berlin*, 70-71.

39. *Walter Benjamin*, 14-15.

40. Scholem described the whole behind-the-scenes development of the letter incident in a letter to me of 31 March 1978. See also *JJC*, 13-15, and *Von Berlin*, 80-83, for an account of the ensuing events. Scholem reported the whole incident to Buber on 10 July 1916, after they had met. The letter has been published in Buber, *Briefwechsel aus sieben Jahrzehnten*, ed. Grete Schaeder (Heidelberg, 1972), I, 445-447.

41. *JJC*, 14, and *Von Berlin*, 94. Scholem filled in details in his letter to me of 31 March 1978. Copies of all the numbers of the *Blauweisse Brille* are in the holdings of the Jewish National Library at the Hebrew University, Jerusalem.

42. The original:

>Aus der Unendlichkeit
>Stieg dir ein Stein [Stern] empor:
>Bis an des Himmels Tor,
>Weit über Raum und Zeit,
>Meintest du trug'er dich
>Gabst dich ihm feierlich
>Es war der Krieg!
>
>Aber er fuhrte nicht,
>Wie du sein Funkeln last,
>Da du ihn steigen sahst,
>Hin zu der Urwelt Licht.
>Es war ein Irrlicht, nur,
>Das durch die Welten fuhr,
>Es war der Krieg!
>
>Gott in der Höhe lacht . . .
>Zündenden Weltenbrand
>Warf er von Land zu Land
>Weit durch die Nacht.
>Gab ihn als Stern uns aus
>Riß uns mit Macht hinaus,
>Hinaus in den Krieg!
>
>Spiel mit dem Irrlicht glückt:
>Wir traun des Himmels Hohn
>Ob auch die Welt uns schon
>Unter den Flammen erstickt.
>Heißen's Notwendigkeit
>Herrliche Gotteszeit:
>Ist doch nur Krieg!
>
>Du aber stehst und schaust
>Hin auf den Feuerherd,
>Bis dich die Flamme verzehrt:
>Leuchtender Blitz aus des Gottes Faust
>Trifft dich, du Sternensohn
>Stört deine Weltvision:
>Dank es dem Krieg!
>. . . Wenn du es kannst!

43. *Von Berlin*, 94-95. See also Scholem's letter to Buber of 10 July 1916 in Buber, *Briefwechsel*, I, 445-446.

44. *Walter Benjamin*, 14, 22, 40. For Benjamin's criticism of Buber on the war, including some veiled references to his Erlebnismystik, see Buber, *Briefwechsel*, I, 448-450.

45. "Farewell," *JJC*, 57-58, originally published as "Abschied—Offener Brief an Herrn Dr. Siegfried Bernfeld und gegen die Leser dieser Zeitschrift," *Jerubbaal* 1 (1918-1919), 127-128. (I have revised the translation on the basis of the original.) On Bernfeld, who was closely associated with Buber, and his journal, see Willie Hoffer, "Siegfried Bernfeld and Jerubbaal," *LBIY* 10 (1965), 150-167.

46. Scholem expressed this position in a discussion in the short-lived Safed Circle, a group of Zionist intellectuals who met in Berlin in 1918. In response to a lecture by Zalman Rubaschoff on the religion of the prophets, Scholem noted: "Gott ist nur vollkommen zudenken; Daath ist nicht Erleben, sondern Wissen Gottes; Diese Klarheit darf nicht durch Mystizismus getrübt werden." The minutes of the Safed Circle are in the Buber Archive 40/11. I thank Steven Aschheim for this reference.

47. "Martin Buber's Conception of Judaism," *JJC*, 127. Scholem revealed in a letter to me of 31 March 1978 that he actually composed such a letter to Buber, but did not send it because it would have led to a break in their relationship. In March 1933, Buber declared in an editorial, "Die Erste," in *Die Jüdische Rundschau* that with the Nazi seizure of power, Zionists should remain in Germany to give spiritual support to the Jewish people. Buber, supported by Ernst Simon, threw himself into Jewish education but, as Scholem must have felt at the time, such efforts were fruitless. Despite a certain view that Scholem created difficulties for Buber when the latter came to Jerusalem, it appears by Scholem's account that he played an important role in securing Buber's position at the Hebrew University. See "Martin Bubers Berufung nach Jerusalem: Eine notwendige Klarstellung," *Frankfurter Hefte* 22 (1967), 229-231.

48. *Walter Benjamin*, 40, 50.

49. *Von Berlin*, 74. In the *Blau-Weiss Brille*, no. 3, Scholem suggested that the Buber and Ahad Ha-am approaches to Judaism might be considered the choices open to young Zionists. See his "Ideologie," 2. See also *Walter Benjamin*, 41: "Benjamins Buber-Kritik gegenüber pries ich die Schriften von Achad Ha-am—von dem er noch nichts gehört hatte—und einige seiner Aufsätze über die Natur des Judentums, die ich ihm Ende 1916 in einer deutschen Auswahl borgte."

50. On Landauer, see Eugene Lunn, *Prophet of Community: The Romantic Socialism of Gustav Landauer* (Berkeley and Los Angeles, 1973). See, further, Ruth Link-Salinger (Hyman), *Gustav Landauer—Philosopher of Utopia* (Indianapolis, 1977), esp. 51-88.

51. Flohr, 150ff.

52. *Walter Benjamin*, 15, *Von Berlin*, 71-73, and 191: "Das anarchistiche Element in manchen, keineswegs unwichtigen Gruppen in Israel kam . . . meiner eigenen damaligen Position sehr nah."

53. "Jewish Youth Movement," *JJC*, 52. The original, on which the translation is based, appeared in *Der Jude* 1 (1916-1917), 822-825. For Scholem's correspondence with Buber, the editor of *Der Jude*, over this article, see his letter of 25 June 1916, where he also criticizes Buber's position on the war in the first number of *Der Jude*: Buber, *Briefwechsel*, I, 441, and

I, 442-443 for Buber's response. Scholem published two other important articles against the youth movements during these years. One appeared in the Blau-Weiss's own journal: "Jugendbewegung, Jugendarbeit und Blau-Weiss," *Blau-Weiss Blätter (Führerzeitung)* 1 (1917), 26-30. The other was the "Abschied" mentioned above. Shatzker has dealt with the Scholem controversy in his *Tenuat ha-Noar*, 199-207.

54. *JJC*, 55: "In *galut* there can be no Jewish community valid before God. And if community among human beings is indeed the highest that can be demanded, what would be the sense of Zionism if it could be realized in *galut?*"

55. "Jugendbewegung, Jugendarbeit und Blau-Weiss," 27. Benjamin criticized Scholem for this concept of education. Benjamin, *Briefe*, I, 144-146, letter from Benjamin to Scholem of 6 September 1917.

56. Scholem's demand that the youth movements return to Jewish sources involved him in an interesting dispute over the right technique for teaching Hebrew. See Marcel Lew, "Hebräische Sprache und hebräische Literatur," *Die jüdische Studenten* 19 (1921-22), 221-225: Lew raised the question whether modern spoken Hebrew should be based on old texts or should be taught as a new language: "Gerhard Scholem und seine Anhänger bejahen den ersten Teil dieser Frage, indem sie sagen: wir müssen uns zu allererst mit Talmud, Midrasch, Bibel, Sohar, etc befassen, um hier wirklich jüdisch erfasst zu werden." Scholem responded to Lew in the journal in October-November 1922, 279-280, denying that he had any one position on the correct method of teaching Hebrew. He further denied that he had any followers. Even if Scholem did not advocate any one pedagogical method, Lew hit upon something basic to Scholem's position: for Scholem, the Zionist movement, including the revival of Hebrew, should be based on a dialectical continuity with Jewish tradition. His position, therefore, led to the conclusion, even if unarticulated, that Hebrew should be taught through old Jewish sources.

57. *JJC*, 59-60. Translation modified from the original, "Abschied," 129. Scholem heard Cohen lecture shortly before Cohen's death. For his rather positive impression, see *Von Berlin*, 90-91.

58. See Karl Glaser, "Oratio pro domo," *Blau-Weiss Blätter (Führernummer)* 1.2 (June 1917), 30-39, and Martin Plessner, "Arbeit," ibid. (August 1918), 87-92, and infra, n. 59. As a result of the controversy, ten Blau-Weiss members in Berlin and six in Leipzig left the Blau-Weiss. See *Blau-Weiss Blätter* 4.5 (February 1918), 198.

59. "Eine Kritik des Blau-Weiss," *Blau-Weiss Blätter (Führernummer)* 1.1 (June 1917), 10-12.

60. Ibid., 3-10.

61. Margalit, *Hashomer ha-Tzair*, 23. The year was 1917 or 1918.

62. Rosenzweig, *Briefe*, ed. Edith Rosenzweig (Berlin, 1935), 355-357 (to Mawrik Kahn, 26 February 1919), 396-397 (to Rudolf Hallo, 25 February 1921), 399-400 (to Hallo, 12 May 1921), 424-431 (to Hallo, 27 March 1922).

63. *JJC*, 20-21. Rosenzweig actually first heard of Scholem from Maw-

rik Kahn while he was in an army hospital. Rosenzweig sent Scholem some of his translations from Hebrew into German and they later met several times. The argument over Zionism occurred in 1922.

64. *Von Berlin*, 195. Rosenzweig wrote to Hallo concerning Scholem: "Du kämpst mit (Scholem), ich habe gleich die Waffen gestreckt und habe von und bei ihm—gelernt." Letter of 12 May 1921 in Rosenzweig, *Briefe*, 399.

65. Rosenzweig, *Briefe*, 482, letter of 30 May 1923.

66. The shift in the Blau-Weiss occurred at the Prunn conference in 1922. Scholem's response appeared in *Die Jüdische Rundschau* 97 (8 December 1922), 638, under the caveat "Ohne Verantwortung der Redaktion." See *Von Berlin*, 190-193.

67. Quoted in *Die Jüdische Rundschau* 97 (8 December 1922), 638.

68. The signers include members of the Jung-Juda group like Erich Brauer but also Hans Oppenheim, who had earlier responded to Scholem's critique of the Blau-Weiss. Oppenheim had evidently parted ways with the Blau-Weiss as a result of the new policy.

69. *Von Berlin*, 109-110.

70. *JJC*, 16-17, *Walter Benjamin*, 68.

71. *Von Berlin*, 110ff.

72. "Agnon—Man into Artist. Portrait of the Author as a Young Man," *Jerusalem Post* (Weekend Magazine), 9 December 1966, 3-4. See also *Von Berlin*, 101.

73. This argument has been made by George Mosse in *Germans and Jews*, 84, and Shatzker, *Mehkarim*, 196-199.

74. Mary Turnowsky, "Die Volksheimidee," *Mitteilungen des Verband der Jüdischen Jugendvereine Deutschlands* 13.2 (April 1922), 46. Shatzker, 198-199.

75. *Von Berlin*, 102. Scholem first heard about the Volksheim from Buber who urged him to participate in it. The impression one gets from his own account is that his participation caused a commotion but no real change.

76. Ibid., 103. Kafka's fiancee, Felice Brauer, was among those who heard Scholem's criticisms and reported them to Kafka who, although he confused him with the Yiddish writer Scholem Alechem, generally agreed with Scholem. See ibid., 102, and "Scholem und Scholem Alechem" *Neue Züricher Zeitung (Morgenausgabe)* 24 (12 January 1968), 13.

77. "Youthful Days With Zalman Rubaschoff" (Hebrew) *Devarim be-Go*, 55-58, and *Von Berlin*, 112-118. According to local wags, Rubaschoff's course on Jewish history at the Volksheim started with Adam and would eventually end with Ber Borochov. On Scholem's evaluation of Rubaschoff as an historian, see "On the History of Sabbatian Research" (Hebrew) *La-Merhav*, 28 June 1960, 5.

78. "Agnon in Germany: Recollections," *JJC*, 117-125.

79. See Hans Tramer, "Gershom Scholem zum 75. Geburtstag," *Mitteilungsblatt des Irgun Olej Merkaz Europa*, 8 December 1972.

80. "S. Y. Agnon—The Last Hebrew Classic?" *JJC*, 93-116.

81. *Von Berlin*, 138-139. Scholem was far less impressed by Berdichevsky's Hebrew anthologies, which he regarded as rewritings of the original sources.

82. Ibid., 136.

83. Letter from Scholem, 31 March 1978.

84. Scholem describes his decision to study the Kabbalah and his studies at Munich in *Von Berlin*, 144ff, and *JJC*, 17-20.

85. *Von Berlin*, 92.

86. Ibid., 92-94, 152, *Walter Benjamin*, esp. 69-110. The best presentation of Benjamin's early thought with reference to his relationship with Scholem is Bernd Witte, *Walter Benjamin—Der Intellektuelle als Kritiker* (Stuttgart, 1976), esp. 1-57.

87. *Von Berlin*, 161.

88. For Scholem's evaluation of Judaism as "unbourgeois" see "Lyrik der Kabbala?" *Der Jude* 6 (1921-22), 55-56, and, much later, *MI*, 308.

89. Jankew Seidmann, *Aus dem heiligen Buche Sohar des Rabbi Schimon ben Jochaj* (Berlin, 1919?). Scholem's review "Über die jungste Sohar-Anthologie" appeared in *Der Jude* 5 (1920-21), 363-369. It is a measure of Buber's tolerance that Scholem's review was published in Buber's own journal.

90. "Über die jungste Sohar-Anthologie," 366.

91. Ibid., 368.

92. *Der Jude* 6 (1921-22), 55-69.

93. Wiener, *Lyrik der Kabbala* (Vienna and Leipzig, 1920), 15: "Nicht so der schlau 'Gottesdienst,' der eher eine Ausserung der Unfähigkeit ist, Gott zu erleben," and 16: "Great creative religious spirits have always separated ethics from religion, and extracted the practical-cultic aspect out of religion or at least limited it, if they only rarely understood the necessity to divide religion from ethics, as did the representatives of Gnosis or religion from cult as did Luther."

94. "Lyrik der Kabbala?" 60. Scholem refers to the "unsuccessful Erlebnis-Simmel," which reveals his hostility toward Buber's teacher from whom Buber took the Erlebnis category. In *Von Berlin*, 99, Scholem describes an argument he had with Buber over some disparaging remarks he made about Simmel.

95. "Kein Mensch durfte bestreiten, dass die Hymnen aller beruhmten expressionistischen Zeitgenossen 'um Gott' ['an Gott'] und was weiss ich in der Tat eine Befreiung dieser Geister von Gott, diesem starksten und umfassendsten aller Erlebnisse, welche sie nicht gehabt haben, oder auch im Sinne jenes Bibelverses eine Befreiung Gottes von Gottes von ihnen, deren treuloses Ende er zu 'erleben' wunscht, sind, und dass mit diesem Satze also das Scheinbare eines anmassenden Mystizismus grossärtig und nicht ohne Ironie erkannt ist, aber der Einigkeit macht die Verallgemeinerungswut vulgärer expressionistischer Theorie ein Ende, die die Jahrtausende nach ruckwärts mit sich zu identifizieren strebt und die den grossen Hymnen aller Volker ob Indern, Griechen, Juden, oder Indianern, ihren eigenen Charakter unterzuschieben sucht." (The contrast between Scholem's later, post-

World War II German style—considered a model by many Germans—and this extraordinary sentence hardly needs comment.)

96. Ibid., 59. This expression is a hidden reference to Peter Wust's *Die Auferstehung der Metaphysik*, which appeared in 1920. Scholem would certainly have rejected Wust's notion of metaphysics which the latter, inspired by a remark by Troeltsch, considered to be the way to rearm Germany spiritually after the war.

97. "Lyrik der Kabbala?" 69.

98. I thank Professor Scholem for generously allowing me to publish this manuscript and for examining my translation.

99. *JJC*, 19.

100. Scholem describes these events in *Von Berlin*, 201-220.

101. Rosenzweig, *Briefe*, 399-400.

4. Theology, Language, and History

1. Adolf von Harnack, *Wesen des Christentums* (Leipzig, 1900); also Ernst Troeltsch, *Die Absolutheit des Christentums und die Religionsgeschichte* (Tübingen-Leipzig, 1902); Uriel Tal, "Theologische Debatte um das 'Wesen' des Judentums," in *Juden im Wilhelminischen Deutschland 1890-1914*, ed. Werner Mosse (Tübingen, 1976), 599-633; Alexander Altmann, "Theology in Twentieth Century German Jewry," *LBIY* 1 (1956), 193-217, and "Zur Auseinandersetzung mit der 'dialektischen Theologie," *MGWJ* 79 (1935) 358-361; Hans Liebeschütz, *Von Simmel zu Rosenzweig* (Tübingen, 1970).

2. The crisis of Christianity was expressed in the idea that Christianity, as originally an apocalyptic movement, is essentially alien to the ethical concerns of modern culture. See esp. Franz Overbeck, *Christentum und Kultur* (Basel, 1919), and Albert Schweitzer, *Geschichte des Lebens-Jesu Forschung*, 2nd ed. (Tübingen, 1913).

3. *Der Begriff der Religion im System der Philosophie* (Giessen, 1915), and *Religion der Vernunft aus den Quellen des Judentums* (Frankfurt, 1919), 13-27, "Entweder nämlich stellt es sich heraus, dass die Religion, als Lehre vom Menschen, in die Ethik hineinfällt, so wird zwar ihr Zusammenhang mit der Vernunft unzweifelhaft, aber ihre *Selbständigkeit*, als Religion der Vernunft, wird dadurch bedroht" (14).

4. For Scholem's analysis of Buber's religious anarchism, see "Martin Buber's Interpretation of Hasidism," *MI*, 245.

5. Buber's *Ich und Du* can be considered a polemic against Otto's *Der Heilige*. Otto's conception of God as the wholly "Other" (*das Andere*) seems to preclude all divine-human communication, while Buber's dialogic philosophy tries to overcome the abyss between God and man. Buber's prewar *Erlebnismystik*, with its silent, intuitive experience of the Absolute, may however be considered a precursor to Otto's philosophy of religion.

6. Buber, *Ekstatische Konfessionen* (Jena, 1909), 11, 16.

7. See his *Beiträge zur Kritik der Sprache* (Leipzig, 1923). The definitive study of Mauthner's linguistic philosophy is by Gershon Weiler, *Mauthner's Critique of Language* (Cambridge, 1970). Mauthner was perhaps the foremost philosopher of atheism in the twentieth century. But out

of linguistic skepticism, which was the position he developed in his main work, he came to a view remarkably similar to Buber's: "I shall attempt . . . to say the unsayable . . . What I can experience (*erleben*) is no longer mere language. What I can experience is real. And I can experience for short hours, that I no longer know anything about the principle of individuation, that there ceases to be a difference between the world and myself. That I become God? Why not?" (quoted in Weiler, 295).

8. *Ekstatische Konfessionen*, 15.

9. Ibid., inscription at beginning. Buber's interest in Christian mysticism went back to his doctoral dissertation, "Zur Geschichte des Individuationsproblems" (1904), which dealt with Nicholas of Cusa and Jacob Boehme. See Flohr, "Kulturmystik," 64ff.

10. *Ekstatische Konfessionen*, 5, 21.

11. *On Judaism*, 88.

12. Buber, *Die Geschichten des Rabbi Nachman*, 7.

13. Ibid., 25.

14. Buber, "Some Comments on the Theory of Hasidism" (Hebrew), *Amot* 2.7 (1963-64), 43ff. On the Ba'al Shem stories, see Buber's "Einleitung" to his collection of *Die Legende des Baalschem* (Frankfurt, 1922). For Scholem's critique of Buber's reliance on the oral tales, see "Buber's Interpretation of Hasidism," *MI*, 233-234. See also "The Historical Image of Israel Ba'al Shem Tov" (Hebrew), *Molad* 144-145 (September-October 1960), 335-357.

15. *Geschichten des Rabbi Nachman*, 28-29. In *Daniel* (1913), trans. M. Friedman (New York, 1964), 31, Buber argued that there is an elevated meaning to words unknown to common usage. On Nachman's theory of silence, see his *Likute ha-Muharan* (Jerusalem, 1969), sec. 64.

16. *Rabbi Nachman*, 4.

17. Ibid., 30.

18. "Ein Hinweis," in *Die Schrift und ihre Verdeutschung* (Berlin, 1936), 311-312. See also his essay from 1960, "Das Wort, das gesprochen wird," *Werke* (Munich, 1962), I, 442-453.

19. See Martin Jay, "Politics of Translation—Siegfried Kracauer and Walter Benjamin on the Buber-Rosenzweig Bible," *LBIY* 21 (1976), 3-24. Jay attributes a metaphysically positive attitude toward language to Buber which more properly applies to Rosenzweig.

20. *Werke*, I, 103, trans. in *I and Thou*, trans. Walter Kaufmann (New York, 1970), 89.

21. *Werke*, I, 81.

22. Ibid., 153, trans. in *I and Thou*, 158.

23. Buber, *Briefwechsel*, II, 196 (24 June 1924), trans. in Franz Rosenzweig, *On Jewish Learning*, trans. Nahum Glatzer (New York, 1965), 111.

24. "Ich und Du," *Werke*, I, 152.

25. Buber, *Religion als Gegenwart*, unpublished lectures held at the Jüdisches Lehrhaus, Frankfurt, from 15 January to 12 March 1922. Buber Archive, MS B/29, VIII, 10-12, quoted in Flohr, 179 (English trans., 337n276).

26. *Walter Benjamin*, 33, 66, 136.

27. *Walter Benjamin*, 107-118. Scholem published the essay in 1970 under the title of "Der Name Gottes und die Sprachtheorie der Kabbala."

28. Benjamin, *Briefe*, I, 142 (17 July 1917). Scholem's translation of the Song of Songs was published by his father's publishing house in 1916.

29. More precisely, Norbert von Hellingrath's book on Hölderlin's Pindar translations. Letter from Scholem, 31 March 1978.

30. Benjamin, "Task of the Translator," *Illuminations*, ed. Hannah Arendt, trans. Harry Zohn (New York, 1969), 69.

31. "Zum Problem der Übersetzung aus dem Jidischen," *Jüdische Rundschau*, 12 January 1917, 16-17.

32. Ibid., 26 January 1917, 35-36.

33. Ernst Simon, "Über einige theologische Sätze von Gershom Scholem," *Mitteilungsblatt des Irgun Olej Merkaz Europa*, 8 December 1972, 3ff.

34. Benjamin was much more hostile to the translation and suggested the inappropriateness of a translation of the Bible into German at a time when Hebrew was being revived. See *Briefe*, I, 432 (letter to Scholem, 18 September 1926), and trans. in Jay, "Politics of Translation," 20. See also Benjamin to Scholem, 29 May 1926, in *Briefe*, I, 429 and Benjamin to Karl Thieme, 9 March 1928, *Briefe*, II, 744-745.

35. Buber, *Briefwechsel*, II, 251-253 (27 April 1926), 371-373 (10 April 1930), 380-381 (22 May 1930).

36. Buber to Scholem, *Briefwechsel*, II, 375, and *MI*, 315.

37. "At the Completion of Buber's Translation of the Bible," *MI*, 316-317.

38. "Lyrik der Kabbala?" *Der Jude* 6 (1921-22), 60.

39. "Über die jungste Sohar Anthologie," *Der Jude* 5 (1920-21), 364.

40. Cf. Benjamin *Briefe*, I, 197: "[Die] Offenbarung . . . die vernommen werden muß, d.h. in der metaphysische akustischen Sphäre liegt."

41. See especially Rufus Jones, *Studies in Mystical Religion* (London, 1909); Rudolf Otto, *Mysticism East and West* (New York, 1932); and Evelyn Underhill, *Mysticism. A Study in the Nature and Development of Man's Spiritual Consciousness* (London, 1926).

42. *MT*, 6.

43. *MT*, 15. On 354n13 Scholem refers explicitly to Buber's *Ekstatische Konfessionen* as his example for the interpretation of mysticism which emphasizes the inadequacy of language.

44. *MT*, 119-155.

45. *MT*, 17.

46. "Der Name Gottes und die Sprachtheorie der Kabbala," delivered first as a lecture at the Eranos conference in 1970, published in *Judaica*, III, 7-71, English trans. in *Diogenes* 79 (1972), 59-80, and 80 (1972), 164-194.

47. "The Name of God," *Diogenes* 79 (1972), 75-76.

48. "The Meaning of the Torah in Jewish Mysticism," *KS*, 41.

49. "The Name of God," 62.

50. *Diogenes* 80 (1972), 194. Scholem's source is in Moses Cordovero's *Pardes Rimonim*, chap. 19, sec. 1. Scholem fails to notice that for Cordo-

vero, the Tetragrammaton does have a meaning, namely, the ten *sefirot* all together, although not the Infinite (*ain sof*) itself. Cordovero seems to have operated with a distinction between *Sinn* and *Bedeutung* such as Frege proposed to distinguish between meaning and reference. For a discussion of these issues, see F. v. Kutschera, *Sprachphilosophie* (Munich, 1971).

51. Simon, "Über einige theologische Sätze," notes the parallel between Scholem's notion of indirect discourse and Kierkegaard's.

52. "The Name of God," 70.

53. Ibid., 60.

54. *MT*, 27, 244-255.

55. "With Gershom Scholem," *JJC*, 48, and "The Name of God," *Diogenes* 80 (1972), 194.

56. "Revelation and Tradition as Religious Categories in Judaism," *MI*, 294.

57. *MI*, 295-296.

58. *MI*, 298.

59. *MI*, 300.

60. "Reflections on Jewish Theology," *JJC*, 296. The essay was originally published as "Jewish Theology in Our Time," *Center Magazine* 7 (March-April 1974), 57-71.

61. Ibid., 268-270. For the various ideas in the Kabbalah about the multifaceted nature of the Torah, see "The Meaning of the Torah in Jewish Mysticism," *KS*, 32-87.

62. Scholem quotes the passage in BT *Menaḥot* 29b about how Moses hears Rabbi Akiva expounding interpretations of Torah which he (Moses) does not understand but which Akiva claims are "teaching given to Moses at Sinai." The implication is that Moses was given teaching at Sinai which he himself did not understand but which would be clarified only by future generations of scholars. *MI*, 283.

63. "Jewish Theology," *JJC*, 270. For Scholem's most extensive treatment of this question, see "Religious Authority and Mysticism," *KS*, 5-32.

64. "Jewish Theology," *JJC*, 271.

65. See, for instance, Gershon Weiler, "On the Theology of Gershom Scholem" (Hebrew), *Keshet* 71 (1976), 123. Baruch Kurzweil, in his numerous articles on Scholem, frequently complains of a similar problem. Simon, in "Uber einige theologische Sätze von Gershom Scholem," turns the issue of Scholem's reticence into a key for understanding his theological and linguistic notion of indirect communication.

66. "Offener Brief an den Verfasser der Schrift, 'Jüdischer Glaube in dieser Zeit,' " *Bayerische Israelitische Gemeindezeitung*, 15 August 1932, 241-244.

67. For Schoeps's political position, see *Wir deutschen Juden* (Berlin, 1934), and *Bereit für Deutschland: Der Patriotismus deutscher Juden und der Nationalisozialismus* (essays written 1930-1939, published Berlin, 1970). On Schoeps, see George Mosse, "The Influence of the Volkish Idea on German Jewry," in *Germans and Jews*, 107-111. Schoeps was influenced by Volkish ideas and, although he rejected Nazi racial views, supported the

notion of a "third force" in Germany to combat both Bolshevism and Western liberalism.

68. See Alexander Altmann, "Zur Auseinandersetzung mit der 'dialektischen Theologie,' " *MGWJ* 79, n.s. 43 (1925), 358-361, which is a discussion and refutation of Schoeps's position. See also the editorial note in the *Bayerische Israelitische Gemeindezeitung* preceding Scholem's review: "der hier unternommene Versuch einer Neugrundung der jüdischen Glaubenslehre mißlungen sei. Eine Reihe von Zuschriften der besten Sachkenner hat dieses Urteil bestätigt."

69. See S.L. Steinheim, *Die Offenbarung nach dem Lehrbegriff der Synagogue* (Frankfurt, 1835), I, 88, and Geiger's letter to Derembourg in 1836, published in *Allgemeine Zeitung des Judentums* (1896), 130. On Steinheim and Kierkegaard, see Schoeps, *Steinheim zum Gedenken* (Leiden, 1966), 32.

70. *Steinheim zum Gedenken*, 34: "unterirdische Kontinuität des Denkens."

71. "Offener Brief," 243. In "Revelation and Tradition," *MI*, 296, Scholem uses precisely the same terms, thus proving that his later analysis (the "Revelation and Tradition" essay was originally delivered as a lecture at an Eranos conference in 1962) was based on earlier theological speculations: "Theologians have described the word of God as the 'absolutely concrete.' But the absolutely concrete is, at the same time, the simply unfulfillable—it is that which in no way can be put into practice." Scholem's analysis of the Kabbalah must therefore be read as a polemic against Barthian theology.

72. Schoeps, *Ja-Nein-und Trotzdem* (Mainz, 1974), 45-54. Schoeps published here for the first time his reply to Scholem of 15 August 1932. In a subsequent visit to Germany, Scholem met with Schoeps and they had an unpleasant argument over the same issues. See Schoeps's account of the meeting, ibid., 54-55.

73. Ibid., 47.

74. Rosenzweig, *Der Stern der Erlösung* (Frankfurt, 1921), 205. See also Buber, *Briefwechsel*, II, 222-223 (Rosenzweig to Buber, 5 June 1925): "The only immediate content of revelation . . . is revelation itself; with *va-yered* it is essentially complete, with *va-yedabber* interpretation sets in." Scholem quotes this letter approvingly in "Religious Authority and Mysticism," *KS*, 30n3. On Rosenzweig's philosophy of language and its relation to Romantics such as Schelling and Baader, see Else Freund, *Die Existenzphilosophie Franz Rosenzweigs* (Hamburg, 1959), 132-154.

75. *Stern der Erlösung*, part 3. Rosenzweig may have been influenced by Schelling, who considered the Jews to be outside of history from a Christian point of view ("ausgeschlossen von der Geschichte"). Rosenzweig may have adopted Schelling's position and turned it into a virtue: history has ceased to be the realm where God manifests his providence and therefore it is only in "eternity" that the Jews realize their dialogue with God. See Alexander Altmann, "Franz Rosenzweig on History," in his *Studies in Religious Philosophy and Mysticism* (London, 1969), 282.

76. Buber, *Briefwechsel*, II, 197, 199 (29 June 1924, 4 July 1924).

77. For Rosenzweig's positive attitude toward the law, see especially *Die Bauleute* (Berlin, 1925), which is a critique of Buber's rejection of the law. Rosenzweig argues that in his search for a living tradition, Buber should not ignore the law but should make it the main focus of his endeavor.

78. "Revelation and Tradition," *MI*, 290.

79. Rosenzweig wrote to his friend Rudolf Hallo, who was disturbed by Scholem's critique of the German-Jewish youth movement: "ich glaube, die Schuld an diesem langen theoretischen Brief . . . trägt der böse Scholem . . . Über das was man tut, läßt sich nicht disputieren. Am wenigsten mit einem Nihilisten wie Scholem." *Briefe*, 431 (27 March 1922). For an identical evaluation of Scholem, see Schoeps, *Ja-Nein-und Trotzdem*, 54, who, after arguing in person with Scholem, concluded: "Nur bestätigte sich mir langsam die Ahnung, daß Scholem eigentlich ein Nihilist sei." For Scholem's definition of religious nihilism, see "Der Nihilismus als Religiose Phänomen," *Eranos Jahrbuch* 43 (1974), 1-4.

80. "Education for Judaism," *Dispersion and Unity* 12 (1971), 211-212.

81. "Jewish Theology," *JJC*, 274. See also "Reflections on the Possibility of Jewish Mysticism in Our Time," *Ariel* 26 (Spring 1970).

82. For one of Scholem's statements of belief in God, see "With Gershom Scholem," *JJC*, 35: "I have never cut myself off from God . . . I don't believe that there is such a thing as the absolute autonomy of man, whereby man makes himself and the world creates itself . . . Faith in God—even if it doesn't have a positive expression in every generation—will reveal itself as a force."

83. Simon suggests the comparison with Maimonides in "Über einige theologische Sätze." Scholem states clearly his objection to theological debates about the essence of God in "Jewish Theology," *JJC*, 281: "the basically sterile and endless discussion about the so-called attributes of God."

84. "Revelation and Tradition," *MI*, 289.

85. Molitor, *Philosophie der Geschichte*, I, 4, quoted in *MI*, 285.

86. "The Name of God," 167.

87. *Judaica*, III, 265.

88. Buber, *Briefwechsel*, III, 367-368 (Scholem to Buber, 27 February 1930).

89. "Rosenzweig's Star of Redemption," *MI*, 323-324. For a more comprehensive presentation of Scholem's view of Rosenzweig, see "Franz Rosenzweig and his book 'The Star of Redemption' " (Hebrew), *Devarim be-Go*, 407-425.

90. For a similar view of historical interpretation, see Simon Rawidowicz, "On Interpretation," *Studies in Jewish Thought* (Philadelphia, 1974), 45-81.

91. *Judaica*, III, 264. See Jürgen Habermas's commentary, "Die verkleidete Tora," *Merkur* (January 1978), esp. 98-99.

92. Scholem translates the mist representing the *sefirah keter* as *Nebel* in *Die Geheimnisse der Schöpfung* (Berlin, 1935), 45.

93. "Zionism—Dialectic of Continuity and Rebellion," in *Unease in Zion*, ed. Ehud Ben Ezer (New York, 1974), 290.

94. The essay was not published in Benjamin's lifetime, but was included in his posthumous *Schriften* (Frankfurt, 1955), II, 401-420. A particularly interesting indication of Scholem's relationship to Benjamin can be discerned in Scholem's essay "Walter Benjamin and His Angel," *JJC*, 198-236. Scholem characterizes Benjamin as an esoteric writer and gives a detailed exegesis of recensions of a "thoroughly hermitic text" entitled "Angesilaus Santander," which Benjamin wrote in August 1933 on Ibiza. The essay leaves one with the inescapable impression that Scholem relates to Benjamin as he might to a Kabbalistic writer and subjects him to the same kind of "decoding."

95. See, for example, his bibliographical essay "Probleme der Sprachsoziologie" (1935), in *Gesammelte Schriften* (Frankfurt, 1972-1974), III, 452-480, and "The Task of the Translator" in *Illuminations*, 69-83.

96. *Walter Benjamin*, 66: "mystische Sprachvorstellungen." See also "Walter Benjamin," *JJC*, 180.

97. The conflicting literature on Benjamin is now considerable. For a partial bibliography, see Martin Jay, *The Dialectical Imagination* (Boston, 1973), 337n127. Scholem's view is expressed in "Walter Benjamin and His Angel," *JJC*, 189-201, *Walter Benjamin*, ibid., 172-197, and "Two Letters to Walter Benjamin," ibid., 237-243. Two works that tend to support Scholem's position are Bernd Witte, *Walter Benjamin—Intellektuelle als Kritiker* (Stuttgart, 1976), and Hans Heinz Holz, "Philosophie als Interpretation," *Alternative* 56/57 (October-December, 1967).

98. Benjamin, *Briefe*, II, 526. See also *Briefe*, I, 136-139, *Illuminations*, 76, and *Walter Benjamin*, 53.

99. A typical example of this renewed interest in Romanticism is Fritz Strich's influential study *Deutsche Klassik und Romantik* (Munich, 1922).

100. For Humboldt's philosophy of language, see his *Über die Verschiedenheit des menschlichen Sprachbaus und ihren Einfluss auf die geistige Entwicklung des Menschengeschlechts* (1830-1835), in *Werke* (Darmstadt, 1963), vol. 3. For Hamann, see his *Sämtliche Werke*, ed. Nadler (Vienna, 1949-1957), II, 199, and on Hamann, Martin Seils, *Wirklichkeit und Wort bei J.G. Hamann* (Stuttgart, 1961).

101. *Briefe*, I, 125-128 (July 1916, no precise date given).

102. Benjamin's first letter to Buber acknowledging the invitation appeared in Buber, *Briefwechsel*, I, 439-440 (May 1916). For Scholem's communication with Buber regarding Benjamin's projected contribution see ibid., 441 (25 June 1916).

103. Cassirer, *Philosophy of Symbolic Forms* (New Haven, 1955), I, 15.

104. *Briefe*, I, 329, trans. in Hannah Arendt's introduction to *Illuminations*, 47. See also "Das Zeichen bezieht sich niemals" (u.p. Benjamin Archiv MS 790), quoted in Rudolf Tiedemann, *Studien zur Philosophie Walter Benjamins* (Frankfurt, 1973), 45. See also *Ursprung des deutschen Trauerspiels* (Frankfurt, 1972), 55. In "Das Zeichen" he asserts: "the sign never refers (*bezieht sich*) to the object because no intention dwells within

it; the object is only attainable [through] intention." In his "Task of the Translator," he developed a distinction between "intention" and "mode of intention," in which the "mode of intention" is the culturally bound conventional meaning of a word which must be stripped away to discover the essence of the object "intended." See *Illuminations*, 74. For Benjamin's relation to phenomenology, see Tiedemann, 43.

105. *Briefe*, I, 197.

106. "The Task of the Translator," 77.

107. Über Sprache überhaupt und über die Sprache des Menschen," *Schriften*, II, 405.

108. *Ursprung des deutschen Trauerspiels*, 176: "Es ist ein grosser Unterschied, ob der Dichter zum Allgemeine das Besondere sucht oder im Besondern das Allgemeine schaut. Aus jener Art entsteht Allegorie, wo das Besondere nur als Beispiel, als Exempel des Allgemeinen gilt; die letztere aber ist eigentlich die Natur der Poesie: sie spricht ein Besonderes aus, ohne ans Allgemein zu denken oder darauf hinzuweisen." The passage is from Goethe, *Sämtliche Werke*, XXXVIII, 261.

109. Arendt, "Introduction," *Illuminations*, 13. Arendt argues that Benjamin's doctrine of linguistic transference was a linguistic metaphor for the Marxist duality between substructure and superstructure. She therefore claims that Benjamin tried to cast his Marxism in a poetic idiom.

110. *Ursprung des deutschen Trauerspiels*, 18.

111. The notion that language is a body of symbols rather than a set of arbitrary signs and that man uses language to give form to sense perceptions suggests Benjamin's intellectual affinity with the Neo-Kantians, particularly Cassirer. See his *Philosophy of Symbolic Forms*, vol. 1. There is no evidence that Benjamin ever read Cassirer, although he knew Rickert, whom he called his "most influential teacher" (*Briefe*, II, 857). In *Ursprung*, 32, he criticizes the Neo-Kantians for their pure metaphysics devoid of historical experience.

112. "Das Zeichen bezieht sich," Tiedemann, 45. See also the second recension of "Agesilaus Santander," published by Scholem in "Walter Benjamin und sein Engel," *Zur Aktualität Walter Benjamin* (Frankfurt, 1972), 100: "However, this name is in no way an enrichment of that which is named," and Scholem's comment, 115: "For Benjamin, the name is projected onto an image, instead of the common conception whereby an image is approximated by an inscribed name."

113. *Illuminations*, 74. See also "Das Zeichen": "Der Name ist ihnen (Gegenstand) nicht rein; sondern an ein Zeichen gebunden."

114. *Illuminations*, 80.

115. Ibid., 74-75.

116. "Man muß die Sprache nicht sowohl wie ein todtes Erzeugtes, sondern weit mehr eine Erzeugung ansehen," *Werke*, sec. 8, p. 55, quoted in Noam Chomsky, *Current Issues in Linguistic Theory* (The Hague, 1964).

117. *Illuminations*, 82.

118. He particularly admired the romantics for this reason: "Denn freilich ist die Romantik die letzte Bewegung, die noch einmal die Tradition

hinüberrettete. Ihr . . . Versuch galt der unsinning orgiastichen Eröffnung aller geheimen Quellen der Tradition." *Briefe*, I, 138 (letter to Scholem of June 1917).

119. *Briefe*, I, 144-146 (6 September 1917).

120. "Education for Judaism," *Dispersion and Unity*, 212.

121. Gershon Weiler, "On the Theology of Gershom Scholem, *Keshet* 71 (1976), 121-128. Weiler's misinterpretations of Scholem are in part because he only used Scholem's "Jewish Theology in Our Time" and ignored other essays.

122. Ibid., 124.

123. *Die Religion der Vernunft*, 68 (English trans. by Simon Kaplan, *The Religion of Reason out of the Sources of Judaism*, New York, 1972, p. 59).

124. Ibid., 79 (English, 69). The best treatment of the *Ursprungsprinzip* is by Hugo Bergmann, "The Principle of Beginning in the Philosophy of Hermann Cohen," (Hebrew), *Kneset* 8 (1944), 143-153, and *Hogai ha-Dor* (Jerusalem, 1935), 194ff.

125. *Religion of Reason*, 84.

126. Ibid., 28.

127. *Religion der Vernunft*, 36 (English, 31).

128. Ibid., 33 (English, 29).

129. Ibid.

130. Ibid., 3 (English, 3): "Es kann nimmermehr gelingen, aus den literrarischen Quellen einen einheitlichen Begriff des Judentums zu entwickeln, wenn dieser nicht selbst . . . als der ideale Vorwurf vorgenommen wird."

131. Ibid., 39 (English, 34): "So hat uns das Prinzip der Vernunft zur Einheit von Religion und Sittenlehre geführt. Und wenn anders die Quellen des Judentums die Religion der Vernunft zur Enthüllung bringen, so wird dadurch auch der Begriff der Vernunft in seiner Religion dem Judentum seine wahrhafte Einheit stiften."

5. MYSTICISM

1. *MT*, 38.

2. See Neumark, *Geschichte der jüdischen Philosophie des Mittelalters* (Berlin, 1907), on the rise of the Kabbalah. Neumark argues: "Von dem hier gewonnenen Gesichtspunkt aus bildet die kabbalistische Bewegung eine latente Parallele zur philosophischen. Die Philosophen kämpfen mit den mystischen Elementen und überwinden sie, aber in den Zwischenstadien dieses Ringens wird mancher Gedanke konzipiert, manches Bild projiziert und manches Wort geschliffen" (I, 181).

3. On Scholem's discussion of Graetz and Neumark, see *Ursprung und Anfänge der Kabbala* (Berlin, 1962), 1-9.

4. "Die Scheidung zwischen dem offiziellen Judentum, das als das Reich der verwesenden Gestalt abgetan wurde, und einem unterirdischen, in dem die wahren Quellen rauschen, war naiv und konnte historischer

Betrachtung nicht standhalten," in "Bubers Auffassung des Judentums," *Judaica*, II, 149.

5. One particularly interesting example is Ahron Marcus (1843-1916), who tried to show that Hartmann's philosophy of the unconscious was already anticipated by Hasidism. See his *Hartmanns inductive Philosophie im Chassidismus* (Vienna, 1888). Scholem first read Marcus in 1914-15 and was greatly impressed by his knowledge of Kabbalah and Hasidism, but he later came to regard Marcus as something of a charlatan who was a defender of orthodoxy. See "Ahron Marcus and Hasidism" (Hebrew), *Behinot* 7 (1954), 3-8. Scholem nevertheless recognized that Marcus may have been partially correct in claiming the similarity between Hartmann's *Ubewußtsein* and the Hasidic *kadmut ha-sekhel* (prerational). See "The Unconscious and the Concept 'kadmut ha-sekhel' " (Hebrew). *Devarim be-Go*, 351-360.

6. "With Gershom Scholem," *JJC*, 32.

7. On the history of the dating of the *Zohar*, see Isaiah Tishby, *Mishnat ha-Zohar* (Jerusalem, 1971) 1, 44-67. For a full bibliography of studies of Jewish mysticism, see Scholem's *Bibliographica Kabbalistica* (1927).

8. For Emden's dating of the *Zohar*, see *Mitpaḥat Sefarim* (Lvov, 1870; repr. Jerusalem, 1970); for his anti-Sabbatian polemics, see esp. *Sefer Shimush* (Amsterdam, 1762). Emden's belief that genuine religious texts must be ancient was based on his view of the history of religions. Christianity was much more legitimate than Sabbatianism because of its antiquity. See the treatise "Resen Mateh" in *Sefer Shimush*, (Amsterdam, 1762), 15a-21a. See also *Torat ha-Kena'ot* (Amsterdam, 1752; Lvov, 1870).

9. M.H. Landauer, "Vorläufiger Bericht in Ansehung des Sohar," *LB Orient* 6 (1845), 322ff.

10. Adolph Jellinek, *Moses de Leon und sein Verhältnis zum Sohar* (Leipzig, 1851), and *Beiträge zur Geschichte der Kabbala* (Leipzig, 1852). Jellinek compared Moses de Leon's known writings with the *Zohar* and came to the conclusion that they were by the same author.

11. David Luria, *Ma'amar Kadmut Sefer ha-Zohar* (Warsaw, 1856). Luria used the same comparative method as Jellinek, but came to the opposite conclusion, namely that the *Zohar* was not stylistically the same as Moses de Leon's writings.

12. Adolph Franck, *La Kabbale ou la philosophie religieuse des Hebreux* (Paris, 1843), and *Die Kabbala oder die Religions-Philosophie der Hebraer* (Leipzig, 1844).

13. Mehlzahagi claimed to have written some 70 books, of which one, *Sefer Ravia* (Ofen, 1837) was published. Another important work exists in manuscript in the National Library of the Hebrew University. See Scholem, *Manuscripts in Hebrew on the Kabbalah* (Hebrew) (Jerusalem, 1930), 13, and G. Kressel, "Writings of Elijakim Mehlzahagi" (Hebrew), *Kiryat Sefer* 17 (1940), 87-94. For Scholem's particularly positive evaluation of Mehlzahagi, see "Die Erforschung der Kabbala von Reuchlin bis zur Gegenwart," *Judaica*, III, 261.

14. See Zeitlin's introduction to the Yiddish translation of Graetz's *Geschichte*, trans. B. Karlinski, J. Leiserowitz, and A. Riklis (Warsaw, 1913). For Zeitlin's studies on the *Zohar*, see "The Antiquity of Mysticism in Israel" (Hebrew), *Ha-Tekufah* V, 280-322, and "Key to the Book *Zohar*" (Hebrew), ibid., VI, 314-334, VII, 353-368, and IX, 265-330. Zeitlin's articles on Kabbalah and Hasidism have been collected in *Be-Fardes ha-Hasidut ve-ha-Kabbalah* (Tel Aviv, 1965).

15. Response to Chaim Nacham Bialik's "Open Letter" to the editors of *Devir* (1925). Scholem's response was written in June 1925, and was published in *ha-Poel ha-Tzair*, 12 December 1967, 18-19, republished in *Devarim be-Go*, 59-63.

16. *Das Buch Bahir* (Leipzig, 1923).

17. The article was Scholem's inaugural lecture at the Hebrew University and was published in *Mada'ai ha-Yahadut* 1 (1926), 16-29.

18. Graetz, *History of the Jews*, trans. Bella Lowy (London, 1904), IV, 12: "His genuine writings however were not sufficiently noticed and had brought him in little fame and money. Moses de Leon then hit upon a much more effective means for opening hearts and purses wider. He commenced the composition of books under feigned but honored names."

19. In his article on the Kabbalah in the *Encyclopedia Judaica*, X, 654, written in 1931, he still held that the question of date and authorship was open. However, in his little book of translations from the *Zohar, Die Geheimnisse der Schöpfung* (Berlin, 1935), he began to reverse his position (see 10-18).

20. *MT*, 156-204: "The Zohar I. The Book and Its Author."

21. See, for example, J.L. Zlotnik, *Ma'amarim* (Jerusalem, 1939), R. Margulies in *Sinai* 5 (1941), 237-240, and, more recently, Samuel Belkin, "Midrash ha-Ne'elam and its sources in early Alexandrian midrashim" (Hebrew), *Sura* 3 (1958), 25-92. The latter is an extensive attempt to prove against Scholem that the *Midrash ha-Ne'elam* can be shown, by comparison to Philonic Midrash, to have been from first-century Alexandria. See R.J.Z. Werblowsky's extensive refutation of Belkin, "Philo and the Zohar," *Journal of Jewish Studies* 10 (1959), 25-45, 113-137.

22. In the letter to Bialik, Scholem mentions a lexicon of the *Zohar* which he had half-completed and which he hoped would put the dating of the *Zohar* on a scientific, philological basis. Although Scholem promised at that time to publish his lexicon, he has not yet done so.

23. *MT*, 208.

24. "Myth and Kabbalah," *KS*, 95.

25. *MT*, 188-189.

26. *MT*, 7.

27. Ibid.

28. *MT*, 23.

29. *MT*, 8.

30. Scholem notes that he took the distinction from Baeck in "Mysticism and Society," *Diogenes* 58 (1967), 8. See Baeck, "Romantische Religion," *Aus Drei Jahrtausenden* (Tübingen, 1958), 42-121. The essay was originally published in 1922. Although Baeck was initially hostile to all mysticism, he gradually came to accept Jewish mysticism as an ethical

force, opposed to other mystical movements which only desired the *unio mystica*. See Alexander Altmann, "Leo Baeck and the Jewish Mystical Tradition," *Leo Baeck Memorial Lecture* 17 (1973).

31. Molitor, *Philosophie der Geschichte*, II, 8.

32. "Die Mystische Gestalt der Gottheit in der Kabbala," *Eranos Jahrbuch* 29 (1961), 141-143. Scholem presents two views of biblical anthropomorphisms: Hermann Gunkel's in *Genesis, übersetzt und erklärt* (Göttingen, 1917), 112, in which the Bible is naively anthropomorphistic, and Benno Jacob's in *Das erste Buch der Tora, Genesis* (Berlin, 1934), 58, in which the Bible has a purely spiritual conception of God. Scholem argues that both authors are partially correct, since an unreflective tension permeates the biblical materials.

33. "Das Ringen zwischen dem biblischen Gott und dem Gott Plotins in der alten Kabbala," *Grundbegriffe*, 10.

34. "Mystische Gestalt," 143.

35. "Tradition and New Creation," *KS*, 121.

36. "Das Ringen" is Scholem's key article dealing with this question; see 9-53.

37. "Kabbalah and Myth," *KS*, 89.

38. *MT*, 28-29; also "Kabbalah and Myth," *KS*, 95.

39. "Kabbalah and Myth," *KS*, 89.

40. A good example is the sixteenth-century codifier of Jewish law, Joseph Karo. See R.J.Z. Werblowsky's *Joseph Karo, Lawyer and Mystic* (London, 1962).

41. "Mystische Gestalt," 144.

42. *MT*, 208.

43. "The Meaning of the Torah in Jewish Mysticism," *KS*, 50-62.

44. "Tradition and New Creation," *KS*, 124. For a similar approach in the history of religions, see Mircea Eliade, *Myth and Reality* (New York, 1963).

45. *Ursprung und Anfänge*, 358ff. On *Rabad*, see I. Twersky, *Rabad of Posquieres* (Cambridge, 1962). Against Scholem, Twersky implicitly deemphasizes the centrality of the new Kabbalah in Rabad's thought.

46. *Ursprung und Anfänge*, 361.

47. Cohen, *Ethik des reinen Willens*, 452, quoted in *MT*, 36.

48. *MT*, 35; "*Sitra Aḥrah*—Good and Evil in the Kabbalah" (Hebrew trans.), in *Pirkei Yisod be-Havanat ha-Kabbala u-Smoleha*, 187-213.

49. The letter was first published in *Encounter* 22 (1964), 51-53, and republished in *JJC*, 300-306.

50. "Mysticism and Society," *Diogenes*, 24.

51. *SS*, 7.

52. "Chapters from the History of Kabbalistic Literature" (Hebrew), *Kiryat Sefer* 4 (1928), 286.

53. *Ursprung und Anfänge*, 373.

6. Myth

1. On the cultural background to the rise of Gnosticism, see Hans Jonas, *The Gnostic Religion* (Boston, 1963), 3-27.

2. *Die Geheimnisse der Schöpfung*, 24.

3. *Gnosticismus und Judenthum*, esp. 14, 30, 55. Graetz interpreted the *pardes* legend (*Ḥagigah* 14b) as a Gnostic allegory. Rabbi Akiva, who was the only one of the four rabbis to survive the flirtation with Gnosticism, was able to wage a successful defense of Judaism precisely because of his familiarity with Gnosticism. His defense was the *Sefer Yeẓirah*, which Graetz dated to the second century, arguing that it was a philosophical polemic against Gnosticism (ibid., 83ff). He later changed his dating of this text, which was to become seminal for Jewish mysticism, to Gaonic times on linguistic grounds, but still maintained his original interpretation of its philosophical charcter. See *Geschichte der Juden* (4th ed.), V, 297n.

4. In *MT*, 40ff, Scholem argues that the Hekhalot literature dated from the fourth or fifth century, but in *Jewish Gnosticism* he claims that he was "not radical enough" and pushes the date much earlier (see 8ff). E. E. Urbach published a major attack on Scholem's early dating of mystical traditions in Scholem's own Festschrift: "The Traditions concerning Mystical Doctrine in the Period of the Tannaim" (Hebrew), in *Sefer ha-Yovel le-Khvod Gershom Scholem* (Jerusalem, 1968), 1-29.

5. *MT*, 49. See Anz, *Zur Frage nach dem Ursprung des Gnostizismus* (Leipzig, 1897), 55-56: "Eine Prüfung der Nachrichten und Quellen, die uns über den Gnostizismus zu Gebote stehen, hat uns die weite Verbreitung der Lehre vom Aufsteig der Seelen gezeigt . . . Und so hat sie sich uns in der That als die gesuchte 'Zentrallehre' herausgestellt." For Scholem on Anz, see also "Zur Frage nach dem Entstehung der Kabbala," *Korrespondenzblatt* 9 (1928), 8, and *Ursprung und Anfänge*, 18.

6. *Jewish Gnosticism*, 36-43.

7. *MT*, 65.

8. *Jewish Gnosticism*, 3, 9. See also *MT*, 359, where Scholem mentions Friedländer, M. Joel's *Blicke in die Religionsgeschichte* (1880), and A. Büchler's essays in *Judaica* (Festschrift für Hermann Cohen, 1912) and in *MGWJ* 76 (1932), 412-456. The thesis that Jewish Gnosticism was the source for Christian Gnosticism was elaborated by Eric Peterson in *Zeitschrift für Neutestamentliche Wissenschaft* 27 (1928), 90-91, and more recently by G. Quispel, "Der gnostische Anthropos und die jüdische Tradition," *Eranos Jahrbuch* 22 (1953), 194-234.

9. *MT*, 65, and *Jewish Gnosticism*, 10-12.

10. *Jewish Symbols in the Greco-Roman Period* (New York, 1953), I; chap. 1 is the most concise statement of Goodenough's position. For his references to Scholem, see 8 and 19. Goodenough's argument is fundamentally an attack on G. F. Moore's definition of normative Judaism. The best critiques of Goodenough are by M. Avi-Yonah, in *The Dura-Europos Synagogue: A Re-evaluation (1932-1972)* (Missoula, 1973), 117-136, and E. Bickerman, "Symbolism in the Dura Synagogue," *Harvard Theological Review* 58 (1956), 127-151.

11. *Jewish Symbols*, I, 19-20.

12. *MT*, 51.

13. *Das Buch Bahir*, 1-2. See Adolf Jellinek, *Auswahl Kabbalistischer Mystik* (Leipzig, 1853), 14.

14. "Zur Frage der Entstehung der Kabbala," 14. See also *Ursprung und Anfänge,* 60ff.

15: "Zur Frage der Entstehung der Kabbala," 15; *MT,* 84.

16. *MT,* 84. For an implicit attack on Scholem's view of the centrality of a mystical aristocracy in the Rhineland, see Haym Soloveitchik, "Three Themes in Sefer Hasidim," *AJS Review* 1 (1976), 311-359.

17. *Moreh Nevukhe ha-Zeman,* 258.

18. *Ursprung und Anfänge,* 94ff; *MT,* 75.

19. On the rise of Jewish Neoplatonism, see Guttman, *Philosophies of Judaism,* 95-152.

20. "Zur Frage der Entstehung der Kabbala," 25; *MT,* 217-218; and "Gott Plotins" in *Grundbegriffe.*

21. "Reste neuplatonischer Spekulation in der Mystik der deutschen Chassidim," *MGWJ* 75 (1931), 172-191, and *MT,* 86. See also "The Footsteps of Gabirol in the Kabbala" (Hebrew), *Me'asef Sofre Eretz Yisrael* (1940), 160-179. Scholem argues against Klausner that ibn Gabirol did not have a direct influence on the history of the Kabbalah. Some of his terminology may have entered the Gerona school through intermediaries, such as the Neoplatonist Abraham ibn Ezra. The Gerona Kabbalists gave ibn Gabirol's ideas a new Gnostic interpretation foreign to their original intent.

22. *MT,* 208; "Zur Frage der Entstehung der Kabbala," 21. For a cogent presentation of Neoplatonic theory, see J.M. Rist, *Plotinus* (Cambridge, 1967).

23. D.H. Joel, *Die Religionsphilosophie des Sohar* (Leipzig, 1849), 179ff. For Scholem's critique of Joel, see *MT,* 209.

24. Scholem's most extensive treatment of the issue of *creatio ex nihilo* can be found in "Schöpfung aus Nichts und die Selbstverschränkung Gottes," *Grundbegriffe,* 53-90. For a partial philological study of the term *creatio ex nihilo,* see H.A. Wolfson, "The Meaning of *Ex Nihilo* in the Church Fathers, Arabic and Hebrew Philosophy, and St. Thomas," in *Medieval Studies in Honor of J.D.M. Ford* (Cambridge, 1948), 355-367.

25. "Zehn Unhistorische Sätze über Kabbala," *Judaica,* III, 267-268: "Hier scheint ein Gefühl dafur mitzuwirken, was mit dieser These von der Identifikation (von En-sof mit dem Nichts) gefährdet wird: ihr fehlt das dialektische Moment im Schopfüngsbegriffe. Es ist dieser Mangel an Dialektik, der diese These dem Pantheismus gegunüber hilflos macht . . . Der Mystiker, der seine Erlebnisse undialektisch verarbeitet, muβ beim Pantheismus anlangen."

26. "Schöpfung aus Nichts," *Grundbegriffe,* 84-89. Scholem shows how the later Kabbalah gave Aristotle's logic a new twist. Their concept of "nothingness" (*ayin*) resembled Aristotle's notion of privation. Since the *ayin* is not the negation of all existence, but only its privation, it becomes the potential for all existence ("die wahre Wurzel allen Seins").

27. *MT,* 264: "[the] conception of the *Reshimu* has a close parallel in the system of the Gnostic Basilides who flourished about 125 A.D. . . . Moreover, we have an early prototype of the *zimzum* in the Gnostic 'Book of the Great Logos.' "

28. "Das Ringen," *Grundbegriffe*, 52. Scholem took this information from F.J. Molitor, *Philosophie der Geschichte*, I, 396.

29. "Gerade diese Ansicht der 'alten Kabbalisten' über das Nichts in Gott ausgesprochen billigend anführt, als ob er die Affinität zwischen der kabbalistischen Spekulation und der des deutschen Idealismus gespürt hätte; vgl. seinen *More Nebboche Ha-seman*, ed. Rawidowicz, S. 306/307. Krochmal ist der einzige bedeutende jüdische Denker des 19. Jahrhunderts, bei dem ich Derartiges gefundet habe." "Schöpfung aus Nichts," *Grundbegriffe*, 83n50.

30. Scholem's most important treatment of Gnostic nihilism is "Der Nihilismus als Religiöses Phänomen," *Eranos Jahrbuch* 43 (1974), 1-50, esp. 7-13.

31. "Redemption Through Sin" (Hebrew), *Keneset* 2 (1937), 347-392. trans. *MI*, 78-141.

32. *MI*, 104.

33. Ibid., 105-106.

34. Ibid., 129-133, and "Der Nihilismus", 35-50.

35. In "Der Nihilismus," 6, he argues that the very nature of the multilevel Kabbalistic approach to reality left the door open to nihilism: "Aber diese mystischen Strukturen werden dann bei weiterem Fortschritt auch ihrerseits ins Amorphe abgebaut, so sehr sie auch noch unter Beibehaltung von traditionellen Symbolen aus der Licht-oder Lautwelt bestimmt werden. Die eigentlichen mystische Erfahrung übersteigt alle Struktur. In ihrer unendlichen Plastizität kann sie neue gebären oder wiederherstellen; sie kann aber auch, wie im Falle der nihilistischen Mystiker, es bei diesem Abbau bewenden lassen."

36. "Unhistorische Sätze," *Judaica*, III, 266-267: "Die Vorwürfe an die häretischen Theologen der sabbatianischen Kabbala, sie hätten die geistigen Mysterien materialistisch miβverstanden, zeigen, wohin die Reise gehen konnte, wenn man einmal versuchte, nach der inneren Logik der Bilder zu denken . . . Die Vorstellung der sabbatianischen Kabbala des Nathan von Gaza . . . ist nur die radikalste Art, diesen Prozess eines dialektischen Materialismus an Gott selber durchzuexerzieren." For further discussion of this aphorism, see Chapter Nine.

37. *Von Berlin*, 152. Scholem studied Semitics with the Assyriologist Fritz Hommel.

38. English trans., *Babel and Bible*, trans. C.H.W. Johns (New York-London, 1903).

39. A particularly interesting example of this comparative tracing of topoi from one religion to another is Robert Eisler's encyclopedic *Weltenmantel und Himmelszelt* (Munich, 1910), which Scholem admired. In *Von Berlin*, 161-169, he relates a number of amusing anecdotes about Eisler, whom he got to know during his period at Munich. Eisler was an eccentric who wanted to organize a society to be called the "Johann-Albert-Widmannstetter-Gesellschaft zur Erforschung der Kabbala." Scholem appears to have been the only "member", and the only sign of life the fictitious society showed was that Scholem's first two books on the Kabbalah (*Das Buch*

Bahir and *Bibliographia Kabbalistica*) appeared as the first and only volumes in the society's projected series of publications on the Kabbalah. Scholem's last contact with Eisler was after the war when Eisler sent him a bizarre plan for solving the Palestine question by shipping all nonreligious Jews back to their countries of origin or, if they still wanted to live in a Jewish state, by creating two autonomous Jewish enclaves in Vienna and Frankfurt. Scholem returned Eisler's manuscript to him with a one word comment: *"Genug."*

40. Jonas, *The Gnostic Religion*, xvii.

41. Jonas, *Gnosis und spätantiker Geist* (Göttingen, 1934, 1964), introduction, esp. 90-91. See also the epilogue to *The Gnostic Religion* ("Gnosticism, Nihilism, Existentialism"), 320-341.

42. In a personal interview, 4 August 1975, Scholem confirmed his association with Jonas but criticized the latter's monistic definition of Gnosticism as alienation from the world. Scholem claimed that there are a variety of definitions of Gnosticism, but one "Gnostic structure of thought." Note his debt to Jonas in "Der Nihilismus," 7-10. He quotes Jonas extensively in "Redemption Through Sin," *MI*, 133-134.

43. Hans Liebeschütz, *Das allegorische Weltbild der Heiligen Hildegard von Bingen* (Leipzig, 1930), 117-118n1.

44. Quoted in Ernst Cassirer, *Philosophy of Symbolic Forms* (New Haven, 1955), II, 3.

45. F.W. Schelling, *Einleitung in die Philosophie der Mythologie*, in *Sämtliche Werke* (Stuttgart and Augsburg, 1856), I, pt. 2, 330ff. English trans. in Cassirer, II, 5.

46. "Kabbalah and Myth," *KS*, 87.

47. Cassirer, II, 4ff.

48. Ibid., 26. See also Alexander Altmann, "Symbol and Myth," *Philosophy* 20 (1945), 162-172.

49. *Walter Benjamin*, 32.

50. *Walter Benjamin*, 44, 79-80. See also *Illuminations*, 226. For Adorno's critique of Benjamin's attraction to myth, see Benjamin, *Briefe*, II, 876, and Jay, *Dialectical Imagination*, 263.

51. *Walter Benjamin*, 79.

52. "The Practical Use of Dream Analysis," in Jung, *Dreams*, trans. R.F.C. Hull (Princeton, 1974), 104.

53. "Psychology and Alchemy," in *Dreams*, 295.

54. "General Aspects of Dream Psychology," in *Dreams*, 33.

55. Ibid., 36.

56. For Scholem's general evaluation of Neumann, see "Erich Neumann," *Mitteilungsblatt des Irgun Olej Merkaz Europa*, 18 November 1960, 4, and "With Gershom Scholem," *JJC*, 30.

57. *The Great Mother*, trans. Ralph Manheim (Princeton, 1963).

58. *Origins and History of Consciousness*, trans. R.F.C. Hull (Princeton, 1954, 1970), 19.

59. Most of the essays published in *KS*, *Grundbegriffe*, and *Mystische Gestalt der Gottheit* were originally delivered at the Eranos conferences

following World War II and were first published in the *Eranos Jahrbuch*. Scholem's appearances at the Eranos conferences marked his return to German intellectual life following the war, although in Switzerland.

60. "With Gershom Scholem," *JJC*, 29.

61. Ibid., 48.

7. MESSIANISM

1. "Die metamorphose des häretischen Messianismus der Sabbatianer in religiösen Nihilismus im 18. Jahrhundert," *Judaica*, III, 198-199.

2. "Toward an Understanding of the Messianic Idea in Judaism," *MI*, 3-4.

3. *MI*, 27: "It is no less wrong, however, in awareness of the great importance of apocalypticism, to underestimate the effect of that other tendency which aimed at removing the apocalyptic thorn. The particular vitality of the Messianic idea in Judaism resides in the dialectical tension between these two tendencies."

4. In response to the question to the Assembly of Notables as to whether the Jews considered Frenchmen their brothers or as strangers, the Sanhedrin ruled: ". . . le Grand Sanhedrin ordonne à tout Israelite de l'Empire Français, de Royaume d'Italie, et des tous autres lieux, de vivre avec les subjects de chacun des États dans lesquels ils habitent, comme avec leurs concitoyens et leurs frères." *Decisions doctrinales du Grand Sanhedrin* (Paris, 1812), 32.

5. Ben Zion Rafael Parrizzi, *Petaḥ Einayim*, I, 39b, and IV, 26a. See Ben Zion Dinur in Jubilee Volume to Y.N. Epstein, 261, and *Be-Mifne ha-Dorot*, 248. See also Harwig Wessely's letter to the Austrian congregations: "Words of Peace and Truth."

6. "Über den Glauben der Juden an einen künftigen Messias," *Zeitschrift für die Wissenschaft des Judentums* 2 (1822), 225. The article to which Ben David replied was written by Baron Sylvester de Sach as a letter to a councilor of the King of Saxony and was published in Paris in 1817. In the Middle Ages, certain Jewish philosophers had already argued that belief in the Messiah was not an article of belief in Judaism, even though Maimonides made it one of his thirteen articles of faith. Nachmanides argued that anti-Messiah position for polemical reasons in his disputation in Barcelona in 1263, but Joseph Albo, in the early fifteenth century, affirmed it sincerely. In the early nineteenth century, orthodox polemicists against Reform tried to show that all true religions must believe in a Messiah by referring to Christianity—surely an unexpected alliance.

7. Y.L. Gordon, "Derekh Bat Ami." See Dinur, *Be-Mifne ha-Dorot*, 248.

8. For example, see his *Nachgelassene Schriften* (Breslau, 1885), II, 120ff. Geiger's messianic doctrine was an implicit polemic against Bruno Bauer who had claimed that, since Christianity is a more universal religion, Jews must renounce their parochial faith before they can undertake the philosophical critique of religion which would lay the basis for emancipation. See Bauer's "Die Fähigkeit der heutigen Juden und Christen, frei zu

werden," in *Einundzwanzig Bogen aus der Schweiz*, ed. Georg Herwegh (1843). A theory similar to Geiger's can be found in the thought of the Reform leader Samuel Holdheim. See Max Wiener, *Jüdische Religion im Zeitalter der Emanzipation* (Hebrew trans.), 128ff.

9. *MI*, 26.

10. *Religion der Vernunft*, 293. See T.W. Rosmarin, *Religion of Reason: Hermann Cohen's System of Religious Philosophy* (New York, 1936), 114-124.

11. *Religion der Vernunft*, 291-292.

12. Ibid., 297-316, and "Deutschtum und Judentum," in *Jüdische Schriften*, II, 237-302.

13. *Reason and Hope*, trans. and ed. Eva Jospe (New York, 1971), 126.

14. "Antwort auf das offene Schreiben des Herrn Dr. Martin Buber an Hermann Cohen," *Jüdische Schriften*, II, 328-340, and "Religion und Zionismus," ibid., 319-327.

15. *Reason and Hope*, 168.

16. Ibid., 183-184.

17. Joseph Klausner, *The Messianic Idea of Israel*, trans. W.F. Stinespring (New York, 1955). See Chapter Eight.

18. Buber, *Werke*, II, 925-942.

19. Buber, *Origin and Meaning of Hasidism*, trans. Maurice Friedman (New York, 1960), 106-112: "redemption does not take place merely once at the end, but also at every moment throughout the whole of time . . . We live in an unredeemed world. But out of each human life that is unarbitrary and bound to the world, a seed of redemption falls into the world and the harvest is God's."

20. Franz Overbeck, *Christentum und Kultur*, Johannes Weiss, *Die Predigt Jesu vom Reiche Gottes*, 2nd ed. (1900), and Albert Schweitzer, *Geschichte des Lebens-Jesu Forschung*.

21. K. Holl, "Luther und die Schwärmer," *Gesammelte Aufsätze zur Kirchengeschichte* (Tübingen, 1927), 420ff; Ernst Bloch, *Thomas Münzer als Theologe der Revolution* (Munich, 1921); Albrecht Ritschl, *Geschichte des Pietismus* (Bonn, 1880-1886); Erich Seeberg, *Gottfried Arnold* (Meerane, 1923).

22. Karl Mannheim, *Ideology and Utopia*, trans. L. Wirth and F. Shills (New York, 1936).

23. W.D. Davies has suggested the analogy between Schweitzer and Scholem in "From Schweitzer to Scholem: Reflections on Sabbatai Sevi," *Journal of Biblical Literature* 95 (1976), 529-558.

24. *SS*, 9. See also *MI*, 9.

25. *MI*, 4.

26. *MI*, 21.

27. *SS*, 282-283.

28. "Education for Judaism," 206. My emphasis.

29. Kurzweil's first articles appeared in *Ha-Aretz*, 25 September 1957 and 2 October 1957. All his articles against Scholem are collected in *Bama'avak al Arkai ha-Yahadut* (Tel Aviv, 1969), 99-243. Werblowsky's "Re-

flections on Gershom Scholem's Sabbatai Zevi" (Hebrew) appeared in *Molad* 15 (November 1957), 539-547. The similarities between Kurzweil's and Werblowsky's critiques were so great that Kurzweil, no great lover of the Jerusalem academics, threatened to sue Werblowsky for plagiarism. In subsequent years, Werblowsky came to moderate some of his criticisms and he even translated Scholem's *Sabbatai Ṣevi* into English. For another negative view of Scholem, see Jacob Agus's review of *MI* in *Judaism* 21 (Summer, 1972), esp. 378.

30. "On Gershom Scholem's Position on the Study of Sabbatianism" (Hebrew) in his *Netive Emunah u-Minut* (Ramat Gan, 1964), 235-275. See 241-245 for Tishby's defense of Scholem. Tishby devotes most of his article to questioning Scholem's interpretations of Sabbatai Zevi's personality and role in the movement and his account of the actual course of events. As such, it is probably the most serious and exhaustive critique of the book.

31. Scholem recounts these events in "On the History of Sabbatian Research" (Hebrew), *La-merhav*, 28 June 1960. The first article Scholem read on Sabbatianism was Rubaschoff's work on Samuel Primo in *Ha-Shiloah* (1912), 36-47.

32. "Die Theologie des Sabbatianismus im Lichte Abraham Cardosos," first published in *Der Jude* 9, Sonderheft 5 (dedicated to Martin Buber) (1928), 123-139, republished in *Judaica*, I, 119-147. "Redemption Through Sin," *MI*, 78-142. See also "Zum Verständnis des Sabbatianismus," *Almanach des Schocken Verlags* (1936-37), 30-42.

33. *MI*, 111, "Sefer ha-Temunah and the Doctrine of Shmitot" (Hebrew), *Ha-Aretz*, 19 October 1945, 506, and *Ursprung und Anfänge der Kabbala*, 407-419.

34. "After the Spanish Expulsion" (Hebrew), *Davar* (Musaf), 22 June 1934, 1-2, and *MT*, 245.

35. "Towards an Understanding of the Messianic Idea of Judaism," *MI*, 1-2. Scholem was criticized for his characterization of Christian messianism by a follower of the Barthian school of dialectical theology. His vigorous reply, arguing that his interpretation and not the Barthian is historically accurate, appeared in *Grundbegriffe*, 168-170.

36. See "The Neutralization of the Messianic Element in Early Hasidism," first published in *Journal of Jewish Studies* (1970), republished in *MI*, 176-203.

37. *MT*, 244-247.

38. "After the Spanish Expulsion."

39. "Abraham Cardosos," *Judaica*, I, 120. See also *SS*, 7ff.

40. "The Kabbala in Safed at the Time of the Ari" (Hebrew), *Doar ha-Yom*, 17 April 1924, 5.

41. *SS*, 377-379. The relevant text is Nathan's letter to the *chelbi* Raphael Joseph, published in Jacob Sasportas, *Ẓiẓat Novel Zvi*, ed. Isaiah Tishby (Jerusalem, 1954), 7-12; trans. in *SS*, 270-275.

42. All of *SS* is aimed at demonstrating this fundamental thesis. See particularly chapter I.

43. *SS*, 65.

44. For a bibliographical discussion of the origins of the Jewish Enlight-

enment, see Azriel Shochat, *Im Ḥilufei ha-Tekufot* (Jerusalem, 1960), 242-246. Shochat's own position, like Scholem's, tries to show the internal preparation of Haskalah. He emphasizes the development of social assimilation as much as a century before Moses Mendelssohn. For a view which, although emphasizing the importance of Mendelssohn, focuses on the internal disintegration of the traditional social structure, see Jacob Katz, *Tradition and Crisis* (New York, 1961), 213-230. See also Nathan Rotenstreich's *Ha-Maḥshava ha-Yehudit Ba-Et ha-Ḥadasha* (Tel Aviv, 1966), 24-26, where he starts his history of modern Jewish thought with Sabbatianism. Rotenstreich studied with Scholem from 1932 to 1937 at the Hebrew University while he was earning his doctorate in philosophy.

45. *Judaica*, I, 142-146.

46. Ibid., 146. "The reality of the Hebrews" ("Die Wirklichkeit der Habräer") refers to Oskar Goldberg's neo-magical Kabbalistic book of the same title, published in 1925. Scholem had certain peripheral connections to Goldberg's theosophical circle in Berlin through Walter Benjamin, who was involved with the group through Erich Unger, another of the group's leaders. Goldberg tried to attract Scholem to his circle when he heard that Scholem had firsthand knowledge of the Kabbalah, but Scholem was just as uninterested in faddish theosophy as he had been earlier in Buber's Erlebnismystik. When Goldberg published his book, Scholem wrote a long critique of it, which he sent from Jerusalem to Walter Benjamin and Leo Strauss in Berlin. See *Walter Benjamin*, 122-126. Scholem also compared Goldberg's magical exegesis with that of the eighteenth-century Frankist Mason, E.J. Hirschfeld, in "Ein verschollener jüdischer Mystiker der Aufklärungszeit," *LBIY* 7 (1962), 261.

47. "Redemption Through Sin," *MI*, 95. Cardozo explicitly compared Sabbatai Zevi's apostasy to the forced conversions undergone by the Marranos. See *Inyanei Shabtai Zevi*, ed. A. Frieman, 1913, 88. Y.H. Yerushalmi, in his study of Cardozo's brother Isaac, argues that Marranism need not necessarily have led to Sabbatianism: Isaac Cardozo was an opponent of Sabbatianism. See *From Spanish Court to Italian Ghetto: Isaac Cardoso* (New York, 1971), 302-350.

48. See "Die krypto-jüdische Sekte der Dönme in der Turkei," *Numen* 7 (1960), 93-122, trans. in *MI*, 142-167. On Frank and Frankism, see "Redemption Through Sin," *MI*, 126-141.

49. *MT*, 320, and *MI*, 137-141.

50. "Wie die Natur, kabbalistisch gesehen, nichts ist als der Schatten des göttlichen Namens, so kann man auch von einem Schatten des Gesetzes, den es immer länger und länger auf die Lebenshaltung des Juden wirft, sprechen Aber die steinerne Mauer des Gesetzes wird in der Kabbala allmählich transparent. Diese Alchimie des Gesetzes, seine Transmutation ins Durchsichtige, ist eines der tiefsten Paradoxe der Kabbala . . . So mußte am Ende dieses Prozesses logischerweise die jüdische 'Reform' stehen: die schattenlose, unhintergründige, aber auch nicht mehr unvernünftige, rein abstrakte Humanität des Gesetzes als ein Rudiment seiner mystischen Zersetzung." *Judaica*, III, 269.

51. *MI*, 140.

52. *MI*, 80; Mauthner, *Erinnerungen* (Munich, 1918), 306. On Hurin, see *MT*, 304.

53. "Ein verschollener jüdischer Mystiker der Auflärungszeit," *LBIY*, and "The Career of a Frankist: Moshe Dobruschka and his Metamorphoses" (Hebrew), in *Meḥkarim u-Mekorot le-Toldot ha-Shabta'ut ve-Gilguleha* (Jerusalem, 1974), 141-219.

54. Review of M.J. Cohen, *Jacob Emden: A Man of Controversy*, in *Kiryat Sefer* 16 (1939-40), 320-338, and "Episodes in the Study of the Sabbatian Movement" (Hebrew), *Zion* 6 (1940-41), 85-100.

55. See the short article by Michael Ha-Cohen Brawer, "Sod ha-Razim," *Ha-Hed* 16(9-12) (1940-41), 21, and Scholem's reply in the same journal, 17(1-2) (1941-42), 14.

56. *Leket Margaliot* (Tel Aviv, 1941). The pamphlet is primarily a refutation of the criticisms of the orthodox scholar, Reuben Margaliot, who himself had published a pamphlet with two essays defending Eibeschütz entitled *Sibat Hitnagduto shel Rabenu Jacob mi-Emden le-Rabenu Yonathan Eibeschütz* (Tel Aviv, 1941). On the history of the controversy and its modern metamorphosis, see F. Lachover, "The Continuation of an Historical Controversy" (Hebrew), *Moznayim* 13 (1940), 177-186, and A. Ha-Shiloni, *La-Pulmus ha-Meḥudash al Shabta-uto shel Yonatan Eibeschütz* (Jerusalem, 1952). Scholem's student, Moses Perlmutter, examined one of the most controversial books of the eighteenth-century polemics and identified it as a Sabbatian tract written by Eibeschütz. See his *Yonatan Eibeschütz ve-Yaḥaso el ha-Shabta'ut*, (Tel Aviv, 1947).

57. See, for example, Leo Strauss, *Spinoza's Critique of Religion* (New York, 1965), 37-86; Ernst Bloch's study of Thomas Münzer; and Erich Seeberg's study of Gottfried Arnold. Karl Mannheim's demonstration of the connections between chiliastic and liberal utopianism is also relevant. See his *Ideology and Utopia*.

58. Albrecht Ritschl, *Geschichte des Pietismus*, II, e.g., 116, 159, 166, 222. See Gerhard Kaiser, *Pietismus und Patriotismus im literarischen Deutschland* (Wiesbaden, 1961), 13-14 and 248n47-51, for bibliography.

59. See Emden's remarks on Sabbatians and *Maskilim* in *Ḥoli Ketem* (Altona, 1775), 24b: "Those two sects . . . make the children of Israel despair of the future redemption by saying that God has left the earth and no longer observes it nor exercises his Providence over this world. They think themselves left to chance." Although Emden did not blame Sabbatianism for causing the Enlightenment, his discussion of Sabbatian views of providence suggests their intellectual connection. For Selig's discussion of Sabbatianism, see his journal *Der Jude* (1779), 79. Scholem discusses his eighteenth-century predecessors in "Die Metamorphose des häretischen Messianismus," *Judaica*, III, 216.

60. On Hurwitz, see Chapter Two. Scholem acknowledges Hurwitz's contribution in *MT*, 418n30. He also mentions V. Zacek, who published documents demonstrating the connections between late Sabbatianism and

Enlightenment in *Jahrbuch für Geschichte der Juden in der Czechoslovakischen Republik* 9 (1938), 343-410.

61. "On the Question of the Connection Between Sabbatianism, Enlightenment and Reform" (Hebrew), *Studies in Honor of Alexander Altmann* (forthcoming). Professor Katz was kind enough to make the galley proofs of his article available to me.

62. "Redemption Through Sin," *MI,* 84.

63. Isaiah Tishby, "The Messianic Idea in the Rise of Hasidism" (Hebrew), *Zion* 32 (1967), 1-45, and Ben Zion Dinur, *Be-Mifne ha-Dorot,* 181-227.

64. Simon Dubnow, *Geschichte des Chassidismus* (Berlin, 1931), I, 108, and Martin Buber, *The Origin and Meaning of Hasidism,* trans. Maurice Friedman (New York, 1960), 107, 111. Scholem discusses the bibliographical literature in "The Neutralization of the Messianic Element in Hasidism," *MI,* 178-179.

65. "Prophetie und Apokalyptik," *Werke,* II, 925-942.

66. *Origin and Meaning of Hasidism,* 252-253, and *Hasidism and Modern Man,* trans. Maurice Friedman (New York, 1958), 27.

67. Introduction to *Der Grosse Maggid* (Frankfurt, 1922).

68. *Origin and Meaning of Hasidism,* 106-112.

69. See Buber's *Paths in Utopia,* trans. R.F.C. Hull (New York, 1958), 1-6.

70. *Origin and Meaning of Hasidism,* 218.

71. Mannheim, *Ideology and Utopia,* 215.

72. *MT,* 329.

73. "The Neutralization of the Messianic Element in Early Hasidism." See also the work of Scholem's students: Joseph Weiss, "Via Passiva in Early Hasidism," *Journal of Jewish Studies* 11 (1960), 137-157, and Rivka Shatz, "The Messianic Principle in Hasidic Thought" (Hebrew), *Molad,* n.s. 1 (1967), 105-111, and *Ha-Ḥasidut ki-Mistika* (Tel Aviv, 1968). Shatz's main contention, based on studies of the writings of the Maggid of Mezritch, is that Hasidism is a quietistic, Jewish version of German pietism.

74. *MI,* 202. See also *MT,* 337.

75. Scholem argues that the mysterious R. Adam Baal Shem who, according to legend, was one of Israel Baal Shem Tov's teachers was actually Heshel Tsoref, an eighteenth-century crypto-Sabbatian. Hasidism emerged out of later Sabbatian traditions and its rejection of Sabbatian apocalypticism was conscious. See *MT,* 331-333, and "Demut Ba'al Shem Shabta'i," *Ha-Aretz,* 22 December 1944, 6.

76. *MI,* 243. "Martin Buber's Interpretation of Hasidism" first appeared in *Commentary* 32 (October 1961), 305-316; expanded in *MI,* 227-251.

77. *MI,* 240.

78. Buber, *Briefwechsel,* II, 86-89 (15 October 1921); Buber's response, 90-91 (19 October 1921).

79. *SS*, xii. The phrase "to pay a very high price" is one of Scholem's favorites. On this evaluation of messianism, see also "With Gershom Scholem," *JJC*, 26.

80. *MI*, 35.

81. *SS*, 929.

8. The Politics of Historiography

1. See the exchange between Kurzweil and Jacob Katz in *Ha-Aretz*, 16 April 1965, 5; 14 May 1965, 10-11; and 28 May 1965, 10-11. See also Isaiah Tishby in *Davar*, 15 January 1965, and in his *Nitive Emunah U-Minut*, 235-275.

2. Kurzweil, *Ba-ma'avak*, 134.

3. Ibid., 111.

4. Kurzweil's other articles dealing with these issues have been collected in *Sifruteinu ha-Hadasha—Hemshekh O Mahapekhah?* (Tel Aviv, 1965), 225-300.

5. Kurzweil, *Ba-ma'avak*, 226.

6. *Judaica*, I, 146.

7. For the historical background on political life in the *Yishuv*, see Noah Lucas, *The Modern History of Israel* (New York, 1975), and Walter Laqueur, *A History of Zionism* (New York, 1972), 270-337.

8. For Magnes's biography, see Norman Bentwich, *For Zion's Sake* (Philadelphia, 1954).

9. In his story "Edo ve-Enam," for instance, Agnon portrays an eccentric scholar in Jerusalem, said by many to be modeled on Scholem. His novel *Shira* also deals with the Jerusalem academic community, and some have professed to find Scholem in a main character role.

10. On Schocken, see Gershom Schocken, "Ich werde seinesgleichen nicht mehr sehen," *Der Monat* 20 (November 1968), 13-30; Siegfried Moses, "Salman Schocken: His Economic and Zionist Activities," *LBIY* 5 (1960), 73-104; and Steven Poppell, "Salman Schocken and the Schocken Verlag," *LBIY* 17 (1972), 93-117.

11. On Brit Shalom, see S.L. Hattis, *The Bi-national Idea in Palestine During Mandatory Times* (Haifa, 1970); Lucas, *The Modern History of Israel*, 146-150.

12. For Scholem's own account of his activity in Brit Shalom, see "With Gershom Scholem," *JJC*, 43-45. See his editorial articles in *She'ifoteinu* 2: "Ha-Matarah ha-Sofit" (August 1931), "Ahad Ha-am ve-Anahnu" (September 1931), and "B'mai Ka Mi'palgi" (September 1931).

13. Y. Burla, "Brit Kishalon," *Davar*, 27 November 1929, and Scholem's response, "Three Sins of Brit Shalom" (Hebrew), *Davar*, 12 December 1929, 2.

14. "Three Sins of Brit Shalom."

15. Laqueur, *A History of Zionism*, 338-383; Joseph Schechtman and Y. Benari, *History of the Revisionist Movement* (Tel Aviv, 1970), vol. 1; and Joseph Schechtman, *The Jabotinsky Story* (New York, 1956-1961), vols. 1 and 2.

16. See Abba Ahimeir, *Ha-Zionut ha-Mahapekhanit* (Tel Aviv, 1966), and his *Brit ha-Biryonim* (Tel Aviv, 1972). On Ahimeir, see Joseph Nedava's introduction to the latter volume. Ahimeir was the ideological leader of the Brit Biryonim group, which was sympathetic to Italian fascism. Ahimeir, like Berdichevsky, developed a counter-history of Jewish militarism.

17. The *Irgun Zvai Leumi* was not precisely an agency of the Revisionist Party, although there were ties between them, and the Irgun considered Jabotinsky its ideological leader until his death in 1940. The Irgun actually originated in a split in the Haganah (the defense force organized by the Jewish Agency) in the late 1930s. The Lehi split from the Irgun after the outbreak of World War II over the issue of continuing terrorist operations against the British during the war and, later, over tactical questions. The independence of these groups from the official Revisionist Party is demonstrated by the fact that in the 1949 Knesset elections, the underground ran its own slate, Herut, which considerably overshadowed the revisionists. In all subsequent elections the Revisionists did not even stand as a party: the underground had successfully swallowed them up.

18. *Ketavim: Lohamei Herut Yisrael* (Tel Aviv, 1959), I, 134.

19. See the memoirs of Lehi leader Geula Cohen, *Woman of Violence*, trans. Hillel Halkin (New York, 1966), 269-270: "In our ecstatic vision of redemption it had always seemed to us that victory in war would coincide with the fulfillment of the dream of ages . . . [We] had believed that when the last British soldier left the country, messianic times would arrive."

20. In the beginning of the poem, the poet relates that his work is really an old book newly discovered, suggesting the classic apocalyptic identification of an early, hidden prophecy with the true understanding of contemporary events. *Rehovot ha-Nahar* (Tel Aviv, 1950-51), 1.

21. Joseph Klausner, *The Messianic Idea in Israel*, trans. W.F. Stinespring (New York, 1955), x.

22. Ibid., 531.

23. Buber Archive (National Library of the Jewish People, Jerusalem), VIII/709.

24. Bentwich relates the incident in his *Mandate Memoirs* (New York, 1965), 150.

25. *Doar ha-Yom*, 20 February 1931.

26. Ibid., 24 March 1931, 3.

27. "Politik der Mystik: Zu Isaac Breuers 'Neuem Kusaril'," *Jüdische Rundschau*, 17 July 1934, 1-2, trans. in *MI*, 325-335. Breuer, the grandson of the German neo-orthodox rabbi S.R. Hirsch, tried to turn his grandfather's rationalist defense of orthodoxy into a mystical alternative to Zionism. Breuer argued for the establishment of a "kingdom of God" in Israel in place of the secular Zionist experiment. In the last paragraph of his critique of Breuer, Scholem explicitly compares Breuer's anti-Zionist mystical messianism with apocalyptic Revisionism. Both injected metahistorical considerations into political questions.

28. Buber, *Briefwechsel*, II, 380-381.

29. "Politics of Mysticism," *MI*, 334.

30. Scholem published the letter in *Walter Benjamin*, 211-217.

31. On this incident, see Laqueur, *A History of Zionism*, 494-497.

32. *Walter Benjamin*, 216. The same formulation appears in his article "B'mai Ka Mi'palgai," *She'ifoteinu* (September 1931), 193-203.

33. "Ahad Ha-am ve-Anahnu," *She'ifoteinu*, 186: "Like us, [Ahad Ha-am] sees the promise of complete redemption through Zionism as a falsification of its mission."

34. "Ha-Matarah ha-Sofit," 156.

35. Ibid.

36. *Walter Benjamin*, 215: "Ich glaube ja nicht, daß es etwas gibt wie eine 'Lösung der Judenfrage' im Sinne einer Normalisierung der Juden, und glaube gewiß nicht, daß in einem solchen Sinn in Palestine diese Frage gelöst werden kann." See also "With Gershom Scholem," *JJC*, 34-35.

37. "Israel und die Diaspora," *Judaica*, II, 58-59.

38. See his expression of the belief in the necessity of a bridge between Israel and the Diaspora, *Judaica*, II, 75-76, trans. in *JJC*, 244-260.

39. In the pages of *Davar*, S. Yavnieli attacked Ahad Ha-am and excluded him from the rosters of Zionism. Scholem responded in "Ahad Ha-am ve-Anahnu," *She'ifoteinu* (September 1931), 185-186, by defending Ahad Ha-am, even though he did not agree with the latter's "bourgeois social views."

40. For Ahad Ha-am's philosophy of historical change, see *Selected Essays of Ahad Ha-am*, trans. Leon Simon (New York, 1962), 54-55, 96.

41. See particularly his "Open Letter to Ahad Ha-am" (Hebrew) in *Ha-Shiloah* 1 (1896), 154-159.

42. *Judaica*, II, 62.

43. "Zionism, Dialectic of Continuity and Rebellion," *Unease in Zion*, 273-275.

44. On the Canaanites, see Ya'akov Shavit, "The Relation Between Idea and Poetics in the Poetry of Yonatan Ratosh" (Hebrew), *Ha-Sifrut* 17 (Fall 1974), 66-91 (including extensive bibliography), and "The Ideology of Israeli Anti-Zionism" (M.A. thesis, Tel Aviv University, 1972). There are parallels between the Canaanites and similar movements, like the Pharonites, in the Arab world.

45. "Zionism—Dialectic of Continuity and Rebellion," 277ff. Also "With Gershom Scholem," *JJC*, 34.

46. It is interesting that the Canaanites, like Schoeps, were prone to an authoritarian, even fascist, ideology. They can be understood as a völkisch revolt against liberal democracy, much as Schoeps was motivated by German völkisch ideas. The romantic desire to return to a prehistorical, mythical period of the true Volk is characteristic of all these movements.

47. *Unease in Zion*, 278. Like Berdichevsky, the Canaanites constructed a counter-history in which all of Jewish history since and even including the Bible has suppressed the true "Canaanite" or "Hebrew" identity of the people. Their historical writings, which seem to suggest a myth of Canaanite origins, are intended actually to demythologize history by return-

ing the people to their original identity: they consider Judaism itself a myth. The Canaanites were more radical than Berdichevsky in that they saw the Zionist movement as a continuation of the myth of Judaism, and they therefore defined themselves as anti-Zionists.

48. Ratosh, perhaps the most prominent leader of the Canaanites, was an editor of one of the Revisionist papers in Palestine in the late 1930s. He split with the Revisionists at about the same time as the Lehi, but while they took up arms he and his followers became politically passive.

49. *Unease in Zion*, 273-274, and "Israel und die Diaspora," *Judaica*, II, 61-62.

50. *Judaica*, II, 60.

51. Ibid., 66.

52. "Rede über Israel," *Judaica*, II, 48. My emphasis.

53. "Abschied," *Jerubbaal*, 129: "Schweigen, Arbeit und Erkenntnis, Reinheit, Strenge, und Verzicht, und welches die Ordnungen sein mögen, die sich im Dasein des Zionisten entfalten sollen, sie alle vollenden sich in einem: Verantwortung." Trans. in *JJC*, 60.

54. *Unease in Zion*, 263.

55. *Judaica*, II, 49.

56. Ibid., 72, and *Unease in Zion*, 269.

57. "Offener Brief," *Bayerische Israelitische Gemeindezeitung*, 244.

58. *Judaica*, II, 39.

59. "Who Is a Jew" (Hebrew trans.), *Devarim be-Go*, 597. See also *Unease in Zion*, 283-284. Scholem strongly opposes the decision of the "who is a Jew" controversy by legal act of the Israeli government. Since he considers Jewish identity as a nondogmatic issue, he opposes any authority, religious or secular, from legislating a dogmatic definition.

60. "Messianic Idea in Judaism," *MI*, 36.

9. COUNTER-HISTORY

1. "The Science of Judaism—Then and Now," *MI*, 310. Trans. revised on the basis of the original, *Judaica*, I, 158.

2. "The Science of Judaism," *MI*, 311-312.

3. Ibid., 312: "The major centers of activity are now in Israel and America . . . The natural tensions will continue to exist and will remain fruitful . . . We must and shall hope that great individuals will accomplish achievements made possible by the new [Zionist] perspective, the new view of the Jewish past and Jewish character."

4. Kurzweil, *Ba-ma'avak*, 168.

5. Ibid., 176-179.

6. See the debate with Jacob Katz in *Ha-Aretz*, 16 April 1965, 5; 14 May 1965, 10-11; and 28 May 1965, 10-11.

7. Kurzweil, *Ba-ma'avak*, 173.

8. Kurzweil, *Ba-ma'avak*, 212, 192: "Eduard Gans and the apostates from the group that founded the Wissenschaft des Judentums arrived by way of their Hegelian philosophy and dialectics to conclusions similar to those of the later Sabbatians and Frankists."

9. Ibid., 174.

10. On Dilthey, see H. A. Hodges, *The Philosophy of Wilhelm Dilthey* (London, 1952) and Georg Misch, *Lebensphilosophie und Phänomenologie* (2nd ed. Leipzig and Berlin, 1931). See also Ernst Troeltsch, "Die Krise des Historismus," *Neue Rundschau* 33 (1922), 572-590, and his *Der Historismus und seine Probleme* (Tübingen, 1922).

11. See Chapter Three, n. 23.

12. Troeltsch, "Die Krise des Historismus," 583.

13. One writer of Scholem's generation who proposed counter-historical interpretations of a number of philosophers in Jewish history was Leo Strauss: see his *Persecution and the Art of Writing* (Glencoe, Ill., 1952), esp. 22-37. Strauss argued that philosophers like Maimonides must be read between the lines to uncover the true esoteric message of their writings. Because the modern age has experienced first-hand the suppression of free expression by totalitarian regimes, modern historians of philosophy are singularly equipped to decode works written in earlier ages of persecution. Strauss was involved with Täubler's *Akademie für Wissenschaft des Judentums* and was also quite influenced by Hermann Cohen and Franz Rosenzweig. Scholem was acquainted with Strauss (see *Walter Benjamin*, 126) and mentions his "subtle investigations" of multilevel philosophical exegeses in *KS*, 51n1.

14. *Illuminations*, 253-264. See the collections of essays, *Materialien zu Benjamins Thesen 'Über den Begriff der Geschichte,'* ed. Peter Bulthaup (Frankfurt, 1975).

15. *Illuminations*, 256.

16. Ibid., 260.

17. Ibid., 257. See Ulrich Sonnemann, "Geschichte gegen den Stricht gebürstet," in *Materialien*, 231-254.

18. "Walter Benjamin," *Judaica*, II, 197-199, and Hannah Arendt, "Introduction," *Illuminations*, 12. Benjamin's technique is reminiscent of Freud's description of psychoanalysis in his essay on "The Moses of Michelangelo": Psychoanalysis "is accustomed to divine secret and concealed things from unconsidered or unnoticed details from the rubbish heap, as it were, of our observations." *Character and Culture*, ed. Philip Rieff (New York, 1963), 92. For Benjamin's relation to Freud, see "On Some Motifs in Baudelaire," *Illuminations*, 160-161.

19. See Scholem's letters to Benjamin in Benjamin, *Briefe*, II, 510-512, 525-529 (20 February 1930 and 31 March 1931), trans. in *JJC*, 237-243. See also Scholem's evaluation of Benjamin's Marxism in "Walter Benjamin," *JJC*, 172-197. On the Benjamin controversy, see Chapter Four, n. 97.

20. Arendt, "Introduction," *Illuminations*, 40. See also, Scholem, "Walter Benjamin," *Judaica*, II, 210, on Benjamin's *Ursprung des Trauerspiels* as a study of the "hidden life" of Baroque allegory.

21. *MI*, 313. Scholem's quotation of Warburg suggests certain striking similarities between him and the great German-Jewish art historian (1866-1929). Like Warburg, Scholem was an inveterate bibliophile from his youth. On the intellectual level, there is also a resemblance between Scholem as a counter-historian and Warburg's history of the underground influ-

ence of pagan myth on Renaissance art. Warburg rebelled against conventional, dogmatic interpretations of the Renaissance and saw that age as a time of conflict between reason and irrationalism, much as Scholem portrays Jewish history. See E. H. Gombrich, *Aby Warburg, an Intellectual Biography* (London, 1970), esp. 10-13.

22. See Scholem's article on Bloch, "Wohnt Gott im Herzen eines Atheisten?" *Der Spiegel*, 7 July 1975, 110-115, and "Walter Benjamin," *Judaica*, II, 211-212. Scholem ridicules Bloch as an "expressionistic" Marxist.

23. Ernst Bloch, *Atheism in Christianity*, trans. J. T. Swann (New York, 1972), 82-83.

24. "Wohnt Gott im Herzen eines Atheisten?" 112. See also Scholem's reference to Arnold in "Mysticism and Society," *Diogenes* 58 (1967), 2. Scholem also referred to his admiration for Arnold in personal conversation (August 1975) and letter (31 March 1978). The best work on Arnold is Erich Seeberg's *Gottfried Arnold* (Meerane, 1923, republished Darmstadt, 1964).

25. Seeberg, *Arnold*, 67, 78.

26. Ibid., 89 and 151. Arnold did not automatically approve of all heresies. The Arians, for example, were rationalists and tried to build a counter-church; they were therefore only slightly better than the orthodox church. Arnold looked instead for those pneumatics, inside and outside the Church, who "imitate Christ."

27. Ibid., chap. 5. Karl Löwith, himself influenced by Barth's concept of Christianity as a religion outside of history, tried to show the continuity of Joachimite ideas into modern times as secularized apocalypticism. See his *Meaning in History* (Chicago, 1949).

28. Seeberg, *Arnold*, 227-233.

29. Ibid., 224-225.

30. *SS*, x.

31. *Judaica*, III, 267. See Habermas, "Die verkleidete Tora," *Merkur*, 101ff, for the best discussion of Scholem's philosophy of history.

32. *Religion of Reason*, 2.

33. Ibid., 3.

34. Ibid.

35. Cohen first developed this epistemological theory in his *Das Prinzip der Infinitesimalmethode und seine Geschichte* (Frankfurt, 1883) and his *Logik der reinen Erkenntnis* (Berlin, 1902), 28-34, 65-78. The theory rests on his notion of the *Ursprungsprinzip*, discussed by Hugo Bergmann in "The Principle of Beginning in the Philosophy of Hermann Cohen" (Hebrew) *Keneset* 8 (1944), 143-153. See also his *Toldot ha-Filosofia ha-Hadashah* (Jerusalem, 1970), 204-213, for a discussion of the history of infinite judgments on which Cohen's logical method is based.

36. *SS*, x-xi.

EPILOGUE

1. "Israel and the Diaspora," *JJC*, 258.
2. "At the Completion of Buber's Translation of the Bible," *MI*, 318.
3. "Against the Myth of a German-Jewish Dialogue," *JJC*, 61-62,

trans. based on original in *Judaica*, II, 7-8. See also "Once More: The German-Jewish Dialogue," *JJC*, 65-70, and "Jews and Germans," *JJC*, 71-92.

4. "Israel and the Diaspora," *JJC*, 253-254.

5. *Devarim be-Go*, 414. See also "With Gershom Scholem," *JJC*, 25-26. In "Reflections on the Possibility of Jewish Mysticism in Our Time" (Hebrew), *Amot* 2 (1964), 11-19, Scholem says "God will appear as non-God. All the divine and symbolic things can also appear in the garb of atheistic mysticism."

Index

Temple Israel

Minneapolis, Minnesota

In Honor of the Bat Mitzvah of

JACKIE DAVIS

September 15, 1979